Lhotse South Face – The Wall of Legends

By Edward Morgan

Bee Different Books

Published by Bee Different Books

7 Honey Lane

Burley, Ringwood

BH24 4EN

United Kingdom

www.fimi.ch

ISBN: 978-0-9935148-0-7

To my parents, who introduced me to the mountain world

Contents

Introduction – An Almost Mythical Story 5
Chapter 1 – A New Era for Himalayan Climbing 12
Chapter 2 – A Problem for the Year 2000 33
Chapter 3 –Daring to Believe Everything is Possible 51
Chapter 4 – Crossing the Line 73
Chapter 5 – Finally a Summit 97
Chapter 6 – Between the Hammer and the Anvil 112
Chapter 7 – Lightweight and Fast 132
Chapter 8 – So Close 151
Chapter 9 – The Tower of Babel 169
Chapter 10 – A Giant has Fallen 186
Chapter 11 – Alone and in Winter 202
Chapter 12 – The New Messner? 213
Chapter 13 – Still More Challengers 231
Chapter 14 – Fighting Huge Snow Mushrooms 252
Chapter 15 – An Infernal Circle 267
Chapter 16 – What Proof is Needed? 285
Chapter 17 – The End of the Golden Age 295
Acknowledgements 310
Sources and Selected Bibliography 312
Index 315

Introduction – An Almost Mythical Story

The spikes of my crampons bit perfectly into the 45° degree hard snow giving a thrilling feeling of power and security as I stepped up. Every few paces I had to pause to gasp for breath, the cold thin air burning my lungs, but the situation was so magnificent that I hardly noticed. It was late October 1990 and we were approaching 7000 metres on the North Peak of Everest, Changtse, a mountain connected to the World's highest summit by the North Col. We were now nearly at the same height as the Col and Everest rose massively on the far side of it. The weather was perfect and, yellowed by a distance of nearly 80 miles, we saw a sublime view of Kangchenjunga, the world's third highest peak. As always at high altitude the pace was slow, but steadily we made progress and the trapezium shaped summit started to look closer. It dawned on me that we were actually going to make it to the top of this huge Himalayan mountain. Changtse was not the highest of course, and the route was of moderate technical difficulty, but for me personally, with experience of only a few seasons of Alpine climbing, it would be a tremendous achievement.

Five days earlier success on Changtese had looked much less likely. We had retreated back to Base Camp tired and dispirited after a first exploration up to the foot of the final face. Whilst down at Base Camp, the weather had turned bad with a day of snowfall and the temperature had fallen sharply. The streams from which we had fetched water when we first arrived had frozen and we now had to painstakingly hack off blocks of ice to melt to get water as it was vital to stay hydrated. Winter was approaching and we knew that the next try on Changtese would be our last. We knew that Everest itself was already deserted having met the last expeditions leaving the Tibetan side of the mountain.

Although climbers on Everest itself had given up for the season, on South Side of massif, two expeditions were battling to try and climb what many considered to be the hardest route in the world, the South Face of Lhotse. Lhotse is the world's fourth highest peak and lies in an analogous position to Changtse on the other side of Everest, connected to it by the South Col. The styles of the two teams couldn't have been more different. One consisted of two Frenchmen, brilliant, bold climbers who wanted to overcome this huge wall in the purest possible lightweight style climbing straight from the top to the bottom in a single push. The other was a large team from the Soviet Union which had spent many weeks forcing their way up a very hard direct route right up the centre of the face, fixing ropes and stocking camps to allow different groups of climbers to attempt the final ridge to the summit. From a snow cave at 8200 metres, three groups had tried and failed to climb the final section. In a desperate struggle they had been slowed to a snailspace by the huge snow mushrooms which festooned the final ridge and finally had to turn round while they could still make it back down. Now it was the turn of two Ukrainians, Sergey Bershov and Vladimir Karataev. After a first night in the snow cave they set out to explore an alternative to the upper ridge on which their companions had failed. They descended down off the final ridge into the gully on its left in the same snowy weather we had encountered before leaving Base Camp. They found that the gully was steep, but looked climable, although they could not see all the way to its top. It was too late and weather too bad to carry on that day, but they returned to the snow cave believing they might have found the key to climbing Lhotse's South Face.

Back on Changtse, as we moved off the steep lower part of the Face onto the easier angled final section the snow conditions started to worsen. No longer did we have firm neve of the lower part, but instead powder snow in which our feet sunk making each step a lung-sapping effort. Even more worrying the powder was covered by a hard crust which sometimes held us and sometimes broke under our weight. We knew this meant a risk of wind-slab avalanche, where a whole wide area of slope can detach if the slab is fractured. The frozen powder underneath can act like ball bearings allowing the whole slab and those on it to slide away. We knew that an avalanche of this type had killed three people on the adjacent slope of the North Col just over a month before. Our success on the mountain no longer seemed a foregone conclusion and, although the weather was still perfect we started to be more worried about our safety than anything else.

I did not know it at the time, but in 1990 an époque of Himalayan climbing was drawing to a close. The history of mountaineering, over its 150 years as a sport, has always seen an evolution, but like biological evolution, rarely one with a constant pace. There have been phases where development was gradual and others where standards jumped, often because attention of the leading climbers had switched to a new form of the sport or geographical arena. This happened at the birth of alpinism in the 1850s and 60s, when most of the great mountains of the Alps were climbed for the first time, and again at the end of the 19th century as guideless climbing led to harder and harder routes being realised on the same mountains. There was a new leap forward in the 1930s, as climbers from Italy, France, Germany and Austria focused on the very hardest faces of the Alps. With labels like the "last great problem of the Alps" and "the three great north faces", these routes attracted the top climbers of the day to tak risks and push climbing standards to an ever higher level. Any jump in standards makes routes and mountains which would have been considered as unclimbable seem realistic objectives and so the process goes on. With a time lag of two or three generations, the same evolutionary process was seen on the World's highest mountains, the Himalayas. All the highest mountains were climbed for the first in the 20 years after the end of the Second World War, but it was not until the 1970s that a new phase of development was reached with climbers tackling the highest mountains by routes of great technical difficulty.

Sometimes the new objectives fall to the challengers fairly quickly once climbing skills, mentality and equipment have reached the required level. Once the English Victorian climbers had focused on making first ascents of the main Alpine peaks, most of them were knocked off without too much difficulty. In the 1860s the main active climbers would meet in the newly formed Alpine Club in London in the winter to discuss which new peaks to climb the following year. One of the active climbers in this era, Edward Buxton, wrote:

"There was a wonderful freemasonry among the worshippers at those shrines, and it would be impossible to exaggerate the devotion and enthusiasm of the votaries during the "sixties." It was the decade following on the formation of the Alpine Club. Within that period, nearly every peak and passage of any importance was discussed at home, minutely examined on the spot, attacked, and finally conquered."

In other cases there have been numerous attempts on a goal before it has finally succumbed. In the 19th century there were numerous rival attempts on the Matterhorn, starting from both the Swiss and Italian sides of the mountain, before Edward Whymper's team triumphed in 1865, although four of them fell to their deaths on the descent. Thirty two years and numerous expeditions passed from the first time Everest was attempted in 1921 to the first ascent in 1953. Several of the other great mountains of the Himalayas like K2, Kangchenjunga and Nanga Parbat also saw multiple attempts, and often major tragedies, before they were finally climbed. Other objectives in the Himalayas however fell at the first or second serious attempt. This included several of the

8000 metre peaks – the 14 highest mountains on the planet which have attracted by far the greatest attention of all the many Himalayan mountains. When the French climbed Annapurna, the first ever 8000er, it was done on the first attempt.

For those objectives which do not surrender easily, each new expedition which fails adds to the reputation of the mountain or route for difficulty. And this growing reputation makes it the place where the leading climbers can prove their talent. This is what happened in 1930s with the North Wall of the Eiger, the largest and one of the steepest faces in the Alps. It became known as one of the last great climbing challenges and was first attempted in 1935 by two young German climbers, Karl Mehringer and Max Sedlmeyer. They made slow progress on the Face and were caught by storms. After five bivouacs on the Face, the climbers were seen for the last time before clouds closed in again. When good weather returned a few days later, the Face was blanketed white in snow and there was no sign of movement – the two climbers had frozen to death. Further attempts the following year by Austrians and Germans resulted in the death of another four climbers in dramatic circumstances. In the climate of 1930s Germany, what seemed like self-sacrificing heroism appealed to the Nazi propagandists and when in 1938 an Austrian and German team combined to conquer the face, the victory was hailed by the Nazis and the successful climbers were personally received by Hitler. The actual motivations of the climbers were certainly more complex and personal than the Nazi ideology suggested, but the glorification of the ascent by the Nazi party certainly gave an unpleasant slant to the climb. The story of the attempts and final success of the North Face of the Eiger were told by one of the first ascentionists, Heinrich Harrer, in a classic book, "The White Spider", one of the first books which fired my interest in mountaineering as a teenager.

More than 20 years after my expedition on Changtse and the Soviet and French attempts on Lhotse's South Face I started to asked myself why there was not a good general book about the golden age in Himalayan mountaineering in the 1970s and 80s when the great walls were climbed for the first time. In the last decades many dramatic accounts published of climbers fighting for their lives in storms and avalanches on Everest and K2 were written, but most of these were about attempts to repeat the much climbed ordinary routes on these mountains. What was missing was the story of the struggles to climb the very hardest routes for the first time. As I thought about how to construct such a history I gradually realised that by telling the story of the attempts to climb the hardest route of all, Lhotse's South Face, it was possible to cover all the key themes and many of the key actors in this golden era. But despite its importance and the dramas which took place there, Lhotse South Face is not well covered in climbing literature – there is no White Spider for Lhotse. So I set out to try and research and write one. This research took me in directions I had not expected and led me to meet fascinating people in many countries from vinyards in France to factories of Silesia, Poland. I met some of those involved in the most dramatic moments, their memories still vivid more 25 or 30 years later. I also met the family and friends of those killed in the mountains, for whom remembering their loved ones was a rewarding but also emotional experience. And the more I looked and read and talked to people, the more fascinating twists and turns in this story I found.

For me, there is an almost mythical quality to the greatest chapters in the history of mountaineering, which tell of men facing desperate challenges and seemingly huge risks for completely intangible rewards. The story of the attempts to climb the South Face of Lhotse has this mythical quality in abundance, but it goes beyond even the heroic and the tragic to include accusations of deceit and foul play. There is no universally accepted version of some of the critical events. For the climbers of certain nations like Poland, France and Slovenia the Face became almost an obsession. The Japanese, the Czechs and Slovaks, the Italians and the Soviets also had an important part to play before the story was finished.

Recounting what happened on the South Face of Lhotse gives a chance to try and explore the motivations of the men, and they are mainly men, who were willing to make such sacrifices, to take such risks in the pursuit of such intangible benefit. They were as the great French climber Lionel Terray wrote, the "Conquistadors of the Useless". They might get fame, but generally only in quite a limited circle of mountaineering enthusiasts. In very rare cases did they win riches. The best most mountaineers could only hope to make a living from the activity they loved. There was glory perhaps. In Plato's Symposium recounts a conversation between Socrates and a wisewoman Diotima where the latter states that "procreation is the nearest thing to perpetuality and immortality that a mortal man can obtain". She then goes on to explain to Socrates that ambition leads to an even greater drive and that "you will be astonished by its irrationality unless you bear in mind ... the desire to win a glory that shall never die has the strongest effects on people. For this … they are ready to run risks, spend their substance, endure every hardship and even sacrifice their lives." In modern times, glory often has a negative conutation: we don't think about "glory hunters" as admirable, but Plato saw glory as a positive motivation.

When the great British climber George Mallory, who disappeared near the summit of Everest in 1924, was asked by a journalist why he was trying to climb Everest his famous reply "because it's there" can be interpreted in different ways. On the one hand it is a clever, but empty reply to the journalist's question, which doesn't say anything other than that he can't really give a good reason – a bit like asking a teenage who says he is going out where he is going, only to get the answer "just out". But it also says something fundamental about human volition – that we do not necessarily know why we do what we do. If we even question free will, then we must look for other reasons, however hard these may be to pin down, as to why men are willing to make huge efforts and sacrifices for such ethereal rewards.

During this golden age of Himalayan mountaineering the home countries of many of the climbers underwent huge changes. In the mid 1970s, when climbers first started to think seriously about this terrifying Wall, the Cold War had frozen the political map of Europe in exactly the same state as it had been since the dust settled at the end of the Second World War and it continued to be so for most of this period. By 1990 when I went to Changtse, the map of Europe was changing fast. Within a couple of years three of countries which feature prominently in this story – Yugoslavia, Czechoslovakia and Soviet Union – no longer existed, whilst for Poland the political situation had changed beyond all recognition. Understanding something of these changes, and how they impacted the ordinary citizens of these countries, helps us comprehend the context in which many of the expeditions to Lhotse's South Face took place.

My role in this story is a mere observer, a recorder of an important period in mountaineering's rich history. I am an enthiastic amateur mountaineer, but have never climbed at anything like the standard of difficulty or had the commitment needed to venture onto this Face. But at one of the critical moments I was very close by, over 7000 metres up on the opposite side of the same mountain group experiencing the same weather and conditions as the climbers on the South Face of Lhotse. Shortly before I visited the Himalayas, the cracks in the political framework of Europe, which had started to open in the late 1980s, became great fissures. Largely thanks to the vision of one man, Mikhail Gorbachev, there was a dramatic weakening in the iron grip which the Soviet Union had exerted over the Eastern half of Europe since the end of the Second World War. As I watched the television images of crowds smashing down the Berlin Wall, I wanted, like many others, to experience this pivotal moment in history at first hand. I drove across West Germany and then into Czechoslovakia before crossing into East Germany and driving to Berlin. It was a strange situation with the old order seemingly having simply evaporated, but a new one not yet arrived. There was an autobahn to Berlin, but it was in such poor condition that it looked as if it had not been repaired since it was built in the Nazi era. The Berlin Wall itself was a bizarre monument to the history of repression. Abandoned by all authorities at that time, it was possible to enter no-man's land through gaps where the Wall had been torn down, stepping over broken glass and barbed wire to climb up the watchtowers where the East German guards had taken potshots at people trying to escape. On the part of the Wall still standing you could simply prize off pieces of concrete to take back as souvenirs of a history which had crumbled shortly before. During this voyage my curiosity as a climber and a collector of mountaineering books caused me to wander into a second hand bookshop in Prague. I found and bought for a pittance some books about the Czechoslovak Himalayan expeditions of the 1970s and 1980s. I could not read Czech or Slovak, but from the pictures and diagrams a sense of what they had done could be gleaned – the spirit of adventure clearly transcended differences in political systems. Here was an exciting chapter of the history of Himalayan mountaineering, which was little known in the English speaking world. And these climbers from the Eastern half of Europe were some of the main protagonists on Lhotse South Face - the story of the Face is also their story.

Chapter 1 – A New Era for Himalayan Climbing

The époque of Himalayan climbing which ended in 1990 had started 20 years before. Most of the world's fourteen 8000 metre peaks were climbed between 1950 and 1960. The only exception was Shisha Pangma which is in Chinese controlled Tibet and was closed to foreign climbers at this time, but climbed by the Chinese in 1964. There followed something of a hiatus in Himalayan climbing, partly because the race to be first climb the highest mountains was over, but also because political turmoil in the India sub-continent meant periods when access to some or all of the mountains was blocked. Many of the 8000 metre peaks, including Lhotse, were left in peace during this period.

Lhotse stands on the frontier between Nepal and Tibet with the South Face standing in Nepal, a country which has followed an uncertain course from monarchy to democracy. When the rest of the Indian subcontinent fell under British Imperial control during the 18th and 19th centuries, Nepal remained independent. In fact after losing the Anglo-Nepalese War in the early 19th century, Nepal had to cede large areas to Britain, but in exchange was allowed to keep its independence and was then left relatively undisturbed until India freed itself from British control in 1947. At this time Nepal was ruled by an absolute monarchy, but the liberty of their much larger neighbour influenced Nepalese intellectuals who had been exposed to the events in India, to press for greater political freedoms. The country, where eight of the world's fourteen 8000ers are situated, started to open to foreigners in the late 1940s, but the first democratic elections were not held until 1959. After only 18 months King Mahendra decided that the experiment with democracy had been a failure, dismissed the government and introduced a new consistution ruled by the monarchy. In the meantime there was also upheal on the other side of Lhotse in Chinese Tibet. The turmoil of the previous decades had allowed Tibet to gain effective autonomy from China, but following the victory of the Chinese Communist Party there was once again a strong government in Beijing which wanted to take control of all the lands of the former Chinese Empire. The events in Nepal and the threat of military action in Chinese Tibet meant that all mountains in Nepal were closed to climbers between 1965 and 1969. At the same time, most of the highest mountains in Pakistan and India were closed to mountaineers due to tensions between the two countries which led to wars in 1965 and 1971. All of this meant that the 1960s were a much quieter period for Himalayan mountaineering than the previous decade.

By the time the mountains started to open again, the climbers who had made the first ascents of the 8000ers were 15 years older, but the next mountaineering generation was active and ready for a new challenge. This new generation had grown up in the post war period when standards in Alpine mountaineering had leapt. The "last great problems" of the pre-war period like the North Faces of the Eiger and the Matterhorn were now routinely climbed by the elite in both summer and winter and harder new routes like the Central Pillar of Freney on Mont Blanc fell. There was also far more climbers active and mountaineering, which had originally been born as a sport for the Victorian elite was now practiced by people from all backgrounds. Once this new generation had cut their teeth in the Alps, they were naturally keen to move onto bigger things. Like in the late 19th century in the Alps, most of the highest peaks in the world had only been climbed by the easiest routes, leaving plenty of other faces and ridges as obvious challenges. In fact by 1970, of the 8000ers, only Everest and Nanga Parbat had been climbed by a route other than that of the first ascent and many of the peaks still awaited a second ascent. That year saw a sudden explosion in Himalayan mountaineering activity.

The climbing seasons in Nepal are governed by the timing of the monsoon, a seasonal series of storms which bring warm humid air from the plains of India creating heavy snowfall and dangerous climbing conditions in much of the Himalayas. Traditionally expeditions have taken place either in the pre-monsoon season, from March to May or the post-monsoon season from September to November. In the pre-monsoon season of 1970 a strong British team led by Chris Bonington attempted the huge South Face of the 8000 metre Annapurna, one of the largest and steepest in the Himalayas. Bonington was a natural leader and chose a fairly young team of climbers who had been performed at the highest technical level in the Alps. Because of the period when the Asian mountains were closed, most of these climbers did not have a lot of Himalayan experience with the exception of Bonington himself and his deputy Don Whillans. Bonington had been to the Himalayas twice before Nepal closed to foreign climbers and had made first ascents of two high 7000 metre peaks – Annapurna II and Nuptse.

Tackling steep faces in the Himalayas required different techniques to those generally used on the ordinary routes. These techniques were developed in the Alps, on climbs such as the first ascent of a direct route of the Eiger Niorth Face in winter, which involved Bonington and another member of his Annpurna team, Dougal Haston. The Eiger Direct, as it came to be known, was a dramatic climb with British-American and German teams competing and extensive press coverage, helped by the fact that the Eiger stands directly above the Swiss ski resort of Grindelwald and is very visible from the Kleine Scheidigg which can be reached by train. Even when climbers were involved in a life or death struggle up on the face, they could be watched by skiers through telescopes on terraces of bars. The Germans planned from the start to fix ropes and have support climbers carrying loads, an approach which would come to be used extensively on the great faces of the Himalayas. Traditionally the rope is used to attach two or more climbers together as they move up a route in a single push from bottom to top. By contrast fixed ropes are anchored to the mountain and climbers can move up and down them multiple times. On the Eiger both teams slept in snow caves when the ground was too steep to place tents. Athough snow caves meant very cold nights, they at least allowed climbers to sleep with the protection from avalanches and rockfall. The British American team, which included the Americans John Harlin and Layton Kor as well as the Scot Haston, reconnoitred the Eiger late in 1965 and then carefully prepared for the climb. They had extra warm double boots, ropes which were known to be resistant to low temperatures and accumstomed their bodies to the cold by skiing without gloves. Bonington was in theory only working as a journalist to photograph and report on the climb, but ended up getting involved in the actual climbing.

Originally the British-American team wanted to climb the route in a single push, but they and the Germans were forced to retreat in the face of a very severe period of weather with 175 kmh winds. The forecast did not give any hope of a fine period long enough to climb the route in a single push, so the British-American team decided to change tactics and use snowholes and fixed ropes like the Germans. Whilst the Germans favoured a route mainly on rock, the British-Americans preferred to tackle the rock bands which go across the Eiger's North Face at their narrowest points. Ice climbing was harder than the rocks, but it was also quicker, especially given Haston's experience of climbing steep Scottish ice. Steadily they made progress up the face, although Haston and the American John Harlin were at one point trapped in a snowhole for five days by bad weather. Initially they were troubled by blown spindrift snow, but after a couple of days the entrance to the snowhole was blocked and things were calmer. The temperatures of around -20 to -25° C were bearable with the help of foam mats to insulate them from the ground. When the food ran out they decided to retreat back down to the valley. When they returned to the mountain it, was Bonington with American Layton Kor who overcame the crucial section of the Central Pillar, clearing the way to the "Spider", the characteristically shaped icefield high on the face which gave the name of Harrer's book on the 1938 first ascent, "The White Spider". But once again bad weather forced everyone back off the mountain before the summit could be attempted. When the good weather returned, the British American saw that the Germans had reached the Fly, a small icefield above the Spider. Not wanting to be beaten to the top, Haston and Harlin hurriedly returned prussiking back up the fixed ropes. Prussiking is a technique using a device which can slide up the rope, but which blocks when it is pulled back down, which would be used frequently on hard Himalayan climbs. Fixing ropes and ascending them in this way avoids climbing hard sections more than once, but also means relying entirely on the equipment. With the traditional method the climber is supported by the rock or ice and the rope serves only as security in the event of a fall, but when ascending fixed ropes on steep ground the climber is at times putting his full weight on the rope and any failure of the equipment can easily be fatal. Tragically this is exactly what happened to Harlin. The last fixed rope below the Spider broke where it ran over the sharp edge of a slab and Harlin fell more than 1000 metres to his death. Harlin, with film star good looks and great determination and ability, had been the inspiration of the British-American team. After his death, both teams contemplated abandoning the attempt, but in the end agreed to join forces and complete the climb. Eventually four of the Germans and Haston made it to the summit in a storm and were able to retreat back down the easier West Face, although with temperatures of -25 °C and 150 km an hour winds, a number of them suffered frostbite.

The techniques used on the Eiger were put to good use by Bonington's team on Annapurna South Face. The route involved many weeks of struggle to put up fixed ropes and a line of camps, overcoming some of the most technical climbing ever done at such high altitudes. They used bottled oxygen to climb the hardest sections believing that they needed the extra power this gave. Bonington rotated the lead between various strong pairs of climbers, following what would prove to be a successful formula for "siege climbing" big Himalayan faces. It allowed teams to come back down to Base Camp and rest at a lower altitude whilst a fresh team went into the lead to push the route ahead. By late

May, Whillans and Haston, the two strongest climbers, were established in a high camp at 7300 metres. They were tough men, brought up in the hard economic climate of post-war Britain, Whillans almost as famous for his ability to get into, and win, fist fights as he was for his many fine first ascents. They had planned to set up another, higher camp, but whilst trying to find a site for it they realised that the upper part of the face was easier and the summit was quite close. So they climbed the last section to the summit unroped. It was a spectacular success, much the hardest route yet climbed on an 8000er, and marked the start of an exciting new era for Himalayan climbing.

Whilst the British were on Annapurna, a Japanese expedition was attempting the South West Face of Everest – the steepest side of the world's highest mountain. They had already reconnoitred the Face the previous year, reaching a height of over 8000 metres. But although the ground was fairly straightforward to reach this height, the difficulties increased significantly in the upper part of the Face, very much like on the South Face of Lhotse which shares the same geology. Even though the 1970 team was much larger than the reconnaissance group, they did not manage to get any higher up the face. It was clear that not all hard routes would fall easily. Climbing big Himalayan faces is a complex business and the best laid plans can be interrupted by bad weather or unexpected technical difficulty.

A few weeks later, an expedition led by Dr Karl Maria Herrligkoffer attempted the Rupal Wall on another 8000er, Nanga Parbat, one of the world's tallest mountain faces. Herrligkoffer was not himself a mountaineer, but was the step brother of the famous German climber, Willi Merkl, who had lost his life on Nanga Parbat in 1934. In 1953, the year Everest was first climbed, Herrligkoffer led an expedition to the then still unclimbed Nanga Parbat. The 1953 expedition seemed likely to fail when the Austrian Hermann Buhl made a bold solo bid for the summit from a camp below 7000 metres. The route involved a very long traverse across a number of subsidiary tops and Buhl only made it to the summit just before nightfall. Unequipped for a bivouac, he was forced to spend a night in the open on a rock ledge just below the summit. A cold or windy night would have almost certainly meant freezing to death, but by luck it was a windless and relatively warm night and he was able to survive and descend the next day to join his teammates, although he paid the price of severe frostbite. For Herrligkoffer, leading the first successful ascent of Germany's "mountain of destiny" was not enough and he returned to Nanga

Parbat with a number of other expeditions in the 1960s, which first successfully climbed the Diamir face and then attempted the Rupal Face, the steepest of the three sides of the mountain. The 1970 attempt was Herrligkoffer's fourth expedition to the face, reflecting a seemingly obsessive determination to conquer the mountain from every possible side. His previous expedition in 1968 had found a feasible route, but had turned back at 7100 metres.

The 1970 team was primarily made up of German and Austria climbers, but also included the Messner brothers, Reinhold and Gunther, natives of the South Tyrol, a German speaking area in the North-East of Italy. During the second half of the 1960s Reinhold Messner was at the forefront of a rapid rise in Alpine climbing standards and a vocal proponent of a purist style. He spoke out against the excessive use of artificial aid - using bolts and pitons not merely to protect the climbers in the event of a fall, but also to pull on to make progress. Artificial techniques, particularly drilling holes in blank rock to place bolts, allow almost anything to be climbed. This led to a trend to try ever more direct routes up rock faces even when there was no natural line of holds to follow. Messner called this "The Murder of the Impossible". He believed the certainty of success guaranteed by artificial climbing had removed the challenge of pitting one's own natural ability against a mountain, which is one of its principle attractions of the sport. Messner said these techniques had polluted the spirit of pure mountaineering. He did not want the sport to become governed by rules and wanted to maintain the freedom for people to climb how they wanted. Instead he threw down the gauntlet, challenging the leading young mountaineers to set their goals not only in terms of what they climbed, but also the style with which they climbed it. Now after achieving some startling ascents in the Alps, Reinhold Messner was ready to test himself in the Himalayas. Reinhold's younger brother, Gunther, who had been his partner on a number of his hardest Alpine climbs, was also included in the team at the last minute.

On Nanga Parbat they followed the classic siege climbing model, establishing camps on the Face, but then a long period of bad weather blocked the lead climbers including both the Messner brothers, on the mountain and it looked doubtful whether a serious bid for the summit could be made. But in late June the weather cleared and there was a chance to continue. By June 26th the Messner brothers and Gerhard Baur were at the highest camp at 7350m. The weather was uncertain and it was crucial to know the forecast, but to save weight they had not taken a radio with them which would allow them to talk to

Base Camp. It had therefore been agreed that flares would be launched from Base Camp to communicate the forecast to the lead climbers. A red flare would indicate bad weather, a blue one good weather and a red followed by a blue flare uncertain weather. The weather forecast was good, but unintentionally a red rocket was launched. When those at Base Camp checked in the box of flares they found that they only had red flares with them so there was no way to countermand the signal they had given.

Up at the top camp the bad weather forecast they thought they had been given was treated with scepticism because it seemed quite settled. Even in the event of bad weather, Reinhold had said he intended to try and get as high as possible and so very early the next morning he set off alone and unroped towards the summit. He lost a lot of time finding a viable route, but pressed on with youthful enthusiasm and daring. According to the plan for that day, Baur and Gunther Messner were supposed to fix ropes above the camp to facilitate a subsequent attempt by the next summit team, but whilst they were preparing to do so the rope became impossible tangled. Gunther threw it down in frustration and without a word, set off unroped to follow his brother. Although he was a few hours behind, Reinhold had lost time finding the route and Gunther was greatly helped by his brother's trail. Pushing himself very hard, Gunther caught up and the brothers made it to the summit together. The events which followed became the subject of a controversy which has continued for 40 years, involved several lawsuits and been the subject of numerous books.

By the time they reached the summit it was late and Gunther was very tired and showing signs of altitude sickness. Reinhold decided to retreat some way down the West Face to a notch on the ridge above the top of what the expedition christened the Merkl Gully. The Messners had climbed the lower part of this gully in the morning, but the upper part was steep and would have been very hard to climb and was impossible to descend without a rope. Here the Messner brothers were forced to spend the night in the open without bivouac equipment, down jackets, food or water. After a very difficult night the condition of Gunther had worsened and Reinhold went to try and get help. He reached the edge of the ridge where he was able to see the second summit team of Felix Kuen and Peter Scholz coming up from below. Reinhold was at the top of the Merkl Gully at a distance which made communication difficult and he and the others were separated by impassable terrain. The exact contents of the shouted conversation which took place are disputed with Messner saying it was clear that he was in difficulty, but Kuen claiming that Messner had said things were OK with the result that he and Scholz continued with their own summit bid. Kuen, who was ahead and heard better, committed suicide a few years later, making it even more difficult to get confirmation of what actually happened. Because the two Messners had left the high camp separately, neither had brought a rope. After the night near the summit, Gunther was not in a condition to be able to descend unroped down the Rupal Face so the brothers decided to try and descend a new route on the somewhat easier angled Diamir Face, directly down the opposite side of the mountain. After surviving a desperate descent and reaching the bottom of the Face, Reinhold, feeling stronger than his younger brother, was scouting ahead to find a way through the crevasses and lost sight of Gunther. For a while Reinhold waited for Gunther and when he didn't come he went back and searched for him. But finding no sign of him, Reinhold started to fear that his brother had been buried under an avalanche.

The exact events and the intentions of Reinhold in descending the Diamir Face have been challenged by some of this team mates. Some suggested it was always his intention to attempt a traverse of the mountain rather than a last minute choice taken in extremis when no other option was open. They questioned whether Gunther died earlier than Reinhold's account suggests. Many years later Gunther's body was found at the foot of the wall, which seemed to support Reinhold's version of events, although the disputes rumbled on. After wandering for a day searching for Gunther at the foot of the face, Reinhold realised that if he was to save his own life, he would have to walk down the Diamir Valley to find help. He set off and the next day encountered local shepherds and despite language difficulties convinced them to carry him down since he could no longer walk due to frostbitten feet and fever. He knew that he would probably die without medical attention soon. Eventually he reached the main valley and the road where he encountered the rest of the expedition who had given up any hope of finding the brothers alive and left the mountain. The actions of Messner and his decision to descend the unequipped Diamir Face were questioned by Herrligkoffer and Messner in turn bitterly complained that a rescue party wasn't sent to try and find him and Gunther. These disputes ended up in the law courts and the controversy about what actually happened and whose fault it was has continued to the present. What is not in doubt is that the Messners had conquered one of the world's highest mountain walls, making a landmark ascent. For Reinhold it was a deeply tragic and traumatic event, but also the start of a stellar Himalayan climbing career.

The successes on Annapurna and Nanga Parbat were followed by others such as the 1971 French ascent of the difficult West Pillar of Makalu, the world's fifth highest mountain. Like the Annapurna and Nanga Parbat expeditions, the French used a heavyweight style with a large team, oxygen and fixed ropes and Sherpas to carry loads. . The term Sherpa, which will be familiar to anyone with even a minimal knowledge of Himalayan climbing, refers to a Nepalese people of ethnic Tibetan origin who live in the area around Mount Everest. From the first attempts to climb Everest in the 1920s until today they have played a vital role in many expeditions as cooks, porters, guides and fully fledged climbers. The French only made a bid for the summit once they had a camp established high on the mountain at 7700 metres. From there Yannick Seigneur and Bernard Mellet reached the summit. Seigneur, one of the strongest climbers on the team, was already thinking about his next goals as he sat on top of Makalu. As they savoured their triumph and looked around at the magnificent view, Mellet said, "say, Yannick", indicating the ordinary route up Makalu by which another French team had made the first ascent in 1955, "if only we had a pair of skis..." Seigneur looked at the ordinary route, which seemed almost easy enough to ski down and reflected on the progress in climbing standards over the past sixteen years. "Instead of that, look at the South Face of Lhotse, Bernard", he said, "When shall we go there?"

This was an exciting period in Himalayan climbing and Yannick Seigneur was certainly not alone amongst the leading players in dreaming of new goals - and Lhotse's South Face was one of the most obvious. Lhotse's summit lies very close to Everest, which it is connected to by the high pass of the South Col and from a geographical point of view is considered by some not to be a separate mountain. One measure of a mountain's separateness is its prominence, defined as how far it rises above the highest col dividing it from a higher peak. A mountain with a prominence of over 1500 metres is referred to as an ultra. Apart from Lhotse, all of the other recognised 8000 metre peaks are ultras and most of them have a prominence of well over 2000 metres. Lhotse, by contrast, only rises 610m above the South Col. Nevertheless it is universally recognised by mountaineers as one of the fourteen 8000 metre peaks.

The key to the first ascent of both Everest and of Lhotse was the Western Cwm, a deep glaciated valley which is encircled by Everest, Lhotse and another mountain, Nuptse, the West Peak of Everest. These three mountains make up a horseshoe of extremely high ridges with Lhotse at the head of the Cwm, the Welsh word for a valley. The route by which Hillary and Tenzing first climbed Everest traverses diagonally across the West Face of Lhotse to reach the South Col, from where they finished by the South East Ridge of Everest. Since before 1950 Nepal was closed to mountaineers, all earlier efforts to climb Everest were from the Northern side of the mountain in Tibet. There are two major valleys on the Northern side of Everest – the Rongbuck and the Kangshung. Everest lies between these two valleys whereas Lhotse only faces the Kangshung valley. After some initial reconnaissance of both valleys in 1921, the British concluded that only the Rongbuck offered a feasible route to the summit of Everest and during the 1920s and 1930s a series of attempts on it were made from this valley. The result was that Lhotse was left undisturbed until the 1950s.

As a mountaineering goal, Lhotse was, of course, never as big a pull as Everest whilst the latter remained unclimbed. But after the first ascent of Everest in 1953, its near neighbour, the 4th highest mountain in the world, suddenly became an attractive objective. In 1955 an international team led by Norman Dyhrenfurth, an American of Swiss origin, made the first attempt. Dyhrenfurth's father, Gunther Oskar, had been one of the pioneers in the previous stage of the evolution of Himalayan mountaineering in the 1930s, when he led two expeditions to attempt 8000 metre peaks, Gasherbrum I and Kangchenjunga. The team included Austrian Erwin Schneider, another 1930s veteran, another Austrian, Ernst Senn, two Swiss and three Americans.

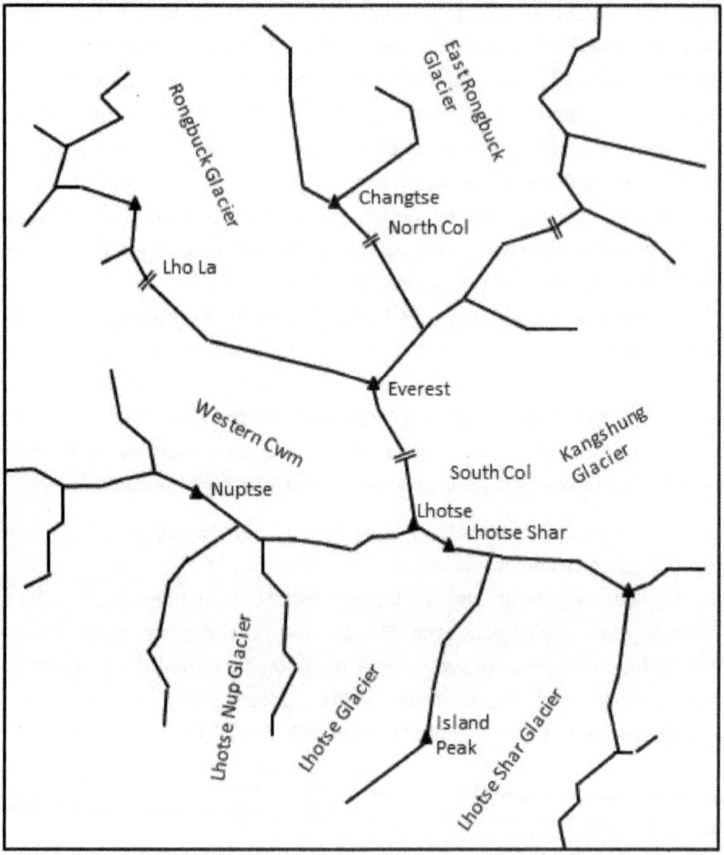

In the few weeks available before the monsoon broke, Dyhrenfurth and Senn explored the south side of Lhotse, as they believed there might be a straightforward way up to the subsidiary peak of Lhotse Shar, from where a ridge led to the main summit of Lhotse. They were thus the first climbers to look seriously at the South side of Lhotse, but what they saw made them sceptical about the prospects of making an ascent from there and they moved on to explore other areas to maintain their acclimatisation and fitness during the monsoon. They were excited to explore the Southern side of the Everest Massif, which had some spectacular peaks and had been completely out of bounds to Westerners until a few years before.

Once the monsoon ended, the team moved to Everest Base Camp to start operations on their primary objective, Lhotse. Following the route of the 1953 British Everest Expedition up the Western Cwm they first had to find their way through the Icefall which blocked its entrance. The Icefall is where the glacier in the Western Cwm, fed by all the snow falling on the surrounding peaks is squeezed out of the narrow exit of the Cwm in a wild tangle of ice. In unbearable heat, Dyhrenfurth's team worked their way through vast chasms, partly filled with huge fallen ice blocks to reach the Cwm itself, which was also called the Valley of Silence by the team which first reached it three years before. Despite frequent snowfall, they placed further camps up the Cwm, but the fifth and highest camp was only at 7600 metres, not as high as Dyhrenfurth would have liked to attempt the 8511m Lhotse. The first summit team was slowed down by deep snow with a hard, but breakable crust and did not make it to 8000 metres. Then four days of storms pinned them down in the tents. When the weather relented, Senn, who couldn't stand the chance of another failure, decided to try alone. Snow conditions were still bad, but he reached the start of the couloir which splits the West Face of Lhotse and provides an obvious route to the summit. Here Senn's oxygen set ceased to function and he pulled off his mask, gasping for air and unable to go on. He returned to Camp V, hoping to make another attempt, but the bad weather blocked him there with diminishing supplies. During his five nights alone at Camp V he realised he had no chance of getting to the top, but the savagery of the storm outside made him he put off the descent. Finally the wind had ripped open one side of the tent and left him no choice but to gather his personal things, put his crampons on and set off down. The wind was so strong that at one point it blew him off his feet and deposited him back on the slope, 15 metres further down. Dyhrenfurth and the rest of team in the next camp down were getting ready to try and relieve Senn when they heard the sound of crampons outside the tent. Senn was a tough character, but, after five days alone and the battle to fight his way down, the relief of seeing his comrades was so great that he could not hold back tears of emotion. Despite the storms, they made another two attempts, but on the second of these a climber, Bruno Spirig, got left up at a high camp alone feeling too unwell to descend. With continued storm conditions and camps damaged by high winds and drifting snow, the situation seemed serious to the expedition leader Dyhrenfurth. The next morning he took all available Sherpas and led a team back up the mountain. Struggling against the fury of the wind, Dyhrenfurth, Fred Beckey and Senn together with a group of Sherpas managed to reach Camp IV. They were met by a scene of desolation with tents half buried under enormous snow drifts, but fortunately Spirig answered their call from the tents and seemed not to be in bad condition. They were able to help the sick man down to Base Camp, but there was no doubt that the first attempt to climb Lhotse was over.

The next year a Swiss expedition set out with the twin goals of making the first ascent of Lhotse and the second of Everest. Two Swiss expeditions in 1952 had pioneered the South Col route on Everest and got to within 200 metres of the top, paving the way for the British the following year during which New Zealander, Edmund Hillary and Sherpa Tenzing made the first ascent. Therefore the Swiss had unfinished business. In 1956 they established a camp at just under 8000 metres, not far below the South Col. From there Fritz Luchsinger and Ernst Reiss, planned to climb Lhotse using the couloir identified by Dyhrenfurth's team. They spent most of the night before the attempt making soup and tea before sleeping fitfully. By 5am they were preparing and saw the sun touch the first peaks in the distance, but slowed by the effects of altitude, they were not ready to leave the camp until 9 am.

They climbed with full bottle of oxygen each, but rejected the option of taking a spare bottle to save weight, making a descent without oxygen likely. In the couloir they found good firm snow allowing relatively fast progress with only occasionally a softer patch where they sunk in up to their knees. They tried to kick a good track in the snow which they could use on the way back down. They gained 150 metres of height in the first hour – excellent progress considering the altitude – but as they got higher they began to feel the lack of oxygen more and more. Luchsinger turned Reiss's oxygen supply up to four litres per minute so that the latter could keep up the hard work of breaking the trail. At noon they reached a zone where the couloir is steeper and blocked by a band of rocks, which they had expected would be the crux of the climb. They found a narrow snow gully which led past this it and, placing a couple of pitons for protection, Reiss managed to overcome the difficulties. After this the couloir opened back up into a funnel shape which acted as a sort of wind tunnel resulting in the climbers being nearly thrown off their feet by heavy gusts. The snow in the upper part was less regular and it became hard work to keep kicking steps. Luchsinger took over the lead, heading for the twin summits, known as the Horns of Lhotse, which stand on either side of the top of the couloir. They could now see that the snow-capped northern peak was higher than the rocky peak on the South side.

The final section was very steep, with a rope's length of 60° hard névé as tough as ice. Given the enormous exposure they cut steps all the way. Just below the highest point, Reiss hacked out a large ledge and leaned against the slope trying to recover his breath. Luchsinger then joined him and the two climbers crouched, waiting for a lull in the wind to haul themselves up to the knife edge ridge of the summit and peer down at the cloud shrouded East and South Faces. They did not say much, overwhelmed by the savagery and magnificence of the situation. The summit was so narrow that they could neither sit nor set down their rucksacks – they had to tie them to their axes driven into the snow. Posing for summit photographs wasn't easy with limited room for manoeuvre and they had to concentrate to avoid a mistake which could have had terrible consequences. They stayed on the summit for 45 minutes, catching occasional glimpses of the camps further down through the drifting clouds. Their oxygen had run out on the summit, but for the descent they put their masks back on to protect their faces from the wind, which had become a gale. By now they had lost feeling in their hands and feet, but they took the utmost care belaying each other, only moving one at a time. They knew that if they moved together and one of them slipped, it would be difficult to arrest a fall on the steep snow with their frozen hands. They overcame the steep narrow section using a rope they had left there on the way up.

As they approached the foot of the couloir they started to realise that they had successfully climbed and got down from the world's fourth highest mountain. When they arrived at the tent at quarter past six they were dismayed to find it was partially collapsed by drifting snow, but it was too late to continue further down. So, despite being close to exhaustion, they had to dig the tent out before being able to crawl into their sleeping bags and starting to make hot drinks. Melting the snow seemed to take for ever and they took occasional breaths of oxygen to restore their strength and warmth. Their feet were still numb and they took off their boots to inspect their toes, but fortunately there were no signs of frostbite. Warmed by the tea and with the monotonous sound of spindrift snow hitting the roof of the tent they drifted off to sleep. At midnight they woke to find that drifting snow had partly crushed the tent, leaving Luchsinger, who was on the side towards the slope, unable to move because of the pressure of the snow. Reiss had no choice but to squeeze out of his sleeping bag, struggle to put on his frozen solid boots and go out into the bitter night to clear the snow. In the morning they completed the descent to the lower camps and the support of their comrades, who made the second ascent of Everest. Reiss and Luchsinger rated the climb extremely difficult by Alpine standards. Today this route has been climbed often and is viewed as steep but fairly straightforward for modern Himalayan climbers. However the couloir on the West Face is a single weak point in Lhotse's otherwise formidable armour. To climb Lhotse by any other route represents an enormous climbing challenge and the vast majority of ascents of Lhotse to date have has been by this route.

Lhotse has three ridges, all of which are complex and narrow making progress along them inevitably difficult and slow. The short North Ridge connecting the mountain to the South Col between Lhotse and Everest, but has a number of large rock towers, which would be difficult to cross. The very long West Ridge, which continues for miles from Nuptse, encloses the Western Cwm on one side. The equally long and even narrower East Ridge passes over two major subsidiary summits, Lhotse Shar and Lhotse Middle, which present a totally different climbing challenge despite not having much prominence from Lhotse. The ridge between Lhotse's main summit and Lhotse Shar is incredibly narrow and jagged and has still not been traversed. Without crossing this ridge any ascent of Lhotse Shar must inevitably start from a completely different valley to that used for the normal route on Lhotse. Between these three ridges there are three faces of Lhotse. The West Face stands at the head of the Western Cwm and is split by the couloir used to make the first ascent. The North East sprawls huge and heavily glaciated above the Kangshung Glacier merging with the East Face of Everest, but does not present appealing lines of ascent for climbers. The lower part is made up of steep rock walls which are topped by shelves covered in hanging glaciers which threaten the lower part of the Face. Then the top part steepens again into vertical cliffs. Unsurprisingly no-one has tried to climb Lhotse from this side, which is also by far the least visited approach to Everest.

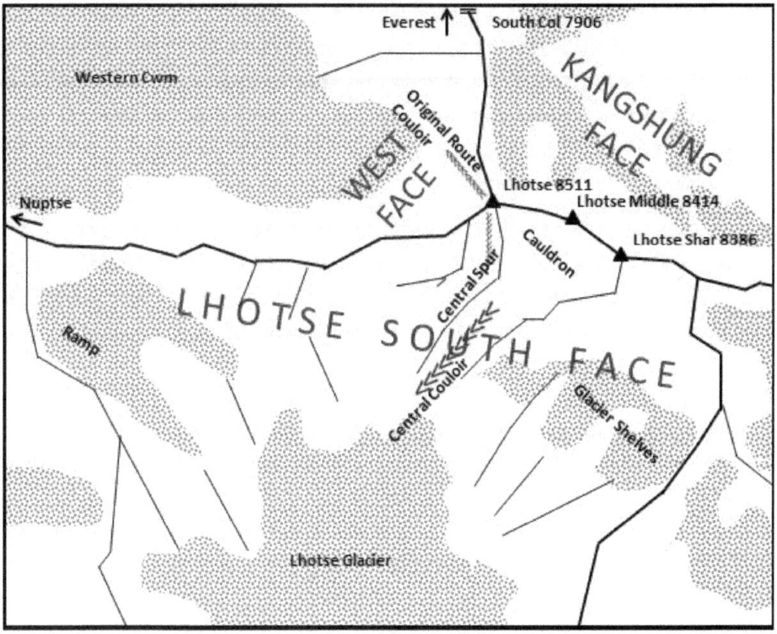

The final Face, the South, is the most obvious aspect of Lhotse, highly visible from the much visited Sherpa region to the South of the Everest Massif. Although from a distance it appears to be a flat wall, the topography of the Face is actually not simple and the main features should be understood if one is to make sense of the history of the attempts to climb it. The Face is very wide, not falling below 7500 metres from Nuptse to Lhotse Shar across a distance of something like 7.5 km, forming a curtain wall which blocks most of the view of Everest from the south. The left side of Lhotse South Face has a broad ice ramp which leads diagonally to the left giving a slightly more easy angled approach to the summit ridge than the central part of the face. The problem with this ramp as a route is that it reaches the ridge some 3.5 kilometres left of the highest point and traversing this section of ridge would be a formidable challenge. The most obvious features of the central part of the Face are a number of very large and vertical or overhanging triangular rock buttresses. The upper part of the centre of Face is also characterised by two large snow basins at around 8000 metres, the right hand one surrounded by the peaks of Lhotse, Lhotse Middle and Lhotse Shar and the left hand below one of the large triangular faces.

Between these two basins a spur leads directly up to the summit, whereas another less distinct spur leads to the summit ridge a few hundred metres to the left of the highest point. Between these two spurs a couloir splits the upper part of the face, finishing on the ridge just to the left of the summit. These different features were of course closely studied by those planning to attempt the face.

Before rising climbing standards made the South Face a realistic objective, the most obvious target on the South side of the Massif was the 8383m Lhotse Shar, which although not rated as a fully independent 8000er was still an important unclimbed summit. It was first attempted by a Japanese team in 1965 by its South East Ridge, which forms the right hand edge of the South Face of Lhotse. In mid-March they established a Base Camp at the foot of the South Face and then a further four camps, the highest at 7000 metres, but then one of the climbers fell and was badly injured. After spending the night in the open, he was also severely frostbitten and the team lost 10 days bringing the injured man down to Camp II. A second party returned to the attack and on May 15th two climbers, Matsuura and Iguchi reached a height of over 8000 metres, but here they found a 200 metre gap and were forced to turn back. Five years later an Austrian expedition completed the route with Sepp Mayerl and Rolf Walter reaching the summit. They had originally contemplated traversing to the main summit of Lhotse, but realised that this was too major an undertaking for their small group. Apart from these attempts on Lhotse Shar, Lhotse was left in peace by the world's mountaineers during the first 17 years following its first ascent.

In the early 1970s with mountaineers looking for ambitious new goals, it was inevitable that a feature as obvious as Lhotse's South Face would attract attention. The first to try it was a Japanese expedition organised by the Kanagawa Mountaineering Federation in 1973. Given the scale of the objective, it was a lightweight team by the standards of the early 1970s with nine climbers supported by only five Sherpas. By contrast the 1970 Japanese attempt on the South West Face of Mount Everest, with the benefit of hindsight a less ambitious objective, had 39 climbers and 26 high altitude Sherpas. The Lhotse team left a wintery Japan on the 10th February 1973 flying via Bangkok and Kolkata to Kathmandu. When I went to Changtse in 1990, Kathmandu was still a strange mixture of chaotic Asian capital and hippy hangout, but also with an almost medieval feel with the narrow dirt streets, horse drawn carts and wooden houses. The Japanese spent a week in Kathmandu organising the permit which is required for any expedition to a high mountain in Nepal and hiring Sherpas for the mountain and porters who would carry loads to Base Camp. Most of the equipment which had been brought from Japan by air was sent by plane to the airstrip Lukla, which is several days' march closer to the mountain than the roadhead. The members of the expedition travelled on foot from the roadhead, the traditional way that expeditions in the 1950s and 60s approached the Everest region, although flying to Lukla became more and more common in the 1970s and 1980s. After leaving the roadhead, they crossed the Bhote Kosi River on a suspension bridge. Soon after the bridge the Japanese leader, Uchida, was surprised to find the Sherpas setting up camp for the night. There were many hours of daylight left and he felt they should really be pushing on given that there was another 130 kilometres to cover to get to the foot of Lhotse. But he resisted the temptation to insist, realising that it was necessary to have a "when in Rome, do as the Romans" attitude. They then settled into the routine of the approach march which was unchanged when I visited the area for the first time more than 17 years later, starting with tea in their tents from the kitchen boy at 5am – something they had been trained to do by the British. Referring to this person who was quite likely a grown man as a "boy" was also something of a vestige of the colonial era. The Japanese followed the well-used path towards Everest Base Camp: one of the world's most popular trekking routes. Every few hours the porters would stop to buy tea or Chang, a local alcohol, from the road-side shops. The whole team halted for a few days at Namche Bazar, the main town of the Solo Khumbu region, in which Lhotse and Everest sit. Here they bought bamboo sticks to mark the way on the glacier and logs to bridge crevasses.

From a hill above Namche Uchida's team saw Lhotse for the first time and it left them speechless. The South Face is dominant and Everest a seemingly insignificant point poking out from behind the enormous mountain wall connecting Lhotse to Nuptse. The lower, but equally dramatic peaks of Ama Dablam, Kangterka and Tamersku formed a picturesque foreground. Further along the path at Imje Khola there was a wooden bridge and the path branched - to the left was the much trodden route to Everest, to the right towards the South side of Lhotse. From the branch it took them a further four days to reach Base Camp on the Lhotse Glacier, which they found to be like a strange moonscape with large rocks and ice blocks standing up and pools of water scattered around. On the first morning at Base Camp, Uchida was woken whilst it was still dark by the kitchen boy bringing tea. He left the tent and looked up at the Face just as the breaking of dawn turned the summit slopes red. Everything was still down on the glacier as if frozen for thousands of years, unseen by human eyes. Based on their experience in Japan, Uchida's team had expected avalanches to occur in the afternoon as the temperature increased, but they were disconcerted to see that on Lhotse they started to come down as soon the sun hit the face in the morning, pouring over the huge overhangs like great white waterfalls and spreading out like fireworks. Even at night when the wind dropped, the avalanches continued and disturbed the climbers' sleep.

The original plan of the Japanese was to climb the highest part of the face leading straight to the summit, the so-called "direttissima". This name was coined in the Italian Dolomites where a trend in the 1950s and 1960s had been to find ever harder climbs by taking more and more direct lines. When this involved crossing blank rock with no natural weaknesses which required artificial climbing techniques it was what Reinhold Messner had called the "Murder of the Impossible". The central line on Lhotse's South Face follows an obvious spur finishing right on the highest point and thus is far from an artificial line. But Central Spur was bound to involve very hard climbing and was beyond the realistic scope of expeditions in the early 1970s. As the first serious visitors to this huge and complex face, the first thing the Japanese did was to explore where a feasible route might lie. Studying photos back home was no substitute for looking at the mountain in the flesh. The mountain was alive with avalanches moving down it, clouds drifting across it, and conditions changing in a way a photo couldn't capture. Uchida sent one team up the glacier to find a route to the foot of the Face and another to climb the opposite side of the valley to study the paths of avalanches coming down the Face to determine which areas were safe and which threatened. After this they decided that the direttissima was too dangerous and asked permission from their liaison officer to change route to a line further left up the ramp leading to the West Ridge of Lhotse. This would then require a very long climb up the ridge or slopes on its left to reach the summit, but that was not at the front of their thoughts, since even reaching the ridge was an ambitious goal. The liaison officer is an employee of the Nepalese Government: one is assigned to each expedition to oversee relations with the locals and ensure the terms of the expedition's permit are respected. He said that Uchida's requested route was covered by the existing permit and so they decided to make their attempt this way.

Although they were not tackling the main part of the South Face, they would nonetheless be tackling unexplored terrain. This was more appealing than the alternative of trying a line further to the right over the already climbed Lhotse Shar.

So they set out to establish a line of camps up the ramp. To reach Camp I they had to climb a steep snow slope and then a 30 metre ice cliff, before another steep ice face led to a flatter area at 5800 metres. It was a good site, flat and around 10 metres square. Climbers would come to understand that having space to camp on was a rare luxury on Lhotse South Face. They spent the next two days carrying loads – 500 kilos in total - to get the camp stocked with provisions. Most of the team went back to Base Camp leaving two climbers, Hiroshima and Sunagawa, in Camp I to push the route further up the mountain. They now started to find that the face had a weather system all of its own, created by Lhotse's position between the humid plains of India and the dry plateau of Tibet and rising nearly 2000 metres above the lower peaks in front of it. The Japanese found there was usually a snowstorm in the afternoon, but during the nights it cleared up again with starry skies. The next section of the route involved crossing three rocky peaks, the first of which was steep and loose making it easy to knock stones off onto climbers below. They set up a 10 metre long rope ladder to facilitate load carrying up this section. Beyond the rock peaks another snow ridge led to the site of Camp II in a flat area at 6400 metres. From there straightforward snow terrain led to Camp III, although they found carrying loads up to it hard work and they carried up logs to bridge some wide crevasses to make the route easier. With Camp III set up at 6850m on May 2nd, the main ridge of Lhotse now seemed quite close. When the weather was good they were very comfortable even at this height – the Wall is of course south facing and with the sun beating down they tended to get too hot and sweaty, but when the afternoon storms arrived it was a different story with temperatures down to -10° C and strong winds.

From Camp III they set off to try and make the route up the final section of the face to the main Nuptse-Lhotse ridge. They were now high enough to see across the face to Makalu, the fifth highest mountain in the world, but the pressure of being a small team climbing on one of the highest and most difficult faces in the world was starting to take its toll. They were unshaven and fatigued and headaches often stopped them from climbing. On May 8th they made a final attempt to climb the last section up to the ridge, but struggled to make progress on steep unconsolidated snow slopes with hidden crevasses. Uchida assessed the situation and decided to abandon the attempt and call off the expedition. His team had reached 7300 metres, made a credible exploration of the face and found a possible route to reach the main ridge. However even after getting there, they would have had an enormous distance to cover to the summit and were unlikely to have had the resources or manpower to make it. Uchida recognised the limitations in their approach and started to make plans to return with a larger team, more Sherpas and more oxygen. He felt this would give a realistic prospect of climbing Lhotse from the South, although he knew it would not be easy. For the moment, the main part of the South Face did not even seem a realistic objective.

Chapter 2 – A Problem for the Year 2000

Before the Japanese could try again, it was the turn of the Italians. The Italian Alpine Club planned a national expedition to the Face, which was now viewed as one of the great unclimbed challenges of world mountaineering. In the first golden age of Himalayan climbing in the 1950s when the 8000ers were climbed for the first time, the first 3 big successes were by French (Annapurna in 1950), British (Everest in 1953) and Germans and Austrians (Nanga Parbat in 1953), so the pride of Italian alpinism received a huge boost when an Italian team climbed K2 in 1954. With the benefit of hindsight, this ascent was perhaps the greatest achievement of any of those in the 1950s. K2 was not climbed again until 1977 and the route is still today considered a major climbing challenge – in contrast to Everest which is routinely climbed with oxygen and fixed ropes by complete amateurs willing to pay a five figure sum to get to the top of the World. In 1954 Italy had needed a boost after the chaos and destruction of the war. In the first half of the 1970s there was a parallel as the British, French and German-Austrian expeditions had made major ascents of some of the hardest faces of the great Himalayan giants. Of course, the first summit pair on the Rupal Face of Nanga Parbat had been the Messner brothers who were German speaking Italians, but this was no substitute for a climb made by a national expedition.

The man chosen to lead the team was Riccardo Cassin, a legendary figure in Italian Alpinism. Cassin was born in 1909 in the Friuli region in North East of Italy. As with many Italians at the time, his father went abroad to find work, but died in a mining accident in Canada. So Riccardo had to start working when he was only 12, initially in a foundry in very tough conditions with an infernal heat, terrible noise and 12 hour working days. When he was 17 he received a letter from a friend advising him to move to Lecco to seek work, as there were opportunities in the engineering sector. Lecco is a small city on Lake Como below the Alpine foothills with a mountain tradition and a concentration of climbers equalled by few places in the World. Above the town is a pair of mountains, the Grigne, which although not high above sea level, tower more than 2000 metres above the lake with limestone eroded into dramatic faces and towers, providing a perfect proving ground for alpinists. The local climbing club, "the spiders of the Grignetta" were very active on these mountains and throughout the Alps. In his youth Cassin was also a good amateur boxer, with a record of 42 victories, 3 draws and a single defeat, but once he his boss took him up the Resegone, a dramatic saw shaped mountain which dominates the town of Lecco, the mountains came to dominate his life and there was no time for boxing. These first excursions were only walks, but it introduced Cassin to a sport which required a balance of strength and courage, and a chance for adventure to escape the mundanity and hard work of everyday life.

By the late 1920s Cassin was using all his free time to go out in the mountains. In 1931 he made the first ascent of the Corno Medale a 400 metre high cliff face which dominates the town of Lecco. There had already been several unsuccessful attempts when Cassin first tried the route the year before with fellow Lecco climber Carlo Corti. Corno Medale is only 1000 metres above sea level and the low altitude means it is very vegetated, almost a jungle with accompanying wildlife. When I climbed Cassin's route in the 1990s I was tied a ledge belaying my partner when a snake appeared from some bushes and slithered towards me. Unable to move, I had a nervous few seconds before the beast decided it liked the look of me as little as I liked the look of it. On the first attempt they were over half-way when Cassin pulled out a loose block whilst tackling a difficult crack. He was 15 metres above Corti, but had a couple of pitons in to protect a fall, but the rock first smashed him on the forehead and then broke into two parts, one of which hit his left hand and the other his right knee. He was sent plunging into space and came to a halt below his partner as one of the pitons was ripped out by the weight of the fall. Cassin was left stunned with his knee hurting badly. There was now no question of carrying on and even getting back down to the foot of the wall was a battle. Undeterred Cassin returned the following year with one of his regular partners, Mario dell Oro. Rapidly passing the previous high point they were so engrossed in the climbing that they had not noticed a storm brewing up and were taken by surprise by the first crack of thunder. With lightning flashing around them and torrents of water created by the downpour washing stones and other debris down on top of them, they hurriedly abseiled down to shelter in a cave. The rain continued all afternoon and they had no choice but to spend the night where they were – Cassin's first bivouac. As the rain eased during the night they could see the lights of the city of Lecco below and even make out their own homes. After a while they saw other lights coming up through the woods below. It was a group of their friends who had come up to check how they were. Cassin told them that they would get soaked and should return home, but they insisting on staying the night in the rain to give moral support to the pair on the face. They were still there with hot drinks and food when the climbers managed to abseil to the bottom in the morning. Cassin was touched and it is clear that this camaraderie was an important part of the mountain experience for him. Again Cassin was not discouraged by the setback and, without telling anyone, he and Dell Oro returned and completed the climb a week later.

During the 1930s Cassin made a series of hard first ascents in the area around Lecco and then more widely in the Alps, including the North East Face of Pizzo Badile in 1937. By now he was one of the world's top climbers and Cassin and his friends spent the next winter preparing to attempt the first ascent of the North Face of the Eiger. They climbed near Lecco in the winter to hone their skills on ice, but when they arrived at the foot of the Eiger they witnessed the German-Austrian group finishing the climb. Not wanting to finish empty handed they turned their attention to another of the last great problems of the Alps, the Walker Spur on the Grand Jorasses near Mont Blanc. Competition to be the first on such routes led climbers to conceal their intentions from potential competitors. Before attempting the Walker, Cassin and Ugo Tizzoni made a reconnaissance and, having concluded the ascent was feasible, telephoned the third member of the team, Gino Esposito, telling him to join them in Courmayeur on the Italian side of Mont Blanc by train. On the train Esposito got talking to a German climber whose bulging sack indicated someone with serious intentions and who seemed suspiciously interested in Esposito's plans. The German said he knew the Mont Blanc group very well and showed him a series of enlarged photographs including one of the North Face of the Grand Jorasses. Esposito was non-committal and said that the Walker Spur must be very difficult, but didn't give any indication of his plans. The German replied that the Walker's first ascent would be one of the hardest climbs yet done in the Alps and it would surely be done by Germans and not some Italians. A week later the Italians had done the climb and were celebrating back in Courmayeur when the same German came up to Esposito and Cassin to complement the Italians on both their climbing skill and slyness. The Walker Spur, on which Cassin led all the way, established his position as one of the World's leading climbers.

During the war years Cassin was leader in Lecco of the partisans who resisted Fascist rule. He freely admitted that he had been a member of the Fascist Party before the war, but at that time he had no interest in politics and was asked to join the party due to his mountaineering achievements. Considering it merely an honorary thing, he accepted, but once Italy had joined the war as an ally to Germany he changed his mind, tore up his Fascist membership card and threw it in Lake Como. A couple of years later he joined the partisans who had formed a rock climbers' group who used the excuse of going into the mountains and their knowledge of the area to carry out resistance activities including helping jews escape across the border into nearby Switzerland.

In 1953 Cassin was part of small group which reconnoitred K2 to prepare for the full expedition the following year, but he was controversially omitted from the 1954 team which went on to be successful. In theory he had failed his medical, but this seems absurd given that he was one of Europe's strongest climbers and in fact Cassin would live to be 100. It seemed more probable that the expedition leader, Ardito Desio, who was not himself a mountaineer, was worried that a well-known figure like Cassin might seem to be more responsible for the success of the expedition than him. Four years later, Cassin showed his exclusion from K2 was an error when he returned to the same Karakorum area to lead an expedition which successfully climbed Gasherbrum IV, a beautiful and difficult mountain just a shade under 8000 metres. By 1975 Cassin was 66, but still active in mountaineering. In fact he would be for many more years: he repeated his first ascent of the North East Face of the Piz Badile to celebrate its' 50th anniversary at the age of 78. In 1997, I was in Lecco at the presentation of a returning successful K2 expedition: a fine achievement for a team from a small city. It was also an emotional occasion as a young climber, Lorenzo Mazzoleni, had died on the mountain and so the triumph was mixed with sadness. The cinema where the presentation was held was packed, with people standing in the aisles – the fire regulations completely ignored. The style of such an event in Italy is very different from a British climbing lecture, where a bearded mountaineer shows slides, whilst giving understated anecdotes about his adventures. In Lecco there was plenty of razzmatazz with attractive young women to present the speakers and the high spot of the evening was when Cassin was invited onto the stage to rapturous applause. He was a short man, but even in his late 80s still sprightly. But the applause was even louder when his even shorter wife, Irma, joined him on the stage. The affection of the whole town for this couple was clearly very deep, not least for their role in the war – where he led the resistance group. He was an obvious leader for the Lhotse team and was able to command huge respect from a team drawn from top climbers all over Italy.

In the spring of 1974 Cassin joined an Italian trekking group in Nepal to have a close up look at the South Face of Lhotse and to study the various logistic and practical problems involved in mounting the following year's expedition. Together with Roberto Sorgato, Cassin climbed to 5300m on the opposite side of the valley from Lhotse and took many photographs. They also explored the base of the Face, but cloudy weather prevented them getting a close up view. However they did identify a seemingly secure spot to place the Base Camp. The following year's expedition was a major enterprise organised by the Italian Alpine Club, which has over 300,000 members and Cassin looked for the strongest and most experienced climbers from throughout the country. The team included men like Alessandro Gogna, from Genova who had made some important first ascents in the Alps including the Zmutt Nose, a huge overhang on the North Face of the Matterhorn, the first winter ascent of Cassin's 1937 route on Piz Badile and the first solo ascent of Cassin's most famous route of all, the Walker Spur.

Reinhold Messner was also part of the team. As a German speaking Italian he managed to participate in expeditions organised in Italy, Germany and Austria. Although later he had enough prestige and finance to organise his own expeditions, in the first years of his Himalayan career being able to participate in different countries' teams helped him to visit the world's highest mountains very frequently. Messner had followed his ascent of Nanga Parbat with a new route on the South Face of another 8000er, Manaslu as part of an Austrian expedition. Messner and Franz Jäger made a bid for the top from a camp at 7400 metres on the edge of the vast summit plateau. On the easy final section Jäger turned back whilst Messner continued to the summit. By now the clouds had descended and in a terrible storm, Messner battled his way safely back to the camp. But there was no sign of Jäger. Two other climbers, Frankhauser and Schlick were at the camp in support and went out to search for the missing man. In the continuing storm, Schlick disappeared too and finally Messner and Frankhauser had to give up hope for their companions and descend. It was Messner's second 8000 metre peak, putting him in a small elite group, but both mountains had cost the life of his companion on the summit climb.

Most of the large Lhotse party left from Milan's Malpensa airport on the 10th of March in a Hercules of the Italian Armed Forces – an indication of the level of national support the effort had. Gogna had left a couple of months earlier and travelled overland to Nepal to join up with the team. After stopping in Tehran and New Delhi, the main team arrived in Kathmandu on the 12th March, before flying on to Lukla, from where they took the same route to the foot of the mountain as the Japanese two years before. The size of the expedition meant they had to fly in two groups, but ten days after leaving Italy, the whole team was reunited at Khumjung in the Sherpa region and caught their first sight of the Face. Cassin studied it carefully with his binoculars, trying to use his 50 years of mountain experience to identify the best line of ascent.

Another seven days and they were at Chukhung, the last village before going onto the glacier. From this close Cassin found Lhotse to be terrifying and completely black, with all fresh snow blown off by the winter winds. This was a quite different appearance from that which he had found in the reconnaissance the previous October when it had snowed almost every day and Cassin felt that an ascent would be possible, although certainly very difficult. Now he was not so sure. Subsequently many of those who visited the Face more than once commented on the fact that the appearance and character could change dramatically from one season to the next, sometimes looking largely rocky, sometimes snowbound with important implications on the difficulty and danger of different routes. When they arrived at Base Camp, the doctor, Franco Chierego, was suffering from altitude sickness. Cassin sent him to bed with tea, but in the night he was vomiting and his condition didn't improve even with bottled oxygen. They got assistance from the doctor of the British Army expedition attempting the neighbouring Nuptse and concluded there was no choice but to take him down to the highest village, from where he was evacuated to Kathmandu and then back to Italy. With altitude sickness there is sometimes no alternative to getting to a lower altitude.

Observing the mountain, Cassin felt that it was alive and treacherous with avalanches not only of snow, but also rocks and ice: one large one contained so much rock that it was practically black. Cassin noted that the whole mass disappeared into the bergschrund – the large crevasse always found between the bottom of a steep face and the glacier. He realised that the absence of debris at the foot of the Face couldn't be taken as evidence of a lack of avalanches in that area. It was clear that the Face was deceptively dangerous and Cassin felt that any route up the centre of the face would be tantamount to suicide. The Italians decided that the only viable route was the one attempted by the Japanese up the large ramp on the left of the face. On the 1st April Messner, Gogna and Lecco climber Aldo Anghileri set out to explore the

Japanese route, while Cassin climbed up a spur on the opposite side of the valley to study the route from a better viewpoint. By now recent snows had left the face very white making features harder to spot, but it was clearly going to be difficult to find good camp sites. In the evening the team exploring the face reported that they had found traces of the Japanese and a possible site for Camp I. Cassin divided the tasks of preparing the route amongst his team and the respect he could command meant that each climber did what was asked with little complaint. Even strong personalities like Messner towed the line. On April 2nd Messner and Fausto Lorenzi reached the site of Camp I, whilst another team improved the route below and fixed ropes to allow Sherpas to carry loads to stock the camp. The next day Messner and Aldo Leviti established and slept in the camp and the following morning climbed 300 metres above, fixing ropes as they went. This was typical Himalayan siege climbing – a gradual step by step progress up a large face with teams alternating to make sure there was always someone fresh at the front. The next day Messner and Leviti descended and Lorenzi and Curnis took over the lead. The day after that it was the turn of Barbacetto and Gogna, who fixed ropes up to the foot of a large serac (an ice cliff formed by the glacier), but had trouble finding a way over it.

During this period, the weather remained favourable, the morale in the team was good and Cassin was very happy with the level of co-operation and commitment. The only exception was Aldo Anghileri who was depressed and homesick. He spoke to Messner about his disappointment with the expedition. When they were in Base Camp there was not much to do – the Sherpas cooked for them. And most of the time on the mountain was spent load carrying and pulling up fixed ropes using jumar clamps, a device to attach the climber onto the ropes which ascends when pushed up the rope, but which blocks if it comes under strain from a fall down. "It's not climbing, it's just hard work" he complained to Messner. He wasn't the first and he wouldn't be the last climber to be dispirited by the tedium of large expeditions using siege techniques, nor to miss his wife and young children when away from home for several months. At the same time, Anghileri was worried about the reaction if he quit of people back in Lecco, many of whom were jealous of the chance he had got to be selected for the expedition. But he realised expedition climbing just wasn't for him. He still wanted to go to the mountains, but not to be away from home for more than two or three days at a time, sufficient to climb most routes in the Alps. Finally he announced to Cassin that he was quitting the expedition and returning to Italy. The leader was disappointed and tried to persuade him to change his mind, suggesting that he could just play a more minor role down in Base Camp, but Anghileri's mind was made up and in the end Cassin accepted his decision.

On the 11th April Messner and Leviti reached Camp II with two Sherpas and placed a Whillans Box there. The camp site was safe and protected by two large crevasses just above which they hoped would catch any smaller avalanches – although if a large part of the ramp above detached they would be in trouble. The Whillans Box was a rectangular structure invented by Don Whillans, who made the first ascent of Annapurna South Face. Whillans had first developed it in Patagonia where ordinary tents struggled to stand up to the winds, which are some of the strongest in the world. The first version was made with a timber frame and was very heavy, but Whillans developed a more sophisticated model for an expedition to the Himalayas two years later and by the time of Annapurna South Face the design had been further improved and consisted of an aluminium frame and a combination of proofed nylon and cotton terylene for the roof and walls. It was 2 metres long and 1 and a quarter metres wide and high, heavier than a traditional high altitude tent, but climbers liked it because they were confident that it would never be blown down and was unlikely to be crushed by powder snow. The rectangular shape of the box gave more headroom than a traditional triangular tent, which was important for climbers spending many weeks on a mountain whilst a difficult route was sieged. On hard routes like Lhotse South Face there is often little scope to move around near the tents because of the steepness of the terrain, which inevitably means a lot of time in the tents. The box would slot neatly into a hole cut into a steep slope and a side benefit was that the snow which collected on the flat roof would melt under the hot daytime sun and provide a source of water, saving the effort of melting snow. Today boxes have been replaced by lightweight dome tents which have some of the same advantages, but are easier to put up and much lighter, but in the 1970s the Whillans Boxes were the state of the art.

With two camps established on face and steady progress things looked promising, but then the weather turned worse with very high winds, which were so strong Messner was afraid the tent would be carried away. He didn't open the tent door until 10 in the morning and when he did the blast threatened to rip the fabric of the tent. He struggled to close it again and then collapsed back inside exhausted. When the storm quietened down Messner tried to look outside, but as if it had been waiting for just this moment, the storm renewed its furious blast of snow and hail. Eventually he managed to get outside the tent and, finding things not too bad, he encouraged Leviti to join him, but although the next few 100 metres did not look too difficult, until the weather improved they had no choice but to hang around in the tents. Base Camp had regular radio contacts with the climbers on the face, but they still felt isolated up there in the storm. Leviti wrote in his diary, while Messner tried to read a book, but the stress of the storm and the avalanche threat from the accumulation of fresh snow made concentration impossible and he tossed the book aside. Eventually they decided to try and climb despite the weather and Messner overcame a steep snow slope and placed an anchor for the fixed rope. As the storm continued to rage, he wiped the icicles of his beard, whilst Leviti, standing further down waist deep in snow, shouted for him to descend. Messner realised there was no alternative and cursed the fact that they had stayed up in the storm for three days and had so little progress to show for it. The descent was nerve wracking because the ropes were buried in snow or coated in ice and it was impossible to see if they had been damaged or frayed.

Back down at Base Camp during the stormy periods people used time to write letters home and update their diaries. Away from home for a long period, the arrival of the mail runner with post from Italy was always a much awaited event. Cassin, who they called "the old man", watched with good natured amusement as those who had received letters teased those who had not. Given the difficulty and danger for Sherpas of carrying loads, Ignazio Piussi proposed constructing a winch to pull loads up the steep ground below Camp II. Piussi, who came from Friuli in the North-East of Italy, was described by Messner as more poacher than mountaineer – once he had carried two Chamois up a 400m rock face in the Alps to avoid being caught by a game keeper. The cableway involved two large wooden supports, suspension and hauling ropes and a winch at the top. On the 17th April a large team consisting of eight Sherpas plus four Italians set off with all the materials to install the winch, with Cassin coming along to film the work. Placing it was an elaborate process, but worthwhile given the amount of effort it would save in load carrying. At the same time, Sereno Barbacetto and Gogna header up to open the route towards Camp III.

This encouraging progress was rudely interrupted by the menace of the Face. Around midnight on 19th April a loud noise was heard by those sleeping in Base

Camp followed by a violent gust of wind. Someone shouted. Cassin put on his head torch and saw that the fabric of his tent was strained by snow pushing against it. At the same time, Messner woke to find himself fighting for his life. His tent had disappeared and he was in the middle of a whirlwind of snow, struggling to breathe before he was completely engulfed by the avalanche. Instinctively he swam with his arms to try and stay high and avoid being buried as blocks which might have been ice or oxygen cylinders flew past him. When he came to his senses he realised the tent was somehow gone, although his feet were still in his sleeping bag. Cassin found Messner disoriented and got him into the shelter of Mario Conti's tent before returning to his own. The pole supporting the ridge of Cassin's tent was broken, but he put off till the morning any attempt to mend it and tried to get some sleep.

At 6 am most of the climbers were sleeping fitfully after the shock of the first avalanche. Cassin went outside the tents to assess the damage and see where the avalanche had come from, which wasn't easy because fresh snow had fallen since. Cassin had just retreated to his tent again when he heard another even louder roar, this time accompanied by a terrifying crack and then a powerful blast of wind which carried away everything in its path. By instinct Cassin put his hand above his head and tried to raise himself, but he was immediately sucked down again. It was hard to tell how long the avalanche lasted, but once everything was calm he struggled out of his tent to survey the scene. The camp was a mess, with no tents left standing, the food and equipment stores swept away and the kitchen, which had been made of dry stone walls covered by a tarpaulin, reduced to a pile of rubble. Messner and Mario Conti were white from head to toe and Cassin escorted them to the Sherpas' tent to try and warm up. He then went around freeing various team members who were trapped, sometimes literally cutting them from their tents using his penknife or hacking them out with his ice axe. Fortunately no one was badly injured and they managed to dry out those who had been soaked by the wet snow and get them into sleeping bags. Some of the cases of food and equipment and oxygen cylinders had been swept more than a kilometre from the camp. Cassin realised that even just collecting everything back together was going to be a long job and radioed the climbers on the Face and told them to descend to help with the clearing up. They were very surprised to hear what had happened, because up on the Face all they knew was that light snowfall prevented them from seeing

Base Camp. Once the sun was up everyone started to search for their personal belongings, but it was three days before everything had been found.

Once the climbers were off the Face, Cassin collected the team together to discuss whether the attempt should continue. He was nervous that the Sherpas would not be willing to carry on, but in the end they agreed. After assessing the damage to the equipment they decided to continue, but with Base Camp in a safer location. Once this was done they returned to the Face, but the weather continued to hamper their efforts. The days sometimes started bright, but very often snow and clouds arrived by mid-morning. A week later there was 80 centimetres of fresh snow at Camp II and Cassin told the climbers to exercise the utmost caution given the avalanche risk. Piussi had got the cable winch working well and they started using it to transport loads. But it continued to snow every afternoon and in late April there were also strong winds and frequent avalanches on the face. By the end of April, Gogna and Leviti at Camp II found that strong winds had half buried the tents, which they spent the whole day digging out. From 20th April to 2nd May the weather was continuously bad and severely restricted activity on the mountain. It was time they could not afford to lose given the expected the onset of the monsoon in the second half of May.

Finally on the 3rd May the day dawned calm and settled and they could start to resupply of the camps on the Face and to try to advance the route above. There was more than one possible way to reach the main Lhotse-Nuptse ridge and it was agreed that Mario Curnis and Messner would explore the first option up the rock face above Camp III. On the first day they fixed all the rope they had - 100 metres - but following a well worked logistical plan, two Sherpas brought up more rope during the day so the Italians could continue the next day. As they progressed further up the rocks Messner led a pitch and then Curnis prussiked up to join him. As Messner set off up the next section the rock was terribly rotten and he had to continuously warn Curnis about falling blocks. They reached a crack which split the second half of this rockwall from left to right. Messner climbed ahead with his gloves dangling off loops and his axe hanging from his wrist. He managed to cross some smooth slabs, his crampons scratching against the rock, and then straddled a chimney to reach a vertical crack where he was able to place a piton as a running belay or "runner". To overcome the crack above he needed to tackle it in a single thrust – if he tried to do it slowly his strength would run out. He knew the piton should hold the rope, but if he fell from the crack he would go twice the distance he was above the piton before the rope came tight. With a deep breath he steeled himself and then went for it, reaching the middle of the crack and standing up on the last two good footholds. Above him he could see no more holds in the very steep rock. He looked down at Curnis belaying and shouted for him to pay attention to the rope – as falling was a real risk now. Just as he was starting to think a fall was inevitable, Messner spotted a rock knob, which he knocked ice off and was able to get a sling round to provide another runner, allowing him to swing across to a ledge on his right and relative safety. He fixed a belay and then told Curnis to come up and join him. Curnis had just removed one of the pitons from the lower stance, leaving the other to anchor the fixed rope, and was about to start climbing, when a rock avalanche hit them. They pressed themselves against the face and put their rucksacks over their heads and waited helplessly while the barrage of rocks passed all around them for over five minutes. When the rockfall stopped there was a smell of sulphur in the air. They had had enough and slid back down the ropes to the tent and then carried on down to Base Camp.

The conclusion of the exploration by Messner and Curnis was that the rock wall above Camp III was too loose and dangerous to be a viable route. Cassin decided that explorations should focus on the continuation of the ice ramp further left, which led to a shoulder which joined the main Lhotse-Nuptse ridge. This upper section was not visible from Base Camp, but they had studied it through binoculars from the village of Chunkung and it seemed to be a possible to traverse round the upper part of the ice ramp and follow a narrow, snow chocked gully to arrive near the main ridge. They planned to place a fourth camp on the ridge, but there would still be a very long distance to cover at high altitude to reach the summit. Following the ridge all the way to Lhotse would be too difficult and instead their idea was to traverse snow slopes on far side of the ridge across the West Face to the foot of the couloir of the original route which would lead to the summit. All this final section would be climbed in alpine style.

In early May Barbacetto and Gogna took up the lead and fixed ropes up to the shoulder of the spur overcoming 55° hard now. The next day they planned to push on up the gully which they had spotted from below. They reached the shoulder where the fixed ropes ended two hours after setting off. With the security of the fixed ropes was behind them, and no radio they had the feeling of being high and committed on a huge mountain, perched 2000 metres above the glacier below. The nature of the task was familiar for Gogna from his long experience in the mountains: the scrape of his crampons on the rocks, thick gloves on his hands, ice on his beard, but he saw poetry in the struggle. They had climbed a further four pitches before fog and snow closed around them. Anyway they had run out of ropes to fix so they had no choice, but to turn back. The remaining ground to the end of the gully was not difficult and they were sure they could finish it and reach the main ridge in the next day or so. Despite bad weather, they had fixed ropes to a height of over 7500m. Barbacetto left his ice axe and hammer attached to a solid piton in a small niche at the high point. They exchanged a few words and slid back down the fixed ropes to the camp. They could look down on the 2200m already climbed, knowing that the ridge was not far above.

On the radio that evening Cassin said that one of them should descend to Camp II for a rest, leaving a place in the lead to Aldo Leviti, who was coming up. Both Barbacetto and Gogna were keen to continue, knowing that the next section to reach the main ridge would give a magnificent view of Everest opposite. They drew lots and it was Gogna lost and descended disappointed, but confident he would be back up a few days later. He recalled years later that he hadn't even bothered to take photos in the gully because it never occurred to him that he wouldn't be back up there. There was a lot enthusiasm and excitement in the team because they had found a viable way onto the ridge, which would be the key to the summit. All the climbers prepared to ascend towards the upper camps, feeling they might be in a position to achieve a victory on one of the world's hardest faces.

Camp III was made up of two box tents placed on a glacier shelf about 50 metres long and 4 metres wide. The tent the climbers slept in was partially protected by the lip of an ice cliff above the camp. The other tent containing the equipment and provisions was in a more exposed position on the outer part of the shelf. Below the camp were steep slopes and ice steps interspersed with easier terrain. Leviti radioed Cassin asking to move the tent further out from the lip of the cliff which overhung it because he was worried about it breaking off and crushing the tent. Messner was with Cassin down at Base Camp and overhearing the conversation, immediately objected saying that if the tent was placed any further out, it risked being carried away by an avalanche. Whilst Cassin was on the radio, Messner made a quick sketch showing the position of the tent relative to the slope and the lip of the crevasse and pushed it under Cassin's nose. He told Cassin to instruct them to dig the tent further in if they wanted, but certainly not to move it further out. Cassin did as Messner said and this probably helped to avoid a catastrophe.

After seeing off Gogna, Barbacetto went inside the tent to prepare hot drinks for Leviti who arrived at 5 pm, tired after a difficult ascent in the usual afternoon storm. Inside the tent, both of them were nervous about the risk of avalanche from the large quantity of new snow which had fallen on the slopes above. Sure enough, soon afterwards it became unexpectedly dark due to a powder snow slide which buried the tent. Leviti went outside and dug the tent clear. They were preparing to face the coming night, when they heard a loud noise and the poles of the tent snapped leaving space inside the tent terrifyingly cramped. They were pushed into the corner, pressed against the fabric of the tent and the ice of the serac behind. With their backs they tried to resist the pressure of the mass of snow, but they were also struggling to breathe due to the lack of air in the compressed space. To make matters worse, the propane stove had been knocked over and extinguished and was now letting out gas, risking to suffocate them. In desperation, Leviti snapped his sunglasses and used the broken glass to cut a hole in the tent. They could then feel some fresh air from a small tunnel which the avalanche had not quite filled due to the obstacle of the serac above. Leviti immediately went into this hole followed by Barbacetto and they started to tunnel their way out. They had to dig for 25-30 metres, literally swimming through the snow, before they emerged out on the mountainside. By now it was 8pm and their relief at escaping suffocation soon gave way to fear of a night in the open at 7200 metres, soaked from their work in the tunnel and without adequate protection from the cold and wind. There was no choice but to start to dig back in towards the tent to try and at least reach their sleeping bags. By midnight they had managed to dig out enough of a hole to get shelter for the night, which was cold, but not insupportable. In the light of the morning they surveyed the damage to the camp. An area of snow 30-40 metres wide had detached from the summit ridge and carried away all the climbing equipment, oxygen and supplies which had been on the shelf outside the tent. The second tent was destroyed and the fixed ropes below the camp had been part swept away and part buried under snow. They radioed Cassin and described the damage, explaining that "everything here is destroyed; some of the tents poles are horribly twisted". Cassin told them to descend back down to Camp II with extreme caution since Barbacetto was without axe or hammer and parts of the fixed ropes were gone. At midday they reached Camp II where Gogna and one of the Sherpas were staying. They were also very worried by the possibility of avalanches.

After this latest setback Cassin had given up any hope of reaching the summit – there was simply not enough time available or undamaged tents available. They discussed the possibility of trying to reach the main ridge of Lhotse and descending into the Western Cwm on the other side, something which even today has not been achieved. Team spirit was still good despite the many setbacks and they worked out a plan to start re-equipping the mountain to achieve this goal. Sherpas were sent up to Camp I but, the weather continued to be against them with heavy snow just when they were most keen to press on. On the 10th May Giuseppe Alippi, Conti and Lorenzi were at Camp II, planning to go up to clean up and remake Camp III. But with 25 centimetres of fresh snow creating significant avalanche risk, Cassin told them to come back down to Base. That night it snowed continuously and in the morning there was 60 centimetres of fresh snow on the Face. The next day they heard on the radio that four British climbers had been killed on the neighbouring mountain Nuptse. They were part of an Army expedition preparing for Everest the following year. The Italians had met the British on the approach march and got on well with them. The British doctor had helped treat the Italians' doctor Chierego when he was ill. On an attempt on the summit two experienced climbers, Owens and Summerton, had fallen to their deaths. A few days later two more climbers, Brister and Pasang, died in another fall. This grim news helped the Italians to decide to abandon their attempt.

As the expedition ended Cassin had mixed feelings. He was pleased with the team spirit and felt that they had done all they could, but in reality he knew that, despite a very strong team, they had not come close to succeeding. It has been a difficult couple of years for Himalayan climbing with no major new route completed since Messner's ascent of Manaslu's South Face in 1972. Actually the luck of Himalayan climbers was about to change and during the next months three important new routes would be climbed. Although Cassin carried on climbing in the Alps for many more years this was his last major expedition. He lived to be 100 and remained lucid and mentally alert well into his 90s, but if he was asked about Lhotse in his later years he claimed not to remember anything at all. Perhaps the canny Cassin had decided to concentrate his aging mental resources on more successful days, of which he had had many.

When the expedition returned to Milan's Malpensa Airport they were met by newspaper reporters – this was a big national expedition and generated a lot of public interest. Messner declared that the wall was currently impossible, at least by traditional techniques of fixed ropes and a chain of camps. In his view it could only be overcome by very talented climbers, fully acclimatised and extremely fit and climbing in alpine style. By alpine style he meant climbing in a continuous push without fixed ropes and camps. He believed that only by minimising the time spent on the face could the risks be kept reasonable.

A few weeks after the Lhotse expedition, Messner returned to Asia to put his ideas into action. He planned to attempt a new route of another 8000 metre peak, Gasherbrum I (sometimes called Hidden Peak) in the Karakoram Range in Pakistan. The scale of this expedition was in complete contrast to the one to Lhotse South Face with only two climbers, Messner and the Austrian, Peter Habeler, no fixed ropes, no oxygen and no porters above Base Camp. The pair had already made some very fast climbs in the Alps including a 10 hour ascent of the North Face of the Eiger and now they were ready to apply this same style in the Himalayas. They likened the lower section of the Gasherbrum route to the North Face of the Matterhorn, involving steep snow and ice and broken rocks. The climbing was at a level which they had done many times in the Alps, but the commitment required at 7000 metres was much higher. Taking it in turns to lead, they both had a good instinct for picking the easiest line, something almost as important as pure climbing ability on a Face like this. Having a turn at going second, using the footsteps of the leader also gave some sort of rest from the lung sapping effort of climbing steep ground at high altitude. After the first day on the face they bivouacked at 7100 metres in a tiny tent. The hardest part of the climb below them and the next day they reached the summit, making only the second ascent of Gasherbrum I.

It was a significant moment in the history of Himalayan mountaineering and Messner showed the way as he would so many times. In 1957 a four-man Austrian team including Hermann Buhl, the first man to climb Nanga Parbat, had made a lightweight first ascent of the 8000er Broad Peak, but Messner and Habeler's ascent went a level beyond this both because they climbed from top to bottom in a single push and because it was a technically harder route. The leading Himalayan climbers took notice. For those who had spent long months on large siege style expeditions, the new alpine style approach gave a refreshing chance to do more real climbing and less load carrying. Although time was still needed to acclimatise before attempting the very highest summits, this could be done on neighbouring lower peaks. Even the question of whether alpine or traditional style expeditions were more risky was not black and white. Clearly the fixed ropes and established camps gave security and a means to escape in the case of storms and illness, but the extra time spent on the route in heavyweight expeditions meant greater exposure to objective hazards like stonefall and avalanche. Messner had already started to think about very ambitious new goals in Himalayan climbing in the first half of the 1970s. He is also a very effective communicator and his ideas influenced many mountaineers. In book, "The Challenge", that Messner wrote about the 1975 expeditions to Lhotse and Gasherbrum I, he contrasts the heavy and lightweight styles of climbing. But the North West Face of Gasherbrum I and the South Face of Lhotse are two very different routes. The face on Gasherbrum is steep, but shorter and much less complex than Lhotse and crucially the main difficulties are below 7000 metres, whereas on Lhotse the hardest section is above 8000. In the next years Messner's attention focused on climbing in ever lighter style and this tended to draw him away from the very hardest technical routes.

In the autumn of 1975 there was also a powerful demonstration of the effectiveness of siege style climbing. A British expedition led by Chris Bonington finally succeeded on Everest's South West Face, which attracted attention as the hardest face of the world's highest mountain. As well as the Japanese attempts in 1969 and 1970, an international expedition in 1971, and a European team led by Karl Herrligkoffer in 1972, Bonington himself tried in 1972. The Japanese tried again in 1973, but gave up at 8400 metres after one of the Sherpas, was killed by an avalanche. In 1975 Bonington had a very strong and experienced team, excellent logistical planning and a large team of Sherpas. They managed to establish six camps up the Face very early in the post-monsoon season with Nick Estcourt and Paul Braithwaite climbing a key section through the Rock Band, the main obstacle to the upper part of the mountain. From a high camp above the Rock Band, Dougal Haston and Doug Scott climbed the final section to the summit. There was a further summit attempt by two more pairs of climbers, Pete Boardman and Sherpa Pertemba and two veterans of the Annapurna South Face, Martin Boysen and Mick Burke. Boardman and Pertemba made it to the summit, but Boysen had to turn back when his oxygen set malfunctioned. As Boardman and Pertemba descended from the summit, the weather started to turn bad, so they were very surprised to meet Burke who had not turned back with Boysen and was still heading up. They tried to persuade him to give up, but the summit was close and the lure of Everest made him carry on. The other two waited just before the South Summit, but the weather continued to worsen and now their lives were at risk too. In the end they had to carry on and hope that somehow Burke would make it down too – sadly he never arrived. The success on Everest following on from that on Annapurna South Face put the British at the forefront of hard Himalayan climbing, but for some of the climbers large siege style expeditions represented a sort of dead end in the development of mountaineering. Scott and Boardman were now more interested in following the example of Messner by tackling hard new routes in Alpine style.

Chapter 3 -Daring to Believe Everything is Possible

The following year the Japanese returned to try and finish what they had started in 1973, led by Kanji Kamei, a member of the previous expedition. They started to fly equipment to Lukla in early February, but this process was slowed by bad weather, which often caused flights to be cancelled – a common delay for expeditions visiting the Everest area. Then their approach to Base Camp was hampered by more bad weather. They first reached it on the 29th February, but their tents were blown down and they had to re-establish it two days later. One lesson they were able to learn from their predecessors was to place Base Camp far enough away from the face to remove any risk from avalanche.

They did not even look at the direct route, but set to work immediately on the left hand route attempted by the previous Japanese expedition and the Italians. The route across the rock towers between Camps I and II was more familiar now, but not easier. The rock was very fragile and the pitons they placed to anchor the fixed ropes did not inspire confidence and had to be handled with caution every time they crossed this section. They now worked to stock the lower camps with the support of their Sherpas, whilst the lead climbers pushed the route out to Camp III, first establishing a provisional camp a little lower, before setting up the full Camp III at 6600 metres, where they found remains of the Italian expedition.

A 150 metre ice wall now blocked their way. The Japanese realised this would be a key passage of the climb and had identified three possible routes up it. They could either follow the right side of this wall, its centre or a steep ice slopes on the left. The latter route was the one the Italians had nearly succeeded the year before. On April 17th the Japanese established a temporary Camp IV at the foot of this wall as a base to try and make the route up it. But it took them nearly two weeks two climb the centre of the wall and they had had to use artificial climbing techniques, which is always a slow process. Three days later another pair managed to climb the wall by its east face and joined the first climbers above. They concluded that this east face route was easier for ferrying loads. It seems that the Italians probably took a different route via the ice slopes on the left referred to by the Japanese. Overcoming this wall seemed to open the way for the Japanese to reach the main ridge, but in practice snow storms and high winds kept preventing them from advancing the route beyond this point.

On the 9th May a team got to a height of nearly 7000 metres where they deposited some loads before descending back down to the temporary Camp IV. Then bad weather set in for an eight day period. The climbers at the temporary Camp IV were cut off from the rest of the team by the bad weather and avalanche risk, although the four climbers there eventually managed to descend back down to Camp III. However, load carrying between Camps II and III had to be interrupted because the Sherpas were concerned about the avalanche danger, with the result that they started to be short of food in the upper camps. On the 19th May the weather improved again and four climbers moved back up to the temporary Camp IV. The next day they tried to make further progress, but the deep snow made this a battle and they went back to Camp III without reaching the previous high point.

The expedition leader, Kamei, talked to the team in Camp III on the radio and decided to stop the expedition within six days because the monsoon was now imminent. In these six days they agreed to try and climb to a height of 7000 metres. So a team of three Japanese and a Sherpa returned to sleep at the temporary Camp IV a final time. Early the next morning two of the climbers set off, but after 10 hours battling in deep snow on the steep face they only reached a little higher than the attempt of 15 days before. This was the expedition's high point, still short of 7000 metres and below what the Italians had managed. Kamei estimated that they were around three hours from the main ridge crest, but this is possibly optimistic given the experience of the Italians. There was no choice but to call off the expedition. This meant that by 1976 three expeditions had attempted the face without getting into a position to make a summit bid and none of them had even tried on the central part of the face. Messner's had stated that the face was a problem for the year 2000, but for many this seemed like an understatement. Messner himself wrote in his 1977 book "The Big Walls" that "the Face may well be impossible".

However such views often ignore rises in climbing standards and the late 1970s saw further dramatic developments in lightweight alpine style climbing in the Himalayas. Once again Messner led the way. After his two man ascent of Gasherbrum I in 1975, he continued to return to the Himalayas every year and in 1978 he and Peter Habeler made the first ascent of Everest without oxygen. In the 1970s Nepal was quite restrictive in the number of permits it granted to expeditions, although it later realised that much more money could be made from permits by selling many for the same mountain in the same year, resulting in serious over-crowding on the most popular routes. Under the 1970s rules, Messner and Habeler would have had to wait several years before getting a permit for Everest, by which time they suspected someone else might have completed the oxygenless ascent. So they paid to get added to the permit of an Austrian expedition under the leadership of Wolfgang Nairz.

Nairz's team was using oxygen and Messner and Habeler planned to climb as independently from them as possible to avoid the accusation that they had only succeeded because of support from climbers using bottled gas. Originally their idea was to try the unclimbed South Pillar, but when they arrived on the mountain they saw that the steepness of this route and its icy condition would make it too difficult. They decided that trying to make two steps forward in one go was too ambitious – climbing the standard route without oxygen was already challenging enough. Prior to the expedition, many people were critical of the planned oxygenless climb saying that it was an unreasonable risk and that if they made it to the summit, they would return as brain damaged vegetables. It was true that people had already climbed high on Everest without oxygen, including several members of the pre-war British expeditions who had none of the advantages of modern lightweight equipment and clothing. As early as 1924, Edward Norton had reached a height of 8600 metres without oxygen. Logically it was not a big step beyond this to go to the summit, but nobody had done it and this constituted a huge psychological barrier. The very highest mountains in the World had always been climbed with oxygen, although there had frequent ascents of lower 8000ers without. Looking back knowing how frequently Everest has subsequently been climbed with oxygen, it is quite very surprising how much controversy the ascent generated at the time. There were accusations that they had stolen oxygen from the Austrian team or even that they had hidden miniature breathing sets. The authoritative Mountain Magazine said that "the current charge of using a "gun belt" of oxygen cartridges is as absurd as the one made after the same pair's alpine style Gasherbum I climb that they employed "invisible Sherpas"". Part of the genius of Messner was his ability to analyse the facts rationally and have the self-confidence and courage to act on his conclusions. This is why he was so often first to make a new step in the evolution of mountaineering, whether climbing in lightweight style, alone or without oxygen. However his skill as a communicator sometimes meant his achievements come across as dominant at the expense of others who were also breaking through the same psychological barriers.

Showing that Everest could be climbed without oxygen was a game changer for alpine style climbing. If oxygen was needed on the highest mountains, then alpine style climbing was impractical because the cylinders and related equipment were simply too heavy to carry in a single push climb. People are needed to carry oxygen up to the point from where it is used. This is most easily done by having fixed ropes, so that load carrying can be done in safety even during bad weather. And the people carrying loads need tents and fuel and so on. The result is that the only feasible way to put a pair of climbers in position to make a bid for the summit from a high camp with oxygen is to have a wide logistical pyramid with many people involved in the supply chain. It is this multiplying effect which creates such a dichotomy between alpine style and siege style climbing. With the necessity for oxygen removed, every goal was theoretically within reach in alpine style.

After Everest, Messner did not sit on his laurels. Just six weeks after returning home from Everest he was back at Nanga Parbat, the scene of his 1970 ascent and the loss of his brother Gunther. This time he was alone and attempted the Diamir face which he and Gunther had descended without ropes, camps or support. He had already tried a solo ascent twice before, in 1973 and 1977, but had turned back through fear of being isolated on such a huge and dangerous mountain. In 1978 he was accompanied by Ursula Grether, a medical student who would stay in support in Base Camp, but on the mountain he was completely alone. Following a new route on the right of the face he set off at 5am on the 7th August. Climbing rapidly because the lower section was threatened by ice cliffs, he covered the lower half of the face in only a few hours and pitched his small tent under shelter of an ice bulge, where he spent the rest of the day and night resting. The following morning he was sitting in his sleeping bag making tea, when there was a sudden tremor followed by cracking and rumbling all around him. Ripping open the tent he saw on all sides, above and below, huge avalanches descending from the mountain gathering into a single enormous flood of snow several kilometres wide, which swept the valley below him. He later learnt that an earthquake had triggered these enormous avalanches, but initially the worrying thing was that the ice tongue which he had climbed the previous day was completely gone, meaning he could no longer descend the way he had come up.

Messner's single mindedness allowed him to put consideration of his descent route to the back of his mind and push on up the mountain. If he had left a day earlier he would have been obliterated by this avalanche. From a rational point of view he knew that he been saved purely by luck and yet this luck made him feel like "a spirit immune from harm", removed his fear and allowed him to push on in a state almost of exaltation. Messner writes in a much more metaphysical vein than many other climbers and talks about a state of merging into infinity on Nanga Parbat. He found himself focusing on existential problems of why humans exist, where they come from and where they are going instead of the basic question of why he was there alone, near the top of one of the world's highest mountains. The drive, determination and concentration on climb seemed to be reasons in themselves and, although he knew this was a circular answer to the question, it seemed the right one at that time. Maybe not revisiting the reasons as to why you are there once you have taken the decision to go is a necessary attribute for Himalayan climbing. Without this it is too easy to have doubts about the difficulties and dangers involved and for resolve to weaken.

After making another camp at 7400 metres, Messner made it to the summit on the third day. To prove his ascent he left a bit of paper with his signature on in an aluminium capsule and attached it to the summit rocks. He also took as many pictures as possible to ensure no doubts could arise about his achievement. The need to find ways to prove a solo ascent was to become significant in the later history of Lhotse's South Face. On the descent he was blocked for a whole day at his top bivouac due to bad weather, but he was carrying plenty of food and fuel so he didn't have to risk descending when it wasn't safe. The next morning he took advantage of a short break in the clouds to get his bearings and made the 3000 metre descent to the glacier below in a straight line through the thick cloud. It was a startling achievement and although it attracted less media attention than the oxygenless ascent of Everest, it was perhaps in retrospect an even greater climb, one which Messner saw as in some ways the high point of his mountaineering career. Messner achieved much more in the coming years, but he didn't pursue his goals with the same animal urge to succeed at all costs on the boldest routes that he had had before.

Nevertheless two years later Messner took the process forward to its logical conclusion by ascending Everest solo, without oxygen and by a new route, albeit one that was partly already climbed and reasonably straightforward technically. Once again he had shown the world's mountaineers that it was possible to climb even new routes on the highest mountains in a very lightweight and pure style. Naturally some climbers started to wonder whether the same techniques couldn't be applied on a route as hard and as high as the South Face of Lhotse.

The next person to venture onto the face, Nicolas Jaeger, wanted to do just that. Jaeger came from a cultured and colourful family background. His maternal ancestors were Burgundy wine makers and his mother was the famous photographer Janine Niepce. She studied art and archaeology at the Sorbonne during the Second World War and managed to make films of the French Resistance and pass them to the allies before participating in the liberation of Paris as a liaison officer. Her commander was Claude Jaeger, who was born in into a wealthy Geneva family in 1917 and studied in Paris with the goal of working in the Ministry of Finance. But he found he was more interested in the cinema and started working as an assistant director. He also became interested in politics and joined the Spanish Communist Party during the period of the Spanish Civil War, but when this ended in defeat for the Left, he returned to France. He was mobilised at the start of the war, but with the swift French defeat he returned to Paris after the armistice. There he mixed in a circle which was artistic and politically active, centred around the famous Café de Flore on the Rive Gauche of the Seine. The actress Simone Signoret, who wrote that she "came alive" when she was introduced to this circle by Claude Jaeger, described it as an "unconventional world, made up of artists, actors, intellectuals, refuges, writers, poets, Communists, Trotskyists and anarchists". Amongst those who were members of this circle were the artists Pablo Picasso and Alberto Giacometti and Jean-Paul Sartre and Simone De Beauvoir were regulars at the Café de Flore too. The Café was also a haven where the German occupiers of Paris rarely if ever ventured. As a communist, Claude Jaeger joined the Resistance and became a colonel with the *nom du guerre* Michelin. He later became a noted film producer, making such political films as "Vive Stalin", as well as many non-political films. The couple married shortly after the liberation of Paris and Nicolas was born in 1946, although his parents divorced after 7 years of marriage.

As a child of divorced parents, he saw his father at weekends and when the weather was good, Claude took young Nicolas rock climbing at Fontainebleau. When the weather was bad they visited friends and relatives and played

Monopoly. Fontainebleau is a town near Paris surrounded by woods which contain sandstone boulders which, although never more than a few metres high, provide a fantastic playground for developing technical climbing skills and have nurtured many generations of Parisian climbers. But strangely given his future, Jaeger didn't become passionate about climbing as a boy. In reality, although he enjoyed his Sunday's there with the long relaxed picnics, Jaeger thought Fontainebleau was not an ideal place for children to climb: the hand-holds were too few and widely spaced for a child's arms and the soles of his shoes slipped on the sandy rock. As he matured as a climber, the simple technical difficulty of rock, which Fountain Belau represents, started to interest him less than the more complete experience of a high mountain environment.

Jaeger didn't start serious mountaineering until the late 1960s when he was already in his early 20s, but within a few years he had become one of the boldest climbers of the day, both technically excellent and with an iron constitution. He had an impressive list of ascents in Alps, including many first solo ascents. Jaeger did not see an interest in searching for artificially difficult lines on faces which had already been climbed by their most logical routes. He was more interested in repeating solo the classic lines established by illustrious climbers of the past. The culture and history of mountaineering made it fascinating for him to follow in the footsteps of men like Alfred Mummery, Giusto Gervasutti, Armand Charlet and Walter Bonatti, sensing the history in ways like recognising the ledge on the Grepon where Mummery and his two companions had drunk champagne during the first ascent in the late 19th Century. Repeating the routes of the legendary names also provided a yardstick to measure his own development.

Although he was happy to climb with others, Jaeger did not suffer from the solitude when climbing alone. In 1973 he made the first complete solo traverse of the Chamonix Aiguilles – an impressive ridge of rocky pinnacles that sit just above France's premier Alpine resort. Two years later he climbed the Bonatti-Gobbi route on the Eckpfeiler Pilier of Mont Blanc before moving directly to the Central Pillar of Freney which he climbed in six hours with a bivouac. Mountain Magazine described this pair of climbs as "a remarkable achievement". The Central Pillar of Freney had been one of the hardest routes of the early 1960s, first climbed by a British-Polish team including Chris Bonington and Don Whillans, but not before a very strong French-Italian team had failed in a week long storm which cost the lives of four of the climbers.

Jaeger interrupted his medical training and eventually started to train as a mountain guide, qualifying in 1975. One part of the guides' course involved a race along the Aiguille Rouges, the rocky peaks facing Mont Blanc across the Chamonix Valley. To pass the test it was necessary to complete the course in less than five and a half hours carrying a 12 kilo pack. The legendary guide, Armand Charlet, waited at the finishing line to cast a critical eye over the candidates. Jaeger decided to play to his reputation as a cultured Parisian and, having checked that he was well out in the lead, he stopped out of sight a few hundred metres before the finish line. There he dried the sweat off himself, put on a clean and well ironed shirt and combed his hair. As a final touch he lit up a cigarette and then strolled across the finished line, bringing a smile even to the face of the gruff old guide Charlet. This time his humour might have won the day, but as a well-educated Parisian and one who was not afraid to call a fool a fool, he did not always endear himself to the Chamoniards. There has always been rivalry between the Chamoniards and the Parisians in the world of French climbing, but Jaeger's character probably accentuated it and probably sometimes meant he was short of climbing partners who were his equals.

In 1977 and 1978 he visited Peru twice and made a number of hard solo first ascents in the Cordillera Blanca. Unlike the Alps, he saw the Andes as still offering plenty of scope for fine new lines. Already in the composition of these first two Peruvian expeditions the evolution of Jaeger's climbing philosophy could be seen. In 1977 he went with a team of 6 including three Chamonix guides, although he himself did most of his climbs solo including several first ascents. With confidence gained from this experience, in 1978 he was only accompanied by a photographer who had no climbing experience meaning that whatever he achieved on the mountains he would do alone. And this is just what he did, making the 4th ascent of Taulliraju by soloing a new route on the South Face in only 8 hours. He also soloed the South Face of the Alpamayo, a fantastically beautiful mountain of just under 6000 metres with dramatic snow flutings. This was the second ascent and he only took two and a half hours.

Having performed strongly in the Alps and the Andes, the Himalayas were the logical next step for Jaeger. His chance came on the 1978 German-French Everest Expedition. He and his partner Jean Afanassief became the first Frenchmen to climb Everest as well as completing a ski descent from close to the South Col. When they stopped on the summit and took off their oxygen masks, Jaeger, in his own inimitable style, lit up a Gitane – the strong filterless

French cigarettes – apparently becoming the first person to smoke on the World's highest point. He enjoyed it, although he was ashamed to be smoking up there as he had throughout the expedition. Claude Deck, the deputy leader of the French team, remembers the smell of cigarette smoke from Jaeger's tent was the first thing they noticed when they woke in the morning in the camps on Everest. Jaeger seemed to suffer few ill effects from smoking and had regular medical check-ups before departing on expeditions, but his family felt he had aged prematurely and that the smoking did not help. Shortly after Jaeger, the expedition leader Pierre Mazeaud arrived with the famous Austrian mountaineer Kurt Diemberger who was making a film of the ascent. Mazeaud was well known and had a much more extrovert style than Jaeger and he made a radio broadcast direct from the summit to the French nation.

Despite the pride in being the first from their country to reach the World's highest point, the ascent of the ordinary route on Everest, which had been repeated several times by the late 1970s, was hardly a major challenge for a strong technical climber like Jaeger. He felt he needed to explain why he was doing this instead of making daring lightweight ascents in the style of Messner and gave three reasons. Firstly there was the irresistible attraction of Everest. For a climber refusing a chance to go there was like an actor refusing to perform Shakespeare. Secondly there was his interest in physiology and the effects of high altitude on the body – as a doctor he wanted to apply his medical knowledge to the problem of altitude. He submitted all members of the expedition and the accompanying journalists to a series of tests. Jaeger himself spent 100 minutes on the summit without his oxygen mask trying to understand what effect the lack of oxygen was having on his body. His final reason for going to Everest was that the publicity of the ascent, which was filmed by French television, would be very useful in trying to get financing for his subsequent plans. Once he had decided to dedicate himself to climbing, raising money was a constant preoccupation and he spent a lot of his time in Paris between expeditions talking to potential sponsors. This wasn't something that came naturally to him and he was much more comfortable alone high on a mountain than making small talk in the salons of Paris with champagne and vol-au-vents, but he realised this was something he had to do if he was to realise his plans. He was a very different character from Pierre Mazeaud, who was a successful lawyer and politician, as well a top level climber, but Jaeger recognised he learnt a lot from Mazeaud about public relations.

To further his understanding of the effects of altitude on the human body, , Jaeger spent two months close to the summit of Huascaran, a 6700 metre mountain in Peru in the summer of 1979. This was a plan he had conceived during the Everest expedition, perhaps because in the midst of the large heavyweight expedition with many climbers, Sherpas and journalists he desired more than anything solitude to appreciate the mountains. He saw his experiment on Huascaran as a crossroads where his two passions of medicine and alpinism met. He used the results of the physiological tests on himself for the final thesis for his medical doctorate as he was finally completing his interrupted medical studies. The stay on Huascaran was also part of physical and psychological preparation for a dramatic ascent he wanted to pull off in the Himalayas which would be much more ground-breaking than his Everest climb.

Before going up to the summit of Huascaran Jaeger went on a trek with various sponsors and his then 11 year old Helene. Jaeger wasn't content to walk ordinary trekking stages and pushed his companions to make longer stages to get his obligation to his sponsors out of the way more quickly and get on with the serious climbing. Whilst Helene as the leader's daughter was allowed to ride on a mule when she was too tired, the sponsors who weren't in peak condition had to struggle on on foot as best they could. But Jaeger seemed to have little sympathy for their fatigue and blisters. This impatience to get as much possible done in aspects of life was an important part of his character, which perhaps even influenced his decisions to get married and have children young and to interrupt his lengthy medical studies. It was almost as if Jaeger felt an overriding sense of urgency, fearing that life was too short to do all of things he wanted. He had courage, determination, a fine mind and a superb physique, so it seemed that the only thing which could stop him realising his goals was a lack of time.

It took 12 days to transport all the material he needed for his long stay on Huascaran with the help of local porters. The way up was a straightforward climb, but this was still a dangerous high mountain environment with a particular threat from falling ice. This danger was emphasised when one of the local porters, who had carried loads up, was killed on the descent. This of course disturbed Jaeger, but did not shake his resolve to carry out his lonely vigil. Close to the summit of Huascaran, the camp where Jaeger was to spend two months consisted of two tents face to face, one in which he slept and ate and the other in which he stored his fragile medical and other equipment.

Huascaran is a popular mountain and so there were fairly frequent visits by other climbers during the day in the early part of his stay when it was still the height of the climbing season. He had installed a fixed rope on the only difficult section between his camp and the summit to allow him to safely reach it to look at the view and assess the weather. This also allowed him to meet other climbers who he helped with hot drinks and advice about symptoms of altitude they might be suffering. But then the climbing seasons ended and in the last weeks of his stay he saw no-one.

Based on this experience in wrote a book, "The Notebook of Solitude", in which he describes his thoughts during his long stay, which range widely from the mundane to the philosophical. The book was entirely written during his stay on the summit and he didn't edit it afterwards so it retains the immediacy of his feelings up there alone. He naturally had a lot of time to reflect on all aspects of his life and in the book tells many anecdotes from his experiences climbing and more generally. He reflects on life in Peru, a country which he had started to know quite well as this was now his third visit, on medicine in sport, on the development of alpinism and so on. Jaeger did not feel loneliness when alone in the mountains. Before he departed for Huascaran many people asked him whether he would be bored, but for him choosing to be alone in the high mountains was incomparable with loneliness which people suffered when friendless in the middle of big city. He quoted Hermann Hesse on the coldness and dignity of mountains which are like another world which does not invite the presence of men and at best tolerates them. But Jaeger himself clearly felt in harmony with that other world. When he talked about the Alpinism of the year 2000 he quoted Ibsen who wrote "Is it really useful to attempt the possible?" He was echoing the ideas of Messner on the need for a continual challenge and striving to find one's limits. This gives us a clue about his motivations – he was not a man who could content himself with the ordinary. But of course he still had some normal human weaknesses, like his smoking. On Huascaran hoped he might be able to give up, but he was obviously not confident of succeeding because he carried up 60 packets of Gitanes for the two months. He also had a chance to reflect at length on his mountaineering plans whilst on the mountain and had worked out an ambitious schedule for the coming years.

By 1980 Jaeger was ready for a dramatic next stage in this development - a solo attempt on Lhotse's South Face. His plans for this climb evolved over time: in his "Notebooks of Solitude" he talks about a four man team attempting a hard new route on a major 8000er without naming Lhotse as the target. He later produced a fund raising brochure for the Lhotse South Face expedition in which he refers to a six man team. I have talked to most of the people who might have known the team composition and how it evolved during Jaeger's planning, but no one is really sure. Helene Jaeger recalls that at one stage he may have invited a British climber. This is possibly Alan Rouse, who was with him in Peru in the weeks before his stay on Huascaran and who died some years later in a terrible storm on K2. Although Jaeger sought sponsors, he did not make any big public announcements about his plans before leaving France – it seems he wanted to show what could be done rather than brag about it before trying. If he succeeded he would certainly have the mountaineering world's attention - this wouldn't just be a step beyond what Messner had achieved, it would be a quantum leap forward. He knew the enterprise was a risky one, but he was certainly not a suicidal maniac who was prepared to throw his life away on a whim. He had enjoyed the time back in France between the period in Peru and the trip to the Himalayas, spending time with his family and helping with the grape harvest at his family's vineyard in Bourgogne.

By the time the team was finalised there were officially 4 members listed: Jaeger himself, the talented French Himalayan climber Georges Bettembourg, Nicolas Berardini and Brigitte Steinmann. Bettembourg was an alpine guide from Chamonix who had made some bold lightweight ascents in the Himalayas during the second half of the 1970s, including a 2 man ascent of Broad Peak with Yannick Seigneur in 1978, one of the early pure alpine style climbs on an 8000er. Bettembourg was also with the Britons Doug Scott, Pete Boardman and Joe Tasker on Kangchenjunga in 1979. They made a brilliant new route in alpine style although Bettembourg did not come on the final summit push. Later in the same year he made the first ascent of the North Ridge of Nuptse with Scott and two other Britons, Brian Hall and Alan Rouse, again in alpine style. These climbs made him one of France's leading Himalayan climbers and a strong candidate for Lhotse South Face. But Hall, who got on well with and climbed with both of them, doubts whether Bettembourg would have been a good choice of partner for Jaeger. Hall remembers him as a joker, erratic and not very dependable. Bettembourg was an artist and great fun to climb and be with whereas Jaeger had much more scientific mentality and could come across as calculating, political and quite stern. Sadly a few years later Bettembourg, who had achieved a lot in faraway places, was killed by stonefall on the Aiguille Verte close to his hometown of Chamonix.

Berardini is the son of the famous French climber Lucien Berardini who was Parisian and, like Jaeger, learnt to climb on the rocks of Fontainebleau where he was one of the pioneers in the post war period. In 1954 Lucien Berardini made an important first ascent on the South Face of Aconcagua, but suffered serious frostbite to his hands and feet. In 1980 his son Nicolas was 19 years old and working in a sports shop in Paris when Jaeger, who he knew through his father, came in. Jaeger asked Berardini about some equipment and then unexpectedly asked whether he would like to accompany him on an expedition to the Himalayas. Surprised but excited, Berardini accepted without hesitation. The final member of the team was Brigitte Steinmann, an anthropologist with a strong interest in Nepalese culture. She had some mountaineering experience, but like Berardini not at the level to go on the face itself with Jaeger. Jaeger had originally envisaged a larger team, before settling on the plan for a solo attempt and in the end his team was less than ten in total including the porters and the liaison officer.

On the way to Nepal, Jaeger had a chance meeting with an American film maker, Bill Rosser, who was to have a significant role in the story of the expedition. Rosser was 26 and about to make his first film with his own money. This was going to be about the snow leopard, the elusive animal which had only been filmed in a brief sequence in Pakistan taken by famed naturalist, George Schaller. Rosser hoped to be the first person to capture extensive behaviour on film. He was on runway in New Delhi airport surrounded by thirty assorted cases of expedition gear, which he was desperate to get loaded onto a plane that had completed boarding and was about to take-off for Kathmandu. Rosser was in a heated argument with the Indian customs official who refused to let his equipment onto the plane. Despite merely being in transit from JFK in New York, the customs officer wanted to send everything to a warehouse for inspection and Rosser knew that if this happened he wouldn't see his gear for a long time, if ever. Looking round in frustration, he saw nearby another huge pile of equipment and a dark-haired Frenchman also arguing furiously to get his things loaded. Rosser continued his pleading and threatening and finally slapped five hundred dollars into the Indian customs officer's hand to resolve the question. He looked around again and the Frenchman and his gear were gone. After checking his material really was on board, Rosser ran up the steps of the plane and the door was closed behind him. He wiped the sweat from his dripping face and looked down the aisle. There was only one seat vacant: and it was next to the Frenchman, who was of course Nicolas Jaeger, who was smiling at him. The pair laughed at the absurdity of the situation: despite each having to pay outrageous bribes, they were both excited to be finally being on the way to Nepal. They told each other about their plans. When Rosser heard about Jaeger's for Lhotse South Face he let out a low whistle. Rosser had heard that even Reinhold Messner considered this "a problem for the next century", so to contemplate a solo ascent was astonishing. They talked non-stop on the flight and agreed to meet in Kathmandu. They both had small teams and were operating on slim budgets and immediately felt an affinity.

A few days later they had dinner in Kathmandu and continued their conversation. Rosser asked the Frenchman if he would come over to his hotel, the Yak & Yeti, and do an interview on audiotape. Rosser didn't have any specific plans what to do with the tape, but a journalistic instinct told him that if Jaeger pulled the ascent off it would stun the whole climbing world and would be big news. Before they parted in Kathmandu, Jaeger told Rosser the date in April he was planning to start his climb on Lhotse and Rosser wrote it in his journal.

After leaving Kathmandu, Jaeger's team flew in to Lukla from where they started their approach march. Some days later, they set up Base Camp below the beautiful 6000m peak of Ama Dablam. Jaeger's plan before approaching Lhotse was to first make a series of acclimatisation climbs on lower peaks in the surrounding area. He did not have permits to climb these, which could in theory get him in trouble with the Nepalese authorities, but fortunately the liaison officer was more interested in smoking mind altering substances than in checking exactly what they were doing. On the acclimatisation climbs, Berardini was very impressed with Jaeger's climbing ability: very fast and sure even on very delicate snow. Berardini didn't find Jaeger a very talkative companion. Rather than the normal Base Camp games of cards and chatting, Jaeger spent a lot of time in his tent writing in his journal, leading to a feeling of distance or even aloofness which created some tension in the small team. But Berardini got on well enough with him, particularly on the mountain where Jaeger seemed to be more at ease and in his element.

Together Jaeger and Berardini attempted Ama Dablam, but did not quite make it to the summit. They then attempted Baruntse, a 7000 metre peak to the East of Lhotse with Brigitte Steinmann. They all reached the col before the final ridge, and Jaeger soloed the final ridge to the summit. Jaeger and Berardini then made a final acclimatisation climb, on a peak between Ama Dablam and Baruntse. On the descent they were on a ridge and Berardini was belaying Jaeger, whilst the latter crossed some rotten schist slabs, when out of sight Jaeger fell. Berardini was not properly belayed, just sitting astride a snow ridge, but fortunately the rope caught on the rocks of the ridge and held. Berardini immediately knew that Jaeger was alright because he heard him swearing. They were then faced with a very long descent coming down into the wrong valley and arriving at the camp long after dark.

After these acclimatisation climbs, Jaeger made a first excursion onto the South Face of Lhotse and reached 6500m, but noted in his journal that there were "enormous risks, frequent avalanches which one does not see coming". They had not moved the Base Camp to the foot of the South Face of Lhotse so the rest of the team did not observe his climb, but Berardini believes he probably attempted the central part of the face. If he did, he was the first climber to venture onto this part of the wall as the two Japanese expeditions and the Italians had all focused on the less steep left hand side without even trying in the centre. In researching this book, I visited the town of Chablis in Bourgogne to search in the archive of Jaeger's slides, which had been carefully stored and labelled by his mother Janine Niepce, who had died a few years before. As a professional photographer she had taken great care of the slides, but she was not a mountaineer and her labelling was quite general. What I was keen to find was evidence of where Jaeger had gone on this first attempt on the Face. This was not easy because he had taken many photos of the area on the different training climbs, but there were a couple of boxes of slides which clearly were taken on this attempt. These seem to show that he got up close to the centre of the Face and camped there, but I found no photographs showing he climbed very far up there. Of course it is possible he may have climbed some way and not taken pictures – he would of course have been engrossed in the actual climbing. One picture shows an avalanche crashing down over the rock ribs at the foot of the Face. Based on the comment in his journal, this seems to have been the type of avalanche that made him conclude this central area was just too dangerous. What the pictures also show is that he climbed quite a long way on the right hand side of the Face, probably on route up towards Lhotse Shar which he planned to take later. It is certainly quite possible he reached a height like 6500m here – the pictures show that he was above the height of the 6200m Island Peak. The pictures did not shed as much light on what he had done when he went off alone for his reconnaissance as I had hoped, but still gave a tantalising glimpse of Jaeger's actions on his penultimate climb. Overall the pictures show a large number of shots of Lhotse South Face from different angles from the foot of the Face and from his different training climbs. Jaeger's fascination, bordering on obsession with the route is clear.

After this reconnaissance he returned to Base Camp and told the others that he decided it was necessary to try another, less exposed, route. He planned to climb the original Austrian route on Lhotse Shar and from there hoped to be able to traverse to Lhotse and descend through the Western Cwm, a fantastically bold plan. There was even some feeling that he felt he could carry straight on over Everest, after descending off Lhotse.

Meanwhile Rosser's film team had lost several weeks in getting all the required permits and organising a flight into the Khumbu Region. His team of four with thirty porters were the first that year to cross over the Mera-La Pass into the uninhabited Hongu Valley. When they arrived in the valley it was so full of snow they realised they couldn't possibly work there. They sat around the camp fire cursing their luck and trying to think of an alternative plan. Rosser took out his journal and his eye lighted on the entry showing Jaeger's planned date to start his climb on Lhotse. He realised there might be a chance to document Jaeger's great adventure. The date was less than a week away, but looking at the map Rosser decided that if he split his team into two groups and travelled light with just his soundman and two Sherpas they might be able to make it. They trekked as quickly as possible, back over the Mera-La, down the next valley, over another pass and straight up the Dudh Khosi River to Lhotse, starting at dawn and arrived five days later in the afternoon. Rosser held his breath as they approached the South Face wondering whether Jaeger would still be there. With excitement he spotted his distinctive red tent.

Jaeger was astonished to see them, especially since he was planning to set off for his final attempt on Lhotse the next morning. Rosser quickly set up the gear for an interview that appears in Rosser's film, "No World for Men". Rosser had to ask the questions and act as cameraman. This meant he had to point the camera at Jaeger and frame it, turn it on, and then run back to sit next to him. They were able to shoot a roll of film before the light faded and forced them to stop. In the interview Jaeger discusses his motivations and his plans. He restates Messner's point that with a big well equipped team it was possible to climb almost any route and that "the real challenge is to climb quickly, with light teams and as little equipment as possible." He said he knew that he could not rely on outside help if things went wrong on Lhotse, but that after a month at the foot of the mountain he felt ready for the attempt. He concluded this last interview saying "once one has spent several years in the mountains, you can end up forgetting that this is no world for men. Every day I need to remind myself that this is not a world for men. It is the only way to survive. It's like when boxing, as soon as a boxer starts to lower his guard he'll be finished very soon". Before setting off Jaeger explained that he knew he could not afford to spend more than 10 days on the mountain, perhaps 15 at maximum. Afterwards his plan was to descend to Everest Base Camp and then, after a short rest, apparently to attempt the West Ridge of Everest, also solo.

Rosser's testimony and films are the last record of Nicolas Jaeger. The next morning, Rosser's group followed Jaeger to a ridge at the base of the South Face of Lhotse Shar. Jaeger was moving fast and soon left them behind, but Rosser still climbed up to 6400 metres. Here he set up his camera with the extreme telephoto lenses, which he had brought to film the snow leopards. It was bitterly cold and very windy, but he filmed all that day and part of the next. On the first day he watched as Jaeger walked to the base of the South Face, climbed a little and bivouacked. Rosser was able to watch him climbing during his second day, moving elegantly up the steep glacier slopes of the lower half of the face. He was obviously in peak physical condition because he was able to climb quite fast with only occasional pauses despite his heavy pack and the altitude. On Rosser's film we can see him tackling steeper ice cliffs without hesitation, swinging his ice axes securely to get placements before stepping up. At the end of the day Jaeger dug a snow hole for a bivouac. He had not taken a tent with him as he felt this would be too heavy: every extra gram of weight would reduce his chances of pulling off the climb. For the same reason, he had refused Rosser's suggestion to carry a small movie camera. Rosser recalls that Jaeger did take freeze dried lasagne with him, which was his favourite climbing food. He also had a bivouac sack made of Gore-Tex, which had just been launched as a material which was waterproof yet breathable.

On the third day, the 27th April, Rosser watched Jaeger climbing with two ice axes up a very steep and long ice face. He recalls that Jaeger reached the top of this long and gruelling section about midday. The Frenchman stood at the top and perhaps put his jacket on, as he must have been sweating from the effort of climbing the steep slope and would have chilled quickly once he stopped. He stood with his hands on his hips looking down at the Face he had just climbed. Rosser guessed that Jaeger felt pride in what he had achieved already. As the American watched him in this pose through his spotting scope, the mist rolled in obscuring both Jaeger and the South Face. Rosser has a clear recollection of the scene, although he did not capture this moment on film.

The ceiling of clouds obscured the upper part of Lhotse and it looked solid and unlikely to clear anytime soon. Rosser and his team were worried that Jaeger might be caught in a heavy snowfall, especially given that he didn't have a tent. At the same time they realised they had to be quick to walk round the base of Nuptse and up to Everest Base Camp in order to film Jaeger's descent down through the Ice Fall if he succeeded in traversing Lhotse. Berardini, Steinmann and the rest of the expedition had already moved to Everest Base Camp to wait for Jaeger. As Rosser's team traversed around the mountain it was windy and bitterly cold. In the end the bad weather lasted for 8 days with low clouds and a lot of snowfall throughout the Everest massif. Those waiting at Everest Base Camp gradually became more and more concerned about whether Jaeger would make it down safely. In the end they realised they had to report him missing.

When they heard the worrying news, Jaeger's family and friends in France moved to organise a search. Leading the efforts tirelessly was Nicolas' mother, Janine Niepce. Her son obviously meant everything to her and she was very worried by his climbing. At one stage she had even fallen into a depression for several months until eventually Nicolas went to her and told her almost brutally that her being depressed would not stop his activities. Jaeger did not plan to carry on extreme climbing for his whole life and when his physical capacity started to reduce he might switch to another sport like ocean sailing, but until he realised his climbing goals he was determined to carry on. Niepce recovered from her depression, but of course her worries about her son's climbing did not go away. Now that he was in trouble she showed great energy and determination to do all she could for him. First she arranged for Jean-Francois Mazeaud flew out to Nepal to assist. Mazeaud, who was nephew of Pierre, was another member of the Everest expedition on which Jaeger had reached the summit two years before. Jean-Francois's own attempt on the summit had been thwarted by bad weather. He was a doctor like Jaeger and the pair had remained friends after Everest. In fact Mazeaud had originally planned to accompany Jaeger to Lhotse, but had had to withdraw after he had been called up for his military service. After Jaeger was reported missing, his mother managed to use her influence to persuade the French army to give permission for Mazeaud to take 15 days leave and go to Nepal to help in the search for him.

After the 8 days of bad weather, it was very fine and Mazeaud was able to make successive helicopter flights to search for Jaeger. At first they looked on the South Face of Lhotse itself, but after talking to Rosser they understood that Jaeger had been going up to the ridge of Lhotse Shar rather than on the Face itself. The Lama helicopter made flights every day for a week to scan the terrain looking for signs of the missing man. Mazeaud knew about his friend's incredible capacity to survive, evidenced by his 60 days at 6600 metres in Peru the year before, and hoped that if he was injured and couldn't move there was a chance he could be found even long after his disappearance. Mazeaud thought Jaeger might have dug a snow hole to shelter, but the location of it would not necessarily be easy to spot from above. In the vast wide snow slopes, brilliant white from the freshly fallen snow, it was hard to spot things with the naked eye. So he took photos which they could scan carefully afterwards. Unfortunately they could not get them developed quickly in Nepal at that time and had to send them off to Bangkok and only got them back two days later. They poured over these with a magnifying glass trying to spot anything which might give a clue to the whereabouts of the missing climber.

Mazeaud, desperate not to leave any possibility untried, also thought Jaeger might have descended down some couloirs on the far side of Lhotse Shar into the Kangshung valley in Chinese Tibet. The helicopter was able to fly up to 7500 metres and tried to fly into Tibet to search for Jaeger there, but this almost caused a diplomatic incident and they were fired on by the Chinese border guards. Mazeaud also contacted a French Military expedition which was making a reconnaissance of the Tibetan side of Everest. Their leader refused to help in looking for Jaeger saying that he had already made illegal ascents in Nepal and that if he had descended into Tibet that was unauthorised and his own responsibility. Naturally Mazeaud was shocked and upset at the refusal of assistance to a climber and fellow countryman in difficulty.

In despair, he even consulted the Lamas at the Swayambhunath (Monkey) Temple in Kathmandu. This is always a lively place with golden stupa draped in colourful Tibetan prayer flags and monkeys scampering around. The Lamas spoke some Buddhist verses and the Head Lama told Mazeaud that he believed Jaeger was still alive and in Tibet. Knowing that he had in mind an impressive traverse there was even some talk that he had managed to traverse Everest and descend down onto the Tibetan side. Later however, the Lama phoned Mazeaud to say that his watch had stopped, which he believed was a sign that Nicolas Jaeger was no longer alive. Mazeaud realised that all hope for his friend was gone.

On the same day that Jaeger was seen for the last time another tragedy occurred. Two other French climbers, Julien Graux and Phillipe Grézat, who had been camping in the same Base Camp as Jaeger's team and who they had spent a lot of time with, made an attempt on Baruntse by its North Ridge. They even borrowed some of Jaeger's spare equipment to do this. But during the climb they apparently dropped their camera and, whilst descending to try and recover it, they both fell to their deaths. This further tragedy combined with the disappearance of Jaeger was traumatic for Berardini, who was still a teenager. In the confusion of the search for Jaeger, he was rather ignored and ended up going back to France alone. I met Berardini at his home near Grenoble many years later. He is still fit and active in the mountains, but he had not been in contact with the Jaeger family since leaving Nepal. When I talked to Berardini 34 years after these climbs with Jaeger he was struggling to access memories he had stored away in the dusty corners of his mind. He has no photos from the expedition because under agreement he had with Jaeger gave the leader all image rights and although he still has a down suit provided for the expedition, it is so warm he has not had the chance to wear it since. After analysing Jaeger's photos, I sent a selection to Berardini and he said that seeing the photos brought back vivid memories and that he felt he could remember each moment shown distinctly.

Whilst the search for Jaeger was going on, Rosser's group, having spent several days at Everest Base Camp, had lost hope of seeing the Frenchman again. They continued through the Khumbu to the Gokyo Valley, and a small, hidden hanging valley at nearly 5000 metres where they baited snow leopards for three and a half months. In this time they didn't seen any other Westerners, so naturally heard no news about Jaeger. In August they made an eleven day hike out to the roadhead in the monsoon rains and went back to Kathmandu. They checked at the French consulate and were told about the fruitless helicopter search. Rosser remembers how sad and frustrated he was, knowing that he had seen Jaeger climb higher than the ceiling at which the helicopters could fly. He was amazed at the bravery of Jaeger's mother in coming to Nepal to try and track down her son and regretted that he wasn't there to give more assistance in retracing his route at the time the search was taking place. At the French Consular Office he reviewed a topo map of Lhotse with the Consul and showed him the last spot he had seen Jaeger. Based on this they estimated that this was at close to 8200 metres. Of course this does not mean he did not climb higher and, like with Mallory and Irvine, nobody knows exactly how high he got. Maybe he made it to the summit of Lhotse Shar and fell attempting the traverse to Lhotse on the incredibly crenelated and difficult ridge between the peaks. Maybe he got even further than that to the summit of Lhotse, which would have been a fantastic achievement completing a traverse still not made today. Or maybe he was overcome by the cold and altitude whilst trying to shelter from storms in a snowhole near the last place he was seen or buried under an avalanche whilst trying to descend. Whatever happened, it was a tragic loss of a man who dared to dream he could achieve the nearly impossible. He certainly made a huge impression on Rosser who named his son after him and later found that that his soundman had done the same thing,

Nicolas Jaeger is an enigmatic presence in the history of mountaineering. He was one of the finest snow and ice climbers of the 1970s and had achieved some very bold solo ascents. In researching this book I spoke to many people who knew and climbed with him and gradually built up a picture of the man and his character and motivations. They all spoke of someone special, not always an easy person to get along with, but someone they were happy to have known. Most of all I was interested to meet his daughter Helene, who was 12 at the time of his disappearance and who Jaeger took into the mountains on a number of occasions. Now in her 40s and living in the Burgundy region where the Niepce family comes from. I arranged to meet her at one of the vineyards she owns and manages in the small town of Chablis. We met in a building at the edge of vineyards, which is normally used for tasting the fine white wines produced by Helene. Since the death of her grandmother, Janine Niepce a few years ago, Helene has maintained the archives about both her grandmother and father. She produced for me boxes with old articles, books and photos about her father's expeditions and we had a long chat. Some aspects of his planning for his Lhotse are hard to piece together – like the composition of the team and how his plans evolved over time. Helene explained to me that Nicolas mother Janine always fought to keep the memory of her son alive, although for others in the family it was perhaps less painful to try and forget. A few years ago they visited the Aiguille du Midi teleferique station in the heart of the Mont Blanc range. At the iconic station, which is always busy with tourists, skiers and climbers, the Club Alpin Francais have installed a display with photos of the most famous figures from French mountaineering history. Nicolas' mother was upset to see that her son was not amongst those displayed, as if he had been airbrushed from history like someone in Stalinist Russia. After her protests to the Club Alpin Francais he was added to the alpinists displayed, but this sense that he was an outsider from the mainstream of French climbing remains. He wrote in his book "Carnets de Solitude" that real heroism was doing a nine-to-five job in Paris, commuting on the metro. As a child Helene recognised that her father was someone special, but sometimes she wished she had an ordinary father who did do a mundane regular job.

Before departing for Nepal, Jaeger had told his mother that if he disappeared above 8000 metres, it would not be worth trying to look for him and although his friends and family did make huge efforts, they found no trace. So ended, far too soon, the life and climbing career of a visionary alpinist. Some accused him of taking risks too far, but all Himalayan climbing involves such risks and there would be many others who shared Jaeger's vision in the decade to come. But in 1980 Nicolas Jaeger was ahead of his time because few yet thought that this was a way realistic approach to an objective as serious as Lhotse's South Face.

Chapter 4 – Crossing the Line

Nicolas Jaeger was a very talented climb and had a bold vision on Lhotse, but the real chances of his succeeding were maybe always low. Although by 1980 many Himalayan climbers believed in Messner's vision for light Alpine style climbing, few yet believed that a route as hard as the South Face of Lhotse could be climbed this way. The next expedition to attempt the face intended to follow a more traditional approach, but seemed equipped to make a much more serious bid for the summit.

This team was officially from Yugoslavia, but was made up primarily of Slovenians. Although Slovenia has a population of only 2 million, it has a very strong mountain tradition. The arc of the Alps finishes here in the Julian Alps, not the highest part of the range at less than 3000 metres, but containing some dramatic limestone peaks which provide fine climbing and a training ground for many top rank mountaineers. In the 1970s the Slovenians were making a name for themselves as top performers in the Himalayas. In 1975 a team led by Ales Kunaver attempted the prestigious South Face of Makalu which had defeated a previous attempt by Kunaver as well as several others, including one by an Austrian team including Messner. Kunaver, with an attention to detail in planning which marked the most successful Himalayan expedition leaders, resolved to learn the lessons of the failure three years before. In 1972 there had been periods of "dead time" when the route had stopped being advanced as the lead teams moved up and down the mountain and times when the Sherpa support team had failed to back up the lead climbers. Kunaver's solution was to take more climbers and less Sherpas on the 1975 expedition. Although Sherpas had been critical in building the supply chain for the large expeditions which had made the first ascents of the 8000 metre peaks, these routes were generally technically easy. On harder climbs, the role they could play was more marginal – at least until they were properly trained as mountain guides. Kunaver decided that Sherpas would only carry loads on the lower part of the Face. This meant more carrying work for the European climbers and meant it was critical for the expedition leader to keep the team motivated. He had to balance giving all these climbers a fair chance of being part of a summit bid whilst trying to give the expedition the best chance of putting at least one team on top. Getting this balance right was not easy, but the most successful expedition leaders, like Kunaver and Chris Bonington, managed it. That was not to say there were never disputes on their expeditions. These were inevitable with strong willed, ambitious and driven lead climbers. And whilst the accounts of expeditions in the 1950s tended to play down or even ignore completely such tensions, Bonington set a new style in his books by openly describing the tensions and disputes between his team members.

Kunaver had a detailed plan, which involved dividing the climbers into five groups and rotating the lead. Other than one short period of bad weather, they managed to stick to the plan and the strength of the team meant that there was no shortage of climbers capable of forming the summit teams. In the end four groups reached the top, including several climbers who were later to form part of Kunaver's team on Lhotse. On 5th October the lead pair of Stane Belak and Marjan Manfreda tackled the last difficulties of the face involving hard rock climbing and steep ice and the next day made it to the summit. Manfreda's oxygen set malfunctioned due to the intense cold, but the pair carried on to complete one of the hardest climbs achieved in the Himalayas so far. Mountain Magazine ranked it alongside the British Ascent of Everest South West Face and Messner and Habeler's two man climb on Gasherbrum I as the finest achievements of 1975. Three days after the first pair reached the summit another four climbers set off for a second summit bid and, although two of them had to turn back, Janko Azman and the 23 year old Nejc Zaplotnik continued to the summit.

Zaplotnik was the inspiration for a generation of Slovenian climbers. In his book "The Way" he set out a vision of climbing which said that "the one who is looking for a goal will remain empty, but those who find the way carry the goal in themselves". The way for him was all the aspects of the mountaineering life, from frostbite and mud and the terrifying creaking of a glacier to nights without sleep and the tired faces and glowing eyes of friends. The important thing for him was the journey not the destination. He was an exceptional performer at altitude, but had unlikely route to becoming a star alpinist. He was a very sickly child and at one point was even given his last rites. He was born in the small village on the outskirts of Kranj, home to a number of Slovenia's top climbers. To recover from an illness he was sent to stay with a cousin who lived in the hills above Kranj, just under the mountain Grintovec. Nejc loved life in the countryside and here he got his first exposure to mountain climbing. Then, like many mountaineers before him, he read the inspirational accounts of the great expeditions of the 1950s like Maurice Herzog's "Annapurna" and Hermann Buhl's "Nanga Parbat Pilgrimage". By his teens he was hooked and after performing impressively in the Alps and Yosemite in the USA he got the chance to go on Kunaver's Makalu expedition.

After Makalu, Zaplotnik's next chance to climb an 8000er came two years later on another Slovenian expedition with the goal of climbing a new route on Gasherbrum I. After the route was prepared, Zaplotnik went for the summit together with 20 year old Andrej Stremfelj, who had the same hungry desire to visit these high places. They left for the summit at 6 am lightweight and without a rope, knowing that at this height speed meant safety. As they progressed the cloud shrouded the mountain and their whole universe narrowed to a small grey and cold area in front of them, their only goal to advance the next few metres. Zaplotnik's thoughts went to the foreign world down below them: a dusty world in which poor people lived in modest huts, sitting by the fire cooking chapattis whilst the children played on the dirt floor. By noon they were standing on the summit, which was nothing special in itself, just a flat area of snow hidden by the fog and snow, with the sun faintly visible through the clouds. They took their backpacks off, embraced and punched each other on the shoulders, tears of joy freezing on their cheeks. For Zaplotnik there was no shame in crying: some people wasted their youth in bars, but they had really achieved something.

Avoiding the temptation to linger, they started down as the wind increased and the snow fell more heavily. In a rock gully, snow slides hit them from behind, threatening to knock them off their feet. When Stremfelj disappeared in the mist, Zaplotnik shouted desperately to make sure they didn't get separated, but the blanket of falling snow muffled the sound. If they didn't find the way back to their bivouac tent they would be in mortal danger, but the rocks played tricks with them in the mist as they struggled to identify the right place to turn off the ridge. Finally at 5 pm with enormous relief they caught sight of the blue fabric of the tent and dived inside, not caring how much snow was blown in as they did so. Icicles were hanging from their beards and they were desperately thirsty, but lacked the willpower to boil water to make drinks. They hadn't expected anyone to have come up from the lower camps given the weather, but after a while Drago Bergar arrived with the intention to make a solo repeat of their ascent. Whilst Bergar congratulated them and made them drinks, the other two tried to persuade him to given up the attempt and accompany them down, but Bergar was determined to sit out the storm and try for the summit. Zaplotnik and Stremfelj had spent too much time at altitude and were becoming exhausted and eventually they gave up trying to make Bergar change his mind and reluctantly left him at the camp. Storms set in for six days and efforts to reach Bergar on the radio proved fruitless. They had to conclude that their companion had been lost on a solo bid for the summit and the expedition ended tragically.

The next major Slovenian expedition, in 1979 under the leadership of Tony Skarja, attempted one of the three main ridges of Everest, the West. This ridge had been climbed by an American team in 1963, but they had avoided both the lower section, by traversing onto the ridge at mid-height from the Western Cwm, and the upper section, where they traversed out left into a couloir on the North Face. The Slovenians aimed to climb the whole ridge from top to bottom. To climb the lower section they had to reach the Lho La, the col at the foot of the ridge, which is threatened by ice avalanches and had been the scene of a major accident in 1974 when one French guide and 5 Sherpas were killed. The Slovenians climbed steep and loose rocks to the left of the line followed by the French. From the Lho La they climbed the slopes which led up to Everest's West Shoulder, where the 1963 American route had joined from the right. But whereas the Americans had traversed left, the Slovenians tackled the steepest section of the ridge above. Although halted for several days by strong winds, they eventually managed to establish a fifth camp at 8100 metres from which Vicki Groselj and Marjan Manfreda made a first summit bid, which failed at 8300 metres due to cold and problems with their oxygen equipment.

A second attempt also failed, but then it was the turn of probably the strongest team of Zaplotnik and the Stremfelj brothers, Andrej and Marko. Marko Stremfelj had problems with his oxygen set and had to turn back, but the pair who had succeeded together on Gasherbrum I, pressed on passing the previous high point and arriving at the final hard section, the so-called Grey Step. This was unexplored terrain and they did not have enough gear to reverse what they were climbing. They knew they would have to find another way down, but despite the commitment they pressed on. Zaplotnik and Stremfelj were young, but a very effective having already climbed together for six years. Zaplotnik had a reputation as a joker, but he looked deadly serious as he took the first lead up the shattered schist. It would not have been hard climbing at sea level in rock shoes, but near the summit of Everest in unwieldy double-boots and crampons and carrying a 15 kilo oxygen tank it took the upmost skill. Suddenly a hold broke and Zaplotnik fell from the rocks onto the snow at the bottom of step.

They were only belayed to one bad piton, but it held. Stremfelj's fear began to increase with the shock of the fall, the huge drop to Western Cwm 2300 metres below and the threat of storms from clouds which now hid the tops of Nuptse and Lhotse. Zaplotnik didn't say anything, but brushed the snow off himself, took off his thick Dachstein mittens and started climbing again. Finding his way with his bare fingers on the difficult rock, Zaplotnik gained height metre by metre, sometimes free climbing and sometimes pulling up on pitons. The whole pitch took an hour and Stremfelj was looking anxiously at this watch – it was already 3 o clock and would be dark by six. He jumared up to join Zaplotnik on the stance, noting that the rope he had pulled up on was attached to one piton not fully driven in. "Do you think it's too late?" asked Stremfelj.

Zaplotnik pulled his oxygen mask of his face, looked Stremfelj in the eyes and said "no". It was the end of the discussion. Stremfelj had complete faith in the decision of his partner and mentor. Technically as climbers they were equals, but, in the savage conditions of the Himalayan death-zone, decision making ability was what counted and Zaplotnik had a knack of making the right calls, of knowing when they could take the chance to climb on and when to turn back. He saw that Stremfelj's first oxygen bottle was empty. To save weight they both took the bottles from their packs and tossed them down the South West Face. With one metallic bang off the rocks, the cylinders disappeared over an overhang and down into the mists of the Cwm two and a half kilometres vertically below. Zaplotnik was concerned about the state of his fingers, which had gone white and numb whilst climbing the critical pitch. He rubbed them and felt the sharp pain of blood returning feeling to the nerves. The skin stayed white and the pain was searing, but he knew that was a good sign.

Emboldened by the resolve of his mentor, Stremfelj pushed on up the next pitch which brought him to the top of the step. As he waited there for Zaplotnik to jumar up, he looked again at his watch. With relief Stremfelj realised that confused by the lack of oxygen reaching his brain, he had mixed up the hands and misread the time - it was still only half past one. They now both knew they were going to make it to the summit. Their partnership had been forged in their youth, climbing and skiing in Slovenia. Those days in the mud and rain and knee deep snow together were now paying off on the greatest prize of all. They crossed narrow snow arêtes and some further rocks steps, fortunately less difficult than those below. The exposure was enormous, but they focused on the climbing and were almost able to enjoy the pleasure of some more technical moves.

Finally crossing another rock step they saw a gentle snow slope which led up to the aluminium tripod left by the Chinese in 1975 and which they knew marked the top. They did not say too much to each other, but they both knew the significance of the moment after completing a major new route on the world's highest mountain. They sat in the snow by the tripod, relieved to not have to go further up and soaking in the glory of the moment, but keeping half a mind of the need to descend. After talking on the radio with Skarja they decided to descend the 1963 American route down the Horbein couloir. Following this another team of Stane Belak, Stipe Bozic and the Sherpa Ang Phu made it to the summit, but got there later than they planned and had to bivouac at 8200 metres during the descent of the Horbein Couloir. A third team, of Borut Bergant, Ivan Kotnik and Vanja Matijevec, were also planning to attempt the summit, but when their companions didn't return before nightfall they abandoned their attempt to try and help. They passed an agonising night where the upper team's radio could send, but not receive calls which meant that the lower group could hear their companions increasing desperate messages, but not reply to re-assure them. The upper team managed to survive the night and continue down, but tragically just before the two parties met, Ang Phu slipped on an easy snow slope and fell to his death down the North Face seemingly without trying to arrest his fall. He was a very experienced Sherpa who had already climbed Everest. The West Ridge climb made him the first person to have climbed Everest by two different routes. After this further attempts were abandoned.

With ascents like those on Makalu and Everest behind them Kunaver was able to select a team with a wealth of first class Himalayan experience for Lhotse. Andrej Stremfelj, for example, had already shown he was one of the very best Himalayan climbers. Unlike the semi-mystical motivations of Nejc Zaplotnik, Stremfelj was attracted to mountain climbing for straightforward reasons. As a child he saw the Kamniske Alps on his way to school and this awakened his curiosity. He wanted to know what it was like up there, to see whether the top of the Grintavec was really such a sharp point. This desire to explore the unknown lured him to the mountains and the realisation that the view got better the higher you went drove him on to climb more and higher. Stremfelj's motivations may seem simplistic, but it perhaps a fully rational explanation for mountaineering simply does not exist. The drive to explore these wild places is perhaps part of man's innate desire to discover new places – the same drive which saw humans explore almost every corner of the globe in prehistoric times.

Since Slovenia was not yet an independent country, the expedition was technically a Yugoslavian one, but with only two non-Slovenian climbing members – Stipe Bozic, from Croatia, and Jovan Popovski, from Macedonia. Bozic in particular was a strong climber who had climbed frequently with the Slovenians, but the inclusion of a Serbian filmmaker was more about making the team seem Yugoslavian to make getting funding from the federal government in Belgrade easier. The Slovenians weren't interested in merely repeating what others had already done, but rather wanted to climb new routes on the hardest and highest peaks. After Makalu and Everest, Lhotse South Face was a logical next step. Kunaver brought with him a nucleus of climbers who had gained experience on the earlier expeditions and who had a strong team spirit. As it was a federal expedition, climbers who wanted to join had to send in an application including a resume' of their main climbs. Kunaver knew personally most of the more experienced ones and the younger ones by reputation. He thought carefully about getting the right mix of both experienced Himalayan climbers and some younger climbers with a record of hard climbs in the Alps. Kunaver sent Zaplotnik and Stremfelj to reconnoitre the Face in 1980 prior to the full assault the following year. Their assessment was somewhat different from that of their predecessors. They judged the right hand, eastern, part of the Face to be too threatened by seracs, but did see potential to make a direct line up the left hand part of the centre of the Face.

The next year the full team arrived and set up Base Camp on the Lhotse Glacier. Being camped under the mountain really brought home to Kunaver the magnitude of what they were undertaking. Lhotse seemed to take up half the sky with its huge triangular overhangs and thundering avalanches. They decided to fix ropes from the very base of the Face allowing climbers to move up and down in full security even in bad weather using jumars and carabiners. A 6m aluminium ladder was used to cross the bergschrund, the large crevasse always found at the base of a mountain face rising above a glacier. To fix ropes they could not often use snow stakes as anchors since just below the surface there was hard ice. So they mainly had to use ice screws and rock anchors. Camp I was placed underneath a rock step, but this provided insufficient protection and avalanches damaged the tents several times. The only way they could get a completely safe shelter was by using laboriously cut ice caves. A cave would take several days to construct, hacking into the rock pitted ice and they frequently broke shovels and ice axes in this construction work. The compensation was that the resulting shelters were completely secure with solid walls.

On the lower part the climbers were often hit by powder snow avalanches which poured over them. These came without warning – one minute they were climbing up the fixed ropes, the next it was as if the lights had been switched off. They wrapped bandanas over their mouths, but it did not stop ice dust entering their lungs, which were lacerated by the razor sharp ice crystals before they melted. But they were secured to the mountain by the fixed ropes and there was nothing to do but wait for the snow to pass. In the first weeks the climbers were alarmed by this bombardment, but they gradually got used to it and understood that the showers of powder snow were not really so threatening.

Above Camp I they installed ladders to assist in carrying loads past a rock step. For the descent they had a rope hanging down the outside of the step and after making a carry higher up it was possible to slide down this rope straight into Camp I – where hopefully a cup of hot tea would be waiting! Above the rock step, the route went up an ice rib which was long, straight and rather boring to climb. The rib was made of a strange mixture of water ice and sand, making it very hard work to ascend in crampons. At the top of the rib there was no sheltered place to situate Camp II and no possibility to dig a snow hole. They could not use tents placed on metal frames like Bonington's team on Everest South West Face. There was no choice, but to hack platforms out from the rock studded ice. It took a week of hard work before they got a decent placement for the camp, which consisted of three tents, each above the last, like steps. After the tents suffered avalanche damage they created a web of ropes above them to try and give some protection. This was not the only discomfort in this camp: the lack of sun also meant that sleeping bags got wet and frozen every night and had to be exchanged for new ones carried up from Base Camp.

They started to understand the pattern of weather – beautiful first thing in the mornings, but then from late morning it would snow and in the afternoons there would always be avalanches. It cleared up again in the evening and the night was usually fine. Kunaver understood the need to keep the team motivated during the hard work of preparing the route, digging snow holes and carrying loads to stock the camps. He ensured that the monotonous diet of dried food was enriched by excellent hams. There was also a lot of card-playing and gambling to kill time and various books did the rounds in Base Camp.

The steepness of the wall made it difficult for the climbers up on the Face to survey the route ahead. Kunaver at Base Camp used binoculars to help explain the nature of the terrain on the radio to the climbers on the Face. From Camp II, they made a long traverse right over an icefield, before mixed ice and rock led back up to the left. This area was in the fall line of all the snow which fell on the upper part of the face and anyone caught here in the afternoon was showered with cascades of powder snow, which nearly led to a serious accident a few weeks later. The whole gully to the left of the big triangular overhang, which dominates the upper part of the Face, is a natural track for avalanches from above. To avoid having a camp exposed to, this they placed Camp III high up under the large overhang. Ivan Kotnik and Zaplotnik were the first to reach the site of this camp at 6800 metres at the height of a storm. All they could do was bury the equipment they had laboriously carried up there in a hole in the steep bank of snow. The job of setting the camp itself was done a few days later by Filip Bence, the Podgornik brothers, Vanja Matijevec and Kunaver. They arrived at the site of Camp III in very bad weather with frequent avalanches and dug out the equipment left by their teammates. When they couldn't dig ice holes, as at the site of Camp III, they tried to place the tents pressed as far into the wall as possible so that avalanches would pass over them without sweeping the tents off the wall.

Matijevec and Kunaver descended back down leaving the others at Camp III. The next day they got ready to fix ropes on the steep section above the camp. The weather was fine, but with high winds and very cold temperatures – around -30 ^{o}c. The terrain was steep rock slabs covered with powder snow. Peter Podgornik took the lead and gradually made progress. He had to clean away the snow away with him hands to find places he could place anchors in the rock. Filip Bence belayed him from just outside the tents whilst Peter's brother Pavel was inside brewing tea. In around three hours work, Peter managed to fix some 120 metres of rope making crucial progress on a difficult section of the route. Around noon it started to snow heavily and snow avalanches soon started to pour over him like waterfalls as he worked on the ropes. Podgornik had had three pairs of gloves on at the beginning of the day, but two of these froze and broke and he was left using only some very thin gloves intended to be worn in the night or for cooking. Once he got back down to the tent it was clear his hands were in a very bad way and it was necessary to try and get him off the mountain, but with a storm raging, this was no trivial matter. In the more critical sections they weren't even sure it was safe to descend the fixed ropes as avalanches poured down. Traversing some couloirs and the rock step above Camp I was particularly serious. When they got back to the glacier at the foot of the Face, Peter inspected his hands again and saw that they were white and feeling very cold. When he showed them to his brother and Filip Bence they went quiet – it was obvious he had frostbite. Within a couple of days they had turned black and it was clear Peter Podgornik would be unable to play any further role on the face. But the doctor was able to treat him at Base Camp and Peter told Kunaver he wanted to stay with the team and his brother Pavel to give moral support. In the end Peter lost some of the end of his fingers, but it didn't stop him carrying on doing hard technical rock climbs in his native Slovenia to this day and participating in several other expeditions.

A huge amount of load carrying was needed to provide provisions and fuel, camping equipment, oxygen, fixed ropes and gear to the chain of camps extending up the Face. The Sherpas played a key role in this on the lower part of the face, but the steep and technical nature of the ground to be covered and the constant risk of avalanche made this risky even with the protection of the fixed ropes. By the 30th April the expedition had been on the Face for more than 40 days. That day two of the Sherpas carried loads of oxygen cylinders up to Camp III and started to descend back to Camp II. But they started too late and were too slow and they found themselves on the long snow field down from Camp III literally in a river of snow. From Base Camp Kunaver watched through binoculars. With the drifting clouds it was hard to spot the Sherpas, but when they did appear Kunaver could see they were moving at a snail's pace on the long traverse towards Camp II. Kunaver had descended the same way himself the day before and knew how bad conditions could be, but down at Base Camp he was powerless to help. The amount of powder snow in the air almost suffocated them and at times they simply stood still, transfixed by the streams of cascading snow and unable to move forwards.

Rajko Kovac, and the Stremfelj brothers were at Camp II and could have gone to the rescue of the Sherpas, but Kunaver had no way to warn them because they had the radio turned off to save the batteries until the scheduled two hours later. The battery life was unpredictable in the cold and damp conditions of the Face so people preferred to turn them off when not in use. Dusk was beginning to fall and Kunaver knew that the onset of night would make the situation very serious for the Sherpas. His inability to help them from Base Camp was maddeningly frustrating. Suddenly, as if by magic, the radio came to life – the team in Camp II wanted to know if the post had arrived in Base Camp. Kunaver didn't have to say any more than "you guys get up the hill to help the Sherpas" and they understood that two lives were at risk. But they still had to get dressed and put their crampons on before they could go out onto the fixed ropes, shouting to the Sherpas that they were on their way to help. It was dark by the time the radio came to life again and Kunaver heard with relief that the Sherpas were safely in the tent and being given hot drinks. No harm had come at the end, but it had illustrated the risks the face and given Kunaver a major fright.

The rock band above Camp IV was one of the hardest sections of the climb. Five teams working one after the other were needed to complete fixing ropes in this section. The middle part was a steep wall which was followed by a traverse into a chimney which acted as a funnel for loose snow blown down from the upper snow field. Being caught in this chimney when a huge volume of snow was cascading down was a nightmarish experience which most of the climbers suffered at one time or another. Once past this section, the snow field up to Camp V was one of the easiest angled parts of the wall. Although technically straightforward to climb, in just about every other respect this section was bad, with lots of soft snow, avalanches and no protected place for Camp V. This camp was established on the 1st May by Bence and Pavel Podgornik just below the so called "Yellow Band". The Yellow Band is a famous geological feature which runs through the sedimentary rocks which make up Everest and Lhotse. When Bence radioed down to report Camp V's establishment to Kunaver he expressed some reservations about the camp's position. It was very difficult terrain in which to dig a cave, but was in an exposed position on the open slope. They spread tarpaulins over it to provide some protection from snow slides, but this meant it was claustrophobic inside and Bence hoped that people wouldn't be afraid to sleep there. He and Pavel Podgornik showed the way by spending that night there.

The next day Marjon Manfreda and Borut Bergant moved up to take their turn at Camp V. They were accompanied by Miro Sustersic and two Sherpas who were carrying loads before returning back down. As they were leaving the cave at Camp IV they met Bence and Podgornik who were on their way back down. They could see in their eyes the strain of a difficult night. Podgornik was also still worried about his brother Peter who was down in Base Camp with frostbite. The team going up passed the difficult section above Camp IV, their crampons screeching on the rocks as they jumared up the ropes. The top of the mountain was already enclosed in clouds which slowly descended towards them. Once the clouds hit them, the wind got up and soon they found themselves in the middle of a blizzard. The thin green rope they were clipped to was their only connection to a human world of safety in the savagery of the storm around them. The snow got harder the avalanches started to rumble around them and still Camp V was nowhere to be seen. They knew they must be close as they continued to follow the ropes, but the tents were so deeply buried that they only saw the camp when they were right upon it. Before they had a chance to dig out the entrance and get inside they were hit by another avalanche from above.

Eventually they got into the shelter of the tent and started to try and make tea, but everything was wet and with damp matches they could not light the stove. Even when they found a cigarette lighter the stove still wouldn't ignite due to the lack of oxygen inside the deeply buried tent. They finished by lying in the tent without drinks, shivering with cold and listening to the thunder of avalanches outside. Eventually Manfreda fell asleep but was soon woken by Bergant shouting that they were trapped by the snow and couldn't get out of the tent. Snow was piled on the outside of the tent restricting the air supply and they knew they urgently had to get some warm liquid and ventilation. At first they were successful in clearing the entrance, but then it started to snow again and the rumble of avalanches restarted. They cursed their bad luck – usually the weather was clear during the night. They took it in turns to use the shovel to keep the entrance clear of snow, but the slides became more and more frequent. Fatigue was enticing them to give up the effort and just sleep, but they knew they could not give in to that temptation and had to keep working.

In panic, they radioed Base Camp during the night to get advice. Bergant got through to Janez Benkovic and asked him to wake up Kunaver. Bergant asked

Kunaver whether they should cut the tent open to get more air. Kunaver strongly advised them against this – the tent was their only protection against the savage elements high on the wall. He told them not to leave the camp until the morning and that the sky above Base Camp was clear and that the Face should eventually clear too. This encouraged them and they agreed to sit tight and wait for the morning. Kunaver said Base Camp would keep the radio open all night, but Camp V should use the radio sparingly to ensure that batteries did not run out and cut them off from contact. Bergant finished by reminding Kunaver that it was his wedding anniversary. During the rest of the night they kept in contact with Base. Even if those below could do nothing to help them, the psychological value of not being completely cut off from the rest of the world was enormous.

After this experience, and others where climbers literally couldn't find the camp because it was so deeply buried in the snow, Kunaver decided to abandon Camp V – it was too hellish a place for anyone to stay. Instead the climbers would move straight through for IV to VI. Camp VI was placed only 300 metres higher up, in a spectacular location protected by a whipped cream roll of snow and was an ideal place to launch a bid for the summit. Marjan Kregar and Viki Groselj were the first pair to stay there and the next day Groselj explored the route above. But a storm was raging and he only managed to progress 50 metres. Although Kregar belayed him directly from the tent, he still suffered frostbite. They spent a further night in the camp, but the storm was still raging and they came back down the next day, Groselj injuring his back during the descent.

On May the 11th a team consisting of Filip Bence and Pavel Podgornik went up to Camp VI. Despite heavy loads, they were able to move quickly from Camp IV to Camp VI quite rapidly passing the now abandoned site of Camp V. From where Camp VI was positioned only a short rock section led to the ridge which they believed could lead to the main summit ridge and be the key to the climb. The top seemed tantalisingly close and Bence felt that all they needed was some more equipment and a renewal of physical strength. Unfortunately the latter was missing for him. He had a bad night, unable to sleep because of the cold and woke feeling little strength and sensitivity in his legs. Bence realised that only a rapid descent to lower altitudes and richer air would revive him. Reluctantly he bid farewell to Podgornik and headed down the fixed ropes leaving his partner alone at the top camp.

Across the whole team the physical and psychological strain of the long weeks on the savage and inhospitable face was gradually taking its toll. Viki Groselj radioed Base Camp to say that Kregar had become overwhelmed by fumes whilst cooking and was suffering gas poisoning. Lack of ventilation was one of the downsides of sleeping inside snow caves and Kregar was in a bad way and it was necessary for him to get down. He struggled to make it down under his own steam and at bottom his companions realised that he needed immediate medical attention and could play no further part in the expedition. Kunaver himself made a last carry up to Camp IV in support of the summit bid. Conditions were difficult with snow pouring down through the gullies they had to pass. After leaving his load he set off down, but knowing that in Camp III there was no gas for cooking. On the way back down he passed two of the Sherpas, Nuvu and Nuru, who were bringing up large loads. He exchanged a few words with them and asked them how they were. They said "OK", but when he asked if they were going to make it to the camp above the answer was ambiguous "Heavy ascent. Very bad, Sahib, much snow". Both he and they knew that it was a tough climb and a vital contribution to the expedition. Meanwhile Stremfelj and Zaplotnik, arguably one of the best pairs of Himalayan climbers in the World at that time, were moving up the mountain to join Podgornik at Camp VI. If anyone could overcome the top section of this wall it was perhaps going to be them. Kunaver reminded them what a great support job the two Sherpas had done in carrying the oxygen up to support the attempt and told them to make sure they gave them hot drinks before they descended.

On the 15th May Podgornik, Stremfelj and Zaplotnik were ready to make a bid for the summit from Camp VI. From the camp at 8200 metres there were only 300 vertical metres to the top, although there was some horizontal distance to cover too. Stremfelj felt that they could make it if they only got some luck with the weather. They woke in the night; the stars set deeply in the black unfeeling sky, and went through the usual ritual of putting on the stove to make tea. As they prepared the oxygen cylinders for the climb, they could see their own breath freezing in front of their faces in the light of the headlamps. With numb fingers they struggled to put on their crampons. Zaplotnik appreciated the magnificent and awe inspiring exposure they faced. For him it was something insanely powerful. They also felt enormous tension – this was perhaps the most risky enterprise of their lives. From the camp they initially traversed around 100 metres to the left in deep snow. They went up following roughly the line of the ridge above which gradually became less distinct and merged into the face.

Soon the going was not straightforward, with steep and friable rock covered with fresh snow. Zaplotnik's crampons slipped on the loose rocks covered by snow – only the will to live seemed to keep him attached to the wall. Stremfelj had to climb one section in bare hands to try to find holds on the compact rock. Clouds started to move in and the first snowflakes fell. Zaplotnik's oxygen was now exhausted and he felt weak, but will power and desperation not to slip kept him going. They were on the last rock step before easier ground that they believed would lead towards the summit ridge, but the climbing was very dangerous and they all felt that they were passing the limit of what was reasonable. The three of them came together to discuss what to do, but in reality they had all already made up their minds. Without saying much, Stremfelj took out the radio and called Kunaver and told him they were turning back. Kunaver urged them to consider staying at Camp VI to see if another attempt could be made. He was reluctant to give up when so much work had been done and they seemed so close. He knew that this section would open the way to the summit if they could overcome it. He told them that Iztok Tomazin was in Camp V and could come up with more oxygen. With four of them, maybe two could carry more oxygen to support an attempt by the other two. Stremfelj tried to convey the difficulty of the climbing they were facing. "It is less a physical problem than a psychological one. The stress of the climbing is killing us. It is like swimming in soft snow with no idea what is under your feet".

Kunaver knew he had to rely on the lead climbers' judgement. He told them that they had made a fantastic effort and if they felt they had no choice but to descend that's what they should do. Stremfelj said they probably would. "We are really tired" he admitted, knowing that they had given it their best shot, but it had not been enough.

Zaplotnik was worried in retrospect whether they hadn't gone too far. He wrote that "Everything inside me broke. Had I crossed a line I should not have crossed? Had I crossed the line I had hitherto always clearly known how to recognise? All I know is that we are escaping, that there is a raging storm and that we are freezing. The me I experienced during the last few hours is completely unfamiliar to me. All the tension of all those long weeks of superhuman effort, the animalistic fear, the feeling of responsibility for my friends, the responsibility for the trust and belief everyone had in our team, everything condensed into a few hours of descent just below the last difficult section, so damn close to the top."

Pavel Podgornik also had this sensation that they had gone beyond what was reasonable. But at least they had survived. All they wanted to do now was get down the mountain, away from the nights in snow-holes, storms and avalanches. But that also meant going away from the place where they and their friends had invested so much. Zaplotnik looked back up at the face in the sunset, at the sharp contrast between the virgin white snow and the intimidating black of the rocks. His longing to stand on top of its narrow summit looking down on the precipices below and across at Everest and Makalu was still there, but right now they all wanted to get down to a world of warmth and friendship.

This was probably the strongest team in the expedition and they had failed to crack the problem of the upper wall, but Kunaver did not give up hope. They had achieved so much and he felt that the only thing stopping them had been the weather – in all the long weeks on the wall they had not had a single day where it had remained fine all day. Now he decided to make a final attempt, not on the summit itself, but to reach the top of the face at a point well to the left. This would allow the expedition to be the first to overcome the face and reach the main ridge, even if they knew that the chances of being able to get along this ridge to the summit were extremely low.

With so many of the team exhausted, injured or ill, the only two climbers left on the face were Franček Knez and Vanja Matijevec. Knez was one of the younger climbers on the expedition, although he had been on the Everest expedition two years earlier. In the second half of the 1970s he was part of a group of Slovenian climbers which had really pushed technical standards in the Julian Alps. Another member of this group called Knez the "guru of modern Slovenian climbing". Matijevec was more of a traditional climber, but had made some difficult climbs in the Alps and only missed out on the summit of Everest two years before when they had to go to the assistance of the second summit team who had got into trouble after reaching the top. With separate partners, Knez and Matijevec had joined up to create a four man team to climb a new route on the North Face of the Grand Jorasses. They were a good pair.

On the night before departure, Kunaver played them some music on the evening radio call to try and raise their spirits for the final push. Everybody knew that the next day was a big one for the fate of the expedition. At 3am they woke and started preparing to go and two hours later they set off. At first they had to drop down around 100 metres and traverse to the left, wading through waist deep snow, before starting to work across the top of the large snow face below the big triangular rock wall on very unstable snow. The weather was poor, visibility zero and it started to snow heavily. Soon avalanches were pouring down the Face like waterfalls all around them. To reach the ridge they main ridge they had to cross this snowfield on a whole series of *zastrugi,* strange unstable snow ridges created by the wind. The distance between one ridge crest and the next one was maybe 20-30 metres, but each gully was something like 10 metres deep so the distance they had to travel was much longer than it would be if the slope was uniform. The snow was soft, especially in the bottom of each gully but could generally support their weight. But when the rope cut into the ridges it sliced off whole sections of them and sent them crashing down into the clouds below, which was very alarming.

They had a radio call with Base Camp at 7.30 am in which the pair up above sounded abrupt. Those below could sense and share the nervousness of the leading team. They knew it was extremely risky climbing and they remembered the climbers' wives back in Slovenia, but the success of the expedition depended on this pair now. From below Kunaver watched the two tiny dots move across the snowfield through binoculars. They seemed to be making encouragingly rapid progress, but soon the usual morning mist moved in and they had to rely on the radio calls to follow what was happening. For Knez and Matijevec the sense of exposure was terrifying, within this huge cauldron and in a way it was comforting when the mist swirled in and partially hid the drop below. They moved up through granular snow on terrain where there was often no way to really secure themselves. The two climbers just had to have faith in each other's ability not to fall. After each gully they climbed up to the rocks to try and get a belay to protect the traverse of the next gully, but the rock was crumbly and they had to remove their outer gloves in order to place some bad pitons in the rocks, which provided more psychological than real protection. Sometimes on the ridges the snow quality was better, but then they had to descend back down into the gullies which were like slides full of soft unstable snow threatening to carry them away.

At eight in the morning Knez had already run out of oxygen and Matijevec's lasted only a little longer. They were puzzled that it had been used up so quickly, but the oxygen sets they were using were anyway heavy and not that reliable and they were quite pleased to get rid of the weight of them. After the long weeks of the expedition they were now at a very high state of acclimatisation and so did not feel the height too much even though they were above 8000 metres. They carried on crossing the snow ridges from one gully to the next. On the edge of the snow ridges were huge cornices which seemed to defy the laws of gravity. They simply could not understand how such a huge quantity of snow managed to remain stuck to such a steep face. As they progressed they radioed Base Camp from time to time. At 12.30 they told Kunaver it was too risky to carry on. He told them they had full freedom to decide and that safety must have priority over reaching the ridge even though they were now so close. Everyone was willing them to succeed, but also wanting them to take upmost care. Through a gap in the mist they could see the crest of the ridge was now perhaps only 200 metres away. Success seemed so close and they decided to carry on, now daring to hope that they could make it, although there were still a number of zastrugi ridges and gullies to cross.

After a while Kunaver opened the radio again and heard fragments of conversation. It was clear Knez and Matijevec had accidently left the radio on and were unaware they were being listened to. In fact all the camps were listening in to the high drama and gradually they understood that the lead team had not turned back and were still pushing on. It was hard to follow exactly what was happening from the snippets of conversation, but the general idea was clear. Knez asked Matijevec how much rope he had left to pay out from where the latter was stopped belaying him. Matijevec replied that there was 8 metres and that he had a good stance. Knez told him that he was trying to reach the rocks, but that the snow he needed to cross was terrible. Matijevec asked if Knez could belay him from the place the latter was standing so that he could move up and free more rope for Knez to climb higher. The friction from the rope pulling across the snow ridges was so great that it was hard for the leader to make progress. Knez moved onto a wide ledge, but as he moved further the ground ran out and suddenly he was flying through the air. Matijevec felt the rope slide through his hands for a moment, but with a climbers instinct he reacted automatically and stopped the rope. The force of the fall pulled him off his feet too and he was flung through the air and onto the vertical wall of the zastruga where he was belayed. The rope between them could have dragged them both to their deaths, but fortuitously it cut deeply into the zastruga between them and held. Matijevec picked up his iceaxe and cautiously moved through the gap in the zastruga. He saw that Knez was unhurt and had a good footing on the face. However Matijevec had lost his radio in the fall.

As they progressed they could see a rock tower which they knew was on the main ridge and only a short steep traverse separated them from this point. Finally Knez made it to the ridge. Looking down he could see the depths of the Western Cwm between gaps in the clouds and the heavy snowfall. A wild wind was chasing the clouds across the ridge. There was no sense of joy despite having reached their objective – the situation was too tense for that. Knez had a modern attitude to climbing where finishing the route rather than reaching the summit was what mattered and he immediately suggested turning round. In reality any serious chance of continuing to the summit had disappeared long before. In the snow and mist they could not see the way ahead up the summit ridge, but Matijevec estimates it would have involved at least a day's climbing.

For Matijevec the ascent had been so dangerous that he was willing to do anything to avoid having to return the same way and he felt their only chance was to descend the other side of the mountain. This would mean breaking through the cornice and going down into the Western Cwm. This meant a descent of the unclimbed and unprepared north face of Lhotse's West Ridge. This face is not as steep as the South Face, but it is still not easy, featureless and crossed by some rock bands. They had both had a chance to study this face from the West Ridge of Everest two years earlier and Matijevec was convinced that it was feasible. If they made it down the face they would then need to find their way through the Western Cwm and then down through the Ice Fall to the safety of Everest Base Camp. Despite the fact that thousands of climbers had gone this way, it was not trivial and they didn't have tents or sleeping bags. They might be lucky and be able to take shelter with expeditions climbing on Everest, but this was an unknown factor. It was a choice born out of desperation, much like that of the Messner brothers on the summit of Nanga Parbat 11 years earlier. They radioed Base Camp and asked if it was possible to arrange a helicopter to pick them up in the Western Cwm.

The request made Kunaver's hair stand on end. What they were suggesting was a descent down an unknown slope with no fixed ropes, no support and no camps. It was in any case clear that a helicopter would not be able to fly to the upper part of the Western Cwm as the air was too thin at that altitude. At best a helicopter might manage to reach a little over 6000 metres, but even this would be dependent on the weather. It was true that the other slope was less steep, but in reality it might well prove to be a death trap and it would no longer be possible for the rest of the team to give them any assistance. Despite their reservations, Base Camp tried to contact Kathmandu airport as the climbers had requested. This was a radio connection they had made many times before, but on this one occasion they were not able to get through. It was approaching evening and the climbers had to make a decision quickly or they would be overtaken by nightfall. Still Knez and Matijevec debated the options. Knez felt that, although the descent the way they had come was hard, it nonetheless represented their only realistic option. Matijevec on the other hand still preferred going down into the Western Cwm. The experience on the zastrugi had filled him with fear and he dreaded the idea of going back the same way. By 6 pm they knew they had to make a decision and in the end there was no alternative but to return the same way, even though it would be very risky operation. Knez simply said "I'm going back down, you do what you want" and they radioed Base Camp to tell them they were descending the same way. Everyone was relieved because they felt descending into the Western Cwm would have been very risky. Then they set off on a desperate descent through the maze of snow and cloud. For Kunaver and the team down below, the fact that they had the strength to start the descent rather than attempting to bivouac was a good sign. Kunaver realised with dread that this was the first time anyone in the team had not been safely in a tent or snow cave after dark. With Knez and Matijevec so high on the face at night he was terribly afraid for them.

Meanwhile the pair pressed on across the snow basin. They desperately needed to rest, but they knew that if they slept for a moment they might never wake up. So they forced themselves to keep moving, having only brief rests. It continued to snow and avalanches rumbled around them in the mist, the storm already wiping away their tracks as they descended. The climbers were too gripped and concentrated on the descent in the dark to have time to open up the radio and the Face was shrouded in cloud so there was no chance for those below to see the lights of their head torches. With no way of knowing how things were progressing above, the tension at Base Camp was almost unbearable. They did not abandon the radio for a second and time seemed to stand still as they waited for news from above. Towards midnight the storm relented and behind the eastern edge of the wall the two climbers could see the faint light of the moon through the mist. Finally around 2 a.m. they reached the end of the fixed ropes, which were their umbilical cord to safety. All that remained to do was slide down the ropes to the camp. Instead of re-ascending to Camp VI where they had spent the night before they went directly down to Camp IV. At 4am they arrived safely at the camp, alive and not even frost bitten. Two Sherpas were waiting for them with hot tea – for Matijevec it was an unbelievable moment of relief and one which remained vivid for him many years later. He and Knez had been climbing for 23 hours, mainly above 8000 metres, fourteen hours up to the edge of the wall and then nine to descend in the dark and the mist. At 4.30 those waiting anxiously at Base Camp finally heard Knez's voice on the radio announcing that they were safely back in the camp. They knew that the decision not to descend into the Western Cwm had been the right one.

The next day the weather was better and Knez and Matijevec were back down at Base Camp. The sun was shining and scene was idyllic with yaks which had been brought up to help with transport going back and forth with bells on their collars ringing. The grass in the valley contrasted with the savage wall of Lhotse above and a great adventure was over. Kunaver and his team justifiably viewed reaching the top of the wall as a major success irrespective of whether or not they had got to the summit. They had achieved far more than the previous Italian and Japanese expeditions. They had not only attacked the central part of the wall, which the previous expeditions had avoided, but they had got very close to the top of it and reached the summit ridge. The international Alpine Clubs' Association (the UIAA) declared the climb to be the most difficult ever undertaken in the Himalayas, whilst the influential Mountain Magazine called it "a most impressive attempt". There was a great national pride in what the Slovenians had achieved and how such a small nation had managed to produce such a strong group of climbers.

1981 Yugoslav Route

In the eight years since Lhotse South Face was first attempted there had been some huge advances in Himalayan climbing. Some of the most important psychological breakthroughs related to an ever lighter style of mountaineering. This movement was led by Messner, with his oxygenless ascent of Everest and his two-man and solo ascents, but others, like French and British climbers played a part too. In 1984 Alan Rouse, who had achieved many fine lightweight ascents in the Himalayas and climbed with Nicolas Jaeger, wrote an article in Mountain Magazine analysing the state of top level British mountaineering. Rouse had recently heard Ales Kunaver give a presentation on the Lhotse expedition in England and he wrote that Kunaver had done "mountaineering a great service, for, by climbing possibly the hardest face in the world, he proved that big expedition climbing had reached a dead end." With the benefit of hindsight, this is very unfair - the Slovenians had achieved something which in terms of difficulty went a big step beyond the greatest climbs of the 1970s and their climb should have an important place in the annals of mountaineering. It would not have been possible without a very strong climbing team, great courage, persistence and teamwork.

In his talk, Kunaver had justified the style of the ascent by stressing that the climbers' safety overrode all other considerations. Rouse was sympathetic to this point of view, but wondered whether it wasn't also luck as well as superb planning that allowed a large group of climbers to spend so long in such a deadly environment without a single very serious accident. Rouse nonetheless felt that climbing the South Face of Lhotse in Alpine Style would be akin to playing Russian roulette with only one barrel left empty. Of course Nicolas Jaeger had already had this plan, but not long after Rouse's declaration, a number of other people started to believe that alpine style was indeed the best way to tackle this route. Rouse's view was that if the heavyweight expedition style was rejected, this route needed to be left to the 21st Century as it could not be climbed in a pure style by the standards of the 20th. But this statement seriously underestimated the speed at which the standards of Himalayan climbing were developing.

When Rouse wrote his article the elite of British Himalayan mountaineering had recently suffered several casualties including Pete Boardman, one of the summit climbers on Everest South West Face, and Joe Tasker who were lost attempting the unclimbed North East Ridge of Everest. Boardman and Tasker had made some very bold alpine style ascents including a new route on Kangchenjunga with Doug Scott. In 1985 Roger Baxter Jones died in the Alps after being hit by a serac fall. He had made the first ascent of the South-West Face of Shisha Pangma in alpine style with Scott and Alex Macintyre. Macintyre himself was killed in 1982 after being hit by stonefall during a very bold attempt on a new route on the South Face of Annapurna. These tragedies meant Britain lost the position it had had in the 1970s as one of the leading nations in Himalayan climbing. Rouse himself died in a storm on K2 two years later, shortly after becoming the first Briton to climb the world's second highest mountain. He did this by the normal route using fixed ropes placed by other expeditions, but after reaching the summit he was caught in a camp high on the mountain with a group of climbers, who were unable to descend due to a furious storm. As the storm dragged on for days, one by one the climbers were overcome by the effects of altitude, cold, hunger and dehydration, either dying in the tents or in vain attempts to exit and try to descend. In the end the only two of them who managed to descend were Kurt Diemberger and Willi Bauer. With the loss of Rouse, British climbing lost another of its stars. Not all leading Himalayan climbers were also top rate rock climbers, but Rouse excelled in all forms of climbing from short very hard rock climbs to major Himalayan routes.

After several years of top level Alpine climbing and visiting the Peruvian Andes, Rouse, together with Baxter-Jones and two other young British climbers, Brian Hall and Rab Carrington, made an Alpine Style ascent of Jannu, a spectacular and difficult mountain of just under 8000 metres. They had a purist alpine style philosophy and after Jannu stated four advantages of the approach. Firstly it removed the tedium of load carrying on fixed ropes; second it reduced the amount of time exposed to objective hazards like rock and ice fall; thirdly it increased the level of personal satisfaction since everyone on the team would get to the highest point reached rather than having a summit pair from a larger team. Their final point was a rather more idealistic one and it was linked with Rouse's view on Kunaver's Lhotse expedition. If unclimbed routes were attacked in a traditional heavy-weight style, then Rouse believed they would all be climbed in a few years. This is what Reinhold Messner had referred to as "The Murder of the Impossible" a decade earlier. If the challenge is viewed as not just in terms of the route to be climbed, but also the style in which it is climbed, then there would be new climbing challenges for many years to come. But if one generation of climbers set out to climb all the available routes in whatever style they were capable of using, then there would be no major new routes left for the subsequent generations.

The question for Rouse was whether the whole mountaineering community would have the self-restraint to leave the major targets untouched until someone managed to climb them in good style. This was certainly in doubt – it is always hard to anticipate what might be considered reasonable and possible in the future and the temptation to climb attractive routes by the ruling standards of the day is great. In fact over the next decade two things would happen. Firstly it became clear that a route as hard as Lhotse's South Face was a tough nut to crack even for strong and determined expeditions using fixed ropes. Secondly some climbers came to believe that even targets like this could be attempted in pure alpine style.

Chapter 5 – Finally a Summit

As well as the philosophical attractions of alpine style climbing, for mountaineers like Al Rouse, financial considerations also played their part. An alpine style expedition is much cheaper than a large siege expedition to organise. Climbers like Rouse and his teammates on Jannu were often fully dedicated to climbing and had few sources of income, particularly in early 1980s Britain when financial times were hard and unemployment high. When not on expeditions they lived nomadic lifestyles shifting between the main climbing centres in Britain, their belongings in rucksacks, sleeping on friends' floors and claiming unemployment benefits. By the mid-1980s, although there were still several top British mountaineers, they were no-longer pulling off the most spectacular climbs as they had in the 1970s. Instead the way was being led by countries in the Eastern half of Europe. From a financial point of view climbers in the Soviet bloc had some advantages over their counterparts in the West. In Communist Czechoslovakia, for example, national expeditions were backed by the state. Climbers chosen for these expeditions were given time off work and the employer had to release them for the duration of the expedition, which might be something like 3 months, and even continue to pay their salary.

In the early 1980s, Czechoslovakia was one of several of the communist nations of Eastern Europe starting to be very active in Himalayan mountaineering. Czechoslovakia is, like Yugoslavia, a country which did not survive the fall of communism, splitting into the Czech and Slovak Republics four years later, although the divorce was much more amicable than the break-up of Yugoslavia. Both republics play a part in their joint mountaineering heritage. Slovakia has more mountains of the two, sharing the Tatra range with Poland, but the Czechs have a long rock climbing tradition, born on the sandstone towers of Saxony. In the early part of the 20th century the hardest rock climbs of the time in the world were being done there. Czechoslovak mountaineers got their first taste of high altitude mountaineering in 1965, visiting the Hindu Kush in Afghanistan and ticking off 17 unclimbed mountains. In the next years they returned to the Hindu Kush and also to the Pamirs in the Soviet Union. For many in Western Europe, the events of the so-called "Prague Spring" and its subsequent crushing coloured their view of Czechoslovakia. At the beginning of 1968 Alexander Dubcek was elected the First Secretary of Communist Party of Czechoslovakia. Dubcek implemented a series of reforms including greater rights for individuals, more democracy and decentralisation of power. Greater freedom was given to travel and to the media. The Soviet Union looked on at these events with concern. Irrespective of their view on the ideological rights and wrongs, they were concerned about the balance of power in the Cold War which was then at its height. On the night of the 20th August, 200,000 troops from the Soviet Union, Poland, Bulgaria and Hungary entered the country. The Czechoslovak armed forces were confined to barracks and, although there was massive passive resistance, the overwhelming weight of force was with the Soviets and their allies and the Czechoslovak's taste of freedom was snatched away.

But this didn't interrupt the activities of the Czechoslovak climbers for long. By 1969 they were ready to graduate on to 8000 metre peaks when Ivan Galfy, the country's own equivalent of Ales Kunaver, led an expedition to Nanga Parbat. Galfy had requested permission from the Pakistan Government to attempt the easier Gasherbrum I, but they replied offering Nanga Parbat, which alarmed Galfy given the mountain's reputation for difficulty and danger. However they tried and although they only reached 6700 metres they had learnt enough to resolve to return and finish the job two years later. The expedition was supported by the Communist Government, who perhaps thought, a year after the Prague Spring, a major mountaineering triumph could start to restore the country's international prestige and help domestic self-esteem. The climbers were less concerned with the politics and just happy to get the chance to travel abroad to the World's greatest mountains. In 1971 they managed to place a small bivouac tent at 7600 metres from where they could launch a summit bid. Without sleeping bags, they relied for warmth on wearing all their clothes and being crammed into the small tent. In the morning, one of the four, Kriššák, turned back quite soon, offering his ice axe to another climber Orolin, who continued with the other two, Záhoranský and Fiala. They needed to belay for some harder sections, but once the terrain looked easier they left the rope to save weight. This proved a mistake because unexpectedly they came to another steep section which they couldn't pass without a rope. Fiala selflessly returned back down 150 metres to pick up the rope – no small matter at this high altitude. This cost them 2 hours and when they continued there was another surprise – a small ice wall, which could not be passed by Záhoranský, who had only brought ski-poles and not an axe. Orolin and Fiala continued to the summit.

Success on Nanga Parbat was the first time a country from the Eastern half of Europe had climbed an 8000er. With this goal achieved, Galfy now wanted to climb a new route on an 8000er. Like the Slovenians, they spotted an attractive line on Makalu: for the Czechoslovaks the South West Buttress. A first attempt in 1973 was unsuccessful and one climber was killed, but three years later Galfy returned with a strong team. For the first time Nepal granted permission for two expeditions to attempt the same mountain in the same season with the result that a Spanish team was attempting the South East Ridge which had a common upper section at the same time as Galfy's team. The Czechoslovaks fixed ropes up the difficult South West Pillar to reach the 8010m South East summit of Makalu. This would have counted as a new route in the Alps, but in the Himalayas they had to reach the main summit for the expedition to be considered a success. This meant climbing the final section of the long South East Ridge, a route pioneered by a Japanese expedition in 1970. A first attempt turned back at a difficult section at 8200 metres. The Spanish team which had been attempting to repeat the South East Ridge was weakened by illness and fatigue and starting to run out of steam and the two expeditions agreed to combine and make a joint summit bid. A combined team of Czechoslovaks Kriššák and Schubert together with the Spaniard Camprubi reached the summit. On the descent Kriššák, who was feeling strongest, pulled ahead and arrived at the camp at 7pm, followed three hours later by the Spaniard. But Schubert, who had been slow on the ascent, did not arrive and a storm was raging outside. The following morning they could hear his shouts from higher up on the ridge, but then they lost contact. Probably he had fallen down the steep South Face. After this success tainted by tragedy Galfy gave his view on how he saw the future goals of Czechoslovak mountaineering. He pointed out that the successes on Makalu and Nanga Parbat could be an inspiration for a new generation of climbers, but there were also many attractive goals on mountains lower than 8000 metres. And in the next years the focus was on lower and generally cheaper objectives in the Soviet Asia, South America and the Alps.

In 1984 Galfy was ready to mount an expedition to attempt a major new objective. He wanted to climb the South Face of 8300m Lhotse Shar, which formed the right hand part of the Lhotse's South Face. This was the first large Federal team for eight years and being a national team, it was chosen by a committee based on climbers' performance in the mountains, although political pressures occasionally entered into the selection process. As he planned for Lhotse Shar, Ivan Galfy could draw on a pool of experienced mountaineers. In 1981 another expedition led by Galfy climbed the North Face of Kangchenjunga.

In addition Josef Rakoncaj had participated in an international expedition which made the second ascent of the North Ridge of K2 in 1983 and had made it to the summit. Rakoncaj had also made hard climbs on Kalanka and Nanda Devi in India. Galfy's team was generally a younger generation than the veterans of the two Nanga Parbat expeditions. Once the 21 man team was selected it was divided into small groups of three or four with specific tasks to prepare for the expedition. This meant co-operation and teamwork started long before the arrival in Nepal. Rakoncaj, for example, had the job of making sleeping bags and tents for the expedition for which he was allocated a budget. Galfy originally received a permit for 1983, but did not have time to organise the expedition or raise the funds that year, so asked to postpone the permit until the pre-monsoon season of the following year. To save the cost of air transporting, all the equipment was taken overland by truck passing through Hungary, Yugoslavia, Bulgaria, Turkey, Iran, Pakistan and India before arriving in Nepal. In fact the expedition was under financial pressure throughout. Galfy had found a number of items had inflated in cost since the expedition to Kangchenjunga three years before. First they had to pay 21,000 rupees in customs' duty – more than twice as much as they had paid for a larger team on Kangchenjunga. Furthermore they had to leave a deposit of 42,000 rupees. Three years earlier the fee for a permit for importing food and climbing equipment was 170 rupees – now it had become 12,400! To try and stay within the budget they had available, Galfy was forced to reduce the number of Sherpas they employed to a bare minimum.

The financial situation almost got a lot worse just as they were setting off on the approach march. During the day Galfy had been dispensing payments from their metal strong box and some local thief had noticed which tent the box was stored in. Galfy was woken at midnight to hear screams from one of the Sherpas saying there was an intruder in the camp. They rushed to the tent where the cash box was stored and saw that it was still there. Instead, an identical box containing personal belongings of Galfy had been taken. They found the missing box a few hundred metres from the camp, broken open and abandoned by the thieves. A few personal possessions of Galfy's were missing, but it was much less serious than if all the expedition's cash – some 180,000 rupees – had been stolen. That would have probably spelt the end of the expedition.

Still the approach march wasn't without its problems. Two Everest expeditions which had preceded them (one Indian and one Bulgarian) had employed more than 1200 porters. Although the Czechoslovaks only needed 185, they still struggled to find them that year. After an approach taking 13 days they set up Base Camp on the 31st March. When team member Jaromir Stejskal reached the place for the first time he was not really in a state to appreciate it due to his lack of acclimatisation. He remembered reading an article by a British climber who likened the effects of altitude to waking up with a hangover –headaches, nausea, unsteadiness on the feet and so on. The team walked between a rocky moraine ridge and the glacier, but found this hollow too narrow to be a good campsite. Finally they came to the Slovenians' campsite and decided to stay there. They found it an uncomfortable and pretty desolate spot, but it was nonetheless better than where the Italians had camped in 1975, which was 200 metres closer to the wall and had been hit several times by avalanches. The nearest source of water was half an hour's walk down to the glacier. Galfy considered it the worst Base Camp site he had ever stayed at. They were sometimes visited by trekkers visited who they always offered tea and biscuits. The only other visitors were birds, who would have finished up in the Czechoslovak's soup, if they hadn't been stopped by the Sherpas who believed that killing any living thing would bring bad luck.

At Base Camp they started studying the Face, the pattern of avalanches and the possible routes. During the approach march, the bottom part was always obscured by the intervening hills. Ales Kunaver had also sent them various photos, which they used for planning purposes, but the Face was rockier than they had expected from these, because most of the winter snow had been blown clear. During the course of the expedition snowfall changed the black bits back to white. Ivan Galfy consulted with the team about the best route to try considering objective danger, technical difficulty and the chances of success. They eventually narrowed down the choices to two: either the pillar which lay directly under the summit of Lhotse Shar or the broad couloir to its left. The pillar went up to about 7000 metres from where a large basin opened up surrounded by the peaks of Lhotse, Lhotse Shar and Lhotse Middle. The couloir led to the same basin, from the right side of which they could reach the peak of Lhotse Shar. The couloir looked to be technically easier, involving mainly climbing on snow, which would generally be faster, although a narrowing at two thirds height would bring some difficulty. The couloir did not seem to be threatened by serac fall, but it was definitely a channel for many powder snow avalanches. The pillar on the other hand would involve several steeper sections, but seem to be largely, although not entirely, protected from the risk of avalanche. Miroslav Smid, one of the top climbers in the team with a string of hard ascents in the Tatras, Alps and beyond, said that he thought he could see a good line to pass the bottleneck in the couloir. Galfy reminded them that the climbers on the wall would receive all of the snow which fell in the upper section of the face as avalanches down this couloir, which acts as a sort of funnel. Even though there had only been 5 centimetres of snow that day, this had still created a large avalanche which had roared down the couloir.

They wondered if the pillar was exposed to serac falls, which would be hard ice. The Slovenians had shown it was possible to live with powder snow avalanches of up to a certain volume, but being hit by serac fall would mean almost certain death. Leopold Palenicek was another experienced climber who had been on both the Makalu expeditions and made many first ascents on the sandstone rocks of the Czech Republic. He was confident that the pillar stood sufficiently away from the Face to avoid the risk of serac falls from the hanging glaciers as its sides. The Slovak climber Igor Novak said that serac falls could potentially hit anywhere, but conceded that the risk of them on the pillar was significantly less than that of snow avalanches in the couloir. The central couloir was also going to offer less scope to find safe campsites. The only option was likely to be snow caves like those used by the Slovenians. The pillar route was also more pleasing aesthetically since it followed a route which came directly down from the summit and meant they were always climbing on Lhotse Shar rather than moving across from Lhotse.

Having weighed up all the options, Galfy finally pronounced that they should start climbing on the pillar the following day, the third of April. He divided up the 14 climbers into three teams who could regularly alternate the lead and hence keep the climbers fresh and momentum going in advancing the route. The first group in the lead would consist of Smid, Ivan's son Robert Galfy, Leopold Palenicek and Ladisclaw Kryc. When they approached the Pillar the next morning, they got proof that this route was safer when huge powder avalanches swept down the couloir, whilst the Pillar remained clear. The first 1000 metres were a rock buttress which gave hard technical climbing with pitches of grade V+. The nature of the rock was changeable with alternating sections of slate and granite. The Pillar was immediately steep and it was necessary to fix ropes from the very foot of the face. They also had to put one rope ladder in place on the way to Camp I, as the Sherpas were not willing to climb overhanging ground on jumars. Bad weather hit them for the first time on the 10th April. Two days of snowfall showed their mess tent was more suitable for camping at the seaside than below one of the world's wildest mountain faces. With some extra anchorage they managed to construct something which would stand up to the weather. Like the Slovenians, they generally found the mornings clear, but clouds moving in during the afternoon and often bringing heavy snowfall, leading to avalanches.

Camp II was set up at 6250 metres under rocky walls which protected it from avalanches. They had thought that the snowy sections in the middle of the wall would allow faster progress, but in reality they had to zig zag through serac cliffs between the second and third camps. Beyond the seracs a 60° ice ridge led up to Camp III at 6800 metres. It was hard work, but very spectacular with the huge triangular overhang of Lhotse Shar above. After this progress slowed, partly because they were now working above 7000 metres, but also because of the 25-40 centimetres of fresh snow every day which necessitating breaking a new trail. By late April they were also facing two serious equipment shortages. The first was that they had run out of gas to cook with, the second that they were running short of rope. Although they had brought 5 kilometres of rope, the difficulty and length of the route meant that they needed another 700-800 metres. They had no choice but to send someone down to Namche Bazar to buy some more. In Namche Bazar, the major town of the Sherpa region, there were shops where it was possible to buy almost anything an expedition could want – climbing gear, clothes, food, medicines and so on, all of which was recycled through the Sherpa economy from other expeditions, but none of which was cheap. Mindful of their budget limitations, the Czechoslovaks managed to buy rope on a use or return basis – they would get their money back for any rope they didn't use. The gas shortage was because the Everest area is a national park, so they were not permitted to use wood for cooking at Base Camp. Gas got used up very quickly in Base Camp and the Sherpas seemed to make no effort to conserve supplies, keeping the stoves burning from morning until night – which made the cook tent cosy, but wasted a lot of fuel.

Up to Camp IV things had progressed pretty much according to plan, but above that progress was slow. On the 2nd May Ivan Galfy knew that time before the monsoon was starting to get short so he asked Rakoncaj and Stejskal, who were taking over the lead, to go straight from Camp III past Camp IV and then fix ropes and place Camp V. They felt this was a very ambitious plan since they knew it took something like 4 hours to get from Camp III to Camp IV and that they then had to climb a section of existing fixed ropes above before placing new ones and the camp. They understood the urgency to advance the route and wanted to avoid conflict and so agreed with Galfy's plan. However by the time they got to Camp IV it was noon and starting to snow, so they decided to stay and sleep there. At this camp they were seriously concerned about the risk of avalanches and during the night. They had problems with snow building up on the back of their tents, which they had to clear several times during the night. They signed off the evening radio call saying that they would start at 7am the next morning to try and advance the route. Rakoncaj and Stejskal set off in the morning as planned, but with all the fresh snow they were only able to advance about 80 metres before it started to snow very heavily again. After another disturbed night, they returned to try again, making 100 metres further progress before the snow returned and they had no choice but to descend, this time right back down to Base Camp. Drlik and Smid took over the lead. Usually when climbers came off the wall, Ivan Galfy always met them in person at the foot of the face and prepared a special meal of stew with cream. The gesture was really appreciated – it was a sign that Galfy knew the value of what they were doing out in the lead. But this time he just grunted a hello from his tent without even coming out to meet them. In the mess tent there was no sign of the special meal and the tension was clear. The next day one of the others told Rakoncaj and Stejskal that Galfy was scared that the slow progress could cost the expedition success, given the possible onset of the monsoon soon. They had been among the stars of the team, but Galfy felt they had let him down or even suspected they were conserving energy for the summit bid and leaving others to prepare the route. After a team meeting at Base Camp these tensions were resolved and a new plan was made to tackle the last part of the route.

Establishing Camp V proved significantly harder than they had expected and was sited in a totally unsuitable place for a camp. The original platform was sloping at an angle of something like 50°. When Stejskal returned to the face with Rakoncaj and Bozik they were very impressed by the difficulty of the route to Camp V. There was a 50 metre run out with only one piece of protection which made them wonder about the sanity of Palenicek who had led it. The final stretch was a long traverse in deep snow overlooking the deep "Cauldron" which was formed by the peaks of Lhotse, Lhotse Middle and Lhotse Shar. Slipping on this stretch despite the fixed rope would have meant a long fall and it was not quite sure the anchors would hold. Weighed down by a tent, sleeping bags and a lot of food, they had to tread carefully across the snow. They found the campsite in a very exposed position on a miserably small platform with part of the tent hanging free in the air. If it wasn't attached securely to the rocks behind, nobody would have risked getting inside the tent. The tent was partly protected from rockfall by the overhang above, but the rest was very exposed. The steepness of the slope in front of the tent made getting inside very awkward and, when they looked inside, they were disconcerted to see that it was completely full of all manner of stuff– food, gas cylinders, cameras, sleeping bags and mats – it looked like equipment for ten people. It was clearly necessary to put a second tent in place, but there was absolutely no space next to the first one. Having arrived from Camp III that morning, they were too tired to climb much higher, but there was no choice but to deposit their rucksacks and carry on further up to try and find a suitable place for another tent. Rakoncaj suddenly came up with the wild idea to place a tent by cutting the top of a sharp snow ridge to flatten it out. Even doing this the tent would hang over both sides of the ridge, but they were at 7500 metres and had to do something to get shelter for the night so they set to work. The first metre was snow, after that it was hard ice and after hacking away for two hours, they had only managed to clear a space half a metre by a metre. They needed at least twice that to place the tent so they kept at it, ice building up round their beards from the effort of the work, taking shorter and shorter turns before having to rest. But it was in vain and as it was getting dark, there was no choice but to give up and try to sleep in the other tent. Even getting inside from the steep slope was easier said than done. Stejskal managed to stick his head in, but then it was necessary to make an awkward squirming manoeuvre to get the torso and legs in too. Rakoncaj tried a different technique going in feet first and then forcing in the rest of his body, but with crampons on, this caused quite a bit of damage to the contents of the tent. Bozik was the last in and got the worst space hanging over the edge. Once inside they tried to get organised and make space to cook, cursing all the things cluttering up the tent and asked what people were going to do with all that junk. On the radio call they told the leader that they had not been able to install a second tent and agreed that the next day they would try and climb 150 metres further up where there was a possible place for another tent.

During the night things got even more cramped as snow started to build up between the tent and the overhang which protected it. Rakoncaj said that somebody should go out and clear it, but it was obvious that he didn't want to, whilst Bozik pretended to be asleep. In the end it was Stejskal who had to make the complicated manoeuvre to exit the tent and clear it. In the morning they knew that they had to find a way to place another tent and went up to investigate a place Ivan Galfy had suggested. It wasn't as good as they had hoped and they had to abandon the idea of a Camp V with two tents side by side. It was hard work to chop out a platform for one tent before returning back to the lower Camp V to fetch their equipment. Rakoncaj had been to the summit of K2 the year before, but for Stejskal this was an altitude record and he wasn't feeling good. He tried to lie as still as possible in the tent to calm his breath, but he had terrible pains in his abdomen and was sure his chances of making it to the summit were very low. He knew that if he went down to Base Camp it would mean the end of the expedition for him. The assault on the summit was only a few days away and there simply wasn't time to go down to Base Camp, recover and then climb back up again for the final push. They knew that on the 15th May three years before the Slovenians had ended their attempt because of the onset of the monsoon and yet the Czechoslovaks had only just placed the penultimate camp. The next day they hoped to fix ropes to at least 7900 metres and place the final camp.

Rakoncaj was tired too, but also did not want to go right back down to Base so they only went to Camp III. On the radio call Galfy told them that they would be replaced in the lead the next day by Smid and Novak. They made some progress, but then there were more lively discussions about the next planned steps. One proposal was that Smid, who was on his own at Camp V, should try and lead the route up and place Camp VI. Rakoncaj pointed out that there was only one difficult section and that apart from that it should be easy snow. Others countered that it was too risky for Smid to operate alone and that there would be no-one there to help him if he fell or collapsed. They were also worried about the season ending before they had had a crack at the summit, especially when the liaison officer warned them that he had heard on the radio that the monsoon was on its way. Finally it was agreed that they would expand Camp V to be able to accommodate more climbers. Zoltan Demjan and Robert

Galfy would move up to Camp V and establish Camp VI and then advance the route beyond this. Nobody wanted to stay in Camp IV which meant a difficult stage from III straight through to V.

This plan represented their last chance for the summit. They had now been on the route for 45 days and this amount of time at altitude gradually wore them down. Everyone had lost weight and several people were suffering illnesses. The expedition was also starting to run short of supplies in particular food and gas, but most of the climbers were fit enough to have a shot at the summit. Ivan Galfy decided to split the ten climbers available into two groups of five. In the first group, Jindra Martis and Karel Jakes had the job of advancing the route Robert Galfy and Zoltan Demjan had made the day before, fixing ropes on any difficult sections. All four of them would attempt the summit together with Smid. At 2am Martis and Jakes left the top camp, followed three hours later by Galfy and Demjan. Those at Base Camp listened to progress on the radio and watched through binoculars. As soon as it was light, Ivan Galfy saw it was windy from the clouds of snow were being blown across the upper part of the face. At about 11am Galfy saw Martis and Jakes turn back at the beginning of some narrow gullies which led up towards the summit ridge. The second pair was about 80-100 metres below them and they met soon after turning around. Martis and Jakes reported that the way was blocked by a rock step. So Galfy and Demjan tried a different line. They each had a hundred and twenty metres of rope to fix in this section. Demjan led out his stretch to reach a rocky island and placed a piton. Robert Galfy followed up, but the rope became tangled up and he lost a lot of time freeing himself and nearly fell in the process. Galfy, who was dehydrated due to stomach problems in the morning, decided to turn round, but Demjan carried on alone.

Later in the day the second summit team of Rakoncaj, Bozik, Palenicek, Drlik and Stejskal moved up the Face and met the descending climbers at an anchor on the fixed ropes. The first to arrive was Smid who just said that he hadn't felt up to it. When they met Robert Galfy, Martis and Jakes they could see huge disappointment on their faces. Jakes had a nose guard on to protect from the sun, his jacket was open, his hood skewed sideways. Galfy had descended without sunglasses and would suffer snow blindness, but probably didn't care. He said the terrain below the summit ridge was harder than they had expected, but that maybe the second team would have more luck if they tried further to the left. The ascending climbers asked where Zoltan Demjan was and Galfy replied that he was still trying, but they did not expect him to succeed. After all, if Martis and Jakes had had to turn round, it seemed unlikely a solo climber would do better. The second summit team carried on up to Camp VI. In trying to dig a platform for it, the previous team had found ice and only been able to make a small and sloping platform with one third of the tent hanging in the air. They were certainly not expecting a comfortable night. It took time to squeeze into the tent and they wouldn't have dared enter at all if it wasn't well anchored to the Face. Once inside, they opened a radio contact to Base Camp and the other camps. Robert Galfy explained in more to his father Ivan the events of the morning. After he had left the tent, he had been violently sick, leaving him terribly dehydrated and weak, which was the main reason he did not go on with Demjan. Ivan Galfy consoled his son. He knew that the chances of succeeding became very low for anyone in less than full health. By now the weather was quite bad, cloudy and snowing and they were worried for the safety of Demjan who was still somewhere up above. They started to boil water, anxiously waiting for his safe return.

When the afternoon was getting late they heard lumps of snow hitting the tent, which could only be knocked down from above by Demjan. Those in the tent didn't have their boots on and were so tightly packed in the tent that it was difficult to get ready quickly so they could not go out to see what was happening. Instead they shouted to ask what had happened. Demjan shouted back that he had made it to the top. Everyone was thrilled and when he arrived at the tent, they dragged him inside the already crowded space. They opened up the radio contact with Base Camp and Demjan told the tale of his ascent. After Robert Galfy had turned back, he noted the route finding problems of Jakes and Martis and took a line further to the left. They asked him if he had been able to leave proof of his ascent. He had thought about building a cairn on top just as people all over the world have done on for thousands of years, but he realised he was too tired to make the effort. He took some photos, but only of a small mascot which his children had given him and without much background because the clouds had closed in. He had planned to take photos of a pennant he had brought up to, but his oxygen deprived brain simply forgot. In the end it didn't really matter, because the next day the second summit party would see signs of his ascent. They put the doctor on the radio to ask Demjan about his condition. His only problem was a painfully dry throat, having drunk hardly anything all day. The doctor was happy he wasn't frostbitten and told

Demjan that they would be opening a bottle of whisky in his honour down in Base Camp. The climbers in the second summit team quizzed Demjan for information about the route. He explained that there was really only one delicate section where he had pushed himself to the limit.

"That's where Karel and Jindra turned round is it?" asked Stejskal. Demjan said it was not and that in fact Martis and Jakes had taken a line further to the right. He explained that after a section where there was a steep snow slope between rocks, there was a choice of going left or right. The right hand line was shorter, but steeper and was where the others had turned back. Demjan said that if they followed the left hand line only bad weather could prevent them reaching the summit. By now he had drunk all the tea they had made and they had to brew up some more. Once he had drunk this, Demjan started preparing to descend down to Camp V. His companions radioed V to tell them to get more drinks ready and make some space for him in the tent.

Then the second summit group got ready for the climb the next day. Trying to rehydrate before the ascent was not easy. They had to reach through the opening in the tent to scoop up snow in a saucepan which melted down to only a centimetre of water. In the crowded tent it was hard to keep the stove upright, but they knew the importance of getting enough liquid so they carrying on cooking, making tea, then lemonade, then more tea and so on. Then they needed more drinks to put in their thermoses for the next day. They put their boots inside their sleeping bags to dry them and get them as warm as possible for the morning – cold boots would significantly increase the risk of frostbite. Rakoncaj, who had already suffered frostbite on K2, put the outer boots under his head and wore the inner ones inside the sleeping bag. With the tent overcrowded they could not sleep and ended up starting to prepare for the summit at half past one in the morning. Those in the two tents shouted to encourage each other, but even with the pull of the summit it was hard to get going. Drlik had already announced that he was not feeling well and was going to go back down, but the others busied themselves getting ready. It was a slow process with so many different things to remember: clothes, climbing equipment, something to eat and all hindered by their brains functioning slowly under the effects of oxygen deprivation.

To avoid the route finding problems which had prevented most of the first summit team from completing the climb, they planned to carry a radio so that

Galfy could direct them through the complex area of couloirs and ribs on the upper part of the Face. In practice Rakoncaj was concerned that using the radio was making his hands cold and was keen to press on more quickly. The first 150 metres were on fixed ropes, but they found the last part of these weren't attached to the anchor, so Rakoncaj tied onto the rope and climbed up to re-fix the anchor, belayed by Stejskal. When they arrived at the rope left by Zoltan Demjan on the hardest section it was so thin it looked more like a shoelace, but it helped them pass and they then replaced it with the more solid rope that they were carrying. Looking down they thought at one stage that Palenicek, who had started later than the others was catching up, but in the end he turned back at the end of the fixed ropes. The other three pressed on. At 8200 metres they left a rucksack with the radio and an empty thermos flask to pick up on the way back. The saving in weight was not great, but at this height everything helped. By half past ten they were on the summit ridge, but it had clouded over and started snowing. Makalu emerged from the clouds for a while, but once it disappeared they just focused on progressing up the snowy ridge in the "white darkness", all the time hoping to come across the top, which never seemed to arrive.

They were all feeling the lack of oxygen with Bozik puffing hard. Demjan had told them this final section was straightforward, but it didn't seem as easy as he'd suggested. Finally the ground eased and there was a text book ridge leading to the highest point, where there wasn't even space for all three of them to stand at the same time. There was not much view with the snow and drifting clouds, but they managed to get one photo with Lhotse Middle in the background to prove that they had been to the summit. They sat down on a rock shelf just below the highest point and tried to take in the significance of the moment. After a short while Rakoncaj roused his two partners, reminding them that they needed to think about getting down. He led off first followed by Bozik, with Stejskal coming last. Stejskal soon fell behind the other two, Rakoncaj with his long legs and Bozik, with the lungs of a former star cyclist. The snow came down more heavily, meaning there was virtually a flowing stream of granular snow as he descended the steep gully. When he found the backpack in which they had left the radio, he was reminded that they had not yet informed Base Camp of the triumph. The descent was now delicate, with mist making the right way hard to find and his crampons balling up from all the fresh snow. When this happens the crampon spikes don't dig into the slope to give a secure grip as usual. Instead the spikes are lost in a ball of snow which can be as slippery as an ice skate. The clouds lifted a little and Stejskal caught sight of Bozik and some red flags which they had placed the day before to help orientation. He knew this would guide him to the top of the fixed ropes which led down to Camp VI, where Rakoncaj and Bozik were waiting for him. Bozik did not feel like descending further that day and stayed at Camp VI, whereas the other two pressed on further down after stopping for drinks.

The next day the whole team were all congregated at Base Camp basking in the success of the expedition and waiting for the yaks to arrive and take them home. Some of the climbers who hadn't made it to the top were a bit subdued, but generally it had been a very successful expedition. This climb has been unfairly overlooked in the history of Himalayan climbing – maybe because Lhotse Shar is not considered a full 8000er. Not only did they climb a hard new route, but it was achieved without any accidents apart from some minor frostbite to the summit climbers. The performance of Zoltan Demjan to find the way to the summit alone was particularly impressive. He had not been one of the leading candidates for the summit and earlier in the expedition had been hit by falling ice which put him out of action for a few days, but he had brilliantly completed the route alone, which required great mental strength as well as climbing skill. Like the Slovenians before them, the Czechoslovaks had found their way to the top of the wall, but the problem of reaching the main summit of Lhotse from the South still remained as the biggest prize.

Chapter 6 – Between the Hammer and the Anvil

"Mountaineering is a complex and unique way of life, interweaving elements of sport, art and mysticism. Success or failure depends on the ebb and flow of immense inspiration. Detecting a single rule governing this energy is difficult – it arises and vanishes like the urge to dance and remains as mysterious as the phenomenon of life itself". So starts an article about how Poland became the world's leading nation for Himalayan climbing for many years, written by one of the top stars, Voytek Kurtyka. In this article Kurtyka proposes that the history of the Polish nation has shaped attitudes, so that the austerity of the mountain world strikes a chord with the Polish psyche. Living between the superpowers of Germany and Russia – what Kurtyka calls "the hammer and the anvil" – the Poles became accustomed to suffering misfortune and hardship in a stoical manner. The first two attempts to get high on Lhotse South Face were from Yugoslavian and Czechoslovakian expeditions. This reflected an increasing role for teams from the eastern half of Europe which had started in the 1970s and gathered pace in the 1980s. By the middle of the 1980s Poland had become the leading country in Himalayan mountaineering with Czechoslovakia and Slovenia not far behind. Poland does not have mountains of its own which rival the Alps in height, but it does have the Tatra which stand on the border with Slovakia in the South. Like the Julian Alps for the Slovenians, the Tatra serve as a great training ground for local climbers as well as a substantial mountaineering arena in its own right.

Andrzej Zawada was Poland's greatest expedition organiser and in 1971 led a team which had conquered Kungang Chhish, one of the world's highest unclimbed mountains. This was hailed as a major triumph by the Polish state, which was keen to have sporting achievement as a proof of the effectiveness of the communist system, which was in reality failing on many economic measures. The climbers were in the vast majority of cases not party members and either didn't care about the communist propaganda or were actively opposed to it. But if allowing the authorities to trumpet their achievements made it easier to get funding, that was good enough for them. In 1974 Zawada started to plan a winter expedition to Lhotse. He had already successfully climbed the 7500 metre Noshaq, the highest mountain yet climbed in winter, and now he felt the next challenge was to try an 8000er in winter. The Poles regretted that they had missed out on a golden period of Himalayan mountaineering in the 1950s, when most of the 8000ers were climbed for the first time whilst the country was devastated by effects of the Second World War, and now wanted to find a new challenge. Zawada said that winter climbing in the Himalayas would be a test to "sort out the top climbers from the others", with physical and mental toughness as important as technical climbing ability.

When Zawada wrote to the Nepalese Government requesting permission to attempt Lhotse in the winter the Nepalese were initially puzzled. It was recognised that there were only two possible climbing seasons in the Himalayas: before and after the summer monsoon rains. Nobody had ever requested a permit for the winter before, but eventually Zawada got one to climb up until the end of the year. Zawada's team had learnt on Noshaq the importance of having climbers in peak physical condition and top quality equipment, particularly clothing to keep the climbers warm and tents to stand up to the savage winter winds. They even had special gas made which would burn more efficiently at high altitudes. Zawada pulled together a strong team including which included Kurtyka.

Initially they did not have too many difficulties in finding a route through the Icefall to the Western Cwm where they set up three camps within 12 days, the highest being at 7100 metres. It seemed that the ascent might prove quite straightforward after all, but then the period of good weather ended abruptly and gave way to severe cold and savage winds. It was as cold as -30° in the Western Cwm and the wind was strong enough to completely destroy Camp II. Even keeping a route open through the Icefall was challenging. The wind scooped snow out of the crevasses making them deeper and wider and causing some of the ice bridges to collapse. It took them over a month to establish Camp IV at 7800 metres near where Luchsinger and Reiss had started for the first ascent 18 years previously. This camp was established by Kurtyka, Rusiecki and Stryczynski, but they arrived too late in the day to dig a platform big enough to place the tent. Instead they had to hang the tent from ice screws and sit in it like a bivouac sack. During a very cold night Stryczynski suffered frostbitten feet. The next day Zawada and Zygmunt Heinrich made a first attempt on the summit. The slopes of the Lhotse Face were in a very exposed position, but the hard ice gave a good grip for their crampons, which avoided the effort of cutting steps and allowed steady progress. Once they got above the height of the Lhotse-Nuptse ridge which surrounds the Western Cwm, they were fully exposed to the savage gale force winter winds. The wind tugged them off balance, causing them to lurch forwards and lean against the slope with their axes dug in to stop themselves being blown away. As snow and ice whirled around they had to decide quickly what to do, and headed for the nearest rocks in the hope of some type of shelter. It was clear they would have to go down and back at the camp they dived into the shelter of the tent. Zawada was so cold he got into his sleeping bag with his boots on. His right hand, which had been holding his ice axe, was painfully swollen and white. They tried to melt some ice, but even inside the tent, the wind kept blowing the flame out. They decided to use oxygen, but Heinrich had to tear the icicles out of his beard before he was able to get the mask on. The wind continued to increase in intensity, tearing at the tent with a terrible roar. They clung onto to the rocks to which the tent was tied; terrified they would be blown away with the tent. The night seemed endless and their hopes that the weather might improve and allow another attempt the next day were dashed. The whole team retreated back down to Base Camp exhausted.

Having recovered their strength they returned to the mountain. On the 17th December, Tadeusz Piotrowski and two of the accompanying film team, Jerzy Surdel and Stanislaw Latallo, were caught in Camp III by bad weather. They finally decided to descend to Camp II despite a very strong winds and blizzard conditions. They climbed unroped, because the steeper sections had fixed ropes, but became separated in the blizzard. Piotrowski made it safely to Camp II, but Surdel was having trouble with his crampons and returned to Camp III to fix them. When he reached the fixed ropes he saw that Latallo was hanging motionless from a jumar clamp. He had been overcome by the cold and was already dead when Surdel reached him. The death of Latallo was big news back in Poland because he was a nationally acclaimed actor and the tragedy captured the public's attention. In a perverse way the higher public profile of mountaineering pressured the Communist Government into more actively supporting the country's climbers. After the accident, the whole team descended to Base Camp in a sombre mood. It was 6 days before they were able to go back up the mountain to bury Latallo. With time running out on their permit, which lasted until the end of December, they decided to make another push for the summit.

On Christmas Eve Heinrich and Zawada were back at the top camp at 7800 metres. They radioed down to Base Camp to exchange seasonal greetings, but there wasn't much Christmas warmth – the thermometer showed -46° the next morning and it took three hours to boil a saucepan of water and another two to get their oxygen equipment ready before they could set out. They were able to make decent progress in the summit couloir and after two hours the top of Lhotse started to look near. Zawada looked at his altimeter and saw that it registered 8250 metres – the highest a human had ever been in winter. Suddenly Heinrich shouted saying that they had to go down. Zawada was startled and didn't know what the problem was, but he soon saw. A feeling of anger and despair welled up in him as he saw the clouds rising swiftly towards them driven by a gale force wind. He dug his axe into the face and braced himself against the blast of icy wind which chilled his whole body. Carefully he reversed back down to where Heinrich was waiting in the couloir. Thankfully their oxygen masks provided some protection for their faces, but surviving the cold and getting down was still a desperate struggle. The cold numbed their senses, making them indifferent to their own survival. It took a huge mental effort to keep going when fatigue was telling them to lie down and rest.

Once down at Base Camp, Zawada wanted to continue the expedition and try and reach the summit during January. He wrote to the Nepalese Government requesting an extension of the permit, but this was refused. Even without reaching the summit, there was no doubt that Zawada and his team had put Poland firmly in the first division of Himalayan climbing nations. Nobody had even attempted this type of winter climb before and the Poles had come close to pulling it off. Zawada's fascination with winter climbing had first arisen in the severe winters of the Polish Tatras. His view was that every climber was only as good as their winter ascents and he coined the phrase "The Art of Suffering" to describe Himalayan winter climbing. The 1974 expedition also started a Polish connection with Lhotse, although Poles were active throughout the Himalayas. In 1975 two twin expeditions, one male and one female, went to the Gasherbrum Group in the Karakoram with the dual objectives of climbing a new route on the 8000m Gasherburm II and making the first ascent of Gasherbrum III, just below 8000 metres and at the time the highest unclimbed peak in the World. They achieved both objectives with Gasherbrum III climbed by the women's team. A major first ascent by a female team was innovation in Himalayan climbing.

The next year a Polish team attempted K2 by the unclimbed North East Ridge. At this time K2, generally considered the world's hardest mountain, had not had a second ascent. Instead of simply repeating the original route, the Poles tackled a difficult new one, overcoming a narrow pinnacled and corniced crest and establishing a camp beyond the hardest section. From there three attempts were launched on the summit, the highest point of 8400 metres, just 200 below the top being reached by Wroz and Chrobak. Although they did not reach the summit, this was a very fine attempt. When the route was completed by an American team two years later, they traversed onto the easier original route above 8000 metres whereas the Poles had been trying to finish up the last section of the North East Ridge. Therefore, although the Americans were the first to follow the ridge and make it to the summit, all the difficulties had been previously overcome by the Poles. By the late 1970s Polish expeditions to the Himalayas were a regular event. The climber who became best known internationally was Wanda Rutkiewicz, who summited on Gasherbrum III. In 1978 she was invited by Karl Herrligkoffer to join the joint French-German expedition to Everest, which Nicolas Jaeger also took part in. Rutkiewicz became both the first Pole and the first European woman to climb the world's highest mountain, reaching the summit on the same day that Karol Wojtyla was elected Pope John Paul II, an event of great symbolic importance for the Polish people.

At the end of 1979 and beginning of 1980 two expeditions were organised by Zawada to Everest, which would try something really ground-breaking: the first winter ascent and, after a break of only a few weeks, a new route on the South Pillar. The winter team attempted the normal route up the Western Cwm. Krzysztof Wielicki, Walenty Fiut and Leszek Cichy reached the South Col for the first time on February 11th and three days later Zawada and Sherpa Pasang Norbu attempted the summit, but turned back at 8300 metres. With many of the team suffering from illness brought on by the savage conditions, Wielicki and Cichy went back up to the South Col a last try at the summit. On the 17th February they set off for the top despite strong winds, severe cold and cloudy skies. To limit the weight they carried only one oxygen cylinder each, but gaining height was still very hard work. Wielicki suffered from frozen legs and would have turned back if it was not for the significance of the ascent. At 14.25 they reached the top, but the descent was very tiring and dangerous with their oxygen running out at the South Summit. They were also hindered by primitive equipment necessitated by the lack of foreign currency available due to the severe economic crisis in Poland. Instead of specialised snow goggles, they only had welding goggles from which they could see poorly and their head torches didn't work because the batteries froze. On the descent Cichy was moving faster and Wielicki fell behind and became disorientated whilst suffering severe pain from frozen toes. Finally he reached the South Col, but could not locate the tents and nearly descended accidentally on the Chinese before finding the tents. Once inside he spent the whole night trying to reheat his feet with the stove. It had been a close thing, but once again the Poles were at the forefront of Himalayan mountaineering. It was also a spectacular start to the Himalayan climbing career of Wielicki, who would go on to play a major role on Lhotse's South Face.

Leaving two climbers at Base Camp to guard the equipment, Zawada returned to Poland to finalise arrangements to finance the second expedition. Like the winter expedition, the South Pillar team was very strong including several very experienced climbers. However the man who would become most famous was a younger climber - Jerzy Kukuczka. Kukuczka was born in 1948 in Katowice in the coal mining area of Silesia in South East Poland. His family had originated from a small village on the slopes of the Tatra Mountains and throughout his childhood he returned to there, where he felt his roots really lay. By trade he was an electrical engineer in the mining industry, although he later became a full time climber. He was introduced to the mountains by the scouts, having tried his hand at weightlifting and athletics. As soon as he started climbing at the age of 17 he knew it was for him. "Perhaps it sounds a bit pompous", he subsequently said, "but after the first touch of my hand on the rock, I knew it was exactly what I had always been looking for".

After tackling some of the hardest climbs in Poland, his career developed abroad in Bulgaria, the Dolomites and the Alps and then in Alaska on Mount McKinley. On the 6000m McKinley, the first really high summit Kukuczka had attempted, he had trouble with the altitude and acclimatised slower than the rest of the team – a surprising start for someone who would go on to be one of the greatest high altitude climbers of all time. Kukuczka himself wasn't discouraged by this – he had persistence in abundance – and climbed his first 7000 metre peaks in the Hindu Kush in Afghanistan. He then took part in an attempt on the East Pillar of Nanga Parbat organised by his climbing club in Katowice in 1977. It was his first visit to an 8000er, the mountains which were going to shape the rest of his life. When the team arrived at the foot of the huge wall they were overwhelmed by the scale of the objective and changed their plans to tackle a variant on the original 1953 route. They were forced to turn back at 8000 metres by a rock wall, leaving Kukuczka bitterly disappointed, but equally determined that he would be back to these huge mountains.

His next chance came on Lhotse in 1979. The expedition's plan was only going to try the original route, at the time the only one on Lhotse. Since they were also going to use oxygen, Kukuczka was somewhat underwhelmed by these goals and suggesting climbing a new variant directly up the West Face, but most of the team were not in favour. To seek a variant a few hundred metres further across a face would have been a valid objective in the Polish Tatra or the Alps, but here on the world's fourth highest mountain it amounted to an artificial search for difficulty. A worthwhile objective would be a completely different side of the mountain, like the South Face, but they did not have a permit for that. So instead Kukuczka decided on another goal – climbing Lhotse without oxygen. Messner's ascent of Everest without oxygen had occurred only the year before and later in the same year some of the Americans who had made the first ascent of K2's North East Ridge had not used oxygen. Britons Doug Scott, Pete Boardman and Joe Tasker had climbed the world's third highest mountain Kangchenjunga without oxygen earlier in 1979.

On Lhotse, the expedition leader gave the summit team of Janusz Skorek, Andrej Czok, Zygmunt Heinrich and Kukuczka the choice of whether to climb with or without oxygen. At the highest camp the climbers debated whether to go with or without. Czok was never in any doubts that he wanted to climb without; whereas Skorek and Heinrich decided they did not want to take this risk and would climb with oxygen. Only Kukuczka wasn't sure. He put on the pack with the bottles and equipment – a weight of around 10 kilos – but did not put the mask on at first. Kukuczka knew that he and Czok would be slower than the other two, but was confident enough to be able to monitor his performance and see whether he needed the extra oxygen. After an hour the pair with oxygen were ahead, but not by that far and Kukuczka made a decision. "Blow this" he said to Czok, "I am dumping this ballast". Gradually the gap between the pair climbing with oxygen and Czok and Kukuczka got wider, but the latter pair managed to keep going. It was slow. 10 steps, before slumping onto their ice axes to try and regain their breath, were all they could manage. Just below the summit, they met Skorek and Heinrich who were heading down. They slapped each other on the shoulders and exchanged mutual congratulations and encouragement. As with Reiss and Luchsinger 23 years before, they found the last metres the steepest of all and weren't quite sure how close they could get to the knife edged, corniced summit. As is surprisingly common, Kukuczka did not feel particularly triumphant – the dominant feeling was relief that the hard work to get there was over. The lack of oxygen created a type of lethargy and mental tunnel vision which made it difficult for him to recall clearly afterwards what he had done on the summit. They descended back down the way they had come with the wind now in their faces. They reached Camp IV and then Camp III and the others wanted to carry on down to Camp II, but Kukuczka felt that with the weather fine it was a pity to rush off the mountain so he stayed at Camp III with the next summit party to savour another night on his first 8000er.

On the return march, the Poles had just set up camp near Namche Bazar when two Sherpas came running up panting and shouting "Mr Messner is coming! Mr Messner's expedition!". Reinhold Messner was at the time, a year after his ascent of Everest without oxygen, a climbing superstar and now Kukuczka and Messner, arguably the two greatest Himalayan climbers of all time, met for the first time. Messner was on his way up to attempt a beautiful 6000er in the Everest region – Ama Dablam. The Poles had just prepared some food so they invited Messner's team in for some soup and tea and, as climbers always do, sat exchanging views and experiences in the mountains. During the conversation the topic of Kukuczka's expedition to Nanga Parbat came up. Kukuczka mentioned that at 8000 metres on Nanga Parbat he had found a torch. Messner, who was surrounded by people seeking his attention, suddenly focused only on what Kukuczka had said. The Pole explained that he had not understood how the torch came to be there because they were climbing a new route. When he described the exact site, Messner was sure that this had been dropped by his brother Gunther following their descent from Nanga Parbat seven years before. For Messner understanding the exact events of those fateful days in 1970 was almost an obsession and he was eager for any additional evidence to support his version of events. He asked Kukuczka to provide him more information and the two exchanged addresses starting a contact between the two great rivals of 1980s Himalayan mountaineering.

A few months later, Kukuczka was back in Nepal with Zawada's 1980 Everest South Pillar expedition. The route involved hard technical climbing and despite a strong team, progress was slow. When the expedition had fixed ropes up to 8300 metres, Kukuczka proposed to abandon the plan of continuing to fix up to 8600 metres and then climb to the summit with oxygen. Instead he wanted to push directly for the summit from the Camp V. He argued that, since it was mid-May, there was a risk that the monsoon would break before they had made a bid for the summit. This argument was logical, but probably the idea also stemmed from a desire to climb in a bold style like Messner and the other leading Himalayan climbers of the day. In the crowded mess tent Kukuczka's suggestion led to a lively debate amongst the team. Andrzej Czok took the argument to the logical next step and proposed that the attempt should be made without oxygen as he and Kukuczka had done on Lhotse the previous year. The consensus was against this on the grounds that it unnecessarily reduced their chances of reaching the summit. Furthermore the delicate question of who should be in the summit party had not yet been raised. The team was exceptionally strong and there were 8 or 9 climbers with valid credentials to be included in the summit bid, but the time and supplies available would not permit them all to try. Czok and Kukuczka were amongst the younger members of the team. They had climbed Lhotse, but some people had dismissed this as an easy route. Somebody suggested Wroz and Chrobak with Heinrich and Olech as alternatives for the summit party. The mood was tense with whispered comments between people in the mess tent. Kukuczka himself spoke up and suggested that four climbers should go in two teams and proposed that he and Czok should be one of these teams. It was clear that some of the senior members of the team felt that they should have priority. Then Heinrich spoke up and acknowledged the work that Czok and Kukuczka had put in to prepare the route. He was a respected figure, but the one who really counted had not yet spoken. The meeting fell silent to hear what the leader Zawada was going to propose. To most people's surprise he suggested that Kukuczka and Czok should go first as they were in the best physical shape and that behind them should come Heinrich and Olech. However there was pressure to abandon the idea of climbing without oxygen. They had managed it on Lhotse, but Everest was higher and they would be on unknown ground rather than repeating a well-established route. Czok pointed out that if they did fail everyone would say it was because of their stubbornness in not taking oxygen. They were disappointed – Messner had set the standard with his oxygenless ascent of Everest two years before – but they felt they had no real choice.

A few days later the pair completed the new route up the South Pillar reaching the South Summit of Everest where they joined the ordinary route. There was still quite a long section of ridge to traverse to reach the summit and both of them had run out of oxygen. They exchanged looks and a few words, but there was never really any doubt that they would go on – the lure of the world's highest mountain was strong. They radioed Base Camp to tell them the situation, but they didn't ask permission to continue. At this stage it was their lungs that had to fight against the thin air and their brains that risked damage through oxygen deprivation. It took two hours to climb the final section, twice the normal time with oxygen. On the summit they went through the motions of taking photos and picking up some rocks as souvenirs, but they were too tired to feel any real elation. It was a battle to get back down and just after the South Summit they were overtaken by nightfall. In the pitch black and with the wind having blown away their tracks they had serious doubts if they could find the top of the fixed ropes and decided to wait for the moon to come up. When the moon's arrival allowed them continued the descent, Kukuczka's foot slipped from under him on an icy section and he fell out of control for 12 metres before he was able to stop himself. As he tried to get back to his feet, he touched something with his hand and realised that with incredible stroke of good fortune he had landed exactly on the start of the fixed ropes which provided a safe way back down. The congratulations of their comrades were muted and they learnt that Zawada had decided that they had taken too many risks and called off further attempts, leading to resentment from those who had been denied a summit chance. They received plaudits when they returned to Poland, but internationally it was not as big an event as the first winter ascent. Furthermore within a few weeks the events at the shipyard in Gdansk had taken climbing out of the public eye in Poland.

The early 1980s was a turbulent period for Poland, with the birth of the Solidarity movement and great economic hardship. Solidarity was a mass trade union movement which sought to improve conditions of the country's people in reaction to the mismanagement of the economy by the ruling Communist Party. Although in some ways a traditional labour movement demanding better economic and working conditions for its members, Solidarity also threatened the authority of the regime. With increasingly bold demands of Solidarity, the period 1980-1981 was overshadowed by the looming fear of a Soviet military invasion to prop up the Communist government, as had happened in Hungary in 1956 and Czechoslovakia in 1968. In 1981, with the power of Solidarity growing and threatening the stability of the regime, the Government of General

Jaruselski decided to impose martial law. The move caught Solidarity by surprise and plunged the Polish people into a dark period of despair so soon after the growth of the movement had given rise to so many hopes of a better, freer society. But this setback for the country seemed to spur its mountaineers on to even greater things. There were now multiple Polish expeditions to the Himalayas every year with different regional clubs in Poland making their own plans.

In 1981 Kukuczka and Voytek Kurtyka, who were to form a highly successful partnership, attempted Makalu's West Face with Alex Macintyre, one of the best British Himalayan climbers. This Face is one of the hardest in the Himalaya's with an upper section which is even steeper than Lhotse's South Face. They reached 7900 metres before retreating when progress slowed to only 20 metres in one day. MacIntyre left for Kathmandu and Kurtyka had had enough for that year. But whilst they were waiting to evacuate Base Camp, Kukuczka announced that he would make one last try. He proceeded to solo a new route on the North West Ridge. It was a stunning achievement – he became only the second man, after Messner, to solo an 8000 metre peak. The next year Kukuczka and Kurtyka climbed the ordinary route on Broad Peak during an expedition to attempt K2 and then the following year the same pair climbed new routes on both Gasherbrum I and Gasherbrum II.

With these ascents an unofficial race started to emerge between Kukuczka and Messner to be the first man to climb all the 8000 metre peaks. Logically it should have been no contest – Messner had climbed his first 8000er, Nanga Parbat, in 1970. Kukuczka by contrast didn't reach his first peak until 1979, by which time Messner had six of the fourteen 8000ers in the bag. But in the early 1980s Kukuczka was visiting the Himalayas or Karakoram several times a year and his incredible endurance and determination meant that he often reached the summit. By the end of 1983 the score was 10-6 to Messner. Despite the race both men were still pursuing other objectives than just pure peak bagging. Kukuczka's goal was to climb all the 8000 metre peaks either by a new route or in winter. This meant he was interested in the South Face of Lhotse, even though he had already climbed the mountain. In 1984 he put his plan into practice by climbing Broad Peak (a mountain he had already "bagged" by the ordinary route) by a fantastic new route which traversed the mountain's three summits, again with Kurtyka as his partner. This ascent did not add a new 8000er and in 1984 neither man added a peak to their tally. But in the winter of

1985 Kukuczka reached the summit of, Dhaulagiri, making the first winter ascent. The odds were still stacked in Messner's favour – Kukuczka still had to climb some of the hardest peaks, like K2 and Kangchenjunga, but for the first time the outcome started to be in doubt.

As preparations started for the Polish attempt on the South Face of Lhotse in the autumn of 1985, the epic race was at its height. Kukuczka was already committed to an expedition to the South-East Pillar of Nanga Parbat in the summer, which meant he would have to join the Lhotse team after they had already started. The temptation to withdraw from a climb on a mountain which wouldn't even add to his score in the 8000er race must have been high, but not as high as the lure of the South Face for a man with the drive and ambition of Jerzy Kukuczka. The Polish team, which was organised by the Mountaineering Club of Katowice and led by Janusz Majer, included some of the strongest Himalayan climbers of the era including both Kukuczka and Krzysztof Wielicki. Katowice is in an industrial area, but with easy access to the Tatra Mountains it was home to many of Poland's climbers. As well as the big names there were also younger rising stars like Artur Hajzer and Rafal Cholda. Three years before this pair, like many Polish climbers in that era, were earning money painting industrial chimneys and preparing to spend the summer climbing in the Alps. Painting was a very useful source of revenue for climbers since it paid as much per day as the normal monthly salary and was also untaxed. Finance was always a problem during the communist era, but the Polish climbers were extremely inventive in raising money and managed to mount an impressive number of expeditions during the 1980s. With Poland under martial law and the country's economy imploding, the more time the climbers could spend out of the country the better. Additionally various artificial aspects of the economy meant that climbers could make good money by selling goods abroad which were artificially cheap in Poland and bring back scarce items to sell on the black economy at home.

In 1982 Hajzer and Cholda worked hard through the week and at the weekends went out climbing to train for the Alps. Unexpectedly, a long standing invitation from Ryszard Warecki came to fruition and Cholda and Hajzer found themselves going to the Himalayas instead of the Alps. The mountain they would attempt, Gaurisankar, wasn't a famous 8000 metre peak, but it was still a chance to prove themselves in the greatest mountaineering arena in the World. On their way to Nepal they were held up in Delhi waiting for their luggage to arrive and, to save money, camping in the grounds of the Polish Embassy. At the same time the 1982 Polish K2 Expedition was also there, on their way back home. The K2 team was packed with some of the biggest names in Polish mountaineering including Kukuczka, Wielicki and Cichy. Most of the established stars like Wojciech Kurtyka remained aloof from the rookies, sunbathing by the pool, but Wielicki, who was a friend of Warecki, spent time telling the younger climbers about the key sequence of events which led to the failure of the expedition. Officially the expedition had failed because of bad weather, but there was more to it than that. At the crucial period of the expedition four climbers were involved in the final assault on the summit and had divided into two teams: Wroz and Chrobak and Cichy and Wielicki, the pair who had climbed Everest in winter. At the top camp Wielicki had seen that Chrobak was not acting completely normally and feared that he was developing signs of severe altitude sickness, which can be fatal very quickly. He couldn't say proper sentences, just individual words. It was clear that somebody would have to take Chrobak down, but no-one wanted to give up their shot at the summit. Wielicki explained that, after some difficult discussions, he had offered to go down, even though Chrobak wasn't even expected to be his partner. The first reaction of Hajzer and the other young climbers was that this had been an unselfish sacrifice from Wielicki. But then Wielicki explained that he had already concluded they had no chance of making the summit anyway – they were simply too far away. He preferred to go down and rest rather than spend energy and take risks on an attempt with little chance of succeeding. Hajzer already had several years climbing experience and thought that he knew everything about decision making in the mountains, but he noted the lesson. Himalayan climbing was a different game to the Alps and sometimes pragmatism and even cynicism had to rule rather than fine principles which might apply in the Alps. Hajzer's Gaurisankar expedition did not reach the summit, but it was a valuable experience. On the way back from the mountain they walked for a couple of days with members of a Yugoslav team which had just climbed a route on the same mountain. For the first time Hajzer heard about Lhotse's South Face and its reputation as the hardest route in the Himalayas. Now three years later he and Cholda were trying to climb it.

The Lhotse expedition was in a difficult financial position from the start. They had little hard cash left once they had paid off the porters who brought their equipment to Base Camp. They knew that a small French team also had permission to attempt the South Face at the same time. In the 1980s the Poles were always looking for inventive ways to finance their expeditions, and thought they could maybe team up with the French in exchange for cash. It did not occur to them that the French could make a serious attempt on Lhotse South Face as a two man team. But when the Poles arrived at Base Camp there was no sign of the French. They spent the first day constructing a solid stone structure as a kitchen. They knew they would be on the mountain for many weeks and so it made sense to invest time building what would be their main communal space. The effort of shifting the heavy stones made them dizzy and reminded them they were still not fully acclimatised to the height of over 5000 metres. As they worked on building the Base Camp, they also discussed the choice of route. Their original plan had been to attempt the Central Couloir, to the right of the route followed by the Slovenians, but because of the danger the Poles decided to look at alternative possibilities. The team divided into three groups: those in favour of attempting the Slovenian route, those wishing to follow the lower part of the Czechoslovak route on Lhotse Shar before moving left towards the main summit of Lhotse and those who were undecided. The supporters of the Slovenian route argued that the Czechoslovak route was too indirect and did not provide an elegant solution to the Face. However the Slovenian route seemed more threatened by avalanches, particularly after bad weather. On arrival in Kathmandu they had met Peter Bozik and Zoltan Demjan, who were en route for Dhaulagiri, who told them that the difficulties of following the Czechoslovak route would essentially be over after 7500 metres. By contrast the Slovenians had been defeated by difficulties above 8000 metres. Not only did the Czechoslovak route offer more chance of success, but since the upper section was expected to be easier it might give multiple teams a shot at the summit. This was an important factor for the climbers who did not expect to be in the first summit team.

Being involved in a team of elite climbers for the first time, Hajzer was able to observe the team dynamics. People's background outside climbing didn't really matter in the mountains. A university professor would respect a miner and vice versa, but the team could still be categorised into two main types, the elite and the bohemians. The elite were the professional climbers who tried to make a living through climbing – not easy in a communist country like Poland. They went to Nepal or Pakistan at least a couple of times a year, were more likely to speak foreign languages, understood the jungle of regulations better and had more flashy western mountain clothes. The other larger group were the "bohemians" who did have jobs back home, although usually only irregular ones, working the minimum needed to make ends meet – for example by painting chimneys – and spending as much time climbing as possible. Miroslaw Falco-Dasal was firmly in this group and was a strong supporter of the Czechoslovak route. He was a geophysicist by training, but worked painting chimneys when not climbing.

As the discussion became a bit more heated Ryszard Pawlowski declared: "I don't care what the rest of you think, tomorrow I am going up that way", indicating the Slovenian route. Pawlowski was a strong climber and probably one of the favourites to be in the summit team. He had already made alpine style ascents of two Himalayan 7000ers and had reached the summit of the 8000 metre Broad Peak. Just at that moment a huge avalanche poured down the section of the Slovenian route he had been pointing to. It seemed almost like the voice of The Wall warning them not to go that way. Even Pawlowski was convinced and on the 2nd September they started to climb on the Czechoslovak route. The way led across the glacier and then up a huge avalanche cone to the foot of the Pillar. The first problem was to locate the start of the Czechoslovak route. On the first day, despite extensively searching, they could not find any sign of their predecessors. Eventually they found what looked like it might be the right route and fixed a few lengths of rope before retreating back to Base Camp. In reality they followed a slightly different line to the Czechoslovaks in the lowest section. In the next weeks they proceeded with the hard and sometimes monotonous task of fixing ropes up the Czechoslovakian Pillar. With Kukuczka still to arrive and several others suffering illness, there was only a handful of climbers available to do this work. Although their predecessors had climbed only a year before and left their fixed ropes on the mountain, the Poles saw little sign of them. Only after 500 metres did they find a rusty piton with a loop of rope attached. At 5700m they found a rope ladder, but above this the Wall was mainly clean. Most of the Czechoslovak ropes had either disappeared under snow or been cut by falling rocks. At least the Poles had the satisfaction that they were climbing the route themselves rather than just pulling up on ropes left by others, although they used what they did find. On a mountain the size of Lhotse, sporting ethical rules of pure climbing did not apply as they would in Europe. In Scotland, in the Polish Tatra or even the Alps the merits of an ascent would depend on its style and pulling on old fixed ropes or in situ gear would tarnish its quality. On an objective as serious as the South Face to climb parallel to and avoiding existing ropes would have been an absurdity.

When the weather was acceptable they made slow, but steady progress and by late September had placed Camp IV at 7100m. On many 8000ers it would have been possible to launch a summit bid directly from this altitude, but the height and difficulty of Lhotse's South Face meant that one or two further camps would be needed. Walenty Fiut and Hajzer established the route towards Camp V, which was one of the hardest sections, helped by a couple of remaining pieces of Czechoslovak fixed rope. They ran out of rope to fix still 100 metres below the ideal campsite. But in their rucksacks they found another length of rope and Fiut lead some tricky sections of rock and ice confidently to reach the campsite. Hajzer had been expecting to partner his old companion Rafal Cholda, but the latter had been unwell early in the expedition so Hajzer ended up in a team with Fiut. Fiut was the oldest member of the team and by training an art historian, although like many of the others he actually earned his money painting chimneys. He had participated in quite a few Himalayan expeditions but, with the exception of Broad Peak the previous year, bad luck had stopped him reaching the summits. He also seemed to suffer a curse which made him to get into traffic accidents, although he always seemed to escape unscathed. On the way to Broad Peak a car he was in had driven off the road at high speed and hit a wall. Fiut didn't even wake up. And on a bus from Delhi to Kathmandu there was a head on collision which killed the local driver and injured several Poles – but again Fiut escaped without a scratch. He was respected by the whole team and was something of a workaholic, which made him popular in expedition life when there are always chores to be done. When he arrived at a camp he would immediately set to work improving and expanding the platform. When he was climbing fixed ropes he would look to improve the placements, tie neater knots and he always carried the heaviest pack.

In total more than 4km of ropes were fixed from the base of the wall up to 7600 metres. At the top of the Czechoslovak Pillar, the Poles' route deviated from that to Lhotse Shar and traversed left into the easier angled basin which lay below the peaks of Lhotse Shar, Lhotse Central and the main summit. Here at the edge of what the Poles called "the Cauldron" they placed Camp V. The next section could not be seen from Base Camp, so their first view of it was when they rounded the ridge into the Cauldron and it was a disappointment. When the Poles met Bozik and Demjan of the Czechoslovak team in Kathmandu they had suggested the next part of the route would be straightforward, but although crossing the Cauldron itself looked fairly easy, the rocks above, which they called "the Great Barrier", looked a formidable obstacle to overcome before they could reach the ridge which led up towards the summit. They had hoped the greatest difficulties were behind them, but now they understood that hardest section of the climb lay above 8000 metres. They were high on the mountain now – of the other peaks they could see only Makalu was higher – and had hoped they were close to being able to make a summit bid, but now they needed to rethink. There were also doubts about whether they had enough equipment, since they had already placed most of their ice screws, snow stakes and pitons to equip the route up to this point. They had not planned to fix ropes above 8000 metres, but now this looked like it would be necessary.

On the evening radio call Base Camp announced there had been a new arrival. Hajzer and Fiut's first thought was that it was the French team and the possibility of new financial resources and manpower. In fact the French still weren't there. They had arrived and dumped some equipment a few days before, but they had now gone off to make some acclimatisation ascents, leaving only their kitchen boy who moved into camp with the Poles. The new arrival was Jerzy Kukuczka, having just made the first ascent of the South East Pillar of Nanga Parbat – a climb he rated as one of the most dangerous he ever undertook. He had been back in Poland, but not for long enough to fully recover from the ordeal on Nanga Parbat. Although he was signed up as a member, some of the team doubted whether he would come, given that he had already climbed Lhotse and was at the height of his race with Reinhold Messner, but they were pleased to know he was here. Although incredibly tired after Nanga Parbat he was still well acclimatised and would certainly strengthen the team. In Base Camp Miroslaw Falco-Dasal recounted to him what they had been doing up on the mountain, feeling that having established Camp IV at 7100 metres, he could talk as an equal to the great man. Kukuczka was impressed with the progress and could see that the lead climbers were pushing to get to the summit as soon as possible. He realised it would lead to tension if he barged his way to the front as soon as he arrived, so he joined the support group ferrying loads to stock the camps. Two days later Falco-Dasal and Wielicki passed Camp V and pushed the route out across the Cauldron to the foot of the

Great Barrier leaving a dump of gear at 7700 metres and returning to camp in an optimistic mood. Having had a closer look at the Great Barrier, Wielicki believed that they could pass the main difficulties with a long traverse left which would lead them onto the Central Pillar which they could follow up to the summit.

On the evening of October 6th it started to snow heavily and Falco-Dasal and Wielicki retreated from the mountain. Falco-Dasal noticed how strange it was that they could be in a severe storm at 7000 metres and then only a few hours later be back down in the safety and relative comfort of Base Camp. The Himalayan veterans recognised the storm as a typical October break in the weather, frequently seen in the post-monsoon season. What they seemed to have been missed was the favourable period of September weather, which should have preceded this break. The next day the French team arrived at Base Camp and set up camp a little way from the Polish team. The Poles invited them over to their camp for tea. They were impressed by their cheerfulness and optimism, given the magnitude of their plans, but privately the Poles didn't rate the French chances of success very highly.

The next few days everyone was blocked in Base Camp by the bad weather, trying to pass time with the usual activities of reading, talking, playing chess and so on. At least the presence of the French team gave a chance to socialise. English was the common language and although their level varied, everyone managed to make themselves understood. It was a week before the weather was settled enough for Hajzer and Kukuczka to move back up onto the Face, followed a day later by Falco-Dasal and Wielicki. But although they made it up to Camp III, the weather then broke again with snow and strong winds and the forecast was for more of the same in the following days. They were starting to run short of food on the Face and the avalanche danger restricted their movement between camps and prevented them descending. Falco-Dasal, Hajzer, Wielicki and Fiut were stuck at Camp III with Pawlowski, Cholda, Kukuczka and Nowak up at Camp IV. Everyone was struggling to sleep as avalanches crashed around at night, accompanied by hurricane force winds and temperatures as low as -40°. On the 19th October things calmed down a bit and both teams moved up. It was agreed that the next day they would try to establish Camp VI and if possible move in. The team at Camp IV would take loads up to V and stay there unless the higher team failed to establish the camp. On the midday radio call the lower group learned that the higher one hadn't done as well as they'd hoped, depositing gear at their high point. When the two groups met up the frozen faces of those who'd gone above told their story – now it was the turn of the other four.

With two pairs ready to go high on the face, it wasn't clear who should take the lead and this was a potential cause of tension, but Wielicki resolved any risk of dispute by suggesting that all four of them climbed together. So on October 21st Hajzer, Fiut, Falco-Dasal and Wielicki headed up to try and site Camp VI below the Great Barrier from where they hoped a summit attempt could be launched. Fiut and Hajzer were climbing as a pair and located a good site at 7800m. Wielicki and Falco-Dasal joined them in the late afternoon taking care in the Cauldron as the snow was loose and they had not fixed any rope in this section, given their shortage of rope and climbing equipment. After an hour's work the four of them had dug out a platform in the steep slope big enough to place the tent. They were pleased to get inside as the cold was starting to bite. With the four of them crammed into a 2 man tent they spent an uncomfortable night, but at least they were warm. A long time was spent brewing tea to make sure they were fully hydrated for the next day. If they could crack the Barrier, the way to the top seemed clear and the prospect of success on such a huge goal was so thrilling that they struggled to sleep.

The next morning was bitterly cold and they brewed more tea before setting out at dawn. Despite all the layers of clothing, their hands were numb even before they had set off. In the cold thin air they crossed snowfields above the camp. Once the sun hit them, it warmed them a little. Their aim was to avoid a direct ascent of the Great Barrier and traverse left up a couloir which ended in a difficult 150 metre chimney which they expected would give access to the Central Pillar. Wielicki took the lead on pitches of grade IV-V followed by Falco-Dasal to reach 8180m just short of the Central Pillar. Hajzer and Fiut caught them up at this point only to be told by Wielicki that the chimney was impassable and that they would have to abandon the attempt for that day. Huge cauliflower-like cornices blocked access from the end of the chimney onto the ridge. Falco-Dasal cursed their luck. Although it was only noon and they were feeling in good shape there was no way to carry on that day – trying to tunnel through or climb over the unstable cornices was simply too risky. Reluctantly they headed down, comforted by the knowledge that there was still enough time for another shot at the summit.

Wielicki didn't seem so sure and was already talking about winding up the expedition, but both Hajzer and Falco-Dasal were keen for another try. On the radio Majer said that their permit lasted until 15th November and there was no reason to give up yet. Besides, there was another team consisting of Rafal Holda, Ryszard Pawlowski and Jerzy Kukuczka moving up the mountain to try and advance the route and if possible reach the summit. The next morning the first group headed down, leaving their sleeping bags, mats and ice axes at the top camp in anticipation of another attempt. Close to Camp IV they met Kukuczka, Pawlowski and Cholda on their way up. Kukuczka was perhaps not fully acclimatised, but then again his teammates were sometimes unsure if he counted as a normal human being. The prospects for the success of the expedition still looked bright.

Chapter 7 – Lightweight and Fast

The small French team, which was attempting the Face at the same time as the Poles, had the same goal, but a very different style: they wanted to attempt an alpine style ascent. The two main climbers, Vincent Fine and Michel Fauquet, had very impressive credentials from the Alps. Fine was one of the first Frenchmen to climb Grade 8 rock and had made the first solo ascent of the North Face of the Dru in winter. The pair had been climbing together for six years and both came from Marseille where they started climbing. The many rock faces around the city and in particular the magnificent sea cliffs of the Calanques, mean that it contains one of the highest concentrations of climbers in the world. The Verdon Gorge, the largest in Europe and a little over an hour from Marseille, was becoming a premier climbing location in the 1970s and 1980s and Fine and Fauquet were also very active there. They would think nothing of climbing one route after another from first thing in the morning until the fall of night stopped them. From Marseilles the Alps are also easily accessible and the pair had also pulled off many fine ascents on the larger mountains. They were young, confident and keen to climb the hardest routes in the perfect style – quick, light and efficient following the example of the likes of Messner and Patrick Berhault. And furthermore they were a well matched pair who had the technical ability, the physical condition and the confidence to succeed at the highest level.

In 1983 Fine and Fauquet had attempted the South Pillar of Baintha Brakk, sometimes known as the Ogre, in the Karakorum as part of a 4 man team. They fixed ropes and set up and stocked two camps on the lower part of the route. The climbing was very technical and so only the lead climber climbed whilst the other three jumared and hauled loads. After a first attempt by all four climbers was defeated by bad weather, Fine and Fauquet made a second attempt. Over a 5 day period they reached the top of the pillar at 6400 metres. It had involved climbing 1000 metres of very technical rock and had required artificial climbing and two pendulums. They used no fixed ropes and mainly belayed with nuts and friends (camming devices which can be placed and removed), rather than drilling in bolts. On the Pillar they had to make hanging bivouacs in a sack attached to the face. From the top of the Pillar there were still 400 metres of snow slopes and 250 metres of rock to go to the summit. On the day they arrived at the top of the Pillar the weather had turned and they were forced to wait in their tent. The following day they set out to cover the final section, but with a metre of new snow progress was slow and they were forced to turn back 200 metres below the summit. It was nonetheless a fine ascent of a new route on which they had climbed all the difficult ground.

In 1985 Fauquet was an aspirant guide in Chamonix, whereas Fine still lived at home, dedicated to climbing. On Lhotse their plan was to climb the South Face, descend the ordinary route and return to Everest Base Camp. "Lightweight and fast" was their motto and they believed these two things were crucially linked. They saw weight as one of the main enemies and they had modern lightweight equipment and made careful preparations, even drilling holes in their pitons. As well as the two principal climbers, Fine and Fauquet, the team included Nathalie LeCable, the girlfriend of Fauquet and Marie-Odile Martine, the girlfriend of Fine. The team was completed by a medical student, Frédéric Potie, who was a friend of Fine. Potie was also active in the Verdon, had climbed with Fine quite a lot. The pair spent two months in the USA visiting various climbing centres including Yosemite. Fine had offered Potie a place in the team feeling he could strengthen the team and his medical knowledge could be useful – although he was only three years into his studies. Their plan was to acclimatise on some lower mountains nearby before making an alpine style attempt on Lhotse. It was a project as bold as any yet attempted in world mountaineering and on a par with the plans of Nicolas Jaeger, who was an inspiration for them.

Their departure from Kathmandu was delayed after their equipment was held up in Sri Lanka for a week due because of the breakdown of an aeroplane. Realising it was necessary to adapt to the relaxed Asian way of viewing things, they decided to pass the time and went on elephant rides and white-water rafting. Rafting on the Trisuli River they alarmed their guide by paddling towards the rapids he told them to avoid and making dangerous jumps down falls. With the monsoon still underway there was little chance of getting a flight to Lukla so they set off to walk the whole way in from the roadhead at Jiri under the monsoon rains. This meant the usual suffering of mud, leeches and crossing swollen torrents on cables where the bridges had been swept away. Their group consisted of 28 porters, the liaison officer and a cook. As they got closer to Lhotse they started to see in some of the roadside lodges stickers saying "Polish Lhotse South Face Expedition 1985". This was a surprise for them as they had expected to have the Face to themselves, but now it seemed they would have to share in with the Poles.

After 8 days walking they set up a Base Camp at the beginning of September at the foot of Thamserku, a beautiful 6600 metre in the Solu Kumbhu region. Marie-Odile Martine, Potie, Fauquet and Fine attempted the North Face starting from the east col but were only able to reach 5500 metres before being turned back by snowy conditions. They bivouacked at 5000 metres and then Fauquet and Fine made another attempt by a direct route. They left at 2am and travelled very light with a few pieces of climbing equipment, some energy bars and drinks. They carried 40 metres of rope, but climbed unroped side by side. Moving fast, they climbed a 1500 metre face of snow and hard ice similar to the North Face of the Dru in the Mont Blanc group and involving pitches as steep as 85°. At 10am they arrived at the summit serac which blocked the top of the face. They now had two alternatives: either they could avoid the serac on the left on very unstable mixed ground or they could turn it on the right on steep ice which led straight to the summit. They roped up and Fine attempted the right hand route, but the ice was so hard that even his ultra-modern ice tools wouldn't grip. After trying for a couple of hours they abandoned the attempt 60 metres below the summit and abseiled back down to the foot of the face on snow mushrooms. They had been on the face for 16 hours and bivouacked at its base. Not reaching the summit was probably not too important as the attempt was an excellent preparation for Lhotse.

They now moved their equipment to the Base Camp of Lhotse where their arrival coincided with four days and four nights of incessant snowfall. At least it gave them a chance to socialise with the Poles who they found not only strong climbers, but also good company. To complete their acclimatisation and to give a chance for the fresh snow to clear from Lhotse, they decided to attempt the West Face of Imjatse (also known as Island Peak), a 6183 metre summit directly across the valley from Lhotse. First, on October 9, Fine and Potie reached 5900 meters, before being turned back by danger of windslab avalanches near the summit. Five days later Fauquet and Fine reached the summit by climbing a direct route on the West Face. The climb took eight hours and although the average angle was 45° there were three 70° pitches. Martine, Fauquet and Fine also got close to repeating the same route on October 18, but there was so much snow around that they almost had to tunnel their way up the mountain. They stopped below the summit pyramid having ploughed up 1100 metres in waist deep snow.

Back at Base Camp they ate well and rested before the climb on Lhotse. They had been camped under the South Face for two weeks and Fauquet and Fine were now prepared for their alpine style attempt. They were going to follow a line to the left of the Poles route, first heading up the Slovenian route before traversing right at around 6500 metres to gain the central spur which led steeply to the summit. Back in France, Vincent Fine had spent a long time studying a magnificent photo of the Face in the famous coffee table book on the Himalayas by the Japanese photographer Shirakawa trying to identify the perfect line. Thirty years later his wife Marie-Odile explained to me that Vincent wanted to climb the South Face simply because it was the hardest route in the world. After packing and re-packing they did not manage to reduce the weight of their rucksacks below 18 kilos each. This included 12 kilos of food and gas which they hoped would last them for the 10 days they expected to be on the route. They had done everything they could to reduce weight, including using ultra-light harnesses and crampons and cutting unnecessary parts off their rucksacks, but it was still a tremendous weight.

On the 23rd October, Fine and Fauquet set off at night to minimise the risk of avalanches on the lower part of the Face. They almost disappeared under the huge rucksacks. On the approach to the Face the snow, which had previously supported them with light sacks, now gave way under each step making progress tiresome. At 5000 metres they reached the start of the huge avalanche cones comprised of irregular rocks and blocks of snow which made walking difficult. At 5200 metres they crossed the first bergschrund on a narrow snow bridge and set foot on the Face proper. They each climbed solo to move as quickly as possible, the rope stored in their sacks to be used on the most difficult pitches higher up. The first difficulty was a mixed band between 5500 and 5700 metres, the first part of which was a short but steep section on snow of dubious quality. Once they had passed this, 60° snow slopes brought them to the foot of some gullies which snaked through rocky outcrops. The ice in these gullies was hard and the walls were sometimes narrow, but they managed to avoid the steepest part by taking a rocky spur which brought them finally onto the huge wide snow slopes which form the lower part of the Face. Here, at 5800 metres they dug out a shelf in the steep slope to place their bivouac tent. It was still quite early, but they didn't want to go too high too fast because of acclimatisation. That day they had covered 800 metres on snow and ice, mostly at an angle of 55°, but with pitches as steep as 80°.

After a dinner of soup, rice and tea they looked out to see the lights of Base Camp flashing at them. It warmed their spirits to know they were being followed from down below by their loved ones. The Poles had also taken note of their progress. They had expected the French to change their plans when they realised the enormity of the face and were quite surprised to see them making a determined push. After folding the tent, they set out again following for 600 metres long monotonous snow arête between the Slovenians first and second camps. Marie Odile took a picture through a telephoto lens which shows two tiny figures, one below the other, dwarfed by the scale of this ridge. During this day they started to be troubled by some rockfall with the projectiles becoming more frequent as the day wore on. Most of the objects falling were not large, but since they had had 1 or 2 kilometres vertically to build up speed they could still be very dangerous. They started to wonder whether they had made the right decision to save on weight by leaving their helmets at Base Camp. They exchanged a glance with each other and it was clear both were keen to go on. At 6500 metres they zig-zagged on ice through some rock bands and followed some avalanche gullies and snow ramps at an angle of 60 or 70°. Two hundred metres higher they had to run to avoid a cascade of rocks rumbling down a couloir. They then climbed the right hand side of the couloir by a very exposed snow slope. At 6900 metres they were surprised by nightfall when climbing a very delicate mixed section without having found any suitable bivouac site. 100 metres higher up they managed to find shelter under a small overhang. That day they had managed to cover another 1200 metres, but their nerves were frayed. Fine had been hit on the wrist and Fauquet had had both his lips cut by a piece of falling ice. It wasn't very pleasant to climb whilst hearing the whistle of falling rocks continuously. That night their sleep was disturbed by the sound of stones bouncing off the roof of the tent.

Meanwhile the Poles were also pushing on with their attempt. As the first team withdrew, a strong team of Kukuczka, Holda and Pawlowski moved into the front to try again. On the morning of their summit push Pawlowski was feeling unwell, so only Kukuczka and Holda set off, travelling light. The rock wall of the Great Barrier proved to be time consuming with sustained Grade V climbing and it took them until 2pm to fix the 80 metres of rope which they had with them. Then Kukuczka abseiled down to join Holda and they started to descend, un-roped, back to the Camp across the Cauldron. The slope was around 45-50 degrees and hard snow in which their crampons gave a good grip, but any slip would be hard to arrest and the slopes steepened at the bottom of the Cauldron before plunging down the Central Couloir to the foot of the face. Kukuczka was only about 15 metres ahead of his companion the last time he saw him, but when he turned again Holda had vanished. There was no shout or visible sign of a fall, but as Kukuczka looked around in desperation he saw, about 200 metres below, a rucksack rolling down the slope. Gradually he realised that Cholda must have fallen to his death. In desperation he radioed to Base Camp asking them to scan the face for signs of Cholda, although in reality he knew there was no hope for him.

The same day was the third for Fauquet and Fine on the Face and they had pushed on to 7200 meters climbing a 50° snow and a rock pitch and traversing right towards an arête which led to the lower rocks of the Central Spur. After climbing a snow slope they stopped for the day on a snow patch in which they set about cutting a ledge for their third bivouac. It was still quite early, but they wanted to be on top form for the next day which would involve tackling some of the most difficult sections. As they dug the ledge their attention was attracted by the sound of an avalanche down the Central Couloir to their right. With horror they saw that there was a body within the debris of the avalanche which plunged down into one of the huge bergschrunds at the foot of the face. They realised that one of the Poles must have fallen from higher up. Deeply shocked by what they had seen, the two climbers then had a long discussion about whether to continue. In the end Fauquet said he wanted to go back down because the risks they were running were too great. At midnight they set off back down, arriving at the foot of the face at 9 o'clock the next morning.

Once they got back down Fauquet decided to go off trekking with his girlfriend leaving Fine without a partner to continue the climb. After they returned to France, Fine wrote an article reporting this version of events. Fauquet wrote another article in which he presented the decision to turn back as a joint one, which caused some tension between the pair. The American Mark Twight who later climbed with Fauquet, wrote that he had "freaked" after seeing Holda fall and had insisted on descending whilst Fine had wanted to continue. This statement needs to be treated with caution because Twight fell out with Fauquet on an expedition to Soviet Union and this probably coloured his view of the Frenchman. The Poles certainly didn't seem to find the descent of the French pair surprising. All the same it is clear from Fine's account that he would have been prepared to go on.

The Polish climbers at Base Camp had been relaxing and killing time, playing chess or reading books, when Kukuczka's call came and they immediately knew something was wrong from his strange voice. Leader Janusz Mayer set about organising a search party. Fiut, Hajzer and Falco-Dasal prepared with heavy hearts to cross the glacier. They took binoculars and the radio and crossed the glacier scanning every area at the bottom of the Central Couloir where it seemed a fall could have ended. They saw nothing and it was really an impossible search, because there were so many crevasses into which a body could have fallen. Eventually dusk fell and without exchanging a word they trudged back across the glacier to Base Camp. It was very cold, but the moon lit their way. At dinner there was semblance of a normal conversation, but the memory of what had happened to Holda hung heavy over the group. Then Wielicki asked how old he was. The realisation that his age was his life span, a life cut cruelly short was too much for Falco-Dasal. He retreated to his tent to be alone with his thoughts of Holda's girlfriend, his mother, his home and of the ultimate futility of what they were doing.

Up on the face the weather was perfect with blue skies and sunshine, but the death of Rafal Holda had demoralised Kukuczka. He talked on the radio with the lower camps and asked "What now? I don't think we will manage this route". This was an unusual position for Kukuczka to take. On previous expeditions he had always been the one who didn't want to turn back when others hesitated, but this time he felt differently. Back at Base Camp the Polish team discussed whether to continue with the attempt or not. Moral was of course shattered and, even though immediately before the accident seven of the eleven team members were in shape to attempt the summit, now everyone was thinking about going home. Kukuczka and Pawlowski were still up on the mountain, but everyone else congregated in the mess tent at Base Camp. There were precedents where someone had died and the remaining members had to decide whether to continue or not. An important one for the Polish climbers was Zawada's 1971 expedition to Kungang Chhish, then one of the highest unclimbed mountains in the world. There had not been a Polish Himalayan expedition for 32 years and, having missed out on the period when all the 8000ers were climbed for the first time, they had a great chance to pull off an important climb. The team members had gathered in front of the mess tent, aware that if they turned back with the restrictions in Communist Poland, they probably wouldn't get another chance to come to the Himalayas. Although it was not a nice fact to face, they knew that the success would relegate the loss of a team member to a thing of lesser importance. But if they turned back after an accident this could affect the chances of getting funding for future expeditions, not only for them, but for all Polish climbers. In the end the 1971 team elected to carry on and the expedition was successful and able to return triumphant to Poland despite the death of one of the climbers. This allowed Zawada to get political and financial support to launch a whole series of further Polish Himalayan expeditions.

The pressure on the 1985 Lhotse expedition was significantly less than on Kungang Chhish, but again it had to be a consensus decision. Janusz Majer had a leadership style which was never intrusive and the result was that his point of view often prevailed. Wielicki opened the discussion by saying that he was pulling out of the expedition and most of the others seemed to take the same view. However Miroslaw Falco-Dasal said he would be willing to carry on if enough people were with him to put a team together. Hajzer was not sure what to do. Naturally the death of Rafal Cholda, who he knew well, had hit him hard, but like Falco-Dasal he was not ready to give up yet. He wandered around Base Camp like a drunk knowing what to do. He was nervous about the difficulties of the Great Barrier and was unsure how good the chances of success were without climbers of the ability of Wielicki and Fiut. He wanted to go in the first assault team, but did not feel ready to lead the key pitches on the Great Barrier. He declared his willingness to go for the summit as long as someone would come to lead the Great Barrier, but there were no takers. There was a majority decision to abandon the expedition and everyone started to make plans to return home.

In the evening the Fauquet and Fine returned to Base Camp and told the horrific tale of seeing the body fall. They confirmed that it was in a crevasse at 5500 metres. The place was too dangerous to reach due to the risk of rock and serac fall and the Poles abandoned the attempt to recover the body. After their attempt on the face the Poles now treated Fine and Fauquet with considerably more respect. At the beginning they had been a bit suspicious of the French, who were competing for the Face, albeit by a different route. They were maybe even a bit condescending towards these two young and small Frenchmen – neither Fine nor Fauquet was taller than 1 metre 67 and both were slightly built – with limited Himalayan climbing experience. The Poles were older and generally well built and had stacks of experience. The Poles had a big enough team to be to lay siege to the mountain in traditional style, but in the eyes of the French they had pretty out of date equipment and the look of a Communist country only just starting to open up. Compared to the "Frenchies" dressed in the latest Millet jackets and state of the art climbing equipment, the Poles seemed almost to be "climbing barefoot". But when the French saw how the Poles were climbing and the fact that even the death of one of their team had not necessarily stopped their desire to reach the objective, they realised that these were climbers who could make up for material disadvantages, with effort, skill and determination.

Artur Hajzer returned to his tent and started the ritual of packing his things for home in the entrance. Whilst he was there Vincent Fine approached him and they struck up a conversation. Fine explained that Michel Fauquet was not willing to return for another attempt. Hajzer said that was a pity. Fine then said that this meant his expedition was over unless Hajzer would accompany him on another attempt. For Hajzer this proposal was a bolt from the blue. He had been impressed with the French climbers' ambition on the Face and this opened his eyes to the fact that a bold approach was possible even on a route as hard as this. He asked Fine if he would lead the key sections on the Great Barrier and the Frenchman agreed. They knew that to have a decent chance of success they would need two teams to tackle the barrier and attempt the summit.

Majer was happy with this plan. He was willing to support whatever the team had planned, and was pleased to see they had not given up. Together they went to talk to Falco-Dasal. He was keen to go up again too, but they knew that the three of them were too few to mount a serious assault. The best chance was Kukuczka and although he was somewhat reluctant he agreed he would follow in support. As they packed for a final attempt on the mountain there was a combined enthusiasm for the French-Polish co-operation. Most of the rest of the team were heading home and Base Camp was partially dismantled. Wielicki said goodbye to Hajzer and wished him luck. He made some cryptic comment about the optimism of youth and did not seem to have any second thoughts about his own decision to quit. Hajzer believed they could pull it off at the last minute as on his previous expedition to Tirich Mir in the Hindu Kush. Vincent Fine was happy to team up with the Poles, although less committed to their route than the direct line he and Fauquet had been attempting. Even if their style of climbing was quite different he liked the Poles as people and could appreciate their determination and skill as climbers. Furthermore now that Fauquet had given up, the Poles were his last chance of climbing Lhotse.

They now had to wait for the weather to be settled for the attempt. On the 29th October Fine and Hajzer left Base Camp. Kukuczka and Falco-Dasal prepared to follow them a day later. As the second pair left in the moonlight on the 30th, the weather was perfect. As they started up the avalanche cone there was a light breeze and their crampons dug nicely in to the snow. Kukuczka was moving like a train and they made it to Camp II in record time arriving at 9 am. They stopped and had a drink and a bite to eat. Then, after an hours nap, it was time to carry on and up to Camp III. The following day they made it to Camp V, their thoughts oscillating between optimism and doubts. It was starting to get cold, but the mornings were bringing very clear and calm weather. Kukuczka and Falco-Dasal spoke to Hajzer at Camp VI in the evening. His plan was to attack the Great Barrier with Fine the next day and try to fix ropes up the main difficulties.

On the morning of November 1, even in Camp V the thermometer showed -30° C. Up in VI Hajzer took longer to prepare than Fine and the latter got cold while waiting for the Pole to be ready. They still managed to leave the camp early in the morning, but after about 100m Fine returned to the tent, because he was cold and feeling unwell. Hajzer reached the end of the ropes fixed by Kukuczka, which was now in the sun and waited for half an hour for Fine to join him, but he did not arrive. So Hajzer returned to the tent to see what was happening. Kukuczka and Falco-Dasal were meanwhile moving up to Camp VI, but when they saw that the pair above had turned round they knew the prospects of success were disappearing. Hajzer spoke to his teammates on the radio and explained that Fine was not feeling well and wanted to rest a day before carrying on. Kukuczka said that at 8000 metres you cannot rest or recover and spending more time there would only weaken them. Hajzer first tried to convince Fine to continue and then to convince Kukuczka to agree to waiting one more day. But Kukuczka was adamant and insisted that they should now abandon the attempt. His teammates were surprised by this, because in all previous expeditions he had always been the one who wanted to press on, even when everyone else was for turning back. Fine, who was suffering from the cold and fatigue from a long period at altitude did not seem to regret the decision to have turned back and felt that at least they had given it their best shot. In any case he was not as committed to the Polish route as he was to the direct line which he and Fauquet had been attempting.

The Polish team were sad and demoralised by the end of the expedition. The loss of Rafal Cholda was a heavy burden for them to bear. For Artur Hajzer it was the first time he had been on an expedition which had not achieved its goals. Hajzer's attitude angered Miroslaw Falco-Dasal who was grieving the loss of their friend, but Cholda's death had hit Hajzer hard too. He was one of the closest to Cholda, they had climbed together frequently and worked together painting chimneys. They had trained, run long distances and partied together. He knew how hard it would be for Cholda's parents back in Poland. He was an only child, a graduate in Metallurgy from the Silesian University of Technology, although he had dedicated all his adult life to climbing. Hajzer knew that things would never be the same when he returned to Poland. They carved a memorial to Rafal Cholda on a rock at the foot of the Face. Above was the Face of Lhotse, brilliant and terrible with the wind roaring and blowing huge plumes of snow from the summit ridge.

At the end of the expedition Falco-Dasal tried to analyse the reasons for their failure. Certainly the weather had not been kind to them, but also the nature of the route with severe difficulties above 8000 metres was a factor. Most Himalayan peaks tend to have straightforward snow slopes in their upper sections so that even tired and oxygen deprived climbers can keep plodding along, but on Lhotse South Face the hardest of the climbing comes right at the top. There were factors in the team dynamics which had perhaps played a part in Falco-Dasal's view. Wielicki had maybe been impatient and Kukuczka indecisive at some key points, but he recognised that it was easy to make such criticisms with the benefit of hindsight. For Falco-Dasal himself, the expedition served as a superb apprenticeship in Himalayan climbing. The Poles realised that they had perhaps underestimated the difficulty of the upper section of the route, but they had found a viable route which could lead to the top. They were determined to come back and finish the job another year. Fine and Fauquet also made plans to return. The rapport between Vincent Fine and the Poles was good and he and Marie-Odile Martine, who later married, visited Poland for Artur Hajzer's own wedding.

After the Lhotse expedition, Kukuczka pressed on with his attempt to complete the 8000 metre peaks with scarcely a pause. When he arrived in Kathmandu, the advance party of a winter expedition to Kangchenjunga was already there. Both Kukuczka and Wielicki were taking part, but were returning to Europe for a three week rest, whereas Artur Hajzer stayed in Nepal to help with the preparations for Kangchenjunga. At first the Kangchenjunga team seemed to Hajzer to be a sort of continuation of Lhotse given the overlap in personnel. In reality the dynamic of the Kangchenjunga team was rather different as it included star climbers from all parts of Poland, but did not the same cohesion as the Lhotse group. As well as Wielicki and Kukuczka, there was Andrzej Czok, who had climbed a new route on Everest and Makalu, Przemek Piasecki, Voytek Kurtyka and several other famous climbers. Hajzer knew that his own credentials were not up to the standards of many of the others and would inevitably limit his chances of having a crack at the summit. But he was happy to participate in the expedition which would be another important stage in his Himalayan apprenticeship. On Kangchenjunga they followed the "ordinary" first ascent route, which in summer is a technically fairly straightforward climb, although still a significant challenge given the height of the mountain. But in the winter the severe cold made things far more difficult. Kukuczka and Wielicki, the two strongest performers at altitude, formed the summit team. On the upper slopes they found traces of old fixed ropes in places and so they left their rope behind and climbed independently using the old ropes as handrails. In the upper section Wielicki passed Kukuczka and arrived on top half an hour before him. Strangely there was no contact between the two on the summit. Having waited half an hour for his comrade, Wielicki actually set off down just before he arrived. Both men commented that one of the effects of severe oxygen deprivation is this type of insularity.

When they got back down to their camp and radioed Base Camp to report the success, the congratulations were very muted. Listening to the radio conversation between Camp III and Base they realised with horror that a tragedy was unfolding. Andrej Czok, Kukuczka's old partner from Lhotse, Everest and Dhaulagiri who had been climbing with Przemek Piasecki, was seriously ill. Czok had not seemed to be acclimatising well and reached Camp IV a couple of hours later than the others, very tired and coughing badly. He and Piasecki had decided to return back down, whilst the others attempted the summit. Normally when losing height, the thicker air makes the strength of a climber suffering from altitude sickness return, but this didn't happen with Czok and he was only able to make it half way down to the camp unassisted. Piasecki went ahead to get help from Artur Hajzer and two other climbers to take up oxygen and bring down Czok. They were now seriously worried that he was developing pulmonary oedema and were in constant radio contact with the doctor at Base Camp. Kukuczka and Wielicki were told to stay put at Camp IV as Camp III was crowded with people getting involved in trying to save Czok. After another very cold night they learnt in the morning that Czok had died during the night. Przemek Piasecki had been in the tent with him and at 9 p.m. Czok had been feeling a bit better and Piasecki prepared another cup of tea for him, but when he passed it to him an hour later he saw that he was dead. Andrzej Machnik, the expedition leader, immediately called off the expedition. They thought about trying to carrying Czok's body down, but they realised this was going to simply be too difficult and instead buried him on the mountain. For Kukuczka it was a heavy moment to say goodbye to his first Himalayan partner, who he had shared so much with both on and off the mountains. Back in Poland there was some criticism of the actions of the two summit climbers, but the hardest moment of all for Kukuczka was going to see Czok's wife to pay his respects. He felt guilty to be the one alive and who had made it to the summit when her husband was left on the mountain.

The next summer Kukuczka had the chance to attempt a bold new route on the South Face of K2, which he had previously tried with Voytek Kurtyka. In the summer of 1986 many expeditions converged on K2 and attempted a variety of new routes as well as the standard Abruzzi Spur. There was a Polish team led by Janusz Mayer, which was attempting the much sought after South-East Ridge. Karl Herrligkoffer was running a semi-commercial expedition, which most participants had paid 12,000 Deutschmarks to join. He had also asked Kukuczka and another Polish climber Tadeus Piotrowski to participate, although of course they didn't have to pay. There were some sharp cultural differences between the Poles and the Swiss, German and Austrian members of the team, who were mainly professional mountain guides. When they first met up on the approach march, one of the Swiss guides introduced himself, saying "so you are this Kukuczka? You don't look much like a mountaineer", whilst looking pointedly at the Pole's somewhat expanded mid-riff. Kukuczka had put on some weight having been inactive in the period since Kangchenjunga whereas the Swiss guides spent their time running around the Alps and were all in great shape. The actual performance on K2 turned out to be quite a different matter. But there were differences in attitudes to danger too. Alpine guides spend a lot of time exposed to high mountain risks and their natural instinct is to try and minimise these. Climbing a route as dangerous as the South Face of K2 did not fit with this. Their reputation as guides would be helped considerably if they climbed K2 by any route and even participating in the expedition was going to look good on their CVs. This was Kukuczka's first expedition with foreign climbers and their attitude to money was eye opening for him. When they were trying to get their baggage through customs in Pakistan the Poles, who were used to preciously guarding foreign currency, were worried at extra expenses they were incurring and called Herrligkoffer for advice. They were very surprised when Herrligkoffer said that they should pay whatever they were asked, an attitude which was completely alien to the Poles. Herrligkoffer's expedition also didn't mind using fuel to heat hot water for washing and good quality food was plentiful – something appreciated but not essential to Kukuczka who had a reputation for having a good appetite whatever the quality of food.

Herrligkoffer's goals were ambitious, including the unclimbed South Face of K2 and a new route on Broad Peak. But most of the team members seemed to find these targets too ambitious and right from the outset there was one group only interested in climbing Broad Peak by its ordinary route. Kukuczka only managed to persuade three of the Swiss guides and one German to join him and Piotrowski on an initial exploration of the South Face. As they set off a gap soon opened up between the Poles and the others. When everyone had arrived at the proposed site of Camp I at 6000 metres, the Swiss told Kukuczka the route seemed far more dangerous than they had imagined. The ground was not very difficult technically, but tiring snow slopes which were threatened by the risk of avalanches and serac cliffs. Kukuczka tried to reassure them that they were over-estimating the difficulty because of lack of acclimatisation, but the next day the others turned back. Gradually more and more of the team became disillusioned with the dangers of trying to make a new route up the South Face. It seemed almost that climbers like Kukuczka had a lower sensibility to danger than their western European counterparts. Eventually the only solution was for Kukuczka and Piotrowski to attempt the South Face in alpine style and without oxygen. It is a measure of Jerzy Kukuczka's drive and ambition as a climber that he was not tempted to divert his attention to the normal route in order to bag what is probably the hardest 8000er. Messner himself had switched to the ordinary route on K2 seven years before, after a fairly brief exploration of the

South East Ridge. The Poles completed the route, one of the hardest and boldest ever on K2, but, as they descended the easier Abruzzi Ridge, Piotrowski lost one of his crampons and fell to his death. Close companions had been killed in each of Kukuczka's last three climbs and it seemed that he was pushing to a level of commitment that was just too much for those around him without his incredible endurance.

After these this climb the score in the 8000er race was 12-11 to Messner. Kukuczka hurriedly organised expeditions to the remaining three summits, Annapurna, Manaslu and Shisha Pangma. However in the space of three weeks in September and October Messner completed the full set of 8000ers and the race was over. On his final climbs he was accompanied by Hans Kammerlander a fellow German speaking Italian from the South Tyrol, who had become his regular partner in the last few years. First they made a lightweight ascent of Makalu, but its normal route. There were other expeditions operating on Makalu at the same time as Messner's group, including a team containing Krzysztof Wielicki, climbing with Marcel Ruedi from Switzerland. Ruedi had already climbed nine 8000 metre peaks, but had flown into Base Camp having arrived practically from sea level and was not properly acclimatised. Wielicki didn't feel fully acclimatised either, but he had taken the drug Diamox, which was becoming widely used to aid acclimatisation, for the first time. From a bivouac at 7800 metres, they went for the summit, unroped and climbing separately. Wielicki soon pulled far ahead of Ruedi even though he was breaking the trail and arrived at the summit long before him. Since it was starting to get dark he decided not to wait for the Swiss, who he passed some way below the summit and still going up. Wielicki gave him his thermos and wished him luck before continuing his descent. By the time he got to the tent he was exhausted and had lost feeling in his legs. Initially he was not too worried about Ruedi as it was a fine moonlit night and his tracks in the snow gave a clear path to follow, but he never returned. Wielicki was himself done in and could not return above 8000 metres to search for his companion and had to carry on down for his own safety. The bond between climbing partners was very different on an 8000 metre peak than it would be in the Tatras or the Alps, where there is an implicit understanding that climbers will stick together whatever happens. In the very high mountains it is understood that each person needs to be fully self-reliant and not expect others to extricate themselves from problems. Ruedi knew this when he had decided to press on despite the late hour and he had paid a terrible price for going too high too quickly.

Meanwhile Messner, now only missing one peak and still full acclimatised, moved to the nearby Lhotse – there was somehow a symmetry that Kukuczka's first 8000er would be Messner's last. Messner and Kammerlander had originally had an ambitious plan to traverse two high cols to go from one Base Camp to the other, but were tired following Makalu and needed to rest and regain some of the lost weight. Messner even talks about a need to declimatise by thinning out the blood at a lower altitude – the reverse of the normal process. So they took a helicopter to Lukla, from where they walked back up to Everest Base Camp. This was Messner's third attempt on Lhotse. As well as his the 1975 Italian South Face expedition, he had also tried in 1980 with just the Sherpa Dati, who in the end declined to make the attempt for religious reasons. Messner tried the ordinary route alone, but turned back. In 1986, he was with another South Tyrolean, Friedl Mutschlechner, and Hans Kammerlander. Messner's team paid a fee to be able to use the route prepared by a Swiss Everest Expedition. This allowed them, already full acclimatised, to rapidly reach a half ruined Swiss camp, at the foot of the summit couloir. Mutschlechner had bad toothache and had to turn back, but the other two continued. They found good snow conditions in the first part of the couloir, but in the narrow section the snow was knee deep, making progress difficult. In the upper part they were helped by the strange wind tunnel effect which others had noted - the wind blowing them up the mountain so strongly that sometimes they only had to lift their feet to be carried forward. The storm was so furious that Messner would have normally turned back, but the release from the quest to climb the 8000ers seemed so near and his team with Kammerlander so fully in tune that they went on. Only in the gap between the two horns of Lhotse did they hesitate, smelling danger, but the summit was so close that they continued. Being blown off their feet in the couloir was not too serious, but the on the very exposed final section they had to cling to their axes to stay on the mountain. Conditions were so extreme they were not even able to get their cameras out. For Messner, the sixteen year quest on the 8000ers was over, but on the summit his overriding desire was to get down to the safety of flat ground, to friends, to home. Up there, wrote Messner, there is not only too little air, but also too little human warmth, too little love. On the summit he stooped over like an invalid staring at the snow at his feet, then shut his eyes and doubled up even more. When he opened them again he could see spindrift snow being hurled vertically into the air – behind it the sky looked almost black. The summit which he called "hell intensified" and the descent was too difficult and dangerous for there to be any joy. When he got back down through the icefall to safe ground, he felt more than anything a sense of release. The chapter in his book on the 8000ers about Lhotse is called "climbed to be free", recognising that Messner had become a prisoner of his own ambition. He still loved the mountains, but now he wanted to be able to enjoy being in them without battling for his life in the death zone.

It is sometimes said that Messner was nothing more than a high altitude peak bagger in last years of the race to climb all the 8000ers. It is true that he focused on climbing the ordinary routes, but he always climbed in good style with lightweight expeditions, he never used oxygen and made first ascents of a number of important new routes. Furthermore he went back and climbed a number of 8000ers a second time, showing that he wasn't merely trying to tick off the list. In the second half of his Himalayan career Messner was more interested in new exploits than climbing the very hardest routes. This included the first ascent of Everest without oxygen, the first solo ascent of an 8000 metre peak, the first solo of Everest and the first traverse of two 8000m peaks (Gasherbrum 1 and 2) in a single push.

Kukuczka had not given up his quest to climb all the 8000ers himself and to do it in his defined style – all new routes or first winter ascents. Whilst Messner was on Lhotse, Kukuczka went to Manaslu and had a permit for Annapurna in the winter, which would leave only Shisha Pangma to complete the 8000ers. He organised the expedition with Artur Hajzer and they had the usual struggles to raise the required cash. Also on the team was Voytek Kurtyka, Kukuczka's old regular partner who had agreed to revisit their old collaboration, Ryszard Warecki and, the Mexicans Carlos Carsolio and Elsa Avila. Carsolio had started climbing on the volcanoes of his home country, introduced to the sport by his mother, and by his early 20s was climbing hard routes in both North and South America. His big break in the Himalayas came in 1985 when he was on the Polish expedition to Nanga Parbat with Kukuczka and made it to the summit. Elsa Avila was also a Mexican and had been on Nanga Parbat. At Manaslu Base Camp they listened to the Nepalese radio broadcast at 9am one morning. Mainly they were interested in the weather forecast, but they left the radio on to hear the news. Like that they heard that Messner had climbed Lhotse and completed the set of 8000 metre peaks. Both Carsolio and Hajzer watched Kukuczka with some trepidation, anxious to see how he would take the news that the epic race was over. There was a moment of silence, eventually broken by Hajzer who said "So? There's no need for us to hurry anymore! We can take this mountain slowly!"

Their goal on Manaslu was the first ascent of the East Ridge which leads to the unclimbed East Summit of Manaslu, only 100 metres less than the magic 8000 line. Reaching the ridge proved problematic due to large quantities of unconsolidated snow. After a first attempt Kurtyka declared that it was too dangerous and quit. They also had a problem of a lack of supplies, having had two barrels of flour and rice stolen at the start of the expedition and being very short of hard currency. Kukuczka sent one of the porters off to see what he could find in the nearest village and he returned triumphant with not only potatoes, but also eggs and even a smuggled bottle of Chinese vodka. On their next attempt, Hajzer and Kukuczka reached 7000 metres where they made a precarious bivouac, but realised they were still too far from the summit. After more than 50 days on the mountain, Kukuczka proposed abandoning the East Ridge and traversing onto the normal route to finish the up that, but after reaching the normal route they were hit by such a ferocious storm that they could not get the tent up and had to pass the night with it wrapped round them. After another retreat, the temptation to give up was strong, but Kukuczka couldn't resist one last try and Carsolio and Hajzer were still keen. They switched to another unclimbed route, the North East face. After four days climbing they made the first ascent of the East Summit and camped on the col between this and the main summit. The next morning the wind was blowing terribly, but Kukuczka felt the main summit was close and persuaded Hajzer to join him. Carsolio was frostbitten and unwell and stayed in the tent. Fighting with the terrible cold, the two Poles made it to the summit, before battling down with the sick Carsolio.

They still had the permit for Annapurna, but Kukuczka had more or less abandoned the idea as the Manaslu expedition had dragged out much longer than expected. So they started organising a winter expedition to the mountain instead. Hajzer was supposed to be completing his studies at the University of Silesia, but was easily persuaded to defer these to participate. They wanted to make the first winter ascent of Annapurna following the original French route on the North Face, which in winter is almost continual shadow, creating an inescable bitter cold which dominated their thoughts all the time on the mountain. With finance again a problem, Kukuczka invited Wanda Rutkiewicz who could bring funding from a film she was making for Austrian TV. Warecki and Krzysztof Wielicki were also taking part. The others were not convinced that Rutkiewicz was ready for such a serious climb, but Kukuczka said he would partner her on the mountain. Since time was running short they started climbing even before Base Camp was properly established. Still well acclimatised from Manaslu, they were able to set up Camp III at 6050 metres within 3 days. Wielicki, Hajzer, Kukuczka and Rutkiewicz then went up to establish Camp IV and then return down to Base Camp before a final push for the summit. Progress up the mountain was slowed by glass like ice which was so hard that their crampons would barely dig in. They were due to go back down to rest, but Kukuczka was still feeling in very good shape and well acclimatised after Manaslu and wondered whether he could make a rapid dash for the summit. When he proposed this, Hajzer who was also well acclimatised, said he wanted to come. Wielicki could probably have made it too, but he was not as well acclimatised as the others and the recent experience with Marcel Ruedi on Makalu was perhaps preying on his mind. He was also worried leaving Rutkiewicz to descend of her own and so he said he'd go back down with her. The next day Kukuczka and Hajzer moved up to 7500 metres, but the weather was bad and they rested for a day. Once the wind was less strong, they set off, but in poor visibility they had route finding problems and difficulty crossing couloirs of hard ice. They reached the summit with only an hour of daylight remaining and headed straight back down. Soon the night fell and by the light of their headtorches they had trouble locating their tent. Finally they stepped on it by pure luck, completely covered in snow. During their summit push half a metre of new snow had fallen lower down and the descent was extremely perilous due to the risk of avalanches. Afterwards Wielicki and Rutkiewicz made another attempt, but Rutkiewicz fell ill and Wielicki did the honourable thing and accompanied his female companion down. Kukuczka felt bad about Wielicki missing out on the summit, but latter seemed to bear him no grudges. With the ascent of Annapurna, Kukuczka had reached 13 8000m peaks. Although Messner had beaten him to the "Himalayan Crown", Kukuczka was now approaching the target himself only months behind the Italian.

Chapter 8 – So Close

Two years after their 1985 attempt, the Poles returned to try and finish what they had started. For many of the 1985 team, this Face had become an obsession, which they felt was "theirs". After hard months of effort exposed to risk of storms, avalanche and stonefall, they had found a viable way to the top which now needed to be completed. Vincent Fine and Michel Fauquet were also still dreaming of the South Face and also had a permit to return in 1987, but Fine was injured and so they had to cancel the expedition. Sadly Fine would lose his life on the Walker Spur the next year and so never got the chance himself to further such a promising career as a Himalayan climber. He had the potential to be one of the greats, but is also remembered fondly as a person. Bernard Vaucher wrote in his history of climbing in the Verdon Gorge, "Les Fous du Verdon" that no-one had left such a mark in the collective memory of Marseille climbers. He described him as bright, warm and humble despite his immense talent. He was a "child of the stars", a sort of Peter Pan for whom the enchanted world was the mountains, with an alpine spirit worthy of Hermann Buhl, but also with honesty, charisma and generosity that those who met him couldn't forget.

The 1987 expedition was led by Krzysztof Wielicki who, though not as well known internationally as Kukuczka or Wanda Rutkiewicz, was starting to build a track record in the Himalayas which few if any could better. Marco Bianchi, an Italian who later climbed a number of 8000ers with Wielicki, described him as having a body only found once in every two billion people. Maybe this is an exaggeration, but he certainly has an exceptional physique for high altitude climbing. Bianchi also talks about his character: nervous, tough and unwilling to compromise – perhaps all characteristics which helped make him such a formidable Himalayan mountaineer. He also seemed able to face great risks with extreme calmness. Once Bianchi and Wielicki were descending a dangerous crevasse field at 6500 metres on Gasherbrum in thick white mist with visibility only a metre and Wielicki seemed to be positively enjoying himself swinging his arm like a windmill and shouting "milk, milk". Unlike Kukuczka, Wielicki wasn't involved in the race to bag all of the 8000 metre peaks, but he eventually became only the 5th man to achieve this feat. After his first winter ascent of Everest in 1980, it was more than four years before he climbed another 8000er. Wielicki has an infectious enthusiasm for life. When I met him in researching this book, he switched into Italian, which he learnt whilst working at Polski Fiat, at high speed when he found I spoke the language. And when I accidentally left my laptop behind, he chased me at high speed through the streets of Katowice, flashing his lights, to bring it back to me.

Following the 1985 expedition, Artur Hajzer and Wielicki spent many long evenings going over the causes of their failure and analysing what they should change in planning for 1987. They recognised that too much time had been spent securing the lower part of the wall. On the other hand they had not fixed ropes across the easier section of the Cauldron and it was from here that Rafal Cholda fell to his death. They realised that it would be safer to have ropes fixed to facilitate load carrying and descent across these slopes. This time they brought more rope – over 6 kilometres of it - purchased in Britain with hard earned foreign currency. Wielicki also felt that the failure in 1985 had been due to a lack of manpower at the critical time and he expanded the size of the expedition. There were not enough climbers from Silesia with the right experience available to come so they also added climbers from Zakopane, the most important resort in the Tatra Mountains. As well as the Poles, they also invited the Italian climbers Alois Brugger and Kurt Walde from the South Tyrol, the home of Reinhold Messner. The Poles increasingly involved foreign climbers in their expeditions, in part to have members who could more easily contribute hard currency to the expedition funds, but also because there was a trend away from hierarchically organised expeditions to looser confederations of friends who came together to organise a trip to a common goal. Chance meetings at the Base Camp and plans brainstormed in mess tents on one expedition could be the genesis of another.

The most difficult issue was whether Kukuczka should be part of the team. Wielicki was opposed to his inclusion, whilst Hajzer, who had made several fine first ascents with him in recent years, was in favour. There were some sharp discussions between them and sometimes Kukuczka was involved too. They even brought in Janusz Majer, the 1985 leader and a conciliatory character, to try and resolve the conflict. Malicious observers felt that Wielicki was afraid that if the expedition was a success, Kukuczka would get all the credit as the famous star. A more balanced explanation, and one that Hajzer had some sympathy with, was that Kukuczka hoped to complete his full set of 8000ers with an ascent of Shisha Pangma immediately before coming to Lhotse. If he succeeded he would not be focused on another climb as serious as Lhotse's South Face immediately afterwards.

There was scope for rivalry between these two great stars of Polish mountaineering. There had been parallels between their careers since 1980, when they had each climbed Everest on Andrzej Zawada's two expeditions that year. Kukuczka made the new route on the South Pillar, but Wielicki had done better than that with the first winter ascent of Everest. In the early 1980s Kukuczka formed his great partnership with Voytek Kurtyka and climbed some fantastic routes, particularly in the Karakoram in Pakistan. In 1984, both Wielicki and Kukuczka were part of a Polish expedition to Broad Peak which included many of the future Lhotse South Face team such as Janusz Mayer, Ryszard Pawlowski and Walenty Fiut as well as Kurtyka. Their original plan was to attempt the unclimbed South Face, but after inspecting this route they decided it was too difficult and dangerous to justify an attempt. Some of the team were happy to climb Broad Peak in alpine style, but Kukuczka, Kurtyka and Wielicki were hungry for something more. The Kukuczka-Kurtyka partnership had planned a very ambitious traverse of two subsidiary peaks to make a major new route on the mountain. It was clear that Wielicki would have liked to join them, but Kurtyka felt that a two man team was better for such a committing route. Instead they tried to interest Wielicki in the idea of making a one day solo ascent of the ordinary route on Broad Peak. Something like this had never been done before, but they knew Wielicki had the physique and the determination to pull off. He left Base Camp just after midnight on a splendid night with a full moon so bright that he didn't need to switch on his head torch. It was very cold and he felt himself freezing even though he was moving very fast. Massaging his feet didn't help and he had to stop at Camp II and wait for the warmth of the daylight. He set off again determined to make up the lost time and reached the tracks of Fiut, Pawlowski and Mayer who were above, going for the summit too. The tracks made things easier and he met the others just below the summit on their way back down. Wielicki himself reached the summit shortly afterwards at 4pm and by 10.30 pm was back in Base Camp after the first ever one day ascent of an 8000er.

In fact the Kukuczka-Kurtyka partnership reached its end not long after their traverse of Broad Peak. Kurtyka wasn't interested in his partner's race for the 8000 metre peaks. Throughout his Himalayan career, Kurtyka fell in love with particular mountains and routes and became obsessed with these. He had too artistic a vision of mountaineering to want to do something as crude as peak bagging, even on the highest mountains in the World. Wielicki and Kukuczka were never a regular partnership, although they went on several expeditions together. The only time they reached the summit of an 8000 metre peak together was the winter ascent of Kangchenjunga. In the end Kukuczka was included on the list of participants, but both he and Hajzer were scheduled to go on an expedition to Shisha Pangma at the same time. Although it was his last remaining 8000 metre and one of the easier peaks, Kukuczka didn't intended to rush up and tag the summit. Instead he took a diverse group with a variety of goals. Kukuczka himself had his eye on both a new route and a ski descent.

Meanwhile the Lhotse team arrived at Base camp in early September. For those, like Wielicki, Fiut and Falco-Dasal who had been in the 1985 team it was strange and yet familiar to be back in exactly the same place. As was normal for the end of the monsoon season, it was raining, but not too hard. They went through the usual ritual of collective work on a stone structure for the team's dining area. There was no big speech from the leader Wielicki to announce the arrival. He just told them they were professionals and knew the job they had to do.

As in 1985 they followed the Czechoslovak Pillar, dividing into two groups to equip the route: one consisting of Maciej Pawlowski and Andrzej Osika, the other of Miroslaw Falco-Dasal, Piotr Konopka and Alois Brugger. The latter team got up at 4.30 am on the first day to start work. Brugger looked outside the tent and declared that the sky wasn't blue, but at least it wasn't raining, so they prepared themselves and set to work. Crossing the glacier Falco-Dasal started to recognise bits of the route from two years before, a descent followed by two large rocks and so on. Konopka looked at his watch – it had taken them 40 minutes, not a bad time for the first day. At the end of the glacier they left their walking poles, put on their harnesses and got out their ice axes and ascended one the vast avalanche cones at the foot of the Face. Brugger took the lead at first, ploughing through thigh deep snow to reach the foot of the rocks. Unlike two years before, they had no difficulty locating the start of the route. For Falco-Dasal each piton, each rock step was familiar, as if he'd never been away. He knew that round this corner in the rock there would be a chimney and at the top of the chimney there would be a ledge with a good piton and so on. Having all this imprinted in his memory of course made progress quicker.

They camped at the site of what had been their interim Camp I in 1985, with the idea of reaching and established the true Camp I the following day. They called Base Camp to report progress and then set to preparing the evening meal of powdered fruit juice, biscuits with meat paste, followed by more fruit juice, then soup with canned meat, more fruit juice and biscuits with jam and finally more fruit juice. Their goal was to try and consume five litres of liquid per day to help acclimatise as quickly as possible and minimise the risk of acute mountain sickness. The long cooking process over, they were dozing in their sleeping bags at midnight when the noise of a huge avalanche woke them with in terror. They had believed that the camp site was quite safe, but they saw with horror that snow was pressing against the side of the tent and the poles were bending. Snow was being forced through a space where the tent door was open. Falco-Dasal threw himself against the wall of the tent to try and keep it up and prevent the poles breaking, whilst Brugger supported the ridge of the tent and Konopka tried to close the zip to stop snow coming in. The pressure did not diminish and they felt the tent shift, the ropes attaching it to the mountainside becoming taught. They wished they'd paid more attention to the strength of the anchors when placing them. Slowly the pressure started to ease and the roar of the avalanche dimmed. They realised they had just been caught in the side blast. If they had been hit directly by an avalanche of that strength, they would not have lived to tell the tale. They cleared the tent of snow and tried to bend the poles back into shape, but one was broken. Then they tried to get back to sleep since there was still a lot of work to do the next day despite their close shave.

They made some progress before going down as the tail end of the monsoon meant the weather was still variable with rain and snow. A few days later Falco-Dasal and Konopka were back up at Camp I preparing for another day's climbing. Looking down before departing, they saw two small figures approaching the foot of the face. Just then they felt a violent gust of air in the couloir to their right and saw a huge avalanche sliding down towards the climbers below. Like in a silent film they saw them stop and then desperately running in vain to escape the path of the avalanche before being engulfed in a huge white cloud. The cloud took minutes to clear and those above watched in suspense trying to fix in their minds the place where Wielicki and Walde had been. After an agonising wait the snow cleared and they saw with relief that the 2 dots were still there and moving normally. After this scare Falco-Dasal and Konopka went back to work on the route, trying to see how much of the old fixed ropes and anchors could be re-used. They found most of the pitons still in place and some ladders useable, but after two years of weathering, falling stones and ice it was necessary to renew the ropes. They continued to work on the route despite rainy weather which would have confined them to Base Camp two years before. A combination of greater familiarity with the route and a determination to outperform what they had done before and make sure they could return to Poland with the route climbed drove them on. Fine weather finally returned on September the 14th. Whilst Pawlikowski and Osika set off to work on the face those at Base Camp enjoyed the sun, with Falco-Dasal opening a sort of barber's shop cutting hair and trimming beards. It was also a chance to have a proper wash for the first time since leaving the village of Namche Bazar. They also used time to make minor repairs to equipment and try to recover fitness.

On September the 15th Falco-Dasal and Konopka were asleep at Base Camp when at 4.00 am they heard the footsteps of three people leaving to work on the Face. It was not their turn that day, so they rolled over and went back to sleep, but before dawn they were disturbed by a strange humming sound and looked out to see snow dust everywhere. With horror they realised that a huge powder snow avalanche had swept the avalanche cones at the foot of the face hitting Brugger, Fiut and Jakiel. In panic they grabbed the binoculars and ran up the moraine above the tent to try and see if their companions were safe. They could only see two figures, one bent over the other and waving his hands. Where was the third? They could hear shouts for help in German. They threw on their clothes, grabbed a thermos of tea and tried to race across the glacier, although they weren't fully acclimatised and their hearts beat wildly at the effort. Falco-Dasal cursed as he realised he had forgotten to bring a shovel, before seeing with relief that there was a third figure on the glacier – so no-one was buried. But relief turned to horror when they got closer. Their doctor, Czeslaw Jakiel, was lying in a pool of blood, his head horribly crushed. They immediately saw that he was dead. Images of the times spent together with Jakiel flashed through Falco-Dasal's head with the horrible sense that it was all in the past. Although the route on the Face followed a protruding rib protected from most of the larger avalanches, the approach across the glacier had no such protection. Brugger had managed to jump into a crevasse and was unhurt, but shaken. Fiut had been struck by the avalanche and carried 150 metres down the slope. When they reached him he was vomiting, his pelvis was damaged and his knee badly twisted. The first thing he asked was about Cekiel. Falco-Dasal told him he was dead, but it wasn't the time to grieve because they had to get the Brugger and the injured Fiut away from the danger of being hit by another avalanche. Fiut was carried down to Base Camp.

This tragic accident underlined the risks of the Face. They usually crossed the exposed areas early in the morning when the risk was less, but when the Face became laden with snow, powder avalanches could come at any time. They radioed Kathmandu to send a helicopter to evacuate Fiut. Wielicki delegated leadership to Falco-Dasal so that he could accompany Fiut. Due to high winds it was two days before the helicopter managed to land and they had to go back and forth across the moraines to the landing place several times whilst it tried and failed to land. Then they turned to the sad task of burying Jakiel. They made a cross with bamboo sticks and wire, took some flowers and candles and looked for a suitable resting place for their comrade. They could not find any crevasse which seemed right and so decided to build a tomb from stones. Maciek Pawlikowski said a prayer and they all joined in. The words "our father who art in heaven" were familiar to them all, but they seemed unexpected and unwanted at this time, in this place. They placed his axe, the flowers and candles on the grave. It was a very subdued atmosphere in the mess tent – the absence of their missing friend heavily felt. For Falco-Dasal, however, it was clear that the expedition would go on - they all knew the risks they were running on Lhotse's South Face. He felt that this had nothing to do with heroism, coldness or insensitivity. Of course they all questioned the sense of what they were doing. On the one hand they knew that mountaineering itself was an irrational activity, particularly in such a savage and dangerous environment. On the other, the sense of being a team to undertake this super-human goal now made them want to achieve something. The death of their friend was of course a terrible price and objectively no mountain could be worth it, but the price was even more pointless if paid for nothing.

The remaining team was pretty small consisting of four Polish climbers – Falco-Dasal, Konopka, Pawlikowski and Osika and the two Italians Brugger and Walde. The Italians seemed to have lost their enthusiasm for the climb, but Falco-Dasal felt that, since the decision had been taken to continue the expedition, they must now restart work on the mountain. If they didn't, then morale would only get worse and expedition's chances would disappear as the autumn drew on.

Ironically, in the days following the accident the weather had been perfect. Three days after the avalanche, Falco-Dasal and Konopka returned to the Face, crossing the glacier very early in the morning and passing the crevasse in which Brugger had managed to shelter. Falco-Dasal felt confident that an avalanche wouldn't strike in the same place again as it was colder now and the snow was firmer. They still wanted to get across the exposed lower section as quickly as possible and they pushed themselves hard to reach Camp I before the sun hit that part of the Face. They were going to carry on to Camp II, but there was no sense in rushing now that the sun was on the Face, so they relaxed and made drinks before moving on. This didn't make the climb up to Camp II any easier, with heavy rucksacks, soft snow and the sun beating down and parching their throats so that they could scarcely speak to each other. They had an unpleasant surprise to find that Camp II was completely flooded, with the sleeping mats floating in a pool of water. Fortunately they were carrying their sleeping bags. They had no choice but to mop up the water and dry out the tent. The grandeur of their situation one third of the way up the Face was in sharp contrast to the cleaning work. Finally the mopping up was finished and they could turn their attention to preparing drinks and dinner.

The weather held the next day and Konopka and Falco-Dasal continued to advance the route. Soon they reached a section where an overhanging snow-ice step barred the way. Armed with two modern ice climbing tools, a Grivel and a Barracuda, Falco-Dasal felt confident in his ability to tackle this step, but instead of hard snow or ice, he found sugary powder in which it was impossible to get a good grip for his ice tools. He felt his arms failing him so he backed down to where there was firmer ice and placed an ice screw for protection. After some rest for his aching arms which were threatening to refuse to obey his brain and hang on, he moved back up again. With the confidence of the protection from the ice screw, he went more quickly, taking small steps and trying to get as much purchase as possible with the ice tools. Pushing himself to the limit, with arms aching and suffering under the intense high altitude sun, Falco-Dasal overcame the bulge. Even then the position was still precarious and a fall could not be contemplated. Finally he managed to get an anchor in and Konopka came up to join him. As they went back down the fixed ropes to Camp II, they knew it had been a bold lead and a good day's work.

Brugger, shaken by the accident, announced that he was returning to Italy. The Poles were sorry to see him go as they had appreciated his sense of humour and his mountain instinct. He wanted to draw back from extreme mountaineering for a while and return to the South Tyrol where he was planning to get married and maybe start a family. Despite only having two pairs of climbers active on the mountain, the Poles continued to advance the route ahead of schedule compared to 1985. Osika and Pawlowski established Camp III at 6600 metres on September 20th and a week later the same pair set up Camp IV at 7100 metres. After 10 days away, Wielicki returned to Base Camp from Kathmandu. He reported that Fiut had had treatment on his fractured hip in in Kathmandu, but had been flown back to Poland for care on the more serious knee injury. Having the leader back helped momentum on the mountain, but the threat from avalanches remained. The day after Wielicki's return, Walde and Falco-Dasal were relaxing in Base Camp, the former sat in the grass studying the Face with binoculars when suddenly he shouted "Herr Gott". Falco-Dasal looked up in alarm to see a huge wall of snow peeling off the slope above Camp IV where Pawlowski and Osika were staying. They saw it first as it covered the camp before a hellish roar reached them. Snow dust covered the whole route and they strained to see through the white veil for signs of their friends. Then they saw first one and then another black dot moving near the tents. Falco-Dasal and Walde breathed a sigh of relief, their throats dry with the tension, wondered how long they could stand this fear of avalanches hanging over them. The atmosphere at Base Camp was nervous and they looked at the reaction of expedition leader Wielicki. He said nothing and paced up and down on the moraines above Base Camp. At one point that Walde started to pack his things to leave, but then he changed his mind and returned to his tent.

They had acquired a new doctor, Steve Boyer, an American who had been on an expedition to Everest and had suffered pulmonary oedema at 7500 metres. He had gone down to recover in the Sherpa village of Periche and when he heard about the tragedy which had happened on the Lhotse expedition, he walked up to their Base Camp and asked if they needed help. After consulting with Wielicki, who was up on the Face, the Poles said they were very happy for him to join them, although they could not pay him anything. He was especially useful since he was not only a qualified doctor, but also a strong climber who later went on to climb the Bonington route on the South Face of Annapurna. He had also been on K2 the year before and had met Janusz Mayer's Polish team there. Uncertain about returning high again so soon after his illness, Boyer remained in Base Camp, but it was still a fascinating experience for him to get to know this group of climbers, who impressed him with their determination and good humour. He reviewed their medical supplies and what they were taking to the upper camps and generally agreed with what they had packed, although a few items were in short supply. Boyer found that the Poles were not only hard workers, but appeared relaxed and to be enjoying the expedition. It interested him that they both despised and laughed at the Communist system, which was forced on their homeland and found climbing an escape from this. He particularly liked Wielicki and said he had never met anyone who loves life as much as him. Boyer's favourite photo of the expedition shows Wielicki juggling snowballs in his long johns, happy despite a period of snowfall which had buried Base Camp in a metre of snow.

On the 7th October Artur Hajzer, Carlos Carsolio, Elsa Avila and Alan Hinkes arrived having completed their expedition on Shisha Pangma. They brought the news that Jerzy Kukuczka had summited Shisha Pangma with Hajzer and so finally become the second person to complete the full set of 14 8000 metre peaks. After a period spent waiting for the weather to be settled, Hajzer and Kukuczka had made an alpine style first ascent of the West Ridge, the hardest on the mountain. The climb went smoothly without any real problems despite some technical sections. It reminded them of the Eagle's Ridge, a climb in the Polish Tatra, only displaced to between 7000 and 8000 metres. Near the summit they met several other members of their team who had come up the ordinary route including Carsolio, Rutkiewicz, Rysiek Warecki and Avila. Shisha Pangma has two summits which are very close in height. The nearer one is much easier to reach, but has been measured to be slightly lower. An Austrian commercial expedition, that reached the nearer summit at the same time as the Poles, turned back, feeling they had bagged the peak. But given the significance of completing the 8000ers, Kukuczka's group felt they had to make the three hour crossing of the narrow undulating ridge to the main summit. Kukuczka completed the last section on skis which his friends had brought up the ordinary route for him. When he arrived he felt a joy and elation that he had rarely experienced before on a summit. He then skied down. Not surprisingly, he returned straight back to Poland to great acclaim, but the other four new members, were fit and keen for Lhotse.

The new team members were warmly greeted – the extra manpower was badly needed after the death of Jakiel and the departures of Brugger and Fiut. Having new faces around Base Camp was also good for morale: Hajzer regaled them with stories of the Shisha Pangma expedition, including about Rutkiewicz, who they called Aunty Wanda. The Poles seemed to treat her as something of a comic figure, but Boyer saw that Hinkes appreciated she was also somewhat tragic, unhappy in her personal life despite all her climbing successes. All the same it was clear she had annoyed or disappointed most of the Shisha Pangma expedition, who found it hard to bear her ambition. Generally the atmosphere was more relaxed, although they could not forget Pawlowski and Osika who were still on their way down from the mountain. But team unity was not guaranteed – the newcomers had all been to the summit of Shisha Pangma recently, were well acclimatised and would be in a position to take advantage of the hard work put in by the others to prepare the route.

Carlos Carsolio and Artur Hajzer went up to fix ropes across the second part of the Cauldron and established Camp VI. Hajzer was familiar with this terrain from two years before: the route was the same, the camps with the same type of orange tents placed on the same platforms. It almost like he had travelled two years back in time. But the grandeur of the Wall – and its difficulty and danger - had not diminished with familiarity. In mid-October the weather broke across the whole Himalayan chain. The climbers were still high on the mountain, and had been hoping that the typical break in the weather often seen in October wouldn't come this year. The monsoon had been so long and heavy, that they somehow hoped all the snow had already fallen. But it wasn't to be and on the morning of October 17th cirrus clouds covered the sky, there was a strong wind and some flakes of snow. Despite this Falco-Dasal and Konopka prepared to set off from Camp IV as planned, to carry loads up to Camp V. They took rope, some anchors, personal equipment, warm clothes and cameras. As always when load carrying, it amounted to a painfully heavy weight. When Falco-Dasal and Konopka arrived at Camp V they weren't impressed with the scene which greeted them. The camp was a mess with sleeping bags thrown in the corner and no karrimats – meaning they'd have to sleep on the cold ground. Furthermore there was nothing to eat and no gas canisters to boil water. Falco-Dasal cursed their luck as they had left behind the burner and some spare canisters back in Camp V. They were supposed to drink five litres a day and now they would go hungry and thirsty, but they had no choice but to wait for the morning radio call.

In the morning the weather was worse – very cold, a gale blowing and heavy snow. On the radio call the climbers in the high camps discussed what to do.

They were all in agreement it would be suicide to try and work on the mountain in these conditions, but they debated whether it was worth staying high on the Face using up supplies and being worn down by the effects of altitude. But if the weather improved quickly they'd be in a position to take advantage if they stayed up. Wielicki was a modern style of leader rather than someone like Kunaver or Cassin who directed his team from below and he gave the climbers the individual choice of whether to stay up or go down. Konopka and Falco-Dasal, who had come back to Camp V with supplies, hesitated. They had everything they needed to sit out the storm if they wanted to, but Falco-Dasal remembered how two metres of fresh snow had blocked people on the Face for days with avalanches roaring around them during the 1985 expedition. He decided to head down and eventually Konopka followed him down. A few hours later Falco-Dasal was sat on a stone at the foot of the face drinking a beer which he and Konopka had deposited there when heading up a few days before. Released from the stress of days spent attached to fix ropes, running the gauntlet of rock and ice fall and avalanches, the cool beer was beautifully thirst quenching on his dry throat. He looked up and saw Konopka descending the avalanche cone and crossing the final rocks to join him. They finished their beers and crossed the glacier to return to Base Camp where they found quite a crowd. As well as most of the team, there were also two visiting Scots and a Bulgarian journalist. As the snow fell outside, the mess tent was crowded with people and filled with multilingual conversations fuelled by tea mixed with alcohol.

In the end the whole team descended to Base Camp to wait out the storm. With continuous heavy snow even Base Camp was threatened by avalanches from the Face and had to be moved after three tents were buried. The days passed with books, conversation and chess, interspersed with excursions out into the storm to dig the tents free of snow. Falco-Dasal borrowed Doctor Zhivago from Konopka who had already finished it and passed time half lying, half sitting in his sleeping bag. Going out in the night to relief themselves was unpleasant in the continuous storm and they lay awake fighting a mental battle to suppress the demands of their bladders. After four days of snow, the sun finally warmed their tired bodies. Despite the storm, there were some important positives - Camp VI was stocked with food, rope and equipment and eight climbers were ready for the job of overcoming the Great Barrier. But with October getting on, the next push up the Face would probably represent the last chance for the summit before winter set in. There were long and sometimes heated discussions in Base Camp about the best way to manage this final assault. Wielicki suggested that Konopka and Falco-Dasal should move up first, but this brought a protest from the pair. They were tired, having done more work high up than anyone, and it didn't seem fair that they would be the ones to tire themselves digging out the camps and excavating the fixed ropes so that others could come through and attempt the summit. Falco-Dasal suggested Walde, Carsolio and Hinkes should go up first and the discussion dragged on. The fatigue and stress of two months on the expedition made people less flexible than usual. Finally they agreed a compromise: Carsolio and Hinkes would go and dig out the ropes up to Camp III and then come back down. Then all teams would go back up and try to finish the job. The next day Hinkes and Carsolio set off as planned.

The main attack began on October 23rd with four pairs of climbers heading up: first Pawlikowski and Osika, then Falco and Konopka, then Hajzer and Wielicki and finally the non-Polish pair of Carsolio and Hinkes. Four waves of climbers each placing fixed ropes for the next to go higher would surely be enough to crack the wall. This running order probably still left some discontentment about peoples roles in the assault, but Wielicki was determined to give the team the highest chance of completing the route and he knew that he himself had the best chance of succeeding and that Hajzer was the best placed to go with him. It seemed they had excess strength to climb the mountain, given the manpower available and how far they'd advanced the route already. In practice, things were not so easy. As they ascended they had to dig out the camps which were buried by snow from the storms. Falco-Dasal and Konopka were the first to try and push the route further up the Great Barrier. On 26th October they woke at 7am in Camp VI. It was cold and they took two hours to get ready. Once they started the sun was on them, but at this height it only gave a little warmth. By late morning the weather conditions had worsened and visibility was down to almost zero. With icicles hanging from their faces and the cold biting, they realised that they would fall far short of their goals and that battling on in this weather would be futile. They hung the equipment at the top of the fixed ropes for the next group and headed down to Camp V. On the way down they met Pawlikowski and Osika who were on coming up to take over the lead. Falco-Dasal could see in their eyes and movements that they were tired too. Both pairs felt that they were doing the hard work to prepare the route for others.

Falco-Dasal thought about asking Wielicki for a more leading role, but he knew that the latter would point to his greater experience of 12 Himalayan expeditions. He also wondered whether he had quite the level of single minded determination of Wielicki. He and Konopka spent the next day at Camp V resting and preparing drinks. During the morning Wielicki and Hajzer arrived, looking fit and confident. They stopped to rest and have drinks and then carried on up to Camp VI. Later Pawlikowski and Osika came on their way down from working on the route above Camp VI. They looked tired, icicles hung from Osika's beard, his eyes were sunken and his voice hoarse. Their experience had been much like that of Falco-Dasal and Konopka the day before, managing to advance the route only a little, hampered by snowfall, cold and wind. The pair in Camp V offered them tea to warm their cold hands and their parched lips. Osika and Pawlikowski knew that the expedition was over for them: they were heading down and the current summit assault would be the final one. They were all hoping for success, but the outcome was of course uncertain.

When Hajzer and Wielicki arrived at the top camp not much progress had yet been made on the Great Barrier. The situation, which only a few days before had looked so promising, had now become a last throw of the die. On the evening radio call Wielicki proposed that he and Hajzer should spend an extra day in front so that they could fix ropes on the Great Barrier, before attempting the summit the day after. It was clear at this point that Hajzer and Wielicki were stronger than the rest of the team. Falco-Dasal and Konopka were not fully happy with this decision, but they agreed to wait in support and maybe to make a second summit bid. On the morning of the 28th October Wielicki and Hajzer left Camp VI. It was very cold, maybe 25-30 ° C below zero, but the weather was not bad and they reached the base of the Great Barrier where the fixed ropes ended quickly. Wielicki took the lead up rocks taking a diagonal ramp further right than the route followed by Kukuczka and Holda two years before. He climbed slowly, but steadily made progress. It was difficult to find good protection and although he managed to place pitons every few metres none of them were very solid. The third pitch was most difficult and he had to remove his gloves to get a better grip on the rock. Hajzer assumed this must lead to frostbite, but Wielicki seemed to have an almost superhuman constitution. As Hajzer followed Wielicki's line he saw the remains of the equipment left by Kukuczka and Cholda two years earlier.

They were pleased with progress and decided to try for the summit the following day. They did not take camping equipment, but did take a stove given the importance of remaining hydrated at altitude. They reached the previous day's highpoint by 8.00 am. Now it was Hajzer's turn to take the lead. He climbed five hard 40 metre pitches of mixed terrain, the most difficult a vertical chimney of water ice interspersed with loose rocks. It was impossible to place protection because there were no cracks for pitons and the ice was too thin to take an ice screw, but Hajzer went for broke, completing a bolder lead than he had ever done before and even surprising Wielicki. They were now past the Great Barrier and on a small col below the final part of the Central Pillar, closer to the summit than anyone had yet been on this side of Lhotse. Seemingly they were past the steepest ground and the summit was in reach, but Lhotse wasn't going to play fair. No sooner had they reached the ridge and caught sight of the final slopes to the summit, than thick cloud moved in and a gale started to blow. It was still only 2 pm, but there was no question of continuing to the top in this weather. The heavily corniced final ridge would require good visibility and careful climbing, meaning that they were unlikely to be able to reach the summit and return to Camp VI that day.

They were at 8300 metres and, given the weather, it would have been prudent to descend to Camp VI for the night, but they hesitated. Returning to Camp VI would mean losing a few hundred metres of height and they were quite tired and had doubts whether they would have strength to return above 8000 metres for a third day running. With only 200 metres to go to the summit they decided to stop for the night. Without a tent they had to find shelter to survive the freezing windy night. After some searching, prodding with their axes in the snow, they found a place where they could dig a snowhole on the upper ridge and set to work. After three hours it was pitch dark, but they had managed to dig a hole large enough that they could sit inside, with their legs sticking out over the precipice. They weren't satisfied with this and carried on digging. At midnight by a combination of digging and building with ice blocks they had a shelter from the outside world. This allowed them to light the stove and start to warm the air a bit. Once they had a first cup of tea, they felt some strength returning and they huddled together to protect their feet from freezing. They did not sleep a wink all night and could hear the wind getting stronger and stronger. They knew that their chances of success were evaporating and to make matters worse, the powdery snow which they had used to build blocks for the shelter kept disintegrating in the wind, which was blowing columns of snow vertically up into the air. By the morning it was a hurricane and not only was there was no prospect of going up, but even getting down would be difficult in a raging storm. They had half hoped that on reaching the summit they would have been able to descend more easily via the Western Cwm, but of course that option was no longer available. They had fixed ropes up the lower part of the Barrier, but above they had run out of ropes to fix and so they had only their climbing rope. In those weather conditions it was too difficult to down climb, so they had to make one abseil attached only to an ice axe and some dangerous traverses to get back down.

Down at Camp V, Konopka and Falco-Dasal were waiting in support, hoping to make a summit bid themselves and anxious to hear news of their companions. When Wielicki and Hajzer didn't call in as scheduled at 7pm they were initially not too worried. The pair had not carried the radio above the camp and it could be a good sign that they had been gone for more time than expected: perhaps they had been able to reach the summit. But as the evening went on and what had started as a fairly moderate wind got stronger and stronger, they began to worry about the fate of their companions. Eventually the tent at Camp V was being shaken like "the crow's nest of a pirate ship in a storm" and they were so alarmed at the prospect of the tent being blown away that they put their harnesses on and attached to the fixed ropes outside. And still the wind got stronger and stronger, almost as if some malignant giant was kicking the tent. They shuddered to think of Wielicki and Hajzer up above facing the elements without a tent. Every hour until midnight they tried to call them on the radio, but each time there was silence. There was nothing they could do to help and no choice, but to wait until the morning and the little warmth which the sun might bring. Any thought of the summit was now forgotten – they were just interested in getting the team off the mountain in one piece. They decided it was anyway a good idea to move up to Camp VI and see if their companions needed support. Konopka had already clipped into the fixed ropes, whilst Falco-Dasal completed his preparations. Suddenly Konopka returned and shouted over the noise of the wind to say he'd seen a figure moving up at Camp VI. Then the radio came to life and Wielicki came on to say that they were alive and well. Their first question to him was "did you make it?"

"No we didn't" said Wielicki and went on to explain the drama of their night digging a snowhole, saying something about cuts and frostbite, but that basically they were safe. Now he and Hajzer were trying to warm up back in Camp VI. The supporting pair offered to come up and help Wielicki and Hajzer descend, but Wielicki told them it wasn't necessary and that Konopka and Falco-Dasal should get off the mountain and take as much equipment down with them as they could. Realising that their chances for the mountain were now gone, the support pair did as their leader asked and descended to organise the withdrawal of the expedition. Falco-Dasal was back down at Base Camp packing just before dark when a figure appeared staggering across the moraines at the foot of the Face. He stopped packing and went across to meet the climber who he recognised as Wielicki when he got closer. The leader threw his helmet down in anger smashing it in two on the rocks of the moraine and flung his ski-pole aside. He swore and asked »and shall we come back again?« Falco-Dasal did not answer and hugged his emanicated leader in silence. All that was left was to return to Katmandu, but even this wasn't easy as the Yaks who would take their equipment from Base Camp couldn't reach it due to the deep snow. Only a week later did they finally manage to get to Kathmandu.

The expedition had come closer than any so far to reaching the summit of Lhotse from the South, but the lead climbers had been forced to turn round when the weather turned bad high on the mountain. Knowing when to make that decision is a key quality to survive in an environment as dangerous as the high Himalayas. Krzysztof Wielicki was one of a rare breed of Himalayan climbers, like Doug Scott and Reinhold Messner who achieved a tremendous amount, participated in a huge number of expeditions and lived to tell the tale. This was partly due to exceptional physique and climbing skill, but also in part because when they found themselves in positions of high peril in the mountains, they knew when to pull their heads from the noose. This meant there was always another chance to return and try again. When the approach used by the Poles is judged against the strict criteria that Al Rouse set out for alpine style climbing a few years before, it could be argued that they were still climbing in traditional fixed rope style. This would be an unfair criticism because there had been notable developments in the approach since the early 1970s. The Poles were not using oxygen despite the fact they were operating on one of the higher 8000ers, spending significant time close to or above 8000 metres and climbing technically difficult ground. By contrast on Annapurna South Face in 1970, 500 metres lower than Lhotse – a significant difference at those heights – and with the main difficulties not right at the top of the route, the British had used oxygen extensively. Furthermore, the Poles did all the load carrying themselves rather than relying on Sherpa support. Both of these choices were driven by economic considerations as well as stylistic ones. People talk about climbing "ethics", but it is sometimes hard to see why the way in which a mountain is climbed is an ethical issue. The big expedition frustrations of load carrying and limited chances to reach the summit were still evident in the accounts of people like Miroslaw Falco-Dasal. Fine and Fauquet had made a credible attempt in a much more lightweight style, but in truth they had not got high enough to start tackling the principle difficulties of the Face, which lie above 8000 metres. The Poles had got higher than the Slovenians seven years before and had climbed in a lighter style, but like the Slovenians they had fallen short.

Chapter 9 – The Tower of Babel

Despite the two narrow misses, Krzysztof Wielicki wasn't beaten and in 1988 he started to organise yet another Polish expedition. Despite completing the 8000ers, Jerzy Kukuczka's appetite for the big peaks wasn't sated either and he mentioned discretely that he would be interested in participating, but there was a surprise in store for him. His old rival Reinhold Messner was organising an attempt on the Face in the spring of 1989 and Wielicki was invited together with a partner – and that partner was Artur Hajzer. Messner was putting together a very strong team and Kukuczka resigned himself to the fact that it was not his fate to be the first one to climb this great wall. Messner's expedition was a sort of super-group of Himalayan climbing bringing together leading climbers from several European countries. This provided a very strong set of climbers, but international expeditions had had a mixed record in the Himalayas with few proving great successes.

Historically the most infamous was the 1971 International Everest Expedition which was a gargantuan enterprise involving climbers from many countries including Germany, USA, UK France, Japan, Switzerland and India. There were ambitious goals including climbing both the West Ridge and the then unclimbed South West Face. Plans and objectives had evolved over time and got more and more complex and they even ended up with two leaders, the experienced Himalayan climber, Jimmy Roberts and Norman Dyhrenfurth, the first man to lead an attempt on Lhotse. In the end the expedition which had started as a small group of friends grew into one of the largest and most diverse teams ever to go to the Himalayas. Lacking a strong natural leader on the mountain, the co-leaders of the overall expedition settled for the compromise of having co-ordinators, Wolfgang Axt for the West Ridge and John Evans for the South West Face. This reflected the desire of Dyhrenfurth, to have a democratic spirit to the expedition, which was an admirable, but probably unrealistic goal. In the relaxed atmosphere of the walk in, climbers from different countries got to know each other and got on well despite some language barriers, helped by plenty of mutual acquaintances. The pre-expedition hype was that the team was so strong that success was almost certain and multiple climbers were likely to reach the summit. Once they started on the mountain things started to not look quite so straightforward. The icefall was in particularly difficult condition, although the climbers worked together well to make the route through it. Once in the Western Cwm they divided into two groups for the two routes. With a lot of equipment to bring up, it was decided that the load carrying burden should be taken by the climbing team as well as the Sherpas. Some of the climbers were not happy with this, perhaps wanting to save their energy for the upper part of the mountain and this shirking of responsibilities caused resentment to build up.

The West Ridge route involved a long traverse across steep snow towards the West Shoulder. After a day's work preparing part of this route the Austrian Wolfgang Axt and the Indian Harsh Bahuguna were descending the fixed ropes as a storm blew up. Axt was starting to lose feeling in his hands and feet and rushed ahead. As he moved out of sight of Bahuguna he saw that the Indian was moving slowly, but was clipped into the fixed roped and waved, seemingly to say that things were fine. By the time Axt reached Camp I the storm was raging and just as he arrived he heard screams of distress from above. Immediately, a rescue party of various climbers set off up through the blizzard. By the time they reached Bahaguna, he was in a bad way having lost a crampon and a glove, his face coated in ice and his clothes pulled up by his harness exposing his midriff to the elements. The rescuers tried to get him across the last steep traverse section, but fury of the wind prevented this. Then they tried to lower him down to the shelter of a crevasse below, but the rope wasn't long enough and he was left dangling 10 metres above the crevasse. It was dark, but Don Whillans managed to crampon across the steep ice to reach the Indian. Whillans realised that there was nothing they could do to save him, and the savagery of the storm meant the rescuers themselves were in grave danger if they did not go down. Bahaguna's death led to recriminations, with several climbers blaming Axt, which made his position as leader of the West Ridge team untenable. After the accident a 10 day period of bad weather set in, blocking many of the climbers on the mountain, with supplies dwindling and morale at rock bottom. Some of the West Ridge team argued that the route was no longer feasible and they should switch to the ordinary South East Ridge route. Dyhrenfurth accepted the decision of the West Ridge team to make switch, but privately he felt that some of them were only interested in the personal glory of reaching the summit and not of the team's goals. Several of the climbers were leading stars back at home, but they were also professionals whose livelihood depended on making noteworthy ascents. Climbing Everest even by the ordinary route would make many of them the first from their country to do so. This was a bigger lure than just contributing to the South West Face attempt.

When the storm ended it was hard to keep the supply chain going through the icefall and co-leader Jimmy Roberts concluded that it was necessary for the expedition to focus on a single goal – either the South East Ridge or the South West Face. The two leaders broadcast messages to all camps asking all the climbers and leading Sherpas to vote on the choice of route. Only the Italian Carlo Mauri and the French Pierre Mazeaud wanted to continue with the ridge, the majority feeling that the Face was a more worthwhile goal. The Swiss husband and wife team of Michel and Yvette Vaucher had not voted because they were descending the mountain, but they joined Mauri and Mazeaud in quitting the expedition, leading to bitter quarrels and accusations. The four climbers considered the decision to focus on the Face a conspiracy aimed at robbing them of the chance of getting to the summit and allowing the two British climbers, Whillans and Dougal Haston to get glory on the new route. Having climbed Annapurna South Face the year before, the British pair had the credentials for the climb and stubbornly stuck at it, placing a series of camps up the South West face, the highest at 8250 metres. But with the monsoon approaching and the hardest section passing the rock band still to overcome, the chances of success started to look thin. Whillans and Haston found a straightforward traverse onto the ordinary route, but they knew that by taking this they would be accused of hypocrisy and having prioritised the summit over the route. So they fixed ropes for another 100 metres up an icy gully in through the rock band. It proved to be a dead end and they were forced to admit defeat. They were accused of hogging the lead and the whole enterprise ended with recriminations as climbers went back home and gave their own versions of events to the climbing magazines. It seemed that international expeditions simply didn't work. It was better to have a tight knit group of climbers who knew each other well, are willing to make sacrifices for each other and have the same attitudes and language. Just putting a lot of star climbers in a team was not a recipe for success.

The lessons of 1971 suggested Messner's 1990 expedition might struggle to work as a coherent team, but there were reasons to think that Messner's expedition might be different. For the Western Europeans at least, the days of great national expeditions were past and climbers were more used to organising and leading their own expeditions, in which consensus decisions were made amongst equals rather than by an autocratic leader. Expeditions were much more frequent and the practice of the Himalayan countries of granting multiple permits to the same mountain meant that active Himalayan climbers came to know each from time spent at common Base Camp sites where plans were often formed for new expeditions in mess tents. Messner was the official leader, but he actually saw himself as more of catalyst to try and create the right chemistry between a team of talented climbers, who could put the strongest team in a position to reach the summit. In advanced publicity for the expedition, Messner said he believed that the accumulated experience of the 16 years of attempts on the Face, should allow them to succeed where others had failed and that he wanted to help the young climbers of Europe to resolve this great problem. Wielicki and Hajzer, of course had an excellent knowledge of the route. Another member was Messner's regular partner of the last few years, Hans Kammerlander.

Kammerlander came from the mountains of the South Tyrol, the youngest child in a family of six. His childhood home in Acereto was at 1500 metres and when he was young there wasn't even a road connecting it to the town of Campo Tures 700 metres below. Life was quite tough when Kammerlander was young – there was rarely meat on the table and the family had to fill up on vegetables from their garden as well as polenta, the staple of much of the Italian Alps. Kammerlander started climbing at the age of eight. At the time his family didn't have a television and he had never been to the cinema. That day he was on his way to the tiny village school when two climbers asked him directions for the Moostock, a 3000 metre peak which dominates the village. There was some difficulty in mutual comprehension because the climbers came from Germany whereas Kammerlander spoke a thick Tyrolian dialect, but he managed to give them directions. The climbers thanked him and continued on their way towards the mountain, but his detailed and rather confused explanations obviously weren't clear. As Kammerlander watched the climbers, he saw they were not heading in the right direction. He whistled to get their attention and then ran to catch them up and explain where they had gone wrong. After they set off again, the young Kammerlander decided to dump his school books behind a bush and follow them discretely. He knew he'd get in trouble for missing school, but seeing two genuine climbers was much more exciting than learning grammar. He knew the route well up to the limit of the pastures, because he was often had to watch over cattle grazing there, but the villagers didn't usually go higher. Cutting hay for animals was hard work and the locals tended to see going into the mountains as a necessity and mock those who climbed for fun.

But the young Kammerlander was fascinated by what these climbers were doing. He felt they were moving excessively slowly, judging their speed from the perspective of a boy with natural fitness from spending his time running around in the mountains. He reached the end of the known area, but his excitement and desire to explore drove me on and up, with his muscles aching from the effort. Before he knew it he was alone on the summit of the Moostock and a lifelong passion for the mountains had been born.

The dominant event of his childhood was the death of his mother when he was ten. It was a terrible loss for the young boy, but it also liberated him to spend a lot of his teenage years in the mountains. His elder sister took over managing the household, but couldn't dedicate time to watching over her young brother and his father was much more laid back than his mother who had always been anxious about her children's' safety. His elder brother was already working as a mountain guide and realised that Hans didn't understand mountain safety and was taking unreasonable risks. He took Hans to one side and told him he was playing with his life climbing without knowing the basics safety techniques. He got Hans signed up for a basic course run by mountain guides and Hans knew that this was how he wanted to spend his life. During the course his brother Alois gave Hans a present of a rope with a significant history – it had come from a friend who had been on an expedition to Aconcagua with Reinhold Messner, a legend in South Tyrolian climbing. A few years later Kammerlander was working for Messner's guiding school and in 1982 Messner invited him on an expedition to Cho Oyu, an 8000er in Nepal. Beaten back by terrible winds, they failed in their goal to climb the South East Face in winter, leaving Kammerlander terribly disappointed. But he had obviously done enough to impress Messner because the following year he was invited on another expedition to the same mountain. This time they were successful, climbing the mountain very rapidly by its South West Face.

The following year the pair made the first ever traverse of two 8000 metre peaks, Gasherbrum I and II. They first climbed Gasherbrum II and descended passing a section which was a funnel for a series of ice cliffs. In ascent it would have been like Russian roulette, but they were able to descend it quickly early in the morning and so spend only a short period in the most dangerous section. Messner had always felt at the limit of his strength when he had summited an 8000er, but this time both climbers felt they had significant reserves as they bivouacked between the two Gasherbrums. They then climbed Gasherbrum I by a new variant passing the place where Messner himself and Peter Habeler had bivouacked on their historic 1975 two man ascent. Only pausing, they pushed on to 7400 metres where a storm forced them to stop and pass a difficult night with the wind threatening to carry the tent away and both of them men suffering hallucinations. It would have been wiser to abandon the traverse, but having completed the first mountain, they weren't sure they would get another chance this good, so despite the stormy weather they pressed on and reached the summit of Gasherbrum I. In the end Kammerlander climbed seven 8000ers with Messner, forming the most productive partnership of the latter's career. Messner had made several great climbs with Peter Habeler including the first ascent of Everest without oxygen, but after the Everest climb the pair fell out when both of them wrote books. Previously Messner had always been the one to write the accounts of the climbs he had made, but time Habeler's book, written a German journalist was published first and the two climbers disagreed about some of the details of the events. They never climbed together again. Kammerlander accompanied Messner as he completed the 8000ers on Makalu and Lhotse. Messner retired from Himalayan climbing, but Kammerlander was 12 years younger and still ready for challenges like the South Face of Lhotse.

Messner also invited Enric Lucas, a Catalan climber who had climbed the South Face of Annapurna five years earlier, one of the finest alpine style climbs ever made in the Himalayas. Lucas and his partner Nil Bohigas followed a pure alpine style model, acclimatising on neighbouring lower peaks and not setting foot on the face until they were ready to climb it from top to bottom. This made for a more pure experience and also minimised exposure to stonefall which severely threatens the lower part of the route and had killed Briton Alex Macintyre on an attempt two years earlier. They took equipment for a single continuous ascent as in the Alps – two ropes for climbing and abseiling, a bivouac tent, climbing equipment and food and fuel for seven days. After acclimatising on smaller peaks and caching equipment at the foot of the wall, a first attempt was thwarted when they found that animals had raided their cache of food, but after a couple of days they tried again. Knowing that speed meant safety, they climbed the first section during the night, untied to move more quickly with the ropes in their rucksacks and reached 6700 metres by dawn. They still were exposed to rockfall for a further two hours during which time there was a regular "hail of death" of stones of all sizes, similar to that experienced by Fine and Fauquet on Lhotse. Finally they escaped the most dangerous area and started to traverse diagonally left. By the time they made a second bivouac at 7100 metres they had been climbing continuously for 20 hours. They now reached a steep rock band which stretched across the face making a barrier which had turned back MacIntyre and the Frenchman Rene Ghillini on their attempt. The Catalans first tried to climb a corner in which they could place pitons for protection. Lucas was hanging on by his axes to an ice sliver when this detached from the rock, resulting in a fall. He tried again, but this time a rock behind which he had placed a piton came away and he fell again. Bohigas tried and took yet another fall, but then managed to climb up a rock pillar with hard free and aid climbing. They now stopped again for the night, digging into the ice to make a platform, but only big enough for them to half sit and half hang into space.

The next day progress slowed as the altitude and the weight of their 25 kg sacks began to take its toll – alpine style climbing is sometimes called lightweight, but that certainly does not mean light packs. Sometimes they managed to fix good belays, but on other occasions they had to climb steep ground moving together making the risk of a fall very serious. For the whole of the fourth day they traversed leftwards underneath a granite rock band, searching for a way to break through onto the upper part of the Face. Eventually this took them onto the line of the Polish Spur and known ground, and they made another bivouac. They radioed their friends down "on earth" at Base Camp and the contact helped them to forget momentarily their desperate isolation on that huge Face. After another night of little sleep, they continued up the Polish Spur with difficult technical climbing on excellent granite. At their next bivouac at 7800 metres they knew the summit was close and so left all their equipment except cameras to climb up to one of the three 8000 metre summits of Annapurna, although they judged the main summit was too far away to reach. It was a huge release after the tension of the climb and they returned to sleep at their last bivouac. Rather than climbing back down as usual on an 8000 metre peak, Lucas and Bohigas planned to abseil all the way to the foot of the Face. They had carried a second rope and plenty of anchors up, but since on each abseil they had to leave the anchors behind, their stock gradually diminished until they had to make the last abseil off only one piton. At the bottom they staggered across the glacier to Base Camp arriving at midnight having made one of the finest alpine style climbs ever. The experience on the Face seemed almost unreal once they were down, but it was an incredibly rich one which would change their lives. It was a climb which showed dramatically that even the biggest, most serious faces could be climbed in a pure alpine style. Some thought that if the South Face of Annapurna could be climbed like this, then the South Face of Lhotse could be too.

Messner's Lhotse team also included a number of French climbers, most notably Christophe Profit who was becoming one of the stars of Alpine mountaineering. Profit came from Normandy, but discovered the mountains during family holidays in the Alps. He started rock climbing at the age of 16 and five years later did his national service in Chamonix with the Groupe Militaire de Haute Montagne, an elite specialised mountain unit of the French army. His military service was only a year, but in the end he stayed two and was very active climbing. By then he had decided to make Chamonix his home and dedicate his life to the mountains. He became a qualified Alpine Guide in 1986 and started to make some very fine and fast solo ascents. In 1982 he free soloed the American Direct route on the Dru in three hours and 10 minutes. It normally took more than a day and the climbing press took note. In the winter of 1984-1985 he made the first one day winter solo of the North Face of the Eiger. The next summer he became the first man to climb the three great north faces of the Alps within 24 hours. Using helicopters to move from one mountain to another, he started up the North Face of the Matterhorn exactly at midnight, taking four hours to reach the summit, before descending the normal route and being whisked by helicopter over to the Bernese Oberland and the North Face of the Eiger. This took 6 hours and 45 minutes – the previous decade Messner himself and Peter Habeler had stunned the climbing world by managing it in 10 hours. Now he moved on to the Grand Jorasses in France reaching the base of the mountain at ten to seven in the evening. It was too late in the day to climb the classic Walker Spur route, so he followed another line and at half past eleven exited out onto the Hirondelles Ridge and continued to the summit. Eighteen months later he repeated the same three faces in winter, taking just under 41 hours including a forced bivouac on the North Face on the Eiger when his head torch batteries ran out. Profit trained every day and was exceptionally fit and technically very strong, the epitome of a modern alpinist. Lhotse was his first expedition to the Himalayas and so he was unproven at high altitude, but as an alpinist he had few equals.

Fulvio Mariani joined the party to make a film of the climb. Mariani came from Italian speaking Ticino in Switzerland and learned to climb on the Denti della

Vecchia, literally the witch's teeth, a mountain of limestone towers above the city of Lugano. His other passion was film making and he was able to combine the two when he went to Cerro Torre, the fantastic rock tower in Patagonia. Messner had seen Mariani's films and liked them. He himself was writing a book and planning to make a film about Cerro Torre and asked Mariani whether he would be interested to assist. Mariani accepted this proposal without hesitation and a few days later went to visit Messner at his castle in the South Tyrol. When he got there Messner did not mention Cerro Torre and instead focused on his new project – the South Face of Lhotse. Messner asked Mariani to join the team and the latter was so excited by this that he was singing with joy on the drive back across North Italy. Messner's fame meant that his expedition didn't have any problem getting funding. So instead of the usual last minute dash for funds, Mariani could focus on running in the hills around Lugano to get fit to avoid making a bad impression amongst the star climbers in Messner's team.

Wielicki had actually been on Lhotse that winter as part of a Belgian team together with fellow Poles Andrzej Zawada and Leszek Cichy, trying to make the first winter ascent by the ordinary route. These three climbers were the leader and both members of the summit team of the first expedition to climb Everest in winter so brought great winter experience to the Belgian team. The summer before Wielicki had had a serious accident. He had led a small expedition, including two veterans of Lhotse South Face, Falco-Dasal and Jan Nowak, to try and make the first ascent of the 1200m high West Face of Bhagirathi II, a spectacular 6500m peak in India. This objective showed that leading Polish climbers were not merely trying to collect 8000 metre peaks, but also climbing technically hard routes on lower mountains in alpine style. The lower part of the Face was not difficult, but after two days they reached technically very hard terrain where progress slowed to only 80-100 metres per day. On the fifth day of the climb they were hit by rockfall which killed Nowak and seriously injured Wielicki. It took the three fit members and the injured Wielicki 24 hours to abseil back to the foot of the mountain. On Lhotse, by the second half of December most of the expedition were suffering illness, a common feature in the Himalayan winter, and the goal was looking beyond the expedition. Near the end of the month the three Poles and Ingrid Bayens went up to a camp in the Western Cwm at 6400 metres. All except Wielicki were ill and wanted to descend, but he stubbornly refused to be beaten, even though his back was a very painful from the accident on Bhagirathi. Alone he went up to Camp III only to find that since they were last there the winter winds had ruined the tents. He spent the night there and the next day went straight past Camp IV and climbed alone by the normal route to the summit. The descent was a nightmare due to the pain from his back after the accident and the normal winter problems of extreme cold, little snow, a lot of bare ice and high winds. When he arrived at Camp III, he met Cichy who, despite being unwell had returned to provide back up to Wielicki – something which the latter appreciated enormously. The climb on Lhotse meant Wielicki had made the first winter ascents of three of the four highest mountains in the world. The one he missed out on, K2, still hadn't seen a winter ascent as of 2015.

On Lhotse, Messner was clear that he would not go on to the actual Face, keeping a promise he had made to his mother that he would retire from top level mountaineering after completing the 8000ers. The year before Reinhold climbed his last 8000er his brother Siegfried was killed in a climbing accident in the Alps and of course another brother Gunther had been lost on Nanga Parbat many years before. With two of her sons killed in the mountains, Reinhold felt he had to reassure his mother about his own future activities. This made his preparations for the expedition less stressful, but also removed the excitement he used to feel when heading off to pit himself against a Himalayan giant and left him feeling slightly depressed. The team congregated in Kathmandu, which gave an opportunity to talk about tactics. Profit and the other French climbers were talking about climbing the "direttissima" route straight up the Central Spur in alpine style. Messner had doubts about whether they understood the real difficulty of the face. Just getting to the mountain was not proving so easy and they were blocked in Kathmandu for a week waiting for a flight to Lukla. This started to be frustrating and Enric Lucas became nervous and asked why someone as famous and important as Messner couldn't get priority on a flight. The delay did at least give the team the chance to get to know each other better. Wielicki told the others stories of his two attempts on the face. The continued delays forced Messner to send part of the team by road to Jiri, eight days march away from the Base Camp, compared to the five it would take starting from the airstrip at Lukla. Eventually the two parts of the expedition met up and they started the walk towards Base Camp. Messner was concerned at a lack of teamwork shown in getting things organised. As usual, there were various tasks to carry out to get the caravan under way, like supervising the weighing of loads for the porters and distributing them so that no-one got away with a light load and so on. Messner felt that people were standing about waiting for these problems to be resolved rather than rolling their sleeves up to try and work them out as a team. He did not expect people to follow a flag bearing leader, but he had expected a bit more team solidarity than he saw at the beginning.

At Dinboche they met up with Artur Hajzer, who had stayed in Nepal after an autumn expedition in which he had climbed a new route on the South Face of Annapurna with Kukuczka. He had just been visiting Everest Base camp where a Polish team was preparing for an attempt on the West Ridge. He made a good impression on Messner, who had not met him before and thought he looked solid and open as well as obviously a fine alpinist. Fulvio Mariani thought Hajzer looked like some sort of Nepalese cowboy, lying topless in a field in dirty torn trousers and smoking a Yak, the Nepalese brand of cigarette. Almost without introducing himself Hajzer started explaining to the film-maker how he was fascinated by the cinema and of his idea to make a film about Himalayan climbing. It would be called "The Story of the Blue Drum" and would tell the story of an expedition from the point of view of the blue plastic drums, which were an ubiquitous feature of Himalayan expeditions in this period. I personally still have a drum like this in my attic which derived from my 1990 expedition to Changtse, although it is green rather than blue. The drums would know all the characteristics of the expedition, its moods and its smells. They would know the secrets and the past of the members, both climbers and Sherpas, like the bottle of alcohol which almost everyone hid in their barrel to celebrate success or fend off homesickness, but also the arguments and tensions between the climbers. The camera would see things from the point of view of the barrels and would follow what happened to them after the expedition too, whether they finished in the house of a Sherpa to brew homemade alcohol or returned to Europe and met up with other barrels from other expeditions. The film was only a passing idea and by now Hajzer had finished his cigarette and he and Mariani set off up the path towards Base Camp together.

On 9th April they arrived at Base Camp and there was immediately a disagreement between two of the Lhotse South Face veterans about the siting of the camp. Wielicki wanted to place it where the Poles had camped in 1985 and 1987, but Messner pointed out that this was the same spot which had been submerged in powder snow during the 1975 Italian expedition. In the end they reached a compromise and placed the camp a little bit higher amongst some large granite blocks. With so many strong and ambitious characters in the team, tensions started to emerge and Messner felt that people were already trying to find excuses and justifications for their actions. On a happy expedition, Base Camp should have been a refuge from hard work and danger on the mountain and a place where camaraderie helped to fend off homesickness, but here the atmosphere was tense. Messner himself also had some family issues to deal with. He had been accompanied to Base Camp by his girlfriend Sabine Stehle and their fifteen month old daughter Magdalena. It should have been an opportunity for them to spend some time together despite Messner's hectic travelling schedule, but things didn't work out as planned. It was so cold and windy at Base Camp, that Magdalena was effectively a prisoner in her tent leaving her mother no choice, but to retreat back to Europe with the child.

The mood was also not helped by finding the Face in an unusual state. It was almost black after several very dry months meaning that sections which would have previously have been straightforward snowfields were now rock which would take longer to climb with much higher risk of stonefall. They judged it to be too dangerous to attempt directly and there were lengthy discussions about the best route to follow. Profit studied the Polish Route through binoculars, but Wielicki told him to move them further right as where he was looking was unclimbable in the current conditions. He recommended following the original Austrian route on Lhotse Shar on the far right side of the South Face and then making a long traverse left to reach the upper part of route followed by the Poles in 1985 and 1987. Not everyone was committed to this route which was a pragmatic but rather convoluted solution to the difficult conditions they found on the central part of the Face. Messner had the impression that Wielicki was trying to stop people going on "his" route and suspected that in the end he and Hajzer would end up making an attempt that way. The leader gave his impressions about the team to Mariani as they studied the Face. Apart from the Poles, he considered Profit to be a very strong climber, although lacking in Himalayan experience. He was used to climbing alone and making his own decisions, but this time that wouldn't do him any good. Of course Kammerlander had masses of Himalayan experience, much of it with Messner himself. Messner felt that Enric Lucas and the others were outsiders who would follow the lead of the stronger characters and make decisions depending on how circumstances unwound. He advised Mariani that if he always kept an eye on what Wielicki, Profit and Kammerlander were doing he was likely to capture the key moments of the expedition for his film.

Two days after arriving in Base Camp the two Poles and Kammerlander set off towards the site of Camp I which they placed at 5800 metres with two of the Sherpas carrying loads in support. Messner was still concerned about the tense mood at Base Camp with everyone seeming to be focused on their own personal ambitions and taking success on the mountain for granted – very reminiscent of the situation on the 1971 Everest expedition. Once the whole team was back at Base Camp, there were further lengthy discussions on the strategy to follow. Finally it was agreed that they would equip the route of the far right side of the face because this would help with acclimatisation and serve as a prepared descent route if they tried to go up another way in alpine style. Trying any other route in the conditions at that time would have been too dangerous. Some of the team who were having some difficulty acclimatising went down to the village of Dingpoche. People coming and going from Base Camp as they saw fit, seemed to Messner to indicate a lack of devotion to a common enterprise and he started to realise the difficulties of an expedition with so many different cultures and attitudes, which were magnified by linguistic difficulties. Because the team had no common language, some people required translation and discussions were going on amongst individual groups in their own language accentuating the feeling that there were cliques within the team.

When good weather finally arrived the 3 French climbers, Profit, Bruno Cormier and Sylvianne Tavernier set off for Camp I, but for Messner it was frustrating to see that they only left after spending hours selecting their equipment – he would have liked to see a bit more dynamism. The good weather didn't last long and within a couple of days the wind had got up again and the mountain was covered above 7000 metres, but Kammerlander and Hajzer continued to work on placing fixed ropes. They arrived at 6700 metres, supported by Wielicki and Lucas. Messner himself went up to Camp I which he found an ideal spot, not much exposed to the wind and with running water during the day. The lead group of the Poles, Kammerlander and Lucas now placed an intermediate camp at 6400 metres in a large crevasse. The following day Lucas wasn't feeling well, but the others arrived at the site of Camp II where they deposited a load of ropes. Michel Arizzi and Mariani went up to Camp I which was definitely in a nicer spot than Base Camp - generally no-one was in a hurry to descend from there to Base Camp. Mariani asked Arizzi to help him by acting as an amateur soundman. The latter was pleased to have something to do, instead of staying in Base Camp listening to the eternal discussions about team work and the choice of route. The day before Messner had lost his temper and said that if they couldn't start working as a team, he was going to return home. The others could do what they wanted, but they could no longer count on his leadership or financing. This discussion lasted more than three hours and Mariani had not only been filming it, but also acting as a translator between those from the South Tyrol, who struggled to communicate with the French, Lucas the Catalan who couldn't understand the English spoken by the Poles, and even helping Kammerlander who despite being Italian was a native German speaker and not fluent in Italian. It was like trying to build the Tower of Babel.

On the 21st April Messner himself ascended to 6700 metres together with Roland Losso to properly place Camp II (his promise to his mother to not go onto the Face seemed not to be absolute), but even getting into action on the mountain did not remove his disquiet about the level of team harmony. Enthusiasm seemed to be evaporating with people making trips down to the neighbouring villages. Only Hans Kammerlander and the Poles seemed to be fully committed to the making a success of the expedition. In addition Mariani impressed Messner with his positive attitude and determination to make a good film. Back down at Base Camp Messner argued with Lucas who he felt didn't want to integrate and contribute to the common effort. Messner felt there was a climate of competition between the different pairs of climbers. He also started to understand that he could not act as an effective catalyst if he was not himself leading the expedition from the front. On all his previous expeditions he had either reached the summit or no-one had and so he could always previously be the one who drove things forward, who decided when to press on, when the weather was uncertain and so on. Doing this from Base Camp was much harder.

By the 24th April Kammerlander, Hajzer and Wielicki had reached 7000 metres and started the long traverse left, but the weather was bad with fog and snow and the arguments continued. The French pair of Bruno Cormier and Michel Arrizzi refused to carry the camera equipment up to Camp II. At Camp I, Fluvio Mariani found Profit alone and depressed. It seemed that Cormier had convinced Arizzi that Profit was making a mistake in joining the others on this route on the far right of the face, rather than the direct line they had planned.

Cormier and Arizzi had descended to Base Camp and declared that they wanted to quit the expedition. Messner did not even try to persuade them to stay as he felt they were making no effort to integrate or contribute to the common goals. Sylvianne Tavernier complained of a persistent sore throat and didn't feel well enough to go up on to the Face, leaving Profit the only French climber still actively involved. The last days of April saw unstable weather, but it started to improve at the beginning of May and Kammerlander and Wielicki went back up to Camp II. Once they arrived the weather closed in again and they found that one of the tents was torn and all the contents including the sleeping bags were soaked. On the 4th May, the weather was splendid, but none of the climbers were up on the Face and Profit and Hajzer set off for Camp II only at midday. The next day they continued to climb, but with some risk of wind-slab avalanche, they had to move with prudence. They set up an intermediate camp and in the afternoon Hajzer continued to equip the route above alone. On the same day, Losso, who had never really properly acclimatised, quit the expedition.

Now that the remaining members were well acclimatised the expedition started to break apart with different sub-teams carrying out different plans, although Messner was still trying to get agreement on a common plan to attempt the summit. On the 7th May Kammerlander and Profit went up to Camp III to attempt the summit.. That night they lay in their tent, protected by the steep rock wall of Lhotse Shar. At 9pm it started to snow heavily and within a short time half a metre had fallen. Less than an hour later powder snow avalanches started to fall all around them. Inside the tent they could feel the vibrations and the currents of air of the avalanches passing nearby and by 11pm the situation had become very dangerous with ever more frequent masses of snow arriving from above. They knew that if one of these buried the tent they were finished. Either they would be buried under metres of snow with no chance of themselves or anyone else digging them out or, more likely, they would be swept down the mountain. Terrified, they decided to quit the tent and run to a nearby crevasse where they were at least protected by solid ice above. At midnight it had almost stopped snowing and when the avalanches stopped falling they decided to return to the tent. They snuggled into their sleeping bags, trying to get warm again after the icy cold of the crevasse, but keeping nervously alert for sounds from outside. After only 10 minutes they heard something fall on the tent which sounded like hailstones. In fear they sprang up and sat tensely waiting to see what would happen next, their hands instinctively protecting their heads. Seconds later three rocks the size of fists smashed through the fabric of the tent and landed in front of them exactly where they had been lying. With a chill they realised that if the rocks had fallen an instant earlier they would have been finished. Two of the rocks landed exactly where they had been lying, whilst the third fell in between smashing down on the saucepan they had been melting snow in with such force that it was embedded in the ground. For the rest of the night they did not manage to sleep a wink, knowing that they had escaped death by a matter of seconds. In shock they descended to Base Camp at first light. During the descent Kammerlander dislocated his ankle and was limping when he arrived in Base Camp. For him the expedition was over and, as if to emphasise this, it snowed the entire day after they arrived at Base Camp.

At the same time, the two Poles decided to try the original Polish line in alpine style, as Messner always suspected they would. Between 11th and 14th May Hajzer and Wielicki climbed to 7100m, but then they were blocked there for three nights due to bad weather. On the third day Hajzer went up to the old 1987 Camp IV to try and scavenge some food left from two years before. By the fourth day they had used up all their food and fuel and, with no sign of an improvement in the weather, they descended by making a long traverse back to the route on the right hand side of the Face, which had been prepared with fixed ropes. To reach the fixed ropes they had to cross the snow slopes below the big triangular face of Lhotse Shar. This was dangerous as the slopes were heavily laden a lot of fresh snow. The risk of triggering an avalanche would have been even greater if they had been roped so they decided to go across this section unroped. Before setting across the perilous slope they drew straws to see who would go first and Hajzer pulled the short one. Tentatively he stepped his way across the slope which fortunately stayed firm. Even going second, Wielicki had his heart in his mouth as he made his own crossing. Once they reached the fixed rope the remainder of the descent was straightforward.

As the Poles descended to Base Camp, Lucas and Profit returned to the mountain for a final attempt, but at Camp III Lucas decided to give up. Profit contemplated a solo attempt, but after considering it he realised that it wasn't a realistic prospect with the Face so charged with snow. Instead he stayed up on the mountain hoping to attempt a parapente descent to Base Camp. But even this wasn't to be as the next morning it was snowing harder than it had at any point during the expedition and he had no choice, but to descend on foot. It took him the whole day to get down in mist and driving snow.

It was an anticlimactic finish to an expedition which had achieved very little, given the strength and experience of the climbing team. This was partly due to bad weather and maybe with more luck they would have got nearer the goal, but it also seems that the international team structure Messner had planned simply proved to be dysfunctional. For Wielicki and Hajzer, who had done so much to try and climb the Face and got closer than anyone it was another disappointment. Wielicki decided it was not worth going back. Even if others had not been subsequently successful he had had enough. He "knew every stone of the Face", but the inner motor which drove him to new challenges didn't work anymore for the South Face of Lhotse. Without this, he asked, what would have been the point of trying to push himself? The failure of Messner's expedition was not as dramatic as that in 1971 on Everest's South West Face, but was nonetheless a major disappointment. Messner had gone with a team with many of the world's top climbers, but they had not made a serious bid on the summit. He had hoped this star team would be the solution to the "last great problem", but the whole had proved to be worth less than the sum of the parts. Bitterness and recriminations were not like those after the 1971 expedition, but still few of the climbers came away with enhanced reputations.

Chapter 10 – A Giant has Fallen

When Jerzy Kukuczka heard the news of the failure of Messner's expedition, he immediately jumped at the challenge and sent a Telex to Nepal requesting a permit. Unlike Messner, Kukuczka had carried on top level Himalayan climbing after completing the 8000 metre peaks with a seemingly undimmed desire to tackle the hardest routes. In 1988 he and Artur Hajzer had climbed a new route on the South Face of Annapurna and had then started planning a traverse of the four high summits of Kangchenjunga, which would involve crossing ridges at very high altitude. When Kukuczka heard that a team from the Soviet Union had completed the Kangchenjunga traverse with a very large team, his attention turned back to Lhotse, which was more than ever the number one unclimbed Himalayan objective. After twice coming so close to completing the Face the Poles felt that the route was rightly "theirs" and for Kukuczka realising this dream would be a crowning moment in his mountaineering career. Kukuczka also saw Lhotse South Face in terms of his rivalry with Messner and the fact that Messner had failed in the spring spurred him to organise his expedition in the autumn. He put together a strong team but, whilst he was travelling in Italy a few months before the expedition, he received shocking and tragic news that the Polish team on the West Ridge of Everest had been hit by an avalanche killing five of climbers, all of whom Kukuczka knew well. As well as the accidents he had been directly involved in, hearing of the deaths of companions had become depressingly frequent for Kukuczka. Of course this dark side to top level mountaineering had always existed, but the frequency of these accidents had been increasing with the ever harder and riskier climbs that the likes of Kukuczka were undertaking by the late 1980s. Even so the loss of five climbers was a particularly heavy blow.

A large team of ten Poles plus Americans, Mexicans, a Briton and a Canadian had been attempting the Slovenian route on the West Ridge of Everest, one of the hardest on the mountain. The Slovenians had reached the Lho La at the foot of the ridge by a loose and dangerous rock face above Everest Base Camp. The Poles avoided this section by traversing the 6000m peak of Khumbutse which lies on the opposite side of the Lho La from Everest. This route was less direct, but seemed a good way to avoid the danger of a direct ascent to the Lho La. Two months after reaching Base Camp, Lhotse South Face veteran Miroslaw Falco-Dasal and Miroslaw Gardzielewski made an unsuccessful bid for the summit which only reached the top of the Horbein Couloir. Two days later another attempt by Andrzej Marciniak and the leader Chrobak succeeded. Others had been planning summit bids of their own, but the weather was bad with heavy snowfall and the priority was to get off the mountain so the whole team descended. Despite all the fresh snow, the climbers decided that the descent route was fairly safe and six climbers set off up the fixed ropes back over Khumbutse in order to return to Base Camp. Even with the fixed ropes it was hard work with a metre of fresh snow to plough through and they had to frequently change the person breaking the trail. At 1 pm they were hit by an avalanche which knocked them down the steep face and broke the fixed ropes. Falco-Dasal, Gardzielewski and Waclaw Otreba did not survive the avalanche. Zygmunt Heinrich, Kukuczka's old companion from Lhotse 10 years before, died soon after and the expedition leader Chrobak during the night. The only survivor was Marciniak, who was left stranded on the Lho La, snowblind, badly injured and without the means to descend. However he managed to crawl back towards the slopes of Everest to reach Camp I and make radio contact with Janusz Majer who was down at Base Camp.

There were various people at Base Camp including Carlos Carsolio and the British climber Alan Burgess, but after trying to get up the face to the Lho La they realised that attempting a rescue of Marciniak from there was out of the question due to severe avalanche danger. So they started urgent efforts to organise a rescue from the other (North) side of the Lho La which lay in Chinese controlled Tibet. Majer first tried to contact Artur Hajzer who was in Kathmandu following the unsuccessful Messner Lhotse expedition. Hajzer was out partying with other climbers in the bars of Kathmandu and it was well after midnight when he returned to his hotel and saw a card pushed under his door reporting the accident. He instantly sobered up and set to work to see what he could do to help his friends. He cycled through the streets of Kathmandu to the Post Office where he could make a call back to Poland, but it was not open yet and he had to wait two hours outside the door smoking cigarette after cigarette. Once he had got things moving in Poland, he contacted the trekking agency which had organised the Lhotse expedition to try and get a helicopter for the rescue. Unfortunately, although a helicopter could be found, there was no pilot who was willing to fly above the normal maximum safe altitude of 5600 metres. The only way to fly higher was in a LAMA helicopter, like the one which had been used to search for Nicolas Jaeger, but apparently there wasn't one in Nepal. Hajzer and his friends desperately tried to get the use of a LAMA with all sorts of options being studied. An American millionaire agreed to help, but unfortunately getting a helicopter across the Pacific from the USA would require refuelling in mid-ocean. Even the possibility to do this was investigated, but soon rejected as impractical. Messner, who was also still in Nepal, tried to help and at one stage seemed to have succeeded with the help of the Italian ambassador. All that was needed was an identification number to get permission to use a Nepalese helicopter, but somehow they were not able to get this number. Things were further complicated because, in the light of political unrest in Nepal, India had imposed an embargo on fuel supplies to the country. By now Marciniak had gone two days without food. He sat helpless in the tent on the Lho La listening to the wind beating the walls, unable to do anything but finger some rosary beads his mother had given him and a mascot given by his girlfriend, praying for a helicopter to come. His snowblindness was so severe that he relied on the radio to know when it was night and when day. Although they had told him of the efforts to get a helicopter, as time passed he started to lose faith that it would actually happen.

Back in Kathmandu and Warsaw, Hajzer and those helping him had indeed concluded that getting a helicopter quickly was impossible, but had not given up hope of saving their friend. Now they started to organise an overland rescue by travelling around the mountain into Tibet and reaching Marciniak on foot. Trying to get into Tibet at all was complicated by the fact that border was closed following the Tiananmen Square protests – the Chinese people were starting to look for the same freedoms as those in Eastern Europe were gaining. Diplomatic contacts involving Poland and China continued to try and organise permission to cross the border. Finally Hajzer received a call from the US Embassy who asked what he would need to carry out a rescue without a helicopter. Hajzer explained that he would need a permit to cross the Kodari Pass into Tibet and a truck or car to pick them up at the border and drive them to the north side of Everest. The woman at the US Embassy said that all of this was arranged and that he could go straight to the Chinese embassy to pick up the paperwork. Hajzer rushed off to complete the formalities, and a hastily arranged team of Hajzer, Rob Hall, Gary Ball and two Sherpas Zangbu and Shiwa travelled by jeep and truck to reach Base Camp on the North side of Everest. They immediately set off towards the Lho La, but it was a full day's march to get up there along the stony moraines of the Rongbuk Glacier to the foot of the Lho La. The next morning they reached Marciniak who had run out of food and was given up hope of being rescued. He had now regained his sight, but his radio was out of battery and so Majer and the others at Base Camp on the South side had no idea whether he was still alive. The rescuers loaded new batteries into Marciniak's radio and called Base Camp. A huge cheer went up from the team there who had started to doubt if there friend was going to make it. There was huge sadness at the loss of the others, but to have managed to save Marciniak was at least something.

This epic rescue happened at a time when fantastic freedoms were opening up back home in Poland. The Solidarity protests of the early 1980s had been crushed by the introduction of martial law by General Jaruselski. It seemed all the protests had achieved little for the Poles, but in reality they were probably critical in showing the Soviet Union that it could not indefinitely keep its iron grip on the satellite countries of Central and Eastern Europe. When the death of Kostantin Chernenko brought Mikhail Gorbachev to power in the Soviet Union, the threat of military invention in Poland faded and the Polish people once again felt able to express their protest against the lack of freedom and economic mismanagement. Massive strikes in 1988 forced the Communist Party to start talking to Solidarity again. This led to an agreement to hold partially free elections, which took place on the 4th and 18th June 1989. Even though they were not allowed to contest all seats, Solidarity was hugely successful where it could and it was clear that the days of Communist Party control were numbered. One of those elected was Janusz Onyszkiewicz, a leading Polish climber from the 1970s. The rescuers on the Lho La noted the coincidence that at the very moment they were fighting to save the life of one Polish climber, another whom they knew personally was part of the move sweeping away 45 years of Soviet rule back home.

Despite the exciting events in his home country, climbing still dominated Kukuczka's thoughts and he was left numbed by the accident on Everest. Many of those lost were people he had known for years and who he had shared rich experiences with. He had climbed his very first 8000 metre peak with Heinrich and also been with him on Cho Oyu and Nanga Parbat. Falco-Dasal was of course a companion from the 1985 Lhotse expedition, Chrobak was with him on Everest in 1980 and so on. With the shock of the tragedy, the team which had been planning to go with him to Lhotse started to fall away too. Hajzer and Majer, who had been involved in the rescue of Marciniak on Everest, unsurprisingly had had enough of the Himalayas for the moment. Wielicki said he was only interested in cutting the grass of his garden on the plains. Only Ryszard Warecki remained enthusiastic, but the two of them needed to put together a new team. Kukuczka didn't want to give up his dream of climbing Lhotse's South Face, but after the tragedy he felt almost embarrassed proposing the expedition to people. When he contacted sponsors to try and get financing he kept getting the same response – it was the wrong moment, he should wait until next year. But Kukuczka understood the competitive nature of Himalayan climbing and the fact that Lhotse South Face had become the number one target for the World's top climbers. Whereas 10 years before there were few who believed it could actually be climbed, now it seemed only a matter of time before someone cracked the puzzle. Having lost out to Messner in the race for the 8000 metre peaks, maybe Kukuczka simply couldn't bear the idea of being beaten to another huge prize. Still he was torn about what to do and even went as far as jotting down the pros and cons. In the end he did what he had always done and followed a sort of inner voice which said "now or never again".

Kukuczka then started to phone round many of Poland's leading climbers to recruit new members for the team. In the end he had a strong team including two other veterans of previous attempts, Ryszard Pawlowski and Maciek Pawlikowski. As well as a Polish core to the team which Kukuczka knew and could rely on, he also asked Fulvio Mariani and the Italian Floriano Castelnuovo who were going to make a film about the climb for Swiss television. Kukuczka also invited Frenchman Yves Ballu, a climber and parapenting enthusiast. Ballu had given the first ever parapenting course at Zakopane in the Tatra mountains a few months before. He was surprised but excited to receive the invitation and although he did not aspire to reach the summit, he hoped to participate in the historic expedition and also to make a parapente descent from high on the mountain.

Arriving in Nepal in late August, by the September 6th they had Base Camp established in the same place as the two previous Polish expeditions. That afternoon it started raining, but next morning it was fine and Kukuczka worked on organising the Base Camp working topless in the hot sun. By the afternoon he had second degree sunburn and had to retreat to his tent with a fever – not a great start for one of the World's greatest mountaineers! Their original plan was to fix ropes only up to Camp II and to acclimatise on neighbouring 6000 metre peaks. A group of climbers would also go on the other side of Lhotse and put a camp at 7400m which would safeguard a descent down the normal route.

This escape route would have allowed them to fix less ropes on the South Face itself, reducing risk by spending less time on the Face and attempting an ascent in partial alpine style. However the bad weather that season put paid to this idea and they had to return to a plan of fixing ropes on the Czechoslovak Pillar much as they had in 1985 and 1987. When Kukuczka explained his plan of attack to the team there was some grumbling. Kopys said it seemed to mean that the team would do the hard work to fix the ropes whilst Kukuczka got acclimatised and then attempted the summit using the route they had prepared. Nevertheless the next day Pawlikowski and Kopys set to work on the Pillar and managed to fix 200 metres of rope. Kukuczka still had a fever and pain in his back and didn't feel well enough to leave his tent. He had hoped that the second week of September would be a good time to start activity, but instead there was low cloud and heavy rain which later turned to snow.

Kukuczka's diaries from this expedition were published posthumously and give a fascinating insight into his thoughts during a Himalayan expedition. They show that he was not a superman and complains of tiredness, aches and pains and the weight of heavy rucksacks. But they do show enormous drive, less in bursts of enthusiasm and energy, but more in a constant determination to pursue his goals in the face of fatigue, perceived shortcomings of his team mates and indifferent weather. The diaries show little introspection or analysis of the motives which were driving him to climb. It doesn't seem to have ever been in doubt for him - it was just something he knew he wanted to do. This is a sharp contrast to the reflections on inner thoughts and motivations which are a frequent feature of the writings of his great rival Messner. Kukuczka, feeling he lacked acclimatisation and fitness, persuaded a couple of team mates to join him on an ascent of Island Peak, the 6000 metre "trekking" peak on the opposite side of the valley from Lhotse. Up on the ridge Kukuczka was moving slowly, when bad weather descended and they lost their way. In the end they had to stop and wrap themselves in the bivouac tent they had been carrying, shivering for two hours until the weather cleared a bit and they realised they had been going the wrong way. They didn't get back to the camp until 11 pm. In the morning Kukuczka felt embarrassed by his performance the day before – he was supposed to be the great star, conqueror of all the world's 8000 metre peaks and he had made mistakes like a novice. To make matters worse, Kukuczka had been carrying three radios in his pack which were now soaked and no longer worked. More than a few jokes were cracked at his expense by his teammates, but he had to grit his teeth and accept them.

The next day Pawlikowski, Piasecki and Kopys went up to continue the work on fixing ropes and Mariani and Castelnuovo planned to film them. But there was a misunderstanding and the Poles raced off before any film could be shot. Mariani tried to explain to them that the film was crucial to the financing of the expedition, but they told him that that was his problem not theirs. Mariani returned to Base Camp in a terrible temper, not helped by the continuous rain. Generally there seemed to be tension between the Swiss/Italian film team and the Poles. Mariani accused the Poles of compromising safety to save money and suspected team members had sold new equipment given by their sponsors and bought cheap replacements leading to a shortage of anchors for the fixed ropes. Perhaps this was just a suspicion, but the different attitudes to security anyway created tensions. On one occasion Castelnuovo was jumaring and compared the fixed ropes attached to single anchors of the Poles with the traditional Czech climbing on soft sandstone cliffs where protection comes on from knotted rope wedged into cracks. But of course the seriousness of the situation on this huge and dangerous wall was much greater than on the modest rock towers in the woods of Bohemia.

Indeed, Kukuczka nearly came to grief by placing too much trust in equipment. Whilst working on fixing ropes above Camp I, he decided to trust some of the old fixed ropes from previous expeditions. On the way down he clipped into an old anchor of Polish origin. The ground wasn't very steep, but the anchor pulled out and he lost his balance. Waving his hands in desperation and shouting "my god" he fell some tens of metres before his hand managed to catch hold of one of the old ropes and stop himself. A religious man, Kukuczka was left thanking god for having given a second life when the first seemed to be over. After this he made a route finding error on the glacier and ended up below Base Camp. Everything seemed to be going wrong. Mariani was distressed about a brand new video camera which was ruined, Kukuczka was still shaken by this brush with death and, to cap it all, the mail runner had not arrived from Kathmandu with news of their friends and loved ones. Throughout the time when the fixed ropes were being placed, the weather was very bad and there was a high risk from avalanches, but they continued to try and work on the route. On the 15th September there was some sign of an improvement in the weather with a full moon in the sky and the next morning dawned bright and cold. Pawlikowski and Piasecki managed to establish Camp II and the next day after Kukuczka returned to the mountain himself with Pawlowski and Kulej. But it took them six hours to get to Camp I and Kukuczka was tired, had a headache and stomach pains and the abundant fresh snow was slowing progress. The expedition doctor was insisting they should all take Diamox – a drug which many climbers swore by as an aid to altitude related problems - but Kukuczka was a bit sceptical that it was doing him any good. The next day they carried on up the mountain and reached at Camp II. As always in the afternoon it had started snowing, but Kukuczka and Pawlowski decided to push on up the snowfield above. After 200 metres in deep snow Kukuczka heard a sudden creaking noise coming from a serac above which froze his blood. If one of these huge blocks of ice detached, they would stand no chance. It was a reminder that even on the relatively safe terrain of the Czechoslovak Pillar, the Wall was alive with danger. They were unsure which way to go, but eventually they traversed left to a snowy ridge which avoided the serac. The next day at Camp II both Kukuczka and Pawlowski were feeling tired and poorly acclimatised and didn't go out climbing. Anyway it started raining before midday, although it cleared up by the evening leaving hope for the next day. But by the morning it was ugly weather again with a grey horizon, cloud cover and light snow. They hesitated about whether to go up, with Kukuczka restless outside the tent watching the weather, listening to the snow slides around them and wondering what to do whilst Pawlowski stayed in his sleeping bag and asked whether it really made sense to persist in this weather. In the end they went up 200 metres, but when they saw even blacker clouds arriving on the horizon they gave up and went back down to Base Camp.

They got there just after Yves Ballu had arrived to join the expedition. His excitement at arriving at the foot of the world's most sought after route was dampened by a terrible period of weather. The Face was hidden in clouds and they heard that the rain had been so violent in Kathmandu that it had turned the roads into torrents. Even despite the bad weather Ballu appreciated the company of the Poles, who he found not lacking in humour or realism. He noted that Kukuczka didn't seem too concerned about the situation. As September drew to a close, the team continued to work on preparing the route and carrying loads, but progress was painfully slow. On the 23rd Kopys, Piasecki and Kulej went back onto the mountain in bad weather with Kukuczka followed progress from Base Camp via radio calls and observing the Face, although the bad weather made viewing difficult. Two days later they had managed to push the route out a couple of 100 metres, but Piasecki complained that powdery snow was making progress insecure and slow. The morale of the whole team was at rock bottom: they had been fighting for 10 days to make the route from Camp II to Camp III, which was supposed to be one of the easiest sections. They knew had to get to Camp V before they could even start to attack main difficulties of the Great Barrier. In the back of his mind Kukuczka was also thinking about the choice of partner for the summit bid – at this stage he had not talked to anyone about this.

On the 27th September Kukuczka went up onto the face with Pawlowski, Pawlikowski and Castelnuovo and by 2 pm they were in Camp II. Kukuczka's plan had been for them to split into two pairs, with one carrying heavy packs to Camp II and the other travelling lighter and attempting to push through and establish Camp III. He was going to give this responsibility to establish the camp to Pawlowski and Pawlikowski, but in the end he changed his mind and decided to push from the front to ensure this actually happened. The next morning they carried on, climbing the ice cliffs and then snow fields with dangerously powdery snow. They picked up gear they had deposited before, making their rucksacks horribly heavy, but they still made it up to 6670 metres where they placed Camp III on a snowy crest. Pawlowski and Pawlikowski stayed up whilst Castelnuovo and Kukuczka went back down to Camp II. Kukuczka expressed concerns about Ryszard Pawlowski in his diary, but it would turn out to be with him that he would attempt the summit.

The next morning Kukuczka went up to replace Maciej Pawlikowski who was feeling unwell. At 6am he left the tent, and was surprised to find thick clouds and the rumble of fresh snow avalanches all around. He stopped, uncertain of what to do next and radioed up to Camp III to share his doubts. Those at Camp III were also uncertain, but Kukuczka convinced them to try and go up a couple of hundred metres to reach a section of old fixed ropes. Unfortunately after only climbing a few 10s of metres they turned back. Kukuczka was disappointed, but there was only so much he could do to push the others. He also descended down to Base Camp making it from Camp II in record time, but arriving soaked to the skin. As usual life in Base Camp had been going on. The doctor had had to extract one of Leszek Czech's teeth, but this didn't stop Czech celebrating his birthday the next day and although they weren't candles, they were up late drinking vodka and homemade 95° proof alcohol. When the weather was good enough, Ballu practised parapenting at 5000 metres, to the interest of the occupants of Base Camp.

On the last day of September the weather was still bad and all climbers were in Base Camp having a siesta in their tents. In the middle of the afternoon, Ballu decided to put his nose outside the tent to find Lhotse finally out of the clouds and glowing in the afternoon autumn sun. He took photos because it was the first time he had seen the Face at that time of day. He thought that everyone else was still asleep in their tents, until he saw Kukuczka outside his tent with binoculars, studying the state of the route intently. The leader's desire and focus were clear. With the beginning of October, there was a different smell to the air, fresher and with perfect blue skies, giving a new optimism about what they could achieve. Kukuczka decided to open a bottle of Champagne to toast the fact that the weather was turning. After waiting for one day for the snow to consolidate, Pawlikowski, Piasecki and Kopys set off with the intention to establish Camp IV. Kukuczka followed the next day with Pawlowski and Kulej, climbing the first section in the dark by light of head torches. Kukuczka waited at Camp I for the others to catch up and then continued up the gully above, which was exposed to risk of stonefall. Before entering it he looked up, but everything seemed quiet so he set off to try and climb this dangerous 15 metre section as quickly as possible. He placed his jumar clamp as high as possible on the rope, dug the points of his crampons into the hard snow and set off. Suddenly he felt a sharp pain above his knee and saw a dark mass disappearing down the gully below him. The pain in his leg was becoming stronger and stronger, but he knew he had to get out of the line of fire as soon as possible. He managed to swing on the rope across to the stance where Pawlowski and Kulej were waiting and crawl to the tent to check the condition of his leg. Nothing was broken – but there was still a lot of pain. After 10 minutes, he told the others that he could continue, although Pawlowski should lead. It was tough, but somehow Kukuczka made it to Camp II despite the pain in his leg.

The next day better weather allowed them to move further up, but it was hard work with a lot of fresh snow and the fixed ropes buried. At least they were moving again and Pawlikowski, Piasecki and Kopys managed to set up Camp IV. Then Kukuczka's group took over the lead, expecting the next section to be quite straightforward, but it proved to be rather hard. Furthermore their sacks were terribly heavy and they were bombarded with pieces of ice. By the time they reached Camp IV they were very tired, particularly the doctor Kulej who didn't want to eat or drink and just slept in a corner of the tent. Despite the fatigue, Kukuczka continued the next day to check the fixed ropes on a long snow slope above Camp IV and fix some new anchors which shortened the route. These slopes ended in a chimney with an unpleasant exit in nearly vertical powder snow, which he remembered from when he had nearly suffocated under a snow slide in 1985. Back at the tent Kulej was still unwell and Kukuczka realised he would probably need to accompany him down, but was also worried this would slow progress further and preoccupied that they had still not reached Camp V. In the end Kukuczka risked letting Kulej descend alone, tired, but not in a bad physical condition. By 4.30 in the afternoon Kukuczka and Pawlowski reached the site of Camp V and dug out a platform. But when he radioed Base Camp they said they could see Kulej descending very slowly. Through binoculars they could see him descend metre by metre, falling in the snow and sometimes resting stationary for 10 or 15 minutes before recovering enough to carry on, before collapsing again. They saw him come to a standstill ten times and each time they feared the worse, but each time he managed to carry on. Only on the 10 pm radio call did those at Base Camp learn from Piasecki that Kulej had arrived at Camp II after a descent lasting 12 hours.

The next day Kukuczka was still worried about the incident and whether he should have accompanied Kulej down and left the job of setting up Camp V to others. But he had felt the need to lead from the front to avoid the expedition losing momentum. Although Kukuczka felt guilty about his choice of priorities, he still did not appreciate Mariani telling him that it was an idiot expedition run by an idiot. Probably Mariani realised he had gone too far too because he produced a bottle of Chianti at dinner in Base Camp to try and rebuild bridges. At least further supplies of much needed climbing equipment had arrived by porter from Namche Bazar. They had been running short of rope, snow stakes and pitons. This lack of equipment had been threatening to slow progress and above Camp IV Kukuczka had had to install 200 metres of fixed ropes without any intermediate anchors. Ryszard Warecki had been supposed to bring supplies from Kathmandu, but had been blocked there by bad weather. The ropes they managed to get from Namche Bazar were twisted and stiff and not ideal for jumaring, but at least they could carry on advancing the route. At this time Ballu, Warecki and Witold Oklek went up onto Island Peak from where Ballu was to attempt a parapente descent. Ballu managed to complete his flight, rigged up with movie cameras to film the event. Kukuczka wasn't enthusiastic as he viewed it a distraction from the real business of climbing.

On the 11th October Kukuczka proposed a new plan to the team – he wanted to climb in alpine style up the central couloir. The team was sceptical and unanimously rejected the plan. For one thing the team who would not participate in the alpine style attempt would then have to tackle the final part of the Polish route without their leading climber. Kukuczka made a further attempt to convince Ryszard Pawlowski, who he believed was the most suitable partner, but even he couldn't be persuaded. Finally Kukuczka decided to stay with the original plan, although he still thought it could be possible to attempt the summit directly from Camp V, maybe with one or two bivouacs. He also decided he needed to try and resolve the tensions between the film team of Mariani and some of the Polish members. He invited Mariani to the mess tent and started off saying "you've offended everyone and above all me. It seems nothing is ever right for you. And now what's wrong?' There was a delay whilst Kukuczka words were translated. Then there was some discussion about money and the leader agreed to give Mariani back some of the money he had contributed to the expedition. Everything seemed to be resolved then, but the next day the Castelnuovo and Mariani still didn't seem to be fully part of the team and went up separately from the others. On a brighter note, they had a radio contact with Everest Base Camp where Elsa Avila told them that Carlos Carsolio together with two Sherpas and four Japanese climbers had reached the summit of Everest. Ever since they had climbed together on Nanga Parbat in 1985, Kukuczka saw Carsolio as a sort of apprentice and took great pleasure in his achievements.

The following day Kopys, Piasecki and Pawlikowski arrived at Camp V in cold and windy weather. Hopes were now higher that, despite the bad weather earlier, they were making enough progress up the mountain to still have a chance of the summit before the winter winds arrived. Kukuczka and Pawlowski were also moving up the mountain, the former irritated by the great weight of the rucksack as he left Base Camp. After passing Camp I, he felt a bit better and by 1 pm they had arrived in Camp II. Kukuczka noted in his diary that it was the anniversary of his solo ascent of Makalu, one his greatest climbs and an achievement which still obviously meant a lot to him.

On the 16th October they woke and started making coffee, but high above they could hear the terrible booming of the wind. It sounded like they were under a railway bridge whilst an express thundered by and they hesitated and then returned to their sleeping bags As if the weather wanted to spite them, when they looked out from the Face they could see brilliant blue skies. They hung around the camp for the day wondering whether they should retreat back to Base Camp, as the wind continued to roar up above. Kukuczka was superstitious and considered it bad luck to have started this attempt on Sunday. As if to support this view, the wind beat the fabric of the tent all night, reminding them they were in a race for time against the autumn winds. These usually got stronger as the year drew on. All they could hope for was a pause, a few days of fine weather to have a tilt at the summit. But they knew it wasn't going to happen that day and made a rapid descent back to Base Camp. There they could see all along the ridge from Lhotse Shar to Lhotse a huge banner of snow whipped off the ridges by the terrible wind. Piasecki, who was one of the strongest climbers in the team, having summited on the first ascent of the South East Ridge of K2, seemed beaten and said he was not going back up again.

The day after coming back down, the 18th October, Kukuczka asked Pawlowski to accompany him again on another attempt. They set off from Base Camp the same day after carefully packing and repacking their supplies, hesitating on each piece of equipment and can of food. They were followed two days later by Pawlikowski and Kopys. This pair did not feel ready to attempt the summit, but agreed to come up to Camp III or IV in support since Kukuczka was now planning to descend the same way instead of traversing the mountain as he had originally envisaged. He knew the expedition was nearly at its end and this was probably the last chance. The desire to return home, the reducing motivation of his companions and the dwindling supplies, all meant that it would be hard to carry on for another couple of weeks to try again. Pawlowski and Kukuczka spent the night of the 18th at Camp II and the following one at Camp IV. On the 20th they slept at Camp V where they found the tent had been damaged by the wind of the previous days and they had to make emergency repairs before they could use it. But for the last two days the wind had dropped and now they felt they had a real chance. On the 21st they established Camp VI at 8000 metres. With the fall in the wind, the temperature had plummeted too and it was as low as -30° during the night, but this was less of an obstacle for them than the wind.

For the rest of the climb they had a small bivouac tent and an ordinary climbing rope. They would climb in alpine style without fixing any more ropes. They bivouacked at 8150 metres on the 22nd, higher than the last camp of the two previous Polish expeditions and just under the first rocks of the Great Barrier. They knew the upper section of the route was difficult and time consuming, so the higher they managed to camp, the greater their chances of success. The first Polish attempts had underestimated the difficulties of this final section and Kukuczka was not going to repeat this error. That day they had had a close shave when Pawlowski slipped on a rocky traverse and took a sharp blow on the foot, but fortunately this was a fright and no more this time. On the 23rd the weather dawned fine and it seemed the mountain was finally going to be kind to them. At 8am they radioed Base Camp to say that the wind was not too strong and they were going on. In the silence of the morning both climbers were thinking the same thing – after all the efforts of three Polish expeditions and the months of hard work, perhaps their dreams would be realised and they might be the lucky people to finally write this chapter in the annals of Himalayan mountaineering. Pawlowski was also thinking about their two companions, Rafal Cholda and Czeslaw Jakiel who had lost their lives on previous Polish expeditions to this Face.

They continued up the Great Barrier towards the crest of the Central Spur. It was still quite early, around 8.30 or 9.00am, as they neared the crest and Kukuczka climbed a steep chimney cover by snow. With the weather set fine and still plenty of time, they had a great chance to reach the summit. Pawlowski was attached to the belay below and watching with great attention every move of the lead climber, whose robust figure was silhouetted against the sky and seemed to be moving rapidly and securely. Kukuczka was just below the col where Hajzer and Wielicki had spent a night at their high point two years previously. A steep rock slab led to what they were sure would be easier ground on the final ridge. Pawlowski held his breath as he watched Kukuczka, concentrated totally on this tricky terrain, covered by powdery snow. It was a long run out without placing a piton, although the difficulty of the terrain was not extreme. His arms were stretched wide searching for holds, the points of his crampons scraping at the rock to get a better grip. "Watch out Jurek" Pawlowski said to himself, realising the seriousness of the situation. Kukuczka was about 70 metres above Pawlowski when without warning he lost his grip on the rocks and came away from the Face. The fall started to be ever quicker and

Kukuczka bounced against the rocks. Naturally Pawlowski was terrified, praying for salvation and asking himself "is this the end?" He grasped the rope with both hands and the force of the falling Kukuczka on the other end threw him against the rocks of the belay. He was sure he would be dragged off the mountain himself, but the rope caught on a sharp rock just above him and cut leaving Kukuczka to fall on into the depths below. Terrified Pawlowski looked towards the dizzying 3 km drop. An instant after he heard the clattering of his partner's ice axe bouncing down the rocks. The final thing he saw was one of Kukuczka's red gloves falling down into the void. Then it was quiet and he was alone.

Pawlowski was not sure what caused Kukuczka to fall – maybe a hold came loose, maybe he simply lost his grip or maybe a thin layer of snow cover the rocks had come off. After the fall Pawlowski was alone on a ledge high on the Face and, despite being a hardened mountaineer, was naturally in a state of shock. Kukuczka had the radio in his rucksack so Pawlowski could not report the accident to the rest of team further down or ask for help. Down at Base Camp they knew something was wrong because they could see Pawlowski descending slowly alone. He down-climbed carefully and managed to reach some old weathered fixed ropes left from one of the earlier Polish expeditions. In the tangled mess of ropes, he managed to cut free a length which looked to be in reasonable condition and which could help him to descend further. By then it was getting dark and he knew he would have to stop for fear of making a fatal mistake - not surprisingly his nerves were frayed. He was quite close to the tent, but he was scared of slipping whilst trying to cross the final rock slabs in the dark. So he rummaged in his rucksack to look for his head torch, but before he was able to get it working, he fumbled and dropped it into the void. Now there was no choice but to stay put for the night. Pawlowski spent the night on a ledge at 8100m and descended the last 100 metres to the tent in the morning. He carried on down and at midday met Kopys and Pawlikowski, who were getting very worried after not hearing news for 2 days. Pawlowski was obviously in a bad way and they helped him down to Camp III at 7000 metres. Two days later his companions found Kukuczka's body at 5400 metres. It was said by some people that the rope broke because they were using a cheap Korean rope which they had bought second hand in Kathmandu. This narrative seems to imply that the economic disadvantage of Poland had finally caught with its greatest climber. The situation is probably not exactly like that. It is true that the 6mm rope was suitable as a fixed rope rather than for lead climbing, but they were using it to save weight rather than money. The ground they were climbing on was not very difficult and the rope was used for psychological protection or to hold a small slip and was not expected to hold a major leader fall. Any rope can be cut by sharp rocks when it takes the impact of a lead climber falling a long distance.

The death of Kukuczka, who at the time was generally considered to be the world's leading mountaineer, was a great shock. He had become a household figure in his home country and well known amongst mountaineers worldwide. It was also a body blow to Polish mountaineering following on from the tragedy on Everest in the spring. The boldness with which the Poles had attacked the hardest objectives in world mountaineering had been embodied in Kukuczka and now he, and many others had paid the ultimate price. They had given so much to try and climb this wall and got so close, but now with three Poles losing their lives, including the country's greatest ever climber, the appetite to try again was diminished and it would be for others to take up the challenge. Given the reputation the route had now built up, there was no shortage of pretenders.

Chapter 11 – Alone and in Winter

Elizabeth Hawley, the famous chronicler of Nepalese climbing, once described Marc Batard as someone who "manages to argue with other climbers" in a report in the American Alpine Journal. This French guide, who was the next to try the South Face, was certainly a divisive figure. He was one of an increasing number who thought that an ultra-lightweight style was the way to succeed on a face like this. Batard had in fact already planned an attempt on the South Face the previous year. In 1988 his life was a mess: he had just split up from his wife, he was still troubled by his repressed homosexuality and was permanently short of money. His combative attitude and short temper caused him no end of problems. But this turmoil drove him to some great climbing feats, particularly during a frantic period in the late 1980s. Batard was originally from the South-West of France and had a troubled childhood in which he suffered abuse from an uncle which scarred him for many years. In his youth he was something of an outsider, very slightly built and short, with an interest in painting and a habit of disappearing for hours on long solitary walks in the countryside. He discovered the mountains when, despairing of his repeated failures at school, his mother sent him to a specialised school in woodwork in Luchon just north of border with Spain. Here he started walking in the Pyrenees and found that he had far greater resistance to fatigue than others around him, even those who appeared physically stronger. To earn money he used to cross the mountains into Spain, where the duty was lower, buy cigarettes and alcohol for his classmates and return back on foot into France. This smuggling trip meant a 20km walk each way and involved crossing a 1200 metre pass. He started to love the mountains, the space they gave him and the chance to expend his seemingly endless supply of energy. When school broke for the summer, he went to join his mother in the Alps and tried rock climbing. He was immediately hooked and by the end of the summer holidays he had no other idea, but to climb. He forged his mother's signature on a letter withdrawing from school and returned to the Alps, where he spent all of his time climbing and soon decided he wanted to make a career as an Alpine guide.

In 1975, he found out that a French team was planning to attempt Gasherbrum II, an 8000 metre peak in the Karakoram which had only been climbed once at the time. Aged 23, he was considered too young to be ready for Himalayan climbing, but he persuaded the expedition leader Jean-Pierre Fresafond to include him in the team after he got the recommendation of the legendary

French climber Rene Desmaison, for whom Batard had reconnoitred a possible route in Peru. The expedition started badly for Batard when he fell down a snow covered crevasse on the Baltoro Glacier. Fortunately his rucksack had wedged him in the crevasse only 15 metres down and his teammates were able to pull him out with only some scratches and cuts. After that he recovered quickly and was one of the strongest performing climbers on the expedition, reaching the summit with Yannick Seigneur, France's top Himalayan climber at the time. Batard became the youngest person to have ever climbed an 8000 metre peak, Vallbut the triumph was soured by events that followed. One of the climbers, Bernard Villaret, was caught in bad weather when trying to repeat the climb and killed. Once back in France, Batard felt, probably with something of persecution complex, that Seigneur was seizing all the glory from their climb. Batard had argued with a French TV journalist on the walk out from Gasherbrum II. This same journalist invited Seigneur, but not Batard, to talk about his ascent on TV and made a point of never mentioning Batard throughout the rest of his journalistic career. Even their names seemed to work for Seigneur and against Batard. Whilst the former launched a line of medallions in the shape of a piton with the strapline "la race des seigneurs" (loosely the "race of lords"), Batard was told by a manufacturer he would have to change his name before he could brand their clothing since with the addition of a circumflex his name mean bastard. He was furious and wanted nothing more to do with the company.

In 1976 he returned to Pakistan to attempt Gasherbrum I in pure alpine style by a new route with Louis Audobert, one of his teammates from Gasherbrum II the year before. With limited resources and facing very bad weather they were defeated at 7000 metres. In the following years he settled into life as a guide, married and had three children. But there was always some dissatisfaction he could neither identify, nor escape, a desire to make something more of his life which continued to burn within him. After a long break from serious Himalayan climbing, he returned in 1987 with a very fast winter ascent of Dhaulagiri with the Sherpa Sundare. They had left Base Camp on December 1st and climbed to 7100 metres where they bivouacked. By 12.30 pm the next day they were on top, despite being hit by the vicious winter winds which Batard measured at 150 km/h. Sundare had climbed Everest five times without oxygen and was, like Batard, a very fast climber at high altitude, but he too was pursued by demons and drank heavily when he was not climbing.

Four months later Batard returned to Nepal with a plan to solo the West Pillar of Makalu – the route originally climbed by the French expedition in 1971 when Seigneur himself had been one of the summiteers. The solo ascent had already been attempted by Yvan Ghirandini who gave up fairly low down. Batard made it, pulling off a spectacular first, although there was some criticism of the fact that he had fixed ropes on the first 2000 metres of the Pillar with Sherpas carrying loads in support. People asked whether on this basis it could still be described a solo. Once the lower part of the route was equipped he left Base Camp on the 27th April at 1 pm. He arrived at a depot at the foot of the Pillar five hours later where he left his companion the Sherpa Onggel. He then set off alone to climb through the night. At 4 am his head torch stopped working and he had to climb in the dark, but he still made it to the summit by 9.45 am the next morning. Alone on the top of Makalu he could savour his success, but he knew he had to get down and he planned to do that by the normal route on the other side of the mountain. This was technically easier than the way he had come up, but there were still a lot of uncertainties involved. He was exhausted and risked losing his way on the long snow slopes of the northern side which were beaten by the icy wind from Tibet. It took him 24 hours to descend, but three days after that he was back in Kathmandu from where he returned directly to France. The whole expedition had lasted only five weeks.

He soon returned to Nepal with an arguably even more ambitious project to climb Everest without oxygen in less than 24 hours from Base Camp. His drive to make these landmark ascents came partly from pent up ambition, but was also influenced by the need to achieve eye catching feats which would interest the media and his sponsors and so allow him to support his family and pay for further expeditions. He left for Nepal in early August and made an ascent of Cho Oyu with Sundare in bad weather to acclimatise. They then went to Everest Base Camp with the rest of the French team of which Batard was a member. This included the famous guide Jean-Marc Boivin who had pulled off both spectacular climbs and parapente descents. Boivin had been denied permission by the Nepalese authorities to parapente from the summit, but Batard learnt that he planned to do it anyway – something which was likely to get Batard, officially listed as expedition leader, into trouble and perhaps banned from climbing in Nepal. Given that his livelihood was dependent on mountaineering achievements in the country, this inevitably led to arguments. Although his preferred partner Sundare decided to quit, Batard set to work with a team of

Sherpas to prepare the ascent. On the 13th September 1989 he made his first attempt, leaving Base Camp in the evening with the Sherpas Onggel and Imam and reaching the South Col exhausted, before strong winds drove them back. Just two days later he tried again, leaving Base Camp at 17.15 pm and picking up the two Sherpas on route so that they were fresh to break the trail for him. Both Sherpas stayed with him up to 7900 metres and Onggel stayed ahead until 8200 metres when he had to turn back, exhausted by the effort of making the trail in the deep soft snow. Batard was feeling too hot and gave his thick jacket to Onggel who descended. This proved an error because by the time he had reached 8500 metres, it had started to snow again and the temperature had plummeted. He reached the South Summit and was left with only 200 metres of horizontal distance and 40 metres climbing to make it to the very top, but he was shivering uncontrollably and he knew there was no choice but to turn back, descending to Base Camp like a zombie.

Batard spent 10 days recovering at Base Camp and during this time Sundare re-appeared, but still the worse for drink. Meanwhile bad weather defeated the Boivin's attempts and Batard wasn't sure what to do. He had got heavily into debt to launch this expedition and it was not an appealing thought to have to abandon it having achieved nothing. He contemplated switching directly to a solo ascent of Lhotse South Face, but in the meantime the mood changed in the community around Everest Base Camp. When he made his first try, everyone at Base Camp had been sceptical, but now people started to believe in him and tell him that he could make it third time lucky. Buoyed by this new wave of optimism, Batard set off again on the 25th September at 5 pm. He traversed the Ice Fall and the Western Cwm under splendid moonlight and arrived at 8 pm arrived at Camp II, where he stopped for some hot chocolate. At midnight he arrived at Camp III where he stopped to sleep for three hours after drinking tea and then continued with Imam. He arrived on the South Col exhausted to the point where he vomited any food or drink he tried to consume. The chances of success seemed slim, but he continued, helped by the trail beaten by thirteen climbers who had left from the South Col that morning, all using oxygen. At 3.30 pm Batard had made it to the summit and achieved his incredible ascent in less than 24 hours. The summit was crowded with the French, Nepalese and Korean climbers who had come up before him and he was there to witness Boivin's parapente flight from the summit. His oxygen starved brain was alert enough to think that he should make sure he got back to France before Boivin to avoid the latter stealing all the headlines. In the end Batard's ascent made news in France and globally, but although the press liked his story, they weren't so keen on his "difficult" character. He still didn't seem to have the ability to project his image to his best advantage, which was important if he was to make a viable living as a leading Himalayan climber.

Batard returned to France only briefly before setting off back to Nepal to try Lhotse's South Face. He wanted to prove to the World that he was capable of climbing an objective in super lightweight style which had defeated top mountaineers using a much heavier style. But things did not proceed so smoothly as on Everest. The autumn was already well advanced when he approached the mountain and a terrible wind from the North was buffeting the mountains creating huge snow plumes on the summit crests. Batard was unnerved when he heard of the death of four Slovak climbers on the South West Face of Everest. The British route of Bonington's 1975 expedition had not been repeated and the Slovaks had a very ambitious plan to climb it in alpine style without oxygen. On October 14th four climbers, including Peter Božík who had climbed Lhotse Shar's South Face four years earlier, started up the South West Face from Camp II. They reached 8100 m on the first day after 15 hours of climbing. The critical gully through the Rock Band, originally climbed by Tut Braithwaite and Nick Estcourt in 1975, proved to be much harder than the Slovaks had expected and they had to bivouac again at 8400, above the Rock Band. Then they made the long traverse across the upper snowfield and bivouacked again below the South Summit. After three nights very high without oxygen they were exhausted and the next day only one of them, Jozef Just, went on to the summit. On the descent down the ordinary route they radioed Base Camp to report that they were descending to the South Col, but moving very slowly and feeling lethargic with one of the climbers unwilling to continue down. They were never seen again. They had made a very hard climb in immaculate style, but they had perhaps pushed the limits too far to a point where the risks became so great as to be unreasonable.

Batard also learnt of other accidents that season, but despite these negative signs he felt he must press on with his plans and flew to Lukla. On the flight he was with a TV journalist, Alain Bourillon, who had accompanied Nicolas Jaeger on his 1980 expedition. Batard had known Jaeger and the two were aspirant guides at the same time in the early 1970s. Batard and Bourillon talked about Jaeger and his attempt on Lhotse and naturally Bourillon urged Batard to be very cautious on Lhotse to avoid the same fate as Jaeger. Batard also heard that the Icefall was in a very dangerous state and was about to be stripped of equipment by the Everest expeditions for the end of the climbing season. His plan was to come down the normal route on Lhotse after climbing the South Face and the thought of descending alone through the Ice Fall without equipment was a frightening one. Batard decided to temporarily abandon the idea of soloing Lhotse's South Face and instead contemplated attempting the easier Lhotse Shar. He moved to the area of Lhotse Shar's Base Camp where a number of expeditions were operating. One was a small French team from Paris who had been attempting a neighbouring 7500m peak, but had failed, with one of their party being killed by a serac fall. Despite this reminder of the dangers involved which depressed Batard's spirits, part of him was tempted to return to his original objective on Lhotse and he decided to make a visit to the foot of the South Face. Once there, his motivation again evaporated. He found the Face huge, but also terrifying, not so much because of the technical difficulty, but more the wind and rock fall. Batard, who has written with great honesty about how often he was terribly afraid during his years of top level mountaineering, then started to be completely overtaken by fear. This was a fear that had stalked him throughout his climbing career, which twisted his stomach, made him vomit and trampled any ray of optimism, undermining even the most firmly resolved plans. He wanted nothing but to run back to France and hug his children. And so he decided to abandon the attempt on the 25th October, although he knew his sponsors would be disappointed. The day he decided to leave the foot of the Face he saw an enormous avalanche sweep the route he had been planning to attempt – this time, as often before, fear had saved his life.

During 1989 Batard was again very active in Nepal with ambitious projects, pushing the limits of the possible. But a streak of bad luck seemed to follow him. In January of that year the magnificent Buddhist temple at Thyangboche in the Sherpa region had burnt down. Devout Sherpas believed this would indicate an unlucky period in the coming months. In April Batard attempted to make the first solo ascent of the South Face of Annapurna following the route of Bonington's 1970 expedition. He would be accompanied by the Sherpa Ang Puri on the lower part of the route. Just as he was about to leave Base Camp he tore his knee which blocked for half an hour and was extremely painful. The pain passed, but it sowed a seed of doubt in his mind about what he would do if the same thing occurred when he was high on the Face. He reached 6150 metres, but, as others had found, this Face was extremely hot and dangerous during the day and he heard many snow avalanches and serac falls around him. Furthermore his knee had blocked again three times. He decided to abandon the attempt, but as he went down he was still racked with doubts about whether he had made the right decision. He thought about how much he had spent on mounting the expedition – money he could ill afford – which would now show no results.

He decided to stay in Nepal and move by helicopter to make a solo attempt on the Bonington route on the South West Face of Everest, an even bolder objective. After another rapid approach, he found himself well up the Face at 7800 metres in the middle of the night with a glacial wind burning his eyes. He couldn't climb without the protection of sunglasses, but with them it was too dark to make progress. His mind was also unbalanced by an event which had occurred a few days before when some of the Sherpas at Base Camp had asked him to identify the corpse of a French climber, which had been exposed by movements of the glacier. He was able to recognise it as the body of Gerard Devouassoux, a Chamonix guide who had been killed there in 1974. High up on the South West Face, Batard knew that he had to get down quickly. The terrible pain in his eyes made the temptation to give way to fatigue enormous, but he knew that the slightest lapse in concentration could see him plunging into the Western Cwm more than 1km vertically below. To make matters worse he started to feel unwell with spasms and vomiting. The descent down to the Cwm seemed to be endless and by the time he reached the foot of the Face he was frozen, exhausted and terrified, his face paralysed by cold. When he arrived at Camp I it was 8am in the morning and there was no sign of movement in any of the tents, but he heard two American climbers talking, so he announced his presence to them and they took him in, gave him shelter, warmed him up and let him radio his friends in Base Camp to report he was safe. He then returned to France with some objects belonging to the dead climber to give them to his family.

The year continued to go badly for Batard and that summer his mother died and he wasn't able to be with her at the end. Then a friend was killed in a wind slab avalanche in the Alps and his Sherpa partner Sundare, drunk on the local spirit raki, decided to drown himself in the Dudh Kosi, the torrent running through the centre of the Sherpa country. Despite these misfortunes, Batard pushed ahead with his plans for another solo attempt on Lhotse's South Face. However he was further shaken to hear the news of Kukuczka's death shortly before leaving for Nepal. Batard had met the Pole and the two were due to see each other again at a mountain film festival in Belgium. The death of as great a climber as Kukuczka made Batard feel very mortal. Only the stress of organising and financing the expedition and making arrangements for his family when he was away managed to distract him from his fear of what would happen to him on Lhotse.

He was accompanied to Nepal by Roland Guenot, a friend who was going to come to the foot of the mountain with him. Batard had at first thought of trying to make a rather gentle acclimatisation by going to Kala Patar above Everest Base Camp and then climbing Island Peak, but he realised this was going to take up too much time and so instead opted to acclimatise on Lhotse South Face itself. He knew the Polish fixed ropes should be in place up to at least 7800 metres and this would provide an easy and safe way to acclimatise. whilst familiarising himself with the route and preparing for the push to the summit. At the same time he knew that if he climbed the Face using the Polish fixed ropes, he would come in for criticism for not having made a true solo as he had on Makalu and for having profited from the work done by the Poles. Such criticism would have been largely unjust – after all the likes of Krzysztof Wielicki recognised that the real problem was climbing the upper section of the mountain above 8000 metres and the fixed ropes would give him no help on that. It wouldn't be a completely pure alpine style ascent like that attempted by Fine and Fauquet, but it would still be a fantastic achievement. Batard detested the mean spiritedness of certain journalists and climbers who would be sure to look to criticise an ascent before even considering its merits. But he closed his mind to this inevitable criticism, thinking that he should not let it influence his choices on the mountain or spoil his pleasure if he did have success.

As the time to set off up the Face approached, Batard was having more and more difficulty in staying calm. His nights were disturbed by terrible nightmares. He tried to remain rational and clear and not let himself be sucked under by negative thoughts, but they kept resurfacing. He arrived at Base Camp with two Sherpas Onggel and Pemba on November 25th. Guenot was not feeling properly acclimatised and had stayed in the lower village of Periche. Batard on the other hand was feeling good and climbed a small 5000 metre summit in the area of

Base Camp, gaining a view of sunset on the slopes of Makalu, a sight so beautiful it allowed him to forget his anxieties. Then he retreated back down to Periche arriving well after dark. He decided to give himself two weeks, until 10th December, to complete the climb. He knew that his nerves wouldn't stand the tension longer than that and with a date fixed it was easier to resist the strain. The next day he went back up to the mountain and climbed the Polish fixed ropes, arriving at their Camp I at 5800m where he found a tent and some bottles of gas. He continued a couple of hundred metres further, expending a lot of energy and time pulling out the fixed ropes, which had in many places been buried under snow despite the fact that the Poles had been up there only a few weeks before. He had made the mistake of setting out without a decent breakfast and the effort exhausted him. As he was taking a rest he saw a beautiful sunset, but the wind had also got up forming a snow plume on the summit and he knew he had to get back down. By the time he arrived in Periche, he was exhausted. His friends were very anxious because they knew he hadn't taken food or a headtorch with him that day. He tried to calm them down by describing in detail his day. He also told them that after careful reflection he had decided to make only one attempt on the summit and that this would take place at the beginning of December.

The next day he returned with the two Sherpas to the foot of the Face where he had left his equipment. All the way from Periche the Face was in front of them savagely huge and inspiring in Batard a combination of attraction and revulsion. In his head he turned over all the scenarios for the coming days, the time he would leave, the height he hoped to reach each day and where he would sleep. But he also couldn't avoid asking himself why, at the age of 38, he was attempting the most difficult face in the World, alone and in winter. And why was he doing this when all he really wanted was to be somewhere secure and warm where he could completely relax. He only had one answer – the innate need to challenge himself against the greatest difficulties, which he had always had from childhood, but which found its clearest expression in mountaineering. The anxiety he felt at the foot of the Face was something he had experienced before all of his most difficult climbs. He felt almost like someone condemned to death with the difference that he was in control of the situation and could always choose to turn round. It needed self-control to recognise the moment when it was not safe to go on. When Batard was attempting to climb Everest and Lhotse in a day, Edmund Hillary, the first man to climb Everest, had written to him saying: "You don't need advice from an old timer like me – but all I would say is take it easy. It's not much of a success if you reach the summits and then don't get safely back down again." He checked his equipment and the state of the mountain. The weather forecast was fine and his chances of success seemed good, but he kept Hillary's words in mind. He decided to spend two days on the Face to assess the situation.

On the 28th November he left in the morning and as he climbed he felt on form and happy. That night he reached the Polish Camp I and settled into their tent, which fortunately was still in good condition. He watched the sunset as he melted snow to make tea. He was now feeling good, in tune with the mountain, despite being alone on that huge Face. He realised that experience of being there was a unique one, difficult to replicate in other fields of human experience. He tried to eat enough to have energy for the efforts of the following day, but just as he was about to settle down to sleep he realised with a fright that he had not checked the anchoring of the tent. If the wind got up in the night, it could carry the tent away with him inside it. When he went out to check and saw that the tent was on a small icy ledge, he decided to tie himself on to the mountain for the night. Whilst he was doing this he also saw that it had now started to snow a bit.

When he woke in the morning the weather was fine again, but very cold. He carried on up the mountain and around 10 am he reached the second Polish Camp at 6200 metres. There was a tent there too, but it was completely collapsed on top of some reserves of food and three mattresses. He tried to dig it out, but it was in a bad state and frozen into the ice. In the afternoon he redescended to Camp I. He knew his next excursion on the Face would be an attempt on the summit. He gave himself a rest day on the 30th November and started preparing for his ascent on the following day. But on that day he only felt a shadow of himself and could think of nothing but his desire to be home. In his frank account of the difficulties of his life written more than 10 years after, he explained that his decision to turn back on the climb was due to nightmares. Despite the fact everything was going to plan, he suffered terrible nightmares every night, in what seemed to be like a general malaise that invaded every part of him and every moment of his existence. He didn't know the cause, but it petrified him, killed all his ambition, his confidence and his courage. Without these he knew he had no chance somewhere on something like Lhotse's South Face. He retreated back to France feeling completely lost.

As he departed from the face, Batard met Enric Lucas and Christophe Profit, who were on their way up to make their own attempt. The pair had been on the Face together with Messner's expedition earlier that year, but now wanted to make an attempt in alpine style. In order to acclimatise, they first spent 40 days trying to climb the ordinary route on Dhaulagiri accompanied by Sylvianne Tavemier, Ana Masip and Pierre-Louis Olland. Their final attempt on Dhaulagiri on 14th November was a lightning assault without even a bivouac, but they were forced to turn back at 7800 metres due to cold and strong winds. They were not too tired out by their time of Dhaulagiri and the eleven days passed between 7500m and 8000m had left them well acclimatised. The time spent together had also consolidated their partnership and they were ready for Lhotse.

After Dhaulagiri, they carried on with the second, and much more difficult, part of their plan to climb the South Face of Lhotse. They transferred to Lhotse Base Camp by helicopter, arriving their on the 5th December. Their plan was to take between 5 and 10 days to climb the face in alpine style. Carrying all the equipment and food for such an attempt required rucksacks weighing at least 20 kg despite things like an ultra-lightweight rope. They wanted to try a similar direct route to that attempted by Fine and Fauquet in pure alpine style. A first attempt was immediately abandoned, but on a second try they reached 6730 metres on December 18, but after two bivouacs there, they were forced to descend due to bad weather. Lucas then decided to abandon the expedition, telling Profit he didn't have the appetite to go back up again and returned to Spain. Profit was not angry with Lucas, but nonetheless found this decision hard to accept and decided to stay on to try and make a solo attempt following the Polish route like Batard. He first tried on the 13th and 14th January 1990 and reached 7150 metres, but his tent was destroyed by the wind and he had to retreat. He then made a final attempt from January 19th to the 21st and reached 7600 metres before turning back. It was a bold try, particularly given the season and Profit was not yet finished with Lhotse's South Face.

Chapter 12 – The New Messner?

By the end of the 1980s an ever increasing number of Himalayan climbers believed that a lightweight approach was the solution to even the greatest challenges. The next man to attempt Lhotse's South Face, Tomo Cesen from Slovenia, was a fanatical exponent of this approach. Although the great successes of Slovenian mountaineering in the 1970s and 1980s gave him many role models, there was no single person who inspired him above all others. But the first ascent of the South Face of Makalu in 1975 when Cesen was 16 and just starting to climb was a significant influence. Ales Kunaver's team on Makalu included many men who would go on to play key roles in the 1981 Lhotse South Face expedition.

Although he started rock climbing, Cesen soon understood that focusing only on short routes of extreme difficulty would not hold a permanent interest for him and instead he pursued many different forms of climbing both on rock and on ice. Solo climbing appealed to him from the beginning and he first soloed a route when he was still only 16. Soloing meant he needed to focus much more than when he had a partner and relying only on himself was a sensation he loved. Before his first hard solo he had done many others of low and medium difficulty, building up his experience and learning important lessons. He realised that he had an unusual level of self-control which he could exercise even in critical moments. This gradual acquisition of self-knowledge and ability to concentrate totally on a task gave him great satisfaction. Sometimes he felt he needed to have that sense of insecurity to give climbing its particular flavour. The Himalayas, which had inspired Cesen to take up climbing, continued to be remote and seemingly unachievable dream for Cesen during his climbing apprenticeship, but gradually the prospect came to seem more real. He first visited the "greater ranges" when he went to the Peruvian Andes in 1979 and climbed a new route of the spectacular Alpamayo. Four years later he got his first experience at really high altitude when he climbed the 7495m Peak Communism in the Soviet Pamirs.

In 1985 Cesen had been climbing for ten years and got his chance to participate in a Slovenian expedition led by Tone Skarja to Yalungkang, an 8505m subsidiary summit of Kangchenjunga in Nepal. Skarja's team was a large traditional style expedition which aimed to make the first ascent of the mountain's North Face. Several of the members were veterans of the 1981 Lhotse South Face expedition, including Filip Bence, Borut Bergant, Francek Knez and Peter Podgornik. Following the tested model they had used on Lhotse, the Slovenians put up fixed ropes and established a series of camps up the Face. The hardest section was climbed by Bence and Podgornik involving grade VI climbing. Two days later Silvo Karo and Knez set up Camp IV at 8100 metres from where a summit bid could be launched.

Bergant and Cesen then moved up to Camp IV for the summit bid. It was the first time Cesen had been over 8000 metres. In the small camp all movement was difficult and they struggled to sleep. To make matters worse, Cesen was sick in the night and only just managed to scramble out of the tent to vomit. After that further sleep was impossible. Cesen was unsure of how he would perform and decided to take some bottled oxygen, which made him feel more lucid and confident. Bergant had decided to climb without oxygen and set off in the lead. The steepness of the slope made the best way forward difficult to identify, but it was clear that they needed to overcome a steep ice bulge. Cesen took over the lead, abandoning the weight of the oxygen equipment, whilst Bergant found a belay. After three hours of difficult ice climbing they had overcome this very steep 40 metres. They continued unroped up the corniced ridge above, but realised this wasn't going to lead to the summit and a long traverse was needed to reach it. Struggling to find their way in the mist shrouded maze of snow ice and rocks, they radioed Base Camp to get guidance. Their colleagues could do little more than encourage them, although time was getting on and it was now 10 hours since they had left the camp. They agreed that if they hadn't made it within 2 hours they would turn back. After a little more than an hour and half they made it to the summit. Both sides of the mountain were covered in clouds and an orange tint marked the approaching evening. At 5pm, knowing that the descent would be very long and difficult, they radioed Base Camp to say that they were leaving the summit. This was the last contact they were able to make for a long time – leaving their companions nervously glued to the radio waiting for news and hearing none.

As they crossed the summit crest onto the North side of the mountain they were immersed in darkness. Bergant wanted to rope up, but Cesen knew that this would cost time. They were having trouble communicating as the oxygen deprivation slowed their mental capabilities. They had inadvertently left their head-torches in the tent and finding their way was becoming very difficult. They knew that the ridge they were on ended on a ledge above the steep ice bulge. This would be too difficult to climb down so they had left some anchors in place to abseil from, but they fumbled around in the dark for an hour and a half before finding the anchors. Cesen tried to keep his concentration, but he realised that Bergant was completely spent; shaking his head to indicate that he couldn't go on. To make matters worse the rope was terribly knotted and frozen, but they had to abseil to get down and so Cesen found an end of the rope and set to work to untangle it. To pull knots through he frequently had to take his gloves off and hold them between his teeth, terrified of the consequences of dropping them. Both of them had now completely lost their sense of time and sensibility for danger. Bergant made the first abseil first and when Cesen joined him, he found him on a tiny stance. Cesen shouted to try and encourage Bergant to stay focused pointing out that in another 20 metres they would be past the worst. Cesen didn't feel secure on his feet and held on with one hand whilst trying to fix an anchor for the next abseil with the other. Then time seemed to stand still as, without making any sound, Bergant leant backwards as if he wanted to sit down and an instant later disappeared into the void. Cesen still had the strength to let out a cry, but of course it changed nothing. He leaned his head against the icy rocks, trying to grasp the situation. He was alone, in the night, at 8350 metres, and almost had the sensation that he was floating in space. He managed to calm himself enough to make another abseil to reach the ledge at the base of the rock band which they had climbed that morning. He struggled to gain a footing on this ledge, which required him to swing like a pendulum on the rope. Each time he swung he landed on steep ice and his crampons skidded without gripping, but fortunately he managed to find a place for his last piton, which allowed him to get down onto easier ground. A little lower he was enveloped in thick fog. Below there was a crevasse zone and in the dark he would have no chance of spotting the holes. The only prudent choice was to bivouac, which meant a night in -40°, with no shelter. He kept repeating to himself that if he wanted to survive he had to keep moving his fingers and feet in order to try and maintain circulation and minimise the risk of frostbite and make sure he didn't fall asleep. If he succumbed to sleep, he knew he would never wake up. His survival that night was done to his nine years of mountaineering experience, which had taught him to be calm even in the most perilous situations. To try and keep warm he moved continuously on that small ledge, 2 metres to the left, then 2 back to the right, repeating the movement like a psychotic bear in a zoo. He kept looking at the eastern sky hoping to see some brightening which would signal the arrival of dawn, but the night seemed to drag on endlessly. Looking back on that terrible night he had the impression that there were moments when he had crossed a mental line. There were long periods of which he had no memory, as if his mind went on to a sort of automatic survival mode and shut off all other functions. All that he could really remember was the need to stay awake and keep moving.

He continued his descent at first light. The radio had been in the rucksack of Bergant when he fell so Cesen could not communicate his situation to Base Camp, although the team there were very preoccupied because they could see a single dot moving on the upper part of the Face. To make matters worse Cesen started to lose part of his sight in his left eye due to a haemorrhage in the retina caused by the lack of oxygen. He didn't stop until he reached the tent at Camp IV, where he tried to get a bit of circulation back into his digits and melted some snow to drink. Up to this point the determination to survive had overridden all other thoughts, but now Cesen was in a more secure place, he was overcome with thoughts about his companion. The couloir down which he had fallen was steep and wide with ice covered slabs and hard snow. He knew that there was no way Bergant could have survived the fall. After a while Cesen continued his descent moving at a slow and irregular speed, half-dead with exhaustion. Down at Base Camp, those watching his progress started to realise that something had gone badly wrong. As he lost height, Cesen started to recover some strength, although only when he reached the security of the fixed ropes was he confident that he was going to make it off the mountain safe and sound. He arrived at Camp I accompanied by various team mates who had waited in support and joined him on the way down. There he was able to take of his boots for the first time in six days. His teammates coaxed him back down to Base Camp and the doctor gave him treatment – Cesen had lost 14 kilos during the ascent. A few days later there was a heavy fall of snow and the wind was buffeting the summit. The porters had arrived for the march out accompanied by their yaks. The bells on the yaks were ringing, but the team only felt sadness at leaving their friend behind on the mountain. Cesen isn't someone who cries easily, but at the end of the Yalungkang expedition everyone was in tears.

Despite the traumatic experience on Yalungkang, Cesen had no thoughts of abandoning Himalayan climbing and the following year he was in the Karakoram with another Slovenian expedition which had permits for Broad Peak and Gasherbrum II. This was the summer of 1986 when it seemed half of the world's top climbers were congregated at K2 Base Camp and two major new routes were climbed by Poles on K2. The Slovenian team involved veterans of the 1981 Lhotse expedition, including Andrej Stremfelj, whose wife was also a member of the team and would become the first Slovenian woman to climb an 8000er. Cesen had a secret ambition to also climb Gasherbrum I, the third of the three low 8000ers which lay in the Karakoram Range close to K2 around the 63 kilometre long Baltoro Glacier. The Baltoro Glacier, one of the longest outside the Polar regions, splits into two main branches at a place called Concordia – named after a similar place on the largest Alpine glacier, the Aletsch glacier in Switzerland. The right hand branch goes off towards the Gasherbrum peaks, two of which are over 8000 metres and two just below, whereas the left hand branch leads up past another 8000 metre peak, Broad Peak to the foot of K2. When Cesen saw K2 for he was so struck by the beauty and majesty of its form that he became obsessed with the idea of climbing it. The Slovenians made a first attempt on Broad Peak, which turned back at 7500 metres due to deep snow. There then followed a long period of bad weather with continuous rain and snow for day after day. With every day the prospects of reaching the summit seemed to get more remote, but some of the team started to return to the mountain despite the adverse weather. Cesen himself stayed down at Base Camp hoping that there would be a real break in the bad weather to get a decent shot at the summit. Finally after 11 days he got ready to depart. He was of course used to climbing solo, but not on a mountain of this scale and initially wasn't certain he wanted to solo Broad Peak. He knew that he would not be completely alone on the mountain because a number of other climbers were up there, including his teammates Viki Groselj and Bogdan Biscak who had already reached the summit and were on their way back down. The success of this first pair had catalysed the rest of the team into action and four of his team members including Andrej Stremfelj had also gone up onto the mountain. In the evening before setting off Cesen ate something, then closed his tent and headed off into the night. It was splendidly calm and so quiet that he almost felt he could hear his own thoughts. The only thing which was missing was the tension which generally accompanied this type of departure – it all seemed too easy for that. 19 hours later he was sat on the summit having made the ascent in 4 hours less than Krzysztof Wielicki. On the summit of

Broad Peak, Cesen looked directly across at the perfect pyramid of K2 and the idea of trying to climb it grew in his thoughts. He felt he was now a prisoner of this idea which he couldn't get out of his mind.

While the rest of the team went off to climb Gasherbrum II, Cesen stayed at the base of K2 studying possible routes from every angle available. The almost perfect symmetry of the pyramid drew the eye and the silver clouds drifting in to hide its upper part added a further air of mystery which became irresistible to Cesen. He had to be quite discrete about his plans because the expedition did not have a permit for K2. At the same time the desire to undertake this climb was so strong Cesen couldn't see how the lack of a piece of paper could rob him of his dream. On K2 he climbed a spur leading to the shoulder high on the "normal" Abruzzi ridge route alone and in only two days. Having already acclimatised on Broad Peak, he did not have many problems with the altitude and was able to move quickly following couloirs and strips of snow at the side of the ridge. Having studied the ridge extensively through binoculars he believed that the lower section would not be too difficult, but the middle looked more problematic and he wouldn't know till he got up there how problematic this would be to climb. In the end this section did not prove as hard as it looked from below and it gave access to the upper section of the spur. Although easier, the upper section was threatened by a giant serac. These huge ice cliffs are part of glaciers, but whereas glaciers move slowly down under the inevitable influence of gravity, seracs move very slowly forward until the front part becomes unstable and breaks off in a huge ice avalanche. This happens rarely, but at a time which is impossible to predict and being hit by huge blocks of rock hard ice as a big as a car or a building means almost certain death. Cesen couldn't keep his eyes of this huge serac and this added urgency to his progress which became a race to get out from under the firing line. Because the night was bright and the dawn promised another splendid day, he pushed himself to the limit without pausing. After 17 hours of climbing he arrived at the top of the spur. This took him to 8000 metres and a day's climb away from the summit.

The weather seemed clear and he had now joined the ordinary route on the Abruzzi Ridge with the major difficulties behind him. He was going at a reasonable pace too, but when he got high enough to see the horizon on the Chinese side of the mountain he could hear the wind becoming ever stronger. The first clouds appeared, as if from nowhere. Within half an hour he found himself in the middle of a violent storm. Snow spun around him at such a speed that it was impossible to tell if it was actually snowing or just wind-blown snow. He had to decide what to do quickly, and although it was hard to give up on such a fantastic mountain, the only rational thing was to head down the ordinary route as quickly as possible and get out of the clouds. He was incredibly relieved to see Camp III because getting shelter had become a life or death matter. He then continued his rapid descent and did not halt until he was down on the glacier, absolutely spent.

When Cesen arrived at the bottom the terrible tragedy which led to the deaths of Alan Rouse and four others was taking place higher up the mountain. Jim Curran, who was at K2 Base Camp throughout the summer of 1986 and chronicled the tragic events, did not even notice the climb of Cesen at the time. In fact there is an appendix to Curran's book "K2 Triumph and Tragedy" called "A Stranger on the Shoulder" which describes Cesen's climb. Curran's book was published before Cesen had become a very widely known climber, but Curran found it the circumstances surprising, particularly since it happened at the same time and almost in the same place as the tragedy at Camp IV where several climbers were stranded. He asked himself "How on earth someone could have blithely soloed up the shoulder, presumably to within metres of Camp IV, and soloed down the Abruzzi without anyone noticing". Of course Curran understood that, since Cesen did not have a permit to climb on K2, he had to avoid drawing attention to himself if he wanted to stay out of trouble with the Pakistani authorities, but he still found it puzzling that no-one had seen him given the number of climbers moving on the Abruzzi ridge during that period. However he did note that Cesen seemed to read the signs of the weather better than the climbers who had chosen to climb to the summit and then tried to sit the storm out high on the mountain, a decision which cost the lives of five of them. Curran also recognised that Cesen had made a fine climb, completing a route tried by the British climbers Al Rouse and Roger Baxter-Jones a few years before.

In 1986 Cesen also claimed some significant climbs in the Alps, including the winter trilogy of classic North Faces, also climbed by Christophe Profit. In 1987 he went on a large Slovenian expedition to Lhotse Shar. This expedition hoped to not only climb Lhotse Shar, but also continue the traverse of the ridge as far as Lhotse Middle, which was still unclimbed. Again there were veterans of Lhotse South face including Filip Bence and Andrzej Stremfelj. The expedition was hampered by bad weather and avalanche danger and only reached 7450 metres. Furthermore they argued with a French expedition which was also attempting Lhotse Shar from the next valley, but whose route overlapped with the Slovenians. The French asked permission to use the Slovenians fixed ropes, which was refused, because they did not have a permit for this route. But the French used the ropes all the same, leading to a lot of bad blood between the teams. After various to-ing and fro-ing with Kathmandu, the French managed to clarify they had permission for the route too and one of their climbers, Yves Tedeschi, made it to the summit alone. The French accused the Slovenians of being bad losers and of having deliberately taken down their ropes to make trouble for them. It doesn't seem to have been a very positive experience for Cesen, who hardly mentions the expedition in his autobiography.

During the winter from 1988-1989 Cesen did climbs in the Alps to prepare himself physically and mentally for harder things he had planned in the Himalayas. Serious hard climbs in the French, Italian and Slovenian Alps tested a variety of different qualities. During his Alpine winter he was thinking obsessively about his next project, a solo ascent of the North Face of Jannu. This is a splendid and difficult mountain, a little short of 8000 metres, but which represents a much more severe climbing challenge than most of the 8000ers. Despite the obsession of many Himalayan mountaineers with the 8000 metre peaks, there are a handful of summits below the height which have a reputation amongst the leading climbers which is equal too and sometimes greater than some of the 8000 metre peaks themselves. Some climbers have focused their activity in the Himalayas almost exclusively on the 8000ers, but others didn't attach quite the same significance to this arbitrary height. Forgetting about the 8000 metre limit, opens up many new potential targets. A good example is the magnificent wedge of Gasherbrum IV, first climbed by an expedition led by Riccardo Cassin in 1958, but which continues to be a major prize for top mountaineers. Jannu is also in this category. It was first climbed in 1962 by a strong French expedition. Several expeditions had tried the huge and very steep North Wall of the mountain, called the "Wall of Shadows" because it receives so little sunlight. Cesen spent a year contemplating attempting this face and weighing the pros and the cons of a route which would be a quantum leap ahead in difficulty and seriousness compared to what he had done before.

The organisation of the expedition was very different to those that Cesen had participated in in the past. Interactions between team members are a big part of Himalayan climbing and conflicts are quite common in larger expeditions. This time Cesen was the only person planning to go on the mountain and so he would be making all the decisions alone. The approach march to the mountain was familiar from his expedition to the nearby Yalungkang, but the incredible countryside was overshadowed by his focus on the objective. Jannu was covered by clouds when they arrived at the last village, but then the top part appeared as a huge nearly vertical rectangular wedge, which sent a shiver down Cesen's spine. They established a pretty modest Base Camp on the edge of the glacier. Before climbing on the Face it was necessary to acclimatise. Cesen tried to use the experience of each expedition he made to increase his understanding of how his physiology adapted to altitude and so to fine tune his acclimatisation programme. He found it was almost an art to find the right balance between spending time at high altitude to adapt the organism whilst trying to remain in peak physical condition. For Cesen the best solution was to make frequent and progressive excursions from Base Camp returning to sleep there, operating on a "climb high – sleep low" principle. Studying the Face closely he changed his mind about the exact route as some features looked different in real life than they had from photos. He also studied the weather patterns and noted that there was almost always a worsening in the afternoon as a powerful wind carried clouds up from the valleys which coated the Face with a sprinkling of snow. During the night the weather usually cleared and was very fine in the morning. This pattern was so regular he was able to plan for it in the timing of his climb. As he completed his acclimatisation, his nerves were on edge and he was tempted to delay in the hope of hitting a period of more settled weather, but it was already late April and if he delayed too long there was a risk that the monsoon would arrive.

At dawn on the 27th April he started to prepare, even though he was not completely convinced about the weather conditions and the sky was covered. For Cesen the final decision on which equipment to bring was an absolutely critical. Various things might conceivably be needed, but since he had to carry everything up steep and difficult ground he could not afford to take too much. He was particularly torn about whether or not to take a bivouac sack. Around midday he set off, accompanied by Jani Kodalj, a doctor who was with Cesen on the expedition. Cesen had been able to study the upper part of the Face, but the bottom part was not visible from Base Camp and so something of a mystery. Although the North Face of Jannu is not greatly threatened by powder snow avalanches and serac falls there is significant danger from rock and ice fall and most of which would be funnelled through an area in the lower section. To keep the risk reasonable he planned to climb this section during the night when colder temperatures reduced rock fall. Once he reached the glacier Kodalj left him and Cesen continued alone, exhilarated by the great adventure. He had pitons and a spare ice axe blade on his harness – if he had only one blade and it broke it would be very serious. He carried two axes, a rope and was wearing crampons and a helmet. His rucksack contained spare clothing, gloves, food and drink, a sleeping bag and the bivouac sack, which he had finally decided to bring. It was an absolutely minimalist set of equipment, considering the magnitude of the undertaking. After four hours climbing it started to get dark in the valley, but up on the Face it was bright enough to carry on climbing. As he had hoped, the ice and rock fall seemed to be easing with the night and he climbed a steep 200 metre couloir which gave access to a large icefield in the middle of the Face. Dawn broke as he reached the top of this icefield. To reach the next icefield he had to tackle the first really problematic section of the route involving very steep ice and granite slabs. The compact crackless rock gave no chance of placing protection and he simply had to press on, aiming for the seracs which marked the start of the next icefield. After overcoming a short rock step he reached the final part of the Face where ice and granite slabs alternated. One of the slabs proved especially difficult. 6000 metres lower, without plastic double boots and crampons, it would have been a straightforward piece of friction climbing, but here it was a completely different matter. He leaned on the slab with his hands, his crampons stuck in the thin ice and he clawed up with his ice axe on some small ice crystals. With enormous relief he managed to lever his weight up and get a firmer placement for his axe. The nearly vertical slabs were 30 to 40 metres high and in the thin air he was incapable of overcoming them without resting, which usually meant perilously hanging off an insecurely placed ice axe. There were around 10 of these slabs and the easiest route through them was almost impossible to spot from below. He had to resort to artificial aid on a number of occasions. He could have climbed free without his crampons, but there was no place where he could remove them and put them on again. Occasionally he managed to rest his arms when he could jam his foot in a crack securely, but otherwise the strain was continuous. After the rock, came hard black or green ice of variable quality. At one point an ice gully ended in a blank granite face. He fixed a piton, descended a little and, by penduluming on the rope, was able to reach the continuation of the ice gully to the left. The difficulty continued right up to the summit ridge and then suddenly he stumbled on to the soft snow of the ridge.

The summit was very close and there were no difficulties left. The huge drive to succeed he had had at the start had all but disappeared and the summit brought only a fleeting moment of euphoria. He was too tired and too anxious to get down for there to be any real joy up there. It was 3.30 pm and the weather was worsening with a sea of grey clouds below him. Rather than reversing his steps, Cesen had decided to descend the Japanese route which took a less steep and direct line to the left of his route of ascent. Given the worsening weather he was keen to get as far down as possible before nightfall. He reached the point where he had to leave the crest of the ridge, but then the technical difficulty increased and he had to use the rope on some steep ice sections of ice. By then there was a real storm, but Cesen didn't even contemplate stopping, until he reached some seracs and darkness and heavy snowfall forced him to seek shelter. He managed to find it in a crevasse where he spent a seemingly endless night, shivering from cold and continuously checking his watch to try and track the passage of time. There is hardly anything more torturous than waiting for time to crawl by to morning in the inhuman conditions of a Himalayan bivouac. Cesen couldn't stop thinking about the similar night on nearby Yalungkang a few years before. He had 800 metres of unknown ground to descend before reaching safety, but there was nothing he could do other than wait for the storm to pass and comfort himself that at least he was sheltered from avalanches in the crevasse.

After waiting for several hours, the storm seemed to calm a little, a few stars became visible in the sky and Cesen decided to immediately continue his descent. Usually he would have waited for daylight, but he did not want to take the risk of being surprised by another storm and anyway the moon was up. He descended between the seracs, but it proved to be the wrong way and he was blocked by a 15 metre ice cliff. Rather than going back up, he decided to try and abseil over this obstacle. He still had two ice screws left, but he was reluctant to waste these as he might need them lower down and so instead he cut out an ice mushroom and wrapped the rope round this. Trusting his weight on the ice required considerable nerves, but he was confident that he had the experience to judge that it would hold his weight. When he reached the lower serac band the ground became less steep and he started to zig-zag between the seracs. As he approached the plateau he had to use the rope to abseil more and more often, sometimes to save time and sometimes because it was simply the only option. The approach of dawn promised another fine day, although the valley was still covered by a layer of low clouds. When he finally reached easier ground and all that remained was to walk across the glacier to Base Camp, the release of tension was so great he hardly had the strength to do it. He staggered along like a drunk leaving a track in the snow which swayed and zig-zagged. Half way to the Camp he was met by Kodalj who greeted him with a wide smile. Re-establishing contact with the rest of the human world was a great feeling for Cesen. It took five hours to reach Base Camp instead of the usual two and he was very hungry after three days of huge exertion, almost without eating. But his stomach couldn't handle food and all he could do was drink huge quantities of liquid.

Cesen's achievement was heralded by the mountaineering press as the start of a new era of Himalayan climbing. It was a long way ahead of what climbers had been able to achieve until recently. Climbs had been made solo, but generally not with great technical difficulty. Climbs of great technical difficulty had been made, but generally in a heavyweight style or at a lower altitude. Now Cesen had combined all of these by climbing a very difficult route on a high mountain in the ultimate lightweight style. For Cesen, what was important was that he had made the climb in the style he had wanted, with faith in his own decisions and climbing ability. But he did not feel he had yet reached a conclusion – there was still scope to take this development further. After the succession of increasingly difficult climbs he had made, Cesen now felt the logical next step was to attempt a route as hard as that on Jannu, but on a major 8000 metre peak. Given the attention given to Lhotse's South Face by the World's leading climbers in the late 1980s, it was a natural choice. Furthermore this Face of course held a special place in Slovenia's mountaineering folklore, following the exploits of the 1981 expedition. By climbing the route he could complete unfinished business for his country. He planned to make the climb in the pre-monsoon season of 1990.

Cesen was accompanied to Lhotse only by a doctor, Janko Kodalj, who had been with him on Jannu and Tomaz Ravnihar, who would make a film of the ascent. When they arrived in Kathmandu they found a climate of political upheaval. This was the People's Movement, a multiparty campaign for democracy and an end to the absolute monarchy. After the police fired on a demonstration in

February killing 12 people, the movement grew and grew and by April two million people were involved in the protests. By the time Cesen arrived, there were daily marches and skirmishes between crowds of demonstrators and the police. Things reached a climax at exactly the time Cesen's team were supposed to be flying to Lukla. Not only was there a strike of the pilots, but also various other demonstrations and even a general strike. The authorities felt threatened and declared a curfew with continuous patrols from the riot police and military. Knowing that they couldn't easily reach Lukla, Cesen's team killed time playing cards and discussing the possible scenarios on how the crisis would play out. Then the King announced that he would become a constitutional monarch, which met the protesters main demand and things calmed down as quickly as they had blown up. The next day Kathmandu was covered by thick fog, but this didn't stop masses of people being out on the streets as the army dismantled the barricades and life returned to its normal chaotic rhythm.

Cesen's team immediately rushed to the airport and paid a small bribe to get tickets for the next flight to Lukla. It was a huge relief to have escaped from the upheaval of Kathmandu and even the normally nerve wracking landing on the beaten earth strip at Lukla seemed trivial. As they proceeded towards the Everest region, Cesen felt the comfortable routine of a Himalayan expedition to which he was well accustomed. Usually the first thing a climber looks for when arriving at Namche Bazar, the Sherpa capital, is a steaming cup of tea, but this time Cesen was more anxious to catch his first glimpse of Lhotse. He raced up the hill above the town as soon as he arrived. He had seen the Face before during his expedition to Lhotse Shar, but its condition this year could determine whether his plan was realistic. He couldn't contain his nerves as he scrambled up the hill, reaching the top out of breath to see the Face completely white from snow cover. This is what he had hoped for and now he started to believe he had a chance of success. Cesen's team spent a couple of days at Namche, waiting for the last loads to arrive, which gave a chance to socialise with friends from other expeditions operating in the region. Once they had collected up everything they moved on to Chukung, the last village before the mountain. Their liaison officer, a Nepalese soldier named Karki on his first expedition, was suffering badly from altitude sickness, but was unwilling to take their advice and descend to a lower level to recover. The doctor Kodalj had to spell out the dire medical consequences of ignoring the signs of altitude sickness before they could persuade him to go back down. They chose a site for Base Camp which was further from the Face than that used by most previous expeditions. Generally teams had camped close to the Face, but this means that there is no water at Base Camp and it tends to be battered by wind all afternoon. Cesen decided that having to walk an hour and a half to the foot of the Face was a price worth paying for additional comfort. For expeditions which spent months fixing ropes and ferrying loads, regularly returning to and from Base Camp, the value of being close was higher than for Cesen who was planning to climb in a single push.

To acclimatise Cesen ascended the South East Ridge of Lhotse Shar. This was familiar to him from three years before, isn't too difficult and, most importantly, isn't dangerous. The fact that Lhotse is 800 metres higher than Jannu made a more thorough acclimatisation necessary. It also gave him a chance to study his proposed ascent route in detail from the side. Navigation on the Face is not always easy and it was critical that he had all the features of the route imprinted in his mind. He made four excursions up onto Lhotse Shar reaching a maximum height of 7200m. After this he felt adequately prepared for the main Face. Cesen knew that timing would be critical to being able to make a safe ascent and that afternoons almost always brought bad weather and increased risk of stonefall and avalanche. Furthermore the latter two risks were most severe on the lower part, making it the most dangerous section. He felt it would be madness to tackle this section during the daytime. Cesen noted that whilst from afar the Face looked a beautiful picture post card mountain scene, close to it was a sinister place. His heart was in his mouth when he reminded himself that he was going to attempt it alone. His plan was to start in the afternoon and climb the most dangerous part during the night. By the 22nd April he felt ready. In his backpack was a bivouac sack and a sleeping bag, two ice axes, 100 metres of 6mm rope, pitons and ice screws, spare gloves, socks and sunglasses, a camera, a radio, special thermal clothing, food and drinks. To attempt Lhotse in the extreme lightweight style meant carrying a very heavy pack. Instead of carrying a stove, Cesen chose to take 3 litres of coffee. For food he brought cheese, chocolate, dextrose, cheesecake, biscuits and cereal bars. Knowing the way the appetite is affected by altitude, all that mattered was bringing things he would find appetising.

Kodalj came with Cesen to the foot of the face and then followed his progress until he lost sight of him. Cesen followed a route much further left than that taken by his compatriots in 1981 and reached the long snow ridge followed by them and Fine and Fauquet (which the Slovenians had called "The Telescope") only in its upper section. Conditions were generally good, particularly in the steepest section of the Face, whilst he had some difficulty on the traverse above the snow field which led to the foot of the huge triangular rock face. He climbed half way up an ice slope which ended in a wide shelf at the left hand side of the big rock face. Following the advice of his Slovenian compatriots he found the easiest place to enter the gully to the left of this shelf. Before tackling this, Cesen bivouacked for the first time. He was at 7500 metres and in need of rest having climbed for 15 hours in a row right through the night. The sun was shining onto the wall creating rockfall danger and making it best to stay still in a sheltered spot. Despite the altitude, it was very warm and he managed to sleep for a while. Resting on that ledge he realised his insignificance in comparison with the enormity of the Face. Even through the most powerful binoculars a climber does not appear larger than a grain of sand when viewed from below. This sense of scale is not so evident for the climber up on the Face when he is stationary, but as soon as he started to move again, the scale became clear. Even moving relatively quickly – which was hard for the human body to achieve at such heights - the summit did not seem to get perceptibly closer.

In the early afternoon he continued his ascent. The beginning of the couloir was a classic chimney, closed in on three sides by steep and narrow walls. Even though the first part was not too steep, he shuddered to imagine what it would be like to be caught there when an avalanche from the wide upper basin was funnelled through there. This was something which happened on various occasions to members of the 1981 expedition, although they were of course attached to fixed ropes. Cesen exited from the chimney and climbed a steep rock wall followed by a delicate traverse to the right, passing several vertical steps. Now only a long snow slope separated him from the foot of the final triangular rock face which led up the summit ridge. He knew that he had to choose his line up this face with extreme care to minimise the risk of being swept away by an avalanche. It was late in the evening when he installed himself at his second bivouac at 8200 metres at the foot of the final pillar, close to where the Slovenians had put their top camp in 1981. This bivouac reminded him of the one he had made high on Yalung Kang, although here the position was much more comfortable. All the same he didn't even want to try sleeping, given the extreme cold at this height. He subsequently learnt that the very same night, four Nepalese climbers had been forced to bivouac close to the South Summit of Everest, across the other side of the Western Cwm from where Cesen was. All four had suffered frost bite and two of them were badly affected. For Cesen, The night was a struggle against the cold and solitude, a struggle which in a few moments of weakness he started to believe he would lose.

The problems of the final pillar leading to the summit, which had defeated the 1981 team, had obsessed Cesen throughout the whole ascent. By looking at photos he had identified a possible line of ascent on the left, but he was aware that at close quarters things might prove much more difficult than they appeared in photos. The sections he had climbed up to this point were known ground from the accounts of the 1981 climbers. Now he was moving onto unexplored terrain. If he couldn't overcome this section, he knew there would be no choice, but to retrace his steps to the foot of the Face. The 24th April dawned calm and clear, exactly as he had hoped. He left all the surplus equipment he could at the bivouac site and set out for the summit. A snowy ramp took him to a steep step. It took him three hours to overcome the next 60-70 metres, climbing at the limit of his ability and using a few pitons for aid. After two days of enormous physical exertion and now quite close to the summit, he didn't care how he did it as long as he overcame this section. Remembering his experience from Yalung Kang he fixed the rope at the top of the difficult section to allow a sure way back down this crux. As he was fixing the rope it started to dawn on him that he had finally solved the puzzle of finding a way up this great Face. The summit was still quite distant, since Cesen's route finishes on the summit ridge well to the left of the highest point, but having come so far he did not even contemplate turning round.

The rest of the climb wasn't difficult, but he started to pay the price for the enormous effort he had already put in and feel the very high altitude. In some stretches there was deep snow which made progress even harder. The weather was typical afternoon weather on Lhotse's South Face – some clouds and a few flakes of snow. The wind troubled him more than the clouds and snow. From time to time the clouds opened up and he got a view of the upper slopes of Everest above the South Col or further away towards Cho Oyu. To the south on the other hand, there was nothing but an endless sea of white clouds. Finally a short descent into a saddle between the horns of Lhotse and a final brief ascent led him to the summit. Cesen established radio contact with Base Camp and announced "Jani, I can't go up anymore, I am on the summit". He didn't feel great joy in completing the ascent, but he did feel satisfaction and even more relief at not having to go up anymore. Naturally the difficulty and danger of the descent down the huge face hung over him.

He wanted to lose as much height as possible before nightfall and managed to follow the ascent line as far as 7800m, before the risk of avalanches made it suicidal to carry on down the couloir which he had ascended. There was no alternative, but to descend by abseiling down the almost vertical rocks to the side which had been one of the hardest sections of the 1981 expedition's route. Unsurprisingly there was no trace of the ropes from 1981, which would have been cut by stone fall or swept away by avalanches long ago, but he was able to find several of the anchors, which proved very useful, saving both time and equipment. Although this section was quite sheltered from large avalanches, he was still showered almost continuously by powder snow making the abseils unpleasant and stressful. Furthermore the day was getting on and the Face was now in shadow. He was tremendously relieved when he finally reached the broad shelf below the rock band, but he still had to complete a complex descent down a steep ramp before reaching the snow field where it would be possible to stop for the night. Visibility was now down to zero with a savage dance of snowflakes blown by the strong wind. Although he couldn't see them, he could hear the roar of avalanches to his right and left. He was forced to bivouac once again at 7300 metres, more than anything else to wait for an improvement of the weather conditions. During this time Cesen continued to receive updates on the weather forecast by radio from Base Camp. The weather down there was bad too, but forecast was for an improvement. Cesen's friends describe him as extremely cool in the face of danger, but during this bivouac he was on the edge of a nervous crisis. Several times the whole mountain seemed to shake as avalanches passed by. Towards midnight, the weather calmed a bit and he managed to see a few stars. He now had to decide whether to wait for the dawn with the risk of being blocked by avalanches for a further day or to immediately continue his descent. Since the bottom part of the Face is not too steep, Cesen judged it feasible to descend it in the dark. During the descent he was continually afraid of being carried away by a river of snow which would sweep away everything in its path. Between 7 and 8 in the morning he reached safe ground. He had been climbing for 62 hours, four days and four nights. Those nights in particular had seemed impossibly long. When Cesen walked back across the glacier to meet his friends at Base Camp, he had seemingly changed the face of Himalayan mountaineering.

Chapter 13 – Still More Challengers

Cesen's ascent stunned the climbing world. The biggest problem of world mountaineering had been solved in exemplary style. It was a quantum leap in standards even greater than Messner's oxygenless ascent of Everest or his first solo of an 8000 metre peak. But other expeditions to the Face were already planned for the post monsoon season and after some hesitation these still went ahead. In fact on a very broad face like the South of Lhotse there are usually several different possible routes which would be fine climbs in themselves. One of the planned expeditions was a large team from the Soviet Union involving many of the country's leading mountaineers. The other was two man attempt involving Christophe Profit, who was returning to the face for a third time, and another Frenchman, Pierre Beghin.

Beghin had established himself as one of the top Himalayan climbers during the 1980s, climbing in perfect style. In 1979 he was a member of a very large French National expedition which attempted the South Ridge of K2, considered one of the great unsolved problems of the Himalayas at that time. Reinhold Messner's writings have had enormous influences on generations of Himalayan climbers and some of the labels he gave to routes have stuck. The South Face of Lhotse was described by him as a Route for the 21st Century. Whether or not this drove climbers to want to attempt it during the 20th Century, it was certainly used a number of times in expedition publicity. Messner referred to the South Ridge of K2 as "The Magic Line". The route was eventually climbed by a Polish team led by Janusz Mayer in 1986 with Wojciech Wroz, Przemyslaw Piasecki and the Slovakian Peter Bozik making it to the summit – the latter two having also climbed on Lhotse's South Face. The 1979 French team was very strong team with veterans of the Makalu West Pillar eight years before, like Yannick Seigneur and the leader Bernard Mellet, as well as younger stars who had driven an explosion in climbing standards in the Alps in the 1970s, like Jean-Marc Boivin. Dividing into three groups of four climbers they gradually built a line of fixed ropes and camps up the ridge following the classic siege model and requiring a lot of time sliding up fixed ropes on jumars carrying loads. Whereas in the Nepal a lot of the load carrying is usually done by Sherpas, the local people in Pakistan have been less commonly used as high altitude porters, although Pakistani climbers have performed very well on the Country's 8000ers. The French used some porters to carry loads on the mountain and one of the strongest of these, Laskar Khan, died of a heart attack whilst jumaring. Beghin asked himself whether European climbers had the moral right to ask porters, who accepted the work because they needed the money, to put themselves in such dangerous situations. This was another disadvantage of siege style climbing. On K2 the weather seemed to play games with them, alternating between good and bad, making it difficult to know when to advance the route and when to retreat back to Base Camp and they ended up spending weeks on end blocked in high camps, the wind battering the tents and shredding their nerves. At the start of September, an improvement in the weather allowed Seigneur and Jean-Claude Mosca to attempt the summit, but they turned back at 8300 metres. Then Yvan Ghirardini, who was to play a part in the story of Lhotse, managed to get slightly higher before spending a terrible bivouac in a tiny cave at 8300 metres.

Next his was the turn of Beghin and his partner Jean Coudray. The route was equipped with fixed ropes up to 8300 metres, the next 100 metres were straightforward, but the final 200 metres to the summit of K2 were an unknown quantity. Coudray turned back without even reaching the end of the fixed ropes, leaving Beghin to try and reach the summit alone. The clouds had closed in and there were flurries of snow. Alone on the avalanche threatened slopes, the 6mm rope gave only a vague psychological protection. When he reached the cave where Ghirandini had bivouacked, he was amazed how he had managed to get inside, let alone spend a night. Beghin recovered two coils of rope which had been left there and set off to try and traverse left to rejoin the ridge. Blinded by the fog it was hard to find a viable route and, even though the crest of the ridge was only a few metres above, he fumbled like an amateur trying to find a way to get protection from the rope. Time was slipping by and suddenly his isolation terrified him. At 8300 metres in a storm, physically and mentally exhausted, he wondered what connection he had to the rest of humanity and felt his very existence was slipping away. His chances of reaching the summit were zero. After three days and three nights above 8000 metres, he was completely spent and had to descend immediately. At Camp IV expedition leader Bernard Mellet greeted him warmly and asked lots of questions about the climb, but for Beghin the time up above already seemed almost like a dream. That evening Daniel Monaci and Thierry Leroy bivouacked at 8400 metres during a last desperate but unsuccessful attempt to finish the route. Then Mosca, Seigneur and Beghin decided to return up the mountain again. But in this strange game of yoyo, they were running on empty. Beghin couldn't stop imagining food and although the views down into China had lost none there fascination, they didn't really have their hearts in the attempt. One by one they turned back and headed down to Camp II, struggling through the deep snow on auto-pilot. A final attempt did not even get high on the mountain. For the French, the failure of this expedition seemed more than anything else to be the failure of the whole philosophy of heavyweight siege style climbing. The sheer effort put in by so many over such a long period seemed disproportionate with the result. In his book, "Les Cinq Tresors de la Grande Neige", Beghin contrasts the boredom and squalor of weeks in high camps, hauling loads up fixed ropes and waiting for storms to pass, with the excitement of a small team trying to make a new route. There are clear parallels with Messner's experience on the heavyweight expeditions in the early part of his career. They failed on K2 despite a team of 15 of France's finest climbers, Government support and a huge budget. The photographers and journalists who greeted their return at Paris airport were less numerous than on the departure and their questions less friendly.

For Beghin it was a delusion, but rather than giving up Himalayan climbing he set about trying to do it in a very different way. He had started climbing as a teenager with his brother Claude and from the beginning had dreamed of achieving great things in the Himalayas. In 1967, when Claude was still only 14 and wearing short trousers, they developed a wild plan to go and try and climb K2. They agreed not to tell their parents, and even went as far as enquiring about the possibility at the Pakistani embassy in Paris. They were greeted by a very polite official who explained to them that Pakistan was a long way away and that the mountains were remote and dangerous and that they should talk to their parents before thinking about undertaking such an enterprise. A year later the brothers did they first serious route and although Claude no longer wore short trousers, there was still some deception of their parents. On the pretext of going for a long walk during a family holiday in Chamonix and with their climbing equipment hidden in the bottom of their rucksacks, they set out to climb the East Face of the Grepon. They had to do it in a day as carrying sleeping bags and heavy coats would have made their rucksacks too large and given the game away. The sense of pride they felt on the top easily compensated the ticking off when they arrived home. As years passed, Pierre's enthusiasm did not diminish and his skills improved. He hesitated about his choice of career because, although the mountains were a central part of his life, he was not sure he wanted to be a mountain guide, like Christophe Profit. What he really wanted was some job which had intellectual interest, but gave him the freedom to pursue his passion for top-level mountaineering. He managed this through a post at Grenoble University.

During the 1970s Beghin continued to pull off some fine ascents in the Alps and in 1974 went to Uli Biaho, a spectacular rock tower in the Karakoram in Pakistan. On the flight they passed over Nanga Parbat and looked down on the scene of the great odyssey of the Messner brothers. Their story had made a big impression on Beghin – it had a mysterious, almost supernatural side to it. Messner's climbing style also appealed greatly to him. In 1979 when the large French team failed on K2, Messner succeeded on the ordinary route with a much smaller team. Messner's team had less porters than had been necessary just for the French TV team. The leader of the French team, Bernard Mellet, asked himself whether such a large expedition was justifiable. His view was that it should not be judged in military terms of victory or defeat. He thought looking at in economic terms of costs and benefits made even less sense. Instead he felt that Himalayan climbing still had to be seen in quasi-mythological terms if any sense was to be made of it. For the Arthurian knight Percival, what is important is not finding the Holy Grail but the quest to search for it, the journey that it takes him on and the challenges that it presents. For Mellet, the K2 expedition had to be seen in the same way as a quest. Beghin saw things differently and resolved that his future expeditions would be lightweight and self-organised, with a climbing style which suited him.

A year after K2 Beghin received an invitation to an expedition to attempt the difficult South West Pillar of Dhaulagiri. After two months the team had managed to establish the route up to 6800 metres, where they placed the fourth of a series of camps, but they knew that the next 600 metres of steep rock and ice were going to be far harder than what they had climbed up to that point. Whilst his partner, Bernard Muller, dug out a snow hole as their base to explore this upper section, Beghin, knowing that winter was approaching, tried to advance the route alone. He managed to climb several icy slabs with auto-belays, before sliding back down the ropes to rejoin Muller. Auto-belaying is a common technique in the Alps and provides security, but the consequences of a fall are greater because there is no companion to amortise the shock. There was still 300 metres to climb before they reached the summit plateau and easier ground. The next day the pair found a chimney which allowed them to advance up the ochre coloured rock of the Pillar on beautiful rock slabs interspersed with thin strips of ice. After a rest day, the next section went up a large open corner, which from Base Camp looked smooth and sold, but from close up was made of strange sandy rock of doubtful solidity. Beghin didn't trust the rock and placed pitons every few metres for security making progress by climbing a couple of metres by jamming his hands into the crack before quickly placing a piton on which he could rest his arms. 4000 metres lower this type of climbing would have been no problem, but Himalayas climbing involved far more than just technical ability. At the end of the day only 50 metres separated them from the shoulder and easier ground, but the wind, which struck the exposed Pillar without mercy, was starting to wear away the walls of their snow cave and they wondered if it would last long enough for a summit attempt. A few days later Beghin completed the last difficult part of the pillar and was rewarded with a fantastic view of the Annapurna group rising from a sea of clouds and smaller mountains. The upper slopes on Dhaulagiri were somewhat easier, but below the 45° snow slopes there was a huge precipice. Supplies were running low, but the strongest Sherpa, Ang Kami made a crucial carry to bring food and gas canisters to Camp IV, covering 2000 metres in a single day on difficult terrain. Ang Kami had climbed a new route on Dhaulagiri with a Japanese team two years before, helping the Japanese climbers lost in a storm near the summit, despite being the only one climbing without oxygen. Beghin suggested he should joint himself and Muller on the summit push, but Ang Kami declined. Sherpas didn't climb for glory and they had their livelihoods to think about. The two French climbers left Camp IV on the 20th October with light equipment – just a stove, sleeping bags, some food and a bivouac tent. But on the upper slopes it proved too difficult to put the tent up and instead they dug a snowhole for shelter. They only managed to construct some type of wall and spent the starry night trying to make drinks and improve their shelter. As the wind bit into them it was impossible to sleep and all they could do was try to keep warm and wait for the morning light when they could set off. After gaining 150 metres of height, they faced a narrow snow ridge which separates the West and South Faces of Dhaulagiri. The wind struck them with a terrible fury. Even with his crampons and two ices dug into the snow, Beghin had the impression he would be blown away. They knew that by continuing they would have a chance to make the summit, but would have to descend exhausted and during the night which would be terribly risky. With heavy hearts they decided to turn back. On the way down to Base Camp, Beghin met Ang Kami who assured them that it was better to renounce the summit and be there to attempt another mountain. Beghin knew this made sense, but still found failure hard to accept. He wondered whether they could make a light weight push, attempting the summit at night under the light of the full moon. His companions pointed out that the camps below 7000 metres were all empty, isolating the team high on the mountain. Beghin was still not ready to break through the psychological barrier of relying on undiscovered reserves of energy – to push things to the limit and see what he had left. He did not yet have the boldness of Hermann Buhl who made one of the greatest ever climbs with a solo push to achieve the first ascent of Nanga Parbat.

Although he had failed on Dhaulagiri, Beghin had learnt how much two highly motivated climbers could do even on very difficult routes at high altitude. He knew that his passion for mountaineering could only be satisfied in this type of lightweight expedition. Although on Dhaulagiri they had used fixed ropes and camps, the team had been compact and he did not feel lost in the midst of a gargantuan organisation as he had on K2. He returned to his work as an engineer, but the high summits of Asia dominated his thoughts on a daily basis. In July 1981 he received a permit to attempt the West Face of Manaslu with a team which again included Muller. This face of Manaslu was extremely dangerous and they limited their activity to between 4 am and 10 am in the morning. Beghin likened this method of advancing "in bounds" to that used by the Slovenians on Lhotse South Face in 1981. He described it as "climbing in the night, burying yourself in the day". On Manaslu placing camps was difficult since the main section of the Face was 2000 metres high, with only one safe campsite. Beghin anyway didn't want to contemplate having climbers going back and forth whilst stocking camps, given the high risk of rock and ice fall. The ropes they did fix were swept on occasions by avalanches of heavy wet snow provoked by the hot sun. But Beghin doubted whether the evolution of mountaineering had yet reached the point where it was reasonable to tackle a route like this without fixed ropes to give a secure connection to the ground and a safe retreat in the case storm. Beghin likened pushing out the fixed ropes to building a bridge across a river that was not yet finished, advancing bit by bit until the whole span was crossed. But he wondered whether it would soon be possible to contemplate a pure alpine style approach on a route like this, given the rapid development of attitudes and climbing techniques. Muller and Beghin established a camp within reach of the summit plateau, but after going to bed on a calm evening, they were awoken at four in the morning by the sound of a storm. Safe in their sleeping bags they were reluctant to move, but the avalanche risk on the lower part of the Face meant they had to try and get off the mountain as quickly as possible. As they headed down conditions worsened and by the time they reached Camp I, it had been snowing continuously for 20 hours. It was too dangerous to descend to Base Camp so they stayed at Camp I. During the night Beghin was woken by the sound of an avalanche. Diving out of the tent he saw a huge wall of snow pouring down the slopes above and threatening to engulf the tents. His companions had been able to take cover, but Beghin was too late. Still in his long johns, he struggled through thigh deep snow in the raging wind, furious and cutting a ridiculous figure. The next morning, soaked to the skin like drowned rats they made it back to Base Camp. The chances of making another bid for the summit seemed slim.

But the fine weather returned and a week later they had attained the summit plateau, which is a wide expanse of snow fields, not technically difficult, but very tiring to cross because of the high altitude and a potential death trap for climbers who are caught there in bad weather as had happened to two of Reinhold Messner's companions in 1972. Most of the plateau was covered with skavras, curious formations made from hard slabs of snow, unstable and eroded at their bases. Beghin and Muller were able to use these to construct walls for a good shelter from the wind. After a poor night's sleep, the pair set off for the summit, deciding to bet on travelling light without bivouac gear and relying on being able to make it to the summit and back before nightfall. They each walked at their own pace using skipoles for support. The skavras were too unstable to support their weight and forced them to continuously make frustrating detours as if through a giant labyrinth. Beghin looked back in at the tent trying to fix its location in his mind as he knew that being lost on this plateau could be fatal. As he approached the foresummit he was close to where he had failed on an attempt on another route on his first expedition to an 8000 metre peak four years earlier. That time, with the rest of team down in Base Camp he and one companion, Thierry Leroy, had turned back exhausted at 7600 metres. By the time they got back down they were suffering from frostbite and had to be carried on the backs of porters to the nearest village and then evacuated by helicopter. This time Beghin was determined to make it to the summit. He used the foresummit as a reference point, knowing the main summit was a kilometre behind it, and tried to keep a regular rhythm. His mind played strange tricks with him producing conversations with friends and loved ones, which never seemed to have a point or reach a conclusion. Suddenly he saw some bamboo poles marking the junction with the ordinary route, which made him feel less alone, even though Muller was out of sight behind him, lost in the contours of the mountain. But then he was hit by stomach cramps, which made caused him terrible pain and feel very alone. He tried to keep moving, focusing his attention on small details of his equipment to distract his own organism from the pain and force it go on when all the built in warning systems were telling him to stop. The final section seemed to be endless, but eventually he came to the top and a spectacular view which seemed to stretch almost infinitely into the distance where he could make out Everest. He had the strange feeling that his consciousness had become discontinuous, as if his brain was halted trying to absorb images which were too rich to take in whilst processing memories and thoughts. As he waited for Muller, Beghin reflected on the achievement of completing a new route on an 8000er in very lightweight style. It was for him the realisation of a dream, but clearly it was also an experience he wanted to repeat. When Muller arrived, Beghin had started to get cold and they exchanged a few words and agreed to meet back at the bivouac before he set off.

The next Himalayan mountain Beghin attempted was Jannu, again with Muller, another member of the K2 team, Xavier Fargeas and Beghin's younger brother Claude. They made a bold attempt on the North Face, climbing difficult rock and ice and equipping the route up to 7000 metres where their way was blocked by an ice cliff. In the middle of October bad weather set in and Claude Beghin and Gerard Bretin were caught up at Camp III with significant risk of avalanches on the ramp they would need to descend. In the end they managed in extremis, sliding down the fixed ropes as quickly as they could with fresh snow everywhere, visibility down to 3 metres and avalanches crashing around them. When the weather cleared, they saw that the lower part of the Face had changed into a steep snow slope and an attempt to clear the route and pull the fixed ropes free as they stood waist deep in new snow was abandoned after 5 hours of struggle. With morale low they decided to end the expedition. Even then Beghin found it hard to give up and, despite the fact that Fargeas and Bretin had returned to France, he told the porters to hold off dismantling Base Camp. On the pretext of recovering material he made a final attempt with

Muller. After a difficult night at Camp II with the wind buffeting their half destroyed tent, Beghin continued alone. Despite the storm he found the fixed ropes intact and he was able to dig a bag of provisions and equipment out of the snow. Camp III however was in a sorry state with the tents buried in the snow and the sleeping bags and mats frozen solid. Still he was not yet ready to give up, but as he tried to kill the empty hours of the afternoon, the solitude started to get to him. The heavy silence was interrupted by the radio and, without thinking, Beghin let slip to the liaison officer that he was planning to try and get to the summit ridge. The liaison officer said this was strictly forbidden under the terms of their permit now that the expedition had ended. Beghin didn't protest and made plans to descend, but was left with the nagging doubt that he hadn't pushed himself to the limit. The next morning, without even getting a hot drink, he went back up the ropes to the previous high point finding all the equipment in a good state. The ice cliff which protected the summit ridge fascinated him. Although he had given his word that he would not go on, the temptation to explore the unknown was almost too hard to resist. Torn between this burning desire and comfort and safety below, he finally headed down and the expedition was over. But this idea to explore what he could do alone became fixed in his mind.

The same year as Beghin's attempt on Jannu, the Soviet Union organised its first Himalayan expedition, attempting Everest. The history of Soviet Mountaineering was quite different than that in the West. It was viewed as a competitive sport with organised competitions. There was no prize money, but nonetheless winning was very important for the Soviet climbers. Although they were late-comers to the Himalayan climbing game, the Soviet Union was one of handful of countries with its own 7000 metre peaks, so they had plenty of experienced high altitude climbers. But they knew there was a big difference between climbing on the highest summits in the Soviet Union, which were less than 7500 metres, and at 8500 metres and this was where they lacked experience. The Soviets had never used bottled oxygen in their home mountains, but considered that this would be necessary when they tried to tackle difficult climbs on the very highest mountains. In the West, there had been persistent rumours, including articles published in The Times, of a secret Soviet Everest expedition through Tibetan China in 1952 which had ended in tragedy. The story had a certain plausibility, occurring as it did at the height of cold war secrecy and the year before Everest was first climbed. The reports of these "phantom expeditions" in the West were quite detailed, even listing the names of members, but over the years their existence has been consistently denied by Soviet mountaineers. There had been some joint climbs and training camps by the two countries in the Chinese and Russian Pamirs in the mid-1950s. This was followed up by a reconnaissance of Everest in October 1958 in which the Chinese invited three Soviet climbers to participate in. There was a strong military flavour to the expedition with the Chinese insisting that the whole team dressed in the winter uniform of the People's Liberation Army. It was late in the year, making cold an inevitable factor, particularly on the Tibetan side of the mountain. They did not reach Rongbuk until mid-November by which time winter had started to close in. At the Rongbuk Monastery they found 70 monks in residence, many more than the handful that were there in 1990 when I visited. In between there had been terrible damage during the Cultural Revolution. The Sino-Soviet team explored the approaches to the North Col and by the 9th December returned to Lhasa where they made plans for a full expedition the following year. But in 1959 a major revolt broke out in Tibet and the Chinese cancelled the planned expedition. In 1960 the situation was more stable in Tibet and the Chinese decided to go ahead with an expedition which eventually succeeded in making the third ascent of Everest and the first from the North Side. But the Soviet climbers didn't take part due to growing political differences between the two superpowers, a decision which delayed the entry of the Soviet Union into Himalayan climbing by 22 years. No publicity was given to the reconnaissance in 1958 at the request of the Chinese for fear that it would lead to further unrest in Tibet.

The 1982 Soviet team was a large one with 25 climbers and planned to climb a new route on Everest. Some had expected that on their first appearance on the Himalayan stage, the Soviets, whose government was keen to use sporting success to enhance the country's international image, would aim for a target which would guarantee a success which could be presented as a triumph rather than trying a hard route with an uncertain outcome. But this didn't see to enter the climbers thinking and, after a reconnaissance in 1980, they decided to tackle a very difficult new route up the left hand side of the South West face, which would involve many sections of hard rock climbing at high altitude. Working in traditional expedition style they fixed ropes and established a series of camps. After a month of hard work, which had to be done almost entirely by the Soviet climbers because the route was too difficult for Sherpas, they were ready for a summit attempt. The first summit team, consisting of Balyberdin and Myslovsky set off for the summit from Camp V on the 4th May. Meanwhile, the second summit team was moving up in support. It included two climbers who would go on to play important roles in the history of Lhotse's South Face, Sergey Bershov and Mikhail Turkevich. Both of these climbers came from the Ukraine. Turkevich was born in the Lviv area of Western Ukraine, but spent most of his life in Donetsk in the East. Unlike some climbers who had discovered the mountains as children, Turkevich didn't even start backpacking until he was 20 and only got introduced to climbing by chance. By the late 1970s he had shown himself to be a star rock climber, winning several competitions at a national level. He had also climbed all the 7000 metre peaks of the Soviet Union and hard rock climbs in the French Alps and Italian Dolomites. Bershov was born in 1947 in the east of Ukraine close to the Russian border. When he was a child, doctors had believed he had a heart condition and prevented him from playing sport, but he was so active that they had to conclude that this diagnosis was mistaken. Also a star skier, Bershov started climbing at 18 and won a number of championships. Bershov also had international climbing experience: in 1975 at the age of 28 he was part of a 6 man group of Soviet climbers who visited the USA to climb with Americans and foster relations which had developed when US climbers participated in an International Camp in the Soviet Pamirs. The group was led by Vitaly Abalakov who was already 69 years old and the father of Soviet mountaineering. Bershov was the youngest member of the group and impressed his hosts with his ready smile and sense of humour – they found he only seemed to be serious when climbing hard rock. The American and Soviet climbers made a hard new route in the Cascade Mountains in Washington State, but there were some differences in style. The Americans, knowing that there were hard rock pitches on the route advised bringing a rope to haul rucksacks, but the Soviets said they were used to always climbing with rucksacks and proceeded to do so.

On Everest Bershov and Turkevich set off from Camp V at the unusual time of 6pm in the evening to attempt the summit and assist the first team on descent. They carried extra oxygen which might be needed by the first pair Balyberdin and Myslovsky who they knew were very tired. Turkevich waited outside the tent whilst Bershov fiddled with his crampons trying to fix them more firmly. Then seeing his partner was ready, Turkevich set off up the fixed ropes. He was feeling fit and moving quickly with the help of the oxygen, barely feeling the weight of his backpack. They reached the end of the fixed ropes quickly and Turkevich got out the climbing rope they would now move together on. A forty metre scree slow led up to the West Ridge. They had an oxygen supply of 2 litres per minute, but they were apparently still going too fast as they were panting for breath. Turkevich tried to slow down to a steady pace, but he was still sweating, which he knew could lead to frostbite. They wanted to climb as far as possible in the two remaining hours of daylight. After an hour they had the first radio contact with Base Camp and learnt that Balyberdin could see them, although they could only hear the higher pair and in fact had just heard the sound of Myslovsky discarding his last oxygen cylinder. Without oxygen, the pair above would inevitably get much slower. As they neared the ridge and night started to fall, they had some route finding difficulties. Balyberdin had told them to always stay to the right of the ridge, but after going along some shelves, they realised it was a wrong turn. Instead the route moved left to climb the grey wall where they saw some the ropes left by Zaplotnik and Stremfelj three years before on the first ascent of the West Ridge. Between the rock steps they also saw some footsteps in the snow which gave them confidence they were going the right way.

The weather was worsening with snowfall. Although some weak moonlight still found its way through the clouds, on the shaded side of the ridge visibility was limited and this slowed progress. Turkevich waited for Bershov to join him and then they removed their oxygen masks in order to shout to their companions, but there was no reply. They knew that it would be easy to miss them and they needed their support. But the top was close and they could not understand how the other two could not have made it down this far yet. They carried on, but Bershov stopped again to call and this time there was an answer from below. The others had lost their way on the descent and strayed off the ridge. They descended about 30 metres and found the summit pair sitting beside a huge boulder at around 8700 metres. Bershov and Turkevich embraced their companions and congratulated them on their success, but Balyberdin and Myslovsky barely had the strength to respond. Bershov and Turkevich gave them food, hot drinks and oxygen on maximum flow, which seemed to revive them a bit, although they were disturbed to find that Balyberdin had a rucksack half full of stones that he was bringing down and that Myslovsky had left his crampons lower down and was now having trouble crossing the snow patches. Turkevich and Bershov started to quiz the others about the route above. The ascending pair was still keen to go to the summit, which was only three hours away, but on a Soviet expedition they needed to get agreement from Base Camp to do this. Turkevich communicated their intentions to the leadership at Base Camp, but the batteries of the radio were freezing and they couldn't get a clear answer back. Then Balyberdin got out his radio and asked the same question. The answer came back "no" – they had to accompany their exhausted colleagues down. But the two Ukrainians were not giving up and Bershov grabbed the radio and asked "why not?" He pointed out that they had two cylinders of oxygen each. After a pause, Base Camp gave them the option to continue if they wanted.

Wishing each other luck, the two pairs went their separate ways. Turkevich and Bershov were worried they would be blamed if anything happened to the others, but the lure of the highest point in the World was strong and they pushed on despite the continued snowfall. They followed a narrow but easy snowy ridge right along the crest with one foot on the south and one on the north side and reached the summit at 10.25 pm, the first people to do so at night. Actually the conditions weren't bad, generally calmer than during the day and with a full moon. They took long exposure pictures, trying to keep still enough to capture the scene by moonlight, but there was simply not enough light. After half an hour they started to descend and caught up with Balyberdin and Myslovsky who were moving very slowly. Then they continued together trying to keep moving, but, given the dark and the huge drop down the North Face, not forgetting to arrange security for the tired climbers on the more difficult sections. Sometimes they had to rely on old worn fixed ropes left by the Slovenians. The other two did not have crampons and needed to move very cautiously. It was also getting colder, the wind had picked up and the moon had fallen below the horizon. Myslovsky was the most tired slipped off several times and Turkevich struggled to hold him. When they reached a relatively flat section, Myslovsky sat down in the snow and refused to go on. They realised he had run out of oxygen so Bershov gave him his bottle, whilst Turkevich gave his crampons. They still struggled to keep the first summit pair going and had to concentrate to avoid missing the turn off from the ridge to get down to their tent. When dawn arrived they found the fixed ropes leading to Camp V, where two of their team mates greeted them. The six of them were squeezed into a 2 man tent. In the night they understood that Myslovsky had severe frostbite and it was a struggle to get him down the fixed ropes with his stiff unbending frozen fingers. In the following days a further seven climbers made it to the summit making a very impressive debut in Himalayan climbing for the Soviet Union.

In terms of climbing philosophy, Pierre Beghin was years ahead of the Soviets and in 1983 he felt ready to make a solo attempt on the World's third highest mountain, Kangchenjunga. After his difficult last night alone on Jannu he wanted to face the challenge of coping with the psychological barrier of solitude. Beghin was recently married and his wife Annie was accompanying him. He wondered whether she wouldn't have preferred a honeymoon in Venice, but she was also an enthusiastic and very competent climber. She accompanied him on the lower part of the heavily glaciated South West Face of the mountain. The Face is cut by a ridge, where they camped together. It was then necessary to descend 200 metres to arrive on a glacier plateau which gave access to the upper part. From here Beghin continued alone. In the upper section the air is extremely thin and he could hear voices talking in his head, which he could recognise as people from his family and friends who he had lost touch with, but none of what they said made any sense. Others have commented on similar hallucinations at very high altitudes. Beghin stayed half an hour on the top, waving to his wife down below, although she was much too far away to see him. He wanted to take photos, but he found that his water bottle had leaked and the camera was completely jammed with ice. Like Messner on Nanga Parbat, he realised the importance of proving his solo ascent – something which Cesen overlooked on Lhotse and which he would come to regret. Beghin found an old oxygen bottle in the snow and scratched his initials and the date on it. He also buried his altimeter, which was the only object he didn't need for the descent. After that he focused on getting down safely, knowing that a friend had been killed in a fall from the long couloir below the summit two years before. Moving slowly and carefully he was overtaken by nightfall half way down the couloir. By now he was exhausted, had not drunk for over 15 hours and had a lacerating pain in his kidneys. After an hour of wandering unsurely he found his tent and relative safety. The next morning he continued his descent and met up with his wife, who he held tightly, trying to hide the fact he was in tears. Beghin had suffered only some minor frostbite and had become the fourth man to make a complete solo of an 8000er, after Messner, Kukuczka and the Japanese Hironobu Kamuro, who climbed Dhaulagiri.

The next year, 1984, Beghin himself returned to Dhaulagiri. It was a feature of Beghin's climbing career that he returned to mountains which defeated him on a number of occasions – as well as Dhaulagiri he did this for K2, Manaslu, Jannu and Everest. This time Beghin and his partner Jean-Noel Roche attempted an alpine style ascent of the South Ridge, first climbed by a heavyweight Japanese expedition in 1978. They had a support and film team which accompanied them on the lower part of the route and fixed 700 metres of ropes here to assist in the descent. On October 1st they set out on their summit push and bivouacked at 6400 metres. The next day they overcame a 300 metre rock face and an unstable snow ridge bristling with snow mushrooms. At 7000 metres they bypassed an overhanging rock step by climbing icy 60° rock slabs and then bivouacked again at 7100 metres. The next day they reached the vast easy angled summit plateau where they had to struggle for 2kms before reaching the summit.

In the following years Beghin continued to visit the Himalayas every year, but he hit a run of bad luck, particularly on the world's highest mountain, which he attempted three times between 1985 and 1987. First with his wife Annie, he attempted the Norton Couloir on the North Face reaching 8200 metres before turning back. The following year he tried again from the North with the Swiss pair Erhard Loretan and Jean Troillet, who were becoming famous for ultra lightweight ultra fast ascents in the Himalayas. Loretan would become the third man, after Messner and Kukuczka, to climb all the 8000 metre peaks. Loretan, Troillet, Beghin and another Swiss climber, Sandro Godio, reached the foot of the mountain at midnight. Troillet carried an ice axe, a walking pole and a rucksack with a stove, a snow shovel and a survival blanket – in total 5 kgs, the sort of weight which might be carried for an Alpine route. They climbed by the light of their head torches up the Horbein Couloir, the steepest and most direct route on the North Face. At 7000 metres Godio had to turn back, but the others carried on through the night, with a steady pace which saw them gain height inexorably. By 10 am the next morning they had reached 8000 metres, where they dug out a platform in the snow and spent the day relaxing in the sun and making drinks. They started to climb again at 9pm before the cold chilled their bodies too much, but Beghin was overcome with an irresistible weariness and for once fell behind his partners. 200 metres higher the others heard him shout to say he was turning back. The other two carried on and completed a fantastic lightweight ascent of Everest. In 1987 Beghin tried the North Face again with a

Spanish expedition during the monsoon season. From a camp at 8200 metres, Beghin and the Spanish climber Fernando Garrido climbed all the way onto the upper part of the West Ridge, but had to turn back only 150 metres from the top when they realised that they would not have been able to summit without bivouacking on the descent. He had more luck on Jannu where he returned with Erik Decamp and made a fine Alpine Style ascent of the North Face. In 1988 he returned to another mountain which had defeated him before, K2, with an expedition which attempted the North Ridge from the Chinese side of the mountain. Very bad weather with never more than three fine days in a row prevented them from getting above 7600 metres. Beghin made a solo bid and got above 8000 metres, but only just managed to return back down again.

By the late 1980s Beghin and other top European climbers were managing to visit the Himalayas two and sometimes three times a year. By contrast, the Soviet climbers had to wait seven years after their Everest expedition before they got another chance to go to the Himalayas. During the 1980s things were changing fast in the Soviet Union. In 1985 Mikhail Gorbachev had been elected General Secretary. Gorbachev was only 54 on attaining leadership, considerably younger than the three previous leaders, Brezhnev, Andropov and Chernenko. Although he was a long standing member of the Communist Party, he was realistic and visionary enough to realise that the position of the Soviet Union was unsustainable. He first focused on modernising industry and agriculture and reducing inefficiency in the country's bureaucracy, but he soon saw that these goals could not be achieved without also introducing additional political freedoms. He set about a programme of reforms called "Perestroika" and openness or "Glasnost". This led to a rapid change in the atmosphere in the Soviet Union, but also caused confusion and feeling of insecurity. Psychologically the increased freedom had a different significance in the Soviet Union, which had not seemed so much an "occupied country" as the supposedly independent states of Central and Eastern Europe. The end of the Soviet Union also potentially meant a loss of prestige and superpower status for the country.

When the Soviet mountaineers started to plan another Himalayan expedition, they again wanted to find an eye catching objective. The South Wall of Lhotse was one the options considered as was a traverse from Lhotse to Everest, but in the end they opted to try and traverse the four main summits of Kangchenjunga, all of which are well above 8000 metres. They would do this from the South West face on which Pierre Beghin had made his solo climb, but the style couldn't have been more different – the Soviet team included 29 climbers plus a film crew of 5. The Soviet climbers spent much longer in preparing their expeditions than Western climbers. Although the expedition was planned for the spring of 1989, an organising committee was set up in November 1986 headed by the Deputy Chairman of the USSR State Sports Committee. During the winter of 1986 and spring of 1987 candidates for the expedition were selected from amongst more than 60 of the Soviet Union's leading climbers. The competitive structure of climbing in the Soviet Union allowed such a list to be put together – something which would not have been possible in Western Europe. Training meets on the 7000m peaks of the Soviet Union were used for selection of team members and reserves and a reconnaissance group including 4 of those who had summited Everest in 1982 visited the foot of the mountain. In the summer of 1988 the team went to the Tien Shan Mountains to practice high level traversing, managing to complete a 10 km traverse along a high ridge at around 7000 metres. This gave them a chance to work out tactics, which would be needed to get a large team well co-ordinated. Then in the autumn of 1988 the expedition and their coaches – no Western climbers had ever had coaches – went to the Black Sea coast to discuss tactics and strategy. There were long arguments about the starting point for the traverse. Should it be the peak of Yalungkang at the western end of the ridge or the South Summit at the eastern end? Several participants were keen on the idea of attempting the South Summit via a new route directly from the Yalung Glacier, but this idea was rejected as the route would have been too hard for the Sherpas who would help in stocking the high camps. To facilitate the traverse they set up a master camp on the plateau and from there a further six camps, 2 each in 3 different directions, towards Yalungkang, the main summit and the South summit. The logistics involved were some of the most complex ever used in the Himalayas.

10 tons of baggage was taken in a Soviet military transport plane to Kolkata, where the team was waiting. They then travelled by bus and lorry to the Nepalese border. It was an expedition of gargantuan size. As well as the large group from the Soviet Union, they had hired 65 Sherpas for load carrying on the face and a total of 600 porters to carry all the equipment and food from the roadhead. Given the size of the party and the fact that some of the passes were still blocked by snow they had to follow a lower route than the normal one for Kangchenjunga, which meant they had to literally cut their way through

bamboo jungles. Working according to the pre-agreed plan, they established camps on the mountain. In the process of doing this a number of ascents of the various peaks of Kangchenjunga were made. The first occurred on the 9th April, which is very early in the season to reach the top of a major Himalayan peak. They made several new routes and oxygenless ascents of the various summits and had achieved a lot before even starting on the planned high level traverse. After these ascents all the team members descended to under 4000 metres in the forests to recuperate and discuss tactics. Since everyone was in good physical shape they decided they would attempt the traverse of the ridge from both directions with two teams of five. On May 2nd they completed traverses of the summit ridge in both directions. In climbing terms the expedition was spectacularly successful. 24 out of the 29 mountaineers in the team had reached at least one of the summits of Kangchenjunga as well as 3 of the five man film crew. In total there were 85 man/ascents of one or other of the 4 summits.

This, much more than the Slovenian climb on Lhotse in 1981 seemed to prove Al Rouse's point that, taken to its logical limit, a strong team of climbers using fixed ropes and oxygen could climb pretty much anything they wanted to. The Soviets had literally clambered all over Kangchenjunga, which is one of the harder 8000 metre peaks. And it is worth recalling that Jerzy Kukuczka had been contemplating a lightweight attempt on the same objective. When the team returned to Kathmandu they had ten days to kill before their flight back to the Soviet Union. They spent time relaxing and sightseeing around the city – spirits were high after the spectacular success of the expedition. Bershov and Turkevich had hatched a plan to try and climb Lhotse's South Face a long time before and with the achievement of Kangchenjunga under their belts, it was a logical next step was to attempt the World's greatest unclimbed challenge. The ease with which they had achieved the traverse of Kangchenjunga gave them optimism they would have the same type of experience on Lhotse. Now they took advantage of being in Kathmandu to submit a request for a permit to attempt the Face.

In the autumn of the same year, 1989, Pierre Beghin took his lightweight climbing concept a step further leading a small expedition to try a new direct route on the South Face of Makalu, first climbed by Kunaver's Slovenian team 14 earlier. The team consisted of only three climbers and the other two with Beghin, Alain Ghersen and Michel Cadot, lacked high altitude experience, although they were fine technical climbers. Their first summit attempt was blocked by a 48 hour uninterrupted storm which deposited a metre of snow. When they returned to their first camp for another try, the inside of the tent was like a swimming pool with clothes and sleeping bags soaked. Fortunately, on the South Face the intensity of the afternoon sun allowed them to get everything dry. The next day they started at midnight, but struggled to find their way in an inky black night and only managed to get back on route when it was light. But once the sun hit them it became unbearably hot. Beghin was ahead and decided to wait for his companions at 7100 metres and they only arrived several hours later. After another bad night with 3 climbers squeezed into a badly pitched two man tent, Ghersen and Cadot decided to quit. This left Beghin in the middle of the face, with 1400 metres of difficult ground to overcome with not much gear and very little food, but he decided to go on. He had to undertake difficult and exposed climbing whilst self-belaying on poor piton placements before joining the Slovenian route. It took him three hours to overcome the last overhang, which he considered one of the most desperate things he had done. The handholds were portable, the pitons could be removed easily by hand, cracks were chocked with ice and it all had to be climbed above a dizzying void. He carried on up very delicate terrains with slabs covered by snow barely thick enough to support his weight, his crampons scratching the rock underneath. Now he was committed and the only way out was to continue to the top and descend the other side. He radioed Base Camp to tell them he was not coming back down the South Face. He bivouacked early because the next morning he wanted to make as much progress as possible before the sun hit the Face. From his bivouac snow slopes seem to lead temptingly towards the West Ridge, but he knew from studying the Face that he could not get through that way. This type of meticulous study and memorisation of the terrain is key for lightweight ascents. As he approached 8000 metres, the way ahead seemed to be blocked by steep verglassed walls, but Beghin remained calm with the same complete concentration which Cesen spoke about in facing extreme difficulty alone. Beghin wrote "curiously, I scarcely feel the precariousness of my situation. I know I have to do what I have to do. Each difficulty requires so much concentration that, in my mind, the previous one disappears instantly".

While auto-belaying his rope caught below him. There was no choice but to cut it loose and continue without protection. Now a traverse allowed him to attain the West Ridge, but it was too late to reach the summit that day and he had to bivouac at 8100 metres. In a fantastic icy night he watched violent electrical storms over the jungles of Nepal too far away to produce any sound. In the morning it was cold, overcast and windy. The ridge was heavily banked in snow creating huge cornices and breaking the trail was hard work. Sometimes he even had to shuffle along "a cheval" with one leg on each side of the ridge. From the summit the view was spectacular, but without hesitation he headed straight down the ordinary route on the North West side of the mountain. Far below he could see four tiny dots, which were the tents of a Spanish expedition attempting the ordinary route. He was able to lose altitude fast, although easy the slopes were overloaded with snow. The tents were quite close when suddenly the whole slope gave way in a windslab avalanche pulling him off his feet and taking him headfirst down the slope. Instinctively he swam to keep his head above the mass of snow and found himself 200 metres further down, having lost his radio and one of his axes, but unharmed. A few minutes later he was at the Spanish tents – they were astonished that he had come from the other side of the mountain. After spending the night with the Spanish he continued his descent, but failed to find the Spanish fixed ropes and ended up in a 45° snow couloir. Half way down he suddenly found himself in an area with a crust over loose snow. With a sense of déjà vu, he was once again carried away by an avalanche, flung about and catapulted over 2 ice cliffs. The snow around him cushioned the impacts, but he travelled 400 metres downhill before he was tossed free. This time he had lost even more – his other axes, gloves, stove and even his camera. This time at least, the lack of summit photos did not put his ascent in any doubt – he could have hardly appeared at the Spanish tents without crossing from the other side. Once off the mountain and out of danger, despite being in a state of nervous exhaustion, he could savour the moment. The richness of the experience made him feel that nothing "will ever really be as it was before".

With these climbs Beghin established himself amongst the very top Himalayan mountaineers and showed how much techniques had advanced over the past decade. A face which a strong Slovenian team had needed siege tactics to conquer in 1975 had been climbed, by a more difficult variant in very lightweight style. Logically the South Face of Lhotse became a realistic target with the same techniques. In the winter of 1990 Beghin ran into Christophe Profit who was just returning from his winter attempt on the Face with Enric

Lucas. Profit's attempt had failed due to the doubts of Lucas and the terrible winter winds, but he had not given up on the idea of climbing the route. Beghin and Profit agreed to mount a joint attempt that autumn. Although they had not climbed together before, the two French climbers felt they shared the same concept of mountaineering. They were only interested in achieving something in good style and had both turned their backs on heavyweight expeditions. In April they were in the middle of preparing for the expedition when they heard the stunning news of Cesen's solo ascent. It was not only a fantastic climb, but also done in a style for which both Beghin and Profit had enormous respect. Of course there was some disappointment that the prize of the first ascent had been taken, but for Beghin this was short lived. The route Cesen had followed, which was essentially a variant on the 1981 line attempted by the Slovenians, was quite different than the one he and Profit planned, which was a line up the centre of the face similar to that attempted by Fine and Fauquet. The situation paralleled that in 1985 with a small French group and a larger Polish one operating on the mountain at the same time, but in different styles. In 1990 the large Soviet team would attempt the Central Pillar at the same time as Beghin and Profit made their attempt. The planned routes were different and the Frenchmen believed they could make their attempt without being disturbed by the presence of the Soviets.

Chapter 14 – Fighting Huge Snow Mushrooms

By chance, I was also planning to visit the Everest massif at exactly the same time as the French and the Soviets. In 1990 I quit my job to travel round the world, but mainly in Asia and with the centre piece of the trip being a commercial expedition to attempt the 7500m Changtse. I had a done few seasons of modest standard Alpine climbing, but felt it should be enough for Changtse which was high, but reasonably straightforward technically. Changtse is in a symmetrical position to Lhotse relative to Everest. The name Changtse means North Peak, whilst Lhotse means South Peak. The South Col of Everest separates it from Lhotse, the North Col from Changtse. The route to the foot of Changtse is common to the normal route on the North side of Everest and then heads off to the right up a final face. The expedition was led by Steve Bell, a former soldier who had left the SAS to become one of the pioneers in organising commercial expeditions to high Himalayan peaks. With only one guide to seven climbers, it was clear nobody was going to drag us up the mountain and we would largely have to depend on our own resources. In our group there were 5 Britons: Bill Bennett, Andy Elliot, Jeremy Edwards, Pete Wilson and myself and two Americans: Paul Dornisch and Russell Lee. All of us had reasonable mountaineering experience, although only a couple had been at really high altitudes. Almost as important, everyone got along well and there were no major tensions during our seven weeks together.

After meeting in Kathmandu we trekked to acclimatise close to the Freedom Highway which goes from Nepal to Tibet. This was a little visited part of Nepal and we passed villages which rarely saw westerners. Some of the villages were several days' walk from the nearest road and it was almost like going back in time to a medieval era with no electricity, cars, windows or chimneys. Curious children crowded around us trying to use the handful of English words they had picked up to engage us in conversation. To be ready for the optimal period for climbing, we trekked at the tail end of the monsoon which inevitably meant rain, wet camp sites and leeches. These little devils drop from plants on to the unsuspecting passer-by or squeeze through bootlaces holes. The leeches inject an anaesthetic so that the victim does not realise his blood is being sucked until he takes his boots off to find his feet a bloody mess where the leech has gouged itself on his blood before bursting. The monsoon, which finished late that year hampering the efforts of the Soviets to establish their route on Lhotse, also meant that we did not see more than a few glimpses of closest mountain group, the Jugal Himal. When we did, its white peaks freshly plastered with snow rising high above the steaming paddy fields made a spectacular sight. After a few days approach we, camped for a week by the lake of Bhairab Kunda at 4150 metres. We made excursions around the camp in terrain which was similar to the English Lake District or the Scottish Highlands, with the rain and clouds the same as well. With the acclimatisation completed, we descended nearly 3000 metres in a single day back down to the Friendship Highway. We rushed past the leech zone, the final part of the descent zig-zagging through paddy fields and finally hitting the road. After the idyllic mountain villages, the shacks lining the side of the road like in some dusty Wild West town were a bit depressing. At least we were able to buy cans of Chinese beer to celebrate our last evening in Nepal.

We then picked up our transport and got ready to cross into Tibet. This was complicated, because the few kilometres of road over the border to reach the customs post a Jangmu was in a terrible state and took hours to cross. When we finally got there met Paul Teare and Rob Anderson, members of an American expedition which had been attempting Everest North Face. They had failed at 7700 metres due to bad snow conditions and looked gaunt and tired – we realised that to summit Changtse we would need to go to nearly the same height. To get the last few hundred metres to our transport in Tibet we had to use Tibetan women porters. These ladies all seemed to be looking for an opportunity to scamper down some side alley with their load, which would then never be seen again. We hung on to our personal things and tried to stay as close to as many of the porters as we could. We ended up only losing a couple of non-critical loads. We then loaded up in a lorry and set off on the drive to Everest Base Camp. As we journeyed across Tibet the scenery got much drier and we soon exited the Nyalam Gorge and got up onto the Tibetan plateau. Here the scenery is fantastic with the massive open plateau of seemingly endless orange brown hills, ruined sand-blasted forts of unknown age and exotic nomads passing on donkeys or camped by the side of the road. We crossed a 5000 metre pass from where we got our first view of Everest and some of the other 8000ers. After a night in Xegar with its impressive stepped fort, we made the final approach up the Rongbuk Valley to Everest, managing to cross the river despite the bridge having been swept away and the lorry driver stalling mid-crossing. We arrived at Base Camp on October 3rd. It was situated in the classic site used by the pre-war British Everest expeditions of the 1920s and 1930s and it was possible to recognise the shape of the moraine hillocks which sheltered the tents from black and white photos in the old books.

The site of Base Camp is magnificent with Everest rising imposingly around 15 kilometres distant. But life can be hard in such a high and inhospitable place and I spent the first evening tent-bound with stomach and back pains and shivering from cold. The next morning I got up at first light. The sun had not yet hit Base Camp and it was very cold, but I was awed by the splendour of the place. I spent the next morning talking to the two Chinese members of our team, who were both interesting characters in different ways. They were provided by the Chinese Mountaineering Association or CMA, which controls expeditions to Chinese Tibet. Our liaison officer was Liu Bin, a young man in his early twenties who, despite being a chain-smoker, was apparently a star rock climber, although we never saw him in action. His father Liu Ta Yi was a senior official at the CMA, who had been on Chinese expeditions to Everest in the 1960s. He had asked for his son to go on an expedition to Shisha Pangma, but this had been blocked by internal CMA politics, so he had ended up on Changtse, which is less prestigious since it is under 8000 metres. An even more interesting character was our translator who westernised his name to Julius for our convenience. He had been one of the protestors in Tiananmen Square the year before and like most of the many thousands involved he left Beijing when the clampdown came and lay low to avoid any government reprisals. His feeling one year after, was that the student protests were never going to succeed because the huge mass of Chinese peasants didn't care about political freedoms as long as they had rising living standards. When news of the clampdown came, some of them reacted by burying their TVs and other consumer goods as they feared these would be smashed by Red Guards in a repeat of the Cultural Revolution. Once they realised that that wasn't going to happen, the peasants were indifferent to the protesters. Julius himself appeared as a bit part in the famous film Bertolucci's "The Last Emperor" as a Red Guard. His only line is to say to the old emperor: "Join us comrade or fuck off".

On the second day at Base Camp, we hiked up the hillside behind to a height of over 5700 metres where there was a splendid view of the North East Ridge of Everest, of Pumori and Cho Oyu and the nearly 8000er Gyachung Kang. The latter peak is a splendid mountain which gets far less attention than it deserves just because it falls slightly short of some arbitrary height. For the next days we were stuck at Base Camp waiting for the yaks, which were going to help us carry equipment to the foot of Changtse. In contrast to the crowded, noisy and polluted state of Tibetan Everest Base Camp today, in 1990 it was very quiet, with visitors being a notable event. There was a small Italian expedition which had been attempting the Japanese Couloir route on the North Face, but they had failed at 7000 metres and were packing up to go home when we arrived. A group of American trekkers came through one time, but apart from that we had the Base Camp and indeed the whole upper Rongbuk Valley to ourselves.

By the time we were at Everest Base Camp, the Soviet expedition had been active on the mountain for several weeks. The Soviets approach to organising the team was in sharp contrast to that of Beghin and Profit, who like most Himalayan climbers of the modern era, just organised the expedition themselves rather than relying on a central organisation and national clubs and committees. But under the leader Shevchenko, there were still some strong characters in the Soviet team, like Sergey Bershov and Misha Turkevich. They were among the driving forces of the expedition even if they had to work within an organised system. The long process of selecting the team for Kangchenjunga already gave many natural candidates for Lhotse, particular those who performed well on the former mountain. As for Kangchenjunga, there was a formal programme over several years aimed at selecting the country's strongest climbers for Lhotse. This involved running on Elbrus, in the South of the Soviet Union, physiological checks in pressure chambers and even psychological tests on the compatibility of the team. The expedition had almost hit a hitch before leaving Russia when Karataev, who was responsible for financial issues, was told that there was no foreign currency available to give to them. Any Himalayan expedition needs a significant quantity of cash to meet expenses locally, pay porters, purchase food and so on. Rumours circulated that the blockage on the cash was because Soviet TV had bought the rights to show a film about the expedition of Profit and Beghin and were worried that the success of a large Soviet team would "spoil the story". This seems farfetched and Bershov makes it clear when recounting these rumours that any skulduggery was certainly done without the knowledge of the French climbers. However in the bureaucratic and Machiavellian world of the Soviet Union just before its break up, strange events did happen. In the end Shevchenko was able to play on rivalry between different parts of the Soviet bureaucracy and to agree that they would make their own film about the climb. After that he was finally able to get the required currency and set off for Nepal.

The team was selected from the cream of Soviet alpinists with many strong climbers who were capable of leading sections of the route and attempting the summit. They divided the 18 man team into four groups and each of these was involved in establishing parts of the route. Generally each group would work for three to five days on the mountain before descending to rest at Base Camp for two to three days' rest. The whole team worked hard on equipping the route, but it was clear to all that the difficulty and complexity would make it likely that only one or two groups would get a chance to go to the summit. There was less internal competition than on Kangchenjunga, where groups from the different Soviet cities and republics, like Moscow, Ukraine, Almay Ata and so on, tended to form groups. But despite the strong team ethic, there was plenty of jostling for position and competition to lead the key pitches and be on the summit team. One of the strongest climbers was, of course, Sergey Bershov. In the first weeks he was in a team with Rinat Khabibulin, Karataev and Alexei Makarov.

The Soviets chose a very direct and logical route up the Central Spur which was hard, but also relatively safe from objective dangers of avalanche and rock and ice fall. They wanted to make the hardest climb yet done in the Himalayas and the success of Cesen in climbing the Face meant that repeating that alone would not be enough. After climbing up the avalanche cones at the foot of the Face they had to cross the bergschrund and then started up a snow couloir. The avalanche risk was highest in this lower part of the wall before the Central Spur become pronounced and it was here that Bershov's group were caught by an avalanche. Down on this lower area the shape of the wall prevented them seeing the higher part, so the first sign they had of an avalanche was a hissing sound. Then one of them shouted to warn the others of danger. It was necessary to make an instant decision to try and find some shelter and his years of mountaineering experience allowed Bershov to react instinctively and grab two of his companions and drag them back down to the bergschrund where they jumped into the shelter of the crevasse. First the air blast of the avalanche hit them followed by the snow which pounded them and plunged them into darkness. After a while there was silence and they realised everyone was OK. Hesitantly they left the shelter of the bergschrund to survey the scene. Everything was calm with the snow dust of the avalanche still settling. Another time, Makarov and Karataev were caught in an avalanche.

Karataev managed to dive into a crevasse, but Makarov took the brunt of the avalanche and was lucky to escape unhurt.

In the lower section the climbing was mainly on snow and was not too hard, but it was difficult to arrange solid protection. There was snow lying over a thin layer of ice which itself was stuck onto rock slabs, but was made unstable by the warm winds blowing from the Indian plain.. It was possible to place ice screws in the ice layer, but it was clear that they would not hold the weight of a fall, so instead they had to hack through the snow and ice to expose the rock underneath and find a crack in which a piton could be hammered in. The route was continuously difficult with no sections easier than grade V from 6000m and above. They established three intermediate camps at heights of 6000 metres, 6500 metres and 6800 metres. Camp II was sheltered under a steep rock face on a snow covered ledge that was so narrow they always had to remain clipped onto the ropes, even when inside the tents and sleeping bags. Camp III was placed to the side of the main route. It frequently had dust like powder avalanches falling from above and sometimes the camp was hit by a forceful blasts of air caused by avalanches. Even if not hit by the avalanches, there was a risk of choking from the snow dust. Sometimes their tents were hit by electrified snow particles creating strange light effects inside the tents. When the tents were hit by avalanches, the occupants would often by lying impotent in their sleeping bags wondering anxiously whether the tents would resist the force of the blast. Camp IV was established at 7100 metres on September 24th. Above this, the wall became more difficult with steep rock faces covered with ice. The difficulty increased above Camp V at 7350 metres with very compact rock offering few chances to get protection for climbing and to fix the ropes.

The late finish to the monsoon, which had made our stay by the lake in Nepal wet and miserable, also added to the Soviet climbers' problems. By 9th September, the date they had established Base Camp, they had been expecting fine post monsoon weather. Instead there was frequent rain and high temperatures. On occasions they even experienced rain above 7000 metres. Their equipment and materials were not designed for such conditions, but following the rule that "necessity is the mother of invention" they looked for ways to adapt, including wrapping plastic sheets over their tents to keep the rain off. They would have preferred to wait for better weather, but they knew the period of good autumn weather before the winter set in was limited and they had to press on if they were to attempt the summit before winter came.

On 30th September they managed to establish Camp V, which consisted of a tent for three people lying down, or five sitting up, attached to a sloping and narrow ledge. Below there was a precipice of 2500 metres and above the most difficult part of the climb.

Originally they had planned to climb the upper part of the route in alpine style, but the technical difficulty of this section forced them to continue to fix ropes. The hardest part was between 7500m and 8000m where there was a steep band of ice covered rocks. Whilst climbing this section they were frequently bombarded by snow avalanches and lumps of ice. Sometimes the climber would disappear in a cloud of snow for several minutes. Initially when this happened they clung on in fear, but in the end they got used to it and almost enjoyed the sensation. This section was tackled by a team comprised of Turkevich, Kopeika, Pogolorev and Khitrikov At the top of it was a sheer 30 metre wall which led to somewhat easier ground. On this wall there was a continuous bombardment of small balls of ice, 2-3 cm in diameter, which pounded their helmets almost like a drumbeat. The physical cause of the formation of these ice balls was not clear. Pogorelov was the first to try this section, but he got stuck part way up on a rock ledge and had to pass the lead to Misha Turkevich. He was one of the stars of the team and had a brilliant rock climbing pedigree having been individual speed climbing champion of the USSR in 1977. But speed climbing, in benign conditions on good rock with good protection and wearing rock boots that let him feel the nuances on the rock, was a completely different situation to that facing him now. Wearing big rigid plastic boots and crampons, heavy clothes and at well over 7000 metres of altitude he had to face ice shattered rock. Turkevich took 40 minutes tackling a 5 metre overhang using artificial climbing techniques. The quality of the rock was very variable and feeling the footholds was not easy since they were climbing in crampons. But he managed to pull through the overhangs and now the way to the top was open. Kopeika filmed the key section using a Panasonic M8 camera which weighed 3.6 kilos and was not easy to manoeuvre. He tried to keep the camera warm, by keeping it under his clothing, but it was a big effort to get it out and shoot film in blizzards, strong winds and temperatures as low as -20°. He had to connect the batteries cables, film the scene and remove the cartridge. By the time he had packed the camera away the rest of the team were usually some way ahead and he had to race to catch up.

Having overcome this section it seemed the summit was in reach for Turkevich's team. From a camp at 8100m, they planned to climb the remaining 400 metres and return to the camp in the same day. So they decided to save weight by travelling light without bivouac equipment such as sleeping bags, stoves and a tent. Since they weren't taking a stove, they also dispensed with food since they knew that without drinks it would not be possible to eat. They only took climbing gear – ropes and pitons – and 2 cylinders of oxygen to give them extra power for a "finishing spurt". By climbing light they hoped to be able to make a quick dash and get back down the same day. Setting out at 6am they were faced with unusual terrain – a steep rock ridge, which was adorned by huge snow cornices and mushrooms. They sometimes had to dig trenches and vertical tunnels to pass through the cornices and making progress was slow work which went on all day. At the same time they did not want to retreat, since they knew that other parties were following them and that if they did not succeed on this attempt they might not get another shot. By 5pm they had reached 8250m, but within an hour it would be dark. There were bivouac sites available, but given that they had no tents, they decided to continue climbing through the night and hope to press on to the summit. But the terrain proved too complicated for night climbing and the cold also slowed them down. By 11pm they had only gained 50 metres of vertical height. They were at a very similar place to where Wielicki and Hajzer had bivouacked three years earlier, but must have been somewhat lower because they subsequently passed signs of the Poles.

There was no choice for Turkevich's team but to stop for the night and try and dig a shelter. Digging in the tightly packed snow, almost of the consistency of ice, was very hard work and by 2am they had only managed to carve a one metre deep niche in the slope, which they struggled to all get inside with their big plastic boots. But it was better to be squeezed in, pressed against their comrades than to be outside where the temperature was 30 degrees below zero. Now they remembered that they had gone all day without food, but all they had with them was a couple of energy bars which Kopeika found in this coat pocket and which they divided between the four of them. They tried to sleep, but it was difficult because of the severe cold. Kopeika bemoaned not even having his down jacket, which someone else had accidently taken from Camp V. Only the quality of the clothing which they had got from Italian sponsors protected them from freezing to death in this bivouac. They knew they could not afford to sleep for long anyway as they had to try and keep moving their toes and fingers to maintain the blood flow and reduce the risk of frostbite. Occasionally Kopeika dozed off and had a recurrent dream about a trolley bus stopping and telling him that it was going to his home, but each time he could not quite raise the energy to climb aboard. This happened again and again and each time he woke up with a start, horrified at the desperate position they were in and the abyss which lay below.

Finally the sun came up and with their spirits raised a little, Turkevich's team steeled themselves to carry on. Getting ready did not take long as they had all their clothes on and had no way to make hot drinks, usually the most time consuming task when leaving a high camp. But the route got no easier. They passed through a fantastic terrain of huge hanging cornices, some of which they had to literally tunnel through. At times they were almost swimming through the snow with progress up the mountain seemingly impossible. When they came to a step, they decided to traverse onto the right wall of the ridge to avoid the steepest part. Unexpectedly they came across pitons hammered into the rocks and tattered strands of rope. They realised with a chill that this was the exact spot where Jerzy Kukuczka had fallen to his death the previous year. They had seen the memorial to Kukuczka at Base Camp, but passing the scene of the fatal accident brought home to them the risks they were facing and reduced their desire to get to the top "at all costs". Time sped by and progress was slow. They were now higher on the route than any of the Polish attempts and at lower altitude or with simpler terrain the top would have been reached quickly. At 5pm they only had 100 metres vertically to go and they tried to use the artificial oxygen to give a boost to push for the summit. Kopeika put his oxygen mask on and hooked up the supply, but he found that it did no good. A high supply of oxygen made him feel stronger, but would have used up the cylinder in half an hour, whereas a low flow seemed to give no benefit. After 20 minutes he pushed the mask away from his face to shout to one of his team mates about getting some protection from the rope and after that he continued without the flow of gas. Even in this short time, the mask had frozen to his beard so firmly that he wasn't able to release it until they reached the camp the following evening. At dusk they saw the summit, but at the pace they were moving it was still half a day away. They had been going for two days without food and water and a second night without shelter at this height would be close to suicidal. It was impossible to carry on up such difficult ground in the dark. They hesitated as the top seemed so near, but they realised their strength was fading and in the end they agreed to turn back. Turkevich radioed Base Camp to inform them. They knew that the descent would have to be undertaken during the night and warned the group who were sleeping in Camp VI to expect their arrival in the coming hours.

The descent was a nightmare, with their legs refusing to obey them and a constant fear they were going to fall through fatigue. In the dark and desperate to get back to the tent, they started to take bigger and bigger risks. They could not easily place pitons in the dark and had to rely on less secure anchors for descent. At one section of the ridge, Turkevich drove his ice axe deep into the snow and immediately proceeded to descend along the rope attached to it. When he reached the end of the rope he screamed for Kopeika to follow him. Pogolorev, who was coming behind Kopeika, stood against the axe belay to stop it being pulled out of the snow. Kopeika approached the edge of steep snow slope with caution, peering into the darkness to try and understand what was below. There seemed to be a steep drop of about 5 metres so he looked for a way down, but before he knew it he had lost his footing and was flying through the dark. As he fell, he flailed around trying to find something to grab. He managed for a second, but couldn't hold on and then his only chance was the rope, which he knew this was only attached by an axe driven into the snow. If it gave way both he and Pogolorev would be plunged into the abyss. Kopeika tried to get a grip on the rocks where he had fallen, but they were steep and he found he was falling further and further down and he realised Pogolorev must have fallen too. After plummeting 15 metres, the rope suddenly became taught. Kopeika was gasping for breath, afraid to move. Slowly he raised his head to see Pogorelov silhouetted against the starry sky, blocked in a narrow gap between rocks. The axe of which they had been belayed had torn out and sent Pogolorev hurtling down the mountain, but by an incredible stroke of fortune, he had jammed in this gap and the rope between them had stopped the fall. With extreme care the two climbers moved to take the weight off the rope and continued the descent.

The same day that Turkevich's team turned back, another team led by Rinat Khabibulin was moving up the face to make their own summit attempt. As well as Khabibulin there was Makarov, Alexander Pitra and Ihor Sverhun. They had moved the highest camp up by some 100 metres to 8150m with the goal of reaching the top for next day. They also knew that Turkevich's group were up above after trying for two days to reach the summit. Without tents and sleeping bags they were likely to be in a bad state. On the radio that night the expedition leader asked Khaibubilin to leave the camp and go up to help Turkevich's group. Khaibubilin, belayed by Alexander Pitra, set off up the ridge above the tent. He could find nowhere to secure the rope and so he asked for Pitra to pay out more rope and carried on further up the ridge in a very precarious position. At that point he heard voices in the darkness and after a while met the higher group. The first to arrive was Misha Turkevich, who still looked in quite good shape, but the rest of the group was in poor condition and some of them needed help to descend. At 3am they all finally arrived at the camp. With eight of them packed in to a four man tent the descending team were finally able to get warm and, most importantly, they had something to drink for the first time in 3 days – tea can rarely have tasted nicer. It was clear that Khabibulin's team could not make further progress with several of Turkevich's group needing help to descend and in any case Sverhun and Pitra in Khabilbulin's team were sick. All eight climbers retreated together. The summit was proving a tougher nut to crack than they had hoped.

When they got back to Base Camp they were all examined by the expedition doctors. Pogolorev and Khitrikov had badly frostbitten hands and were immediately put on a helicopter to Moscow. Khitrikov's fingers were so badly swollen with blisters that they had to cut his wedding ring off with wire cutters. Kopeika was not in such a bad way, but had lost all feeling in the last joints of his fingers and toes. However he was not yet ready to withdraw from the attempt to climb the mountain. Using electrical stimulators the medics were able to get the feeling back into his hands and he and Turkevich eventually returned up the mountain. In his account of the expedition written 30 years later, Sergey Bershov attributes the determination of this first summit group to keep going seemingly at all costs to the fact that with a big team there was effectively a queue to get into the lead. If they failed to reach the summit when it was their turn, they would return to the back of the line again. The climbers knew that the additional fame and reputation with the Soviet sporting authorities that would go to the summiteers could be crucial to their future climbing careers. The situation was not so different from that of Western climbers in the large expeditions of the 1970s. For those wanting to make a career in mountaineering, making the summits could make a huge difference to their chances. But for Kopeika and even more so Turkevich, the driver more than anything else seemed to be a burning ambition to climb this great wall to its top.

Whilst the Soviet team were setting up their fixed ropes and camps, Pierre Beghin and Christophe Profit had established themselves at a Base Camp not far from the Soviet one and were ready for their first attempt on the Face. They were going to start up the Central Couloir to the right of the Soviet route on the Central Pillar. The lower part of this route was much more exposed to stonefall and avalanche risk than the Pillar, but they could climb this steep snow much more quickly and, more importantly, only climb it once, which would minimise the danger. Early one morning they crossed the bergschrund and climbed the first few hundred metres up to the foot of the Central Couloir at 5700 metres. They found a safe place to shelter before the sun hit the Face and then waited until the onset of night to freeze the stones and rocks to make an ascent of the lower part of the couloir an acceptable risk to take. As they waited for the day to pass, Beghin tried to read a trashy thriller, but was unable to concentrate and ended up tearing up the book to dry out the condensation which had formed on the groundsheet of the bivouac tent. The couloir carried constant reminders of the continuous erosion of the mountain from the huge avalanche cones at its base to the constant fall of rock and ice from above. From time to time the wind deposited a thin layer of snow on top of their tent.

They waited in shelter until the sun had set and the glacial night had arrived and put a stop to the constant fall of rock and ice. They had a significant weight to carry with equipment in their rucksacks for what could be a long climb – leading maybe even to the summit. 1500 metres separated them from the part of the Face which is relatively sheltered by the big overhangs above and it was imperative to reach this area before the sun hit the Face the next morning. A traverse to the right took them into the centre of the Couloir. Here they were hit by cascades of fresh snow which came from some undefined place above. When the volume of snow increased they had to stop, hugging the wall, their heads hunched into their shoulders like turtles. Their head torches traced strange silhouettes in the air, creating a spooky atmosphere. Beghin made a false move and his ice axe slipped from his grip. "Merde that's a good start" he shouted as the axe bounced down the slope and disappeared from view, but there was nothing to be done. Below Profit left his belay and started climbing up to where Beghin waited, his headtorch creating a halo of light in the fog. At a certain point he stopped and with surprise saw Beghin's ice axe stuck in the snow. They started to feel that perhaps their luck was going to hold after all.

The lower part of the route was monotonous with one 50 metre rope length following another. The belayer risked being overcome by sleep and Beghin kept doing things like adjusting his helmet and checking knots and carabiners just to keep occupied and his mind alert. A little after midnight they gave themselves a short, but well-earned rest. Beghin got out his drink bottle, which had been boiling when they set off, but was now already cold. The mixture of coffee and a caffeine and vitamin C drink should have been enough to wake the dead, but it didn't work – all he Beghin wanted to do was lay down and sleep. He knew that only the arrival of the day would rid him of this torpor. Profit took the lead and they set off again. As they slowly approached the top of the Couloir the dawn light started to be visible in the east. They wanted to move faster because they knew that it could be deadly to be caught in the middle of the Couloir when the sun was full on it loosening rocks and ice from the overhangs above. But at 7000 metres, and after a night of hard work, their bodies were unable to do more. They were now in a vast amphitheatre surrounded by unclimbable walls. On the right some rectangular snow channels, which seemed offered a possible escape to the eastern part of the Face where the Polish route went.

At 8am the sun struck the face and within minutes the heat became oppressive and the brightness overwhelming. Icicles detached from the rocks above and splintered into thousands of pieces. Protected by the overhangs above they gained another 100 metres of height before reaching a point which was no longer sheltered. As they started to traverse diagonally across the couloir the bombardment started. Missiles of ice and rock of all shapes and sizes seemed to come from the sky without warning. With a rising crescendo of noise the missiles came hurtling through the air and landed around them, making dull noises as they thudded into the snow. With fear tightening their stomachs they climbed as quickly as possible, not worrying about belaying. Three rope lengths would be enough to reach the protection of the huge overhang which stood above the couloir. Just at the moment that they were looking for a place to bivouac Beghin was hit in the thigh by a rock, a few seconds later another hit his arm. At the same time Profit was hit. Under a constant barrage, Beghin cursed everything around him, the mountain, the fact they were later than planned and the choice of route. Anger almost allowed him to forget his fear.

At 10am they threw themselves against the first rocks of the huge cliff above. A few metres away from them the ground was pockmarked with holes from the bombardment of stones. With their backs literally to the wall they worked to hack out a miserable bivouac site. There wasn't even space to fully place the tent, which hung out over the abyss. As the hours passed in their bivouac, Beghin found himself more and more taken over by anxiety at their position, but Profit seemed to be able to forget their precarious situation. Beghin felt they seemed to be in some sort of vertical cul-du-sac without an obvious means of escape. To return down the couloir was unthinkable. On the right was the channel through which all the avalanches from the upper basis were channelled. On the left a ramp, which had looked promising from below, now proved a delusion. Below it, at the same height as them, was a series of thin ice plates lying on top of grey rocks. Under the effect of the sun bits of these were regularly shattering off with the sound of broken glass, but this was nonetheless the only route open to them. It involved 200 metres of very exposed climbing on hollow sounding ice.

To their surprise at the steepest part of the climb they suddenly found themselves face to face with the Soviet climbers who were fixing ropes up the Central Spur. The isolation and danger of their position a short while earlier now seemed somewhat absurd as they found themselves next to a chain of fixed ropes which led safely down to the bottom of the Face. Even if the Soviets had accepted it, it would have completed changed the character of the French pair's climb if they were to ascend the Soviets' fixed ropes. To climb parallel to the ropes without touching them would have been highly artificial. In the end they felt they had no choice but to go down.

After a few days in Base Camp, Beghin and Profit were ready to attempt the Face again. This time they tried a direct route through the Central Couloir and further to the right than their first attempt, but to the left of the Polish route. After three days of effort in the cold and the wind and overcoming a difficult rock section between 7100m and 7500m they had reached 7600 metres. But weather conditions were against them. In the cauldron between Lhotse and Lhotse Shar the wind was so strong that the falling snow didn't even manage to descend. The plume of snow blown from the summit ridge was of a startling height. In these conditions it was clear that they would have needed several bivouacs above 8000 metres if they were to reach the summit. To make matters worse, the burner on their gas cooker had broken. Without the possibility to make drinks, their lifespan at this height was very limited. They had no choice but to turn back. So they folded their small tent and started their first abseil. It was the first of many before they arrived at the foot of the mountain. Sometimes these even took them into space where the Face was overhanging. And always they were frightened that the ropes might block leaving them stranded on this enormous wall. They were disappointed to not achieve their goal, but had no regrets. They knew that the long hours lived in this strange high altitude world would remain precious moments of their lives. Despite his exhaustion, despite the uncertainties and risks of the descent, Beghin realised that they were privileged to be able to go and pursue such wild dreams. As a team he and Profit had been highly effective without any conflicts poisoning the atmosphere. This team would go on to make one great climb together, but it would not be on Lhotse.

Chapter 15 – An Infernal Circle

At the same time as Beghin and Profit were attempting Lhotse, our expedition was well established at Everest Base Camp on the other side of the massif. The terrain on the north side of the Everest massif is quite different from the south. Because the mountain rises from the Tibetan plateau which is much higher than the Nepalese plains, the approach is flatter and it is also much drier on the North side. These factors allow yaks to be used to transport equipment to only 2400 metres vertically below the summit. We were held up because our yaks arrived three days later than planned, although at least we improved our acclimatisation during this time. Impatient after the delays we set off well ahead of the yaks, which was to have unforeseen consequences. Base Camp is at the side of the Central Rongbuk Glacier, but our route went up the East Rongbuk Glacier, which is on a side valley on the left, to reach the foot of the North Col. I was feeling very lethargic and sick by the time we reached the turn off for the East Rongbuk Glacier and slipped behind the rest of the team. We were following the true right bank of the Glacier, which we knew was the route taken by the pre-war British expeditions. Our goal was to get half way up the glacier so that we could make an Advanced Base Camp or ABC below the North Col on the following day. After a while I seemed to recover a bit and managed to struggle along, but relief that we were getting close to the campsite turned to dismay when I saw the others descending on to the glacier. Getting to the same place as the yaks was critical since they were carrying the tents, sleeping bags and stoves. So I followed the others down and caught them up just as they spotted the yaks high up on the moraines on the far side of the glacier and still moving forward. We later found that the reason for the confusion was that since the 1920s the conventional route had changed from one side of the Glacier to the other. By relying on the historic books to research the route we had ended up going the wrong way. The glacier was wide and finding a way through the ice pinnacles and crevasses was time consuming and tiring. We jumped across a glacial stream in the middle which took us to little icy hollow bound in by ice cliffs and with the stream swishing round it in an arc cut into the far wall. Above a 40 metre ice pinnacle stood guard, but the glacier seemed so immobile in the cold Tibetan air that I did not feel it constituted a threat. We needed to ascend the far slope to where the yak herders were setting up camp, but I was too physically and mentally spent to carry on and I told Steve I would bivvy where I was. Jerry generously offered to stay there with me and Steve said he would go on to the camp and bring our sleeping bags and mats back to us. By the time Steve returned we had realised that this hollow was going to be an extraordinarily cold place to spend the night with the stream bringing bitterly cold air. Steve said we should return to the camp and we agreed and struggled up the final slope to the camp where, fortified by some hot tea, we had a comfortable, although sleepless night. I did not know how to account for my performance on that day, which was both a puzzle and a worry to me after being fine on the earlier acclimatisation trips, but I was too tired to think through the implications for the rest of the expedition.

I woke a little bit fresher the next day to find that we were camped in what was effectively a rubbish tip at 5800 metres, with old tin cans and the burnt remains of packaging scattered around – the scars of decades of expeditions' passage. At the time it didn't really matter because the weather was good and the situation so impressive. I was very pleased to feel fit enough to carry on, albeit slowly and sticking close to the yaks. The route now led up the central moraine of the East Rongbuk Glacier, gently ascending and with magnificent views of Everest, Changtse and the various 7000ers surrounding the glacier. The moraine we toiled up is a long wide trench in the Glacier between ice towers which looks like the parting in a frozen Red Sea. We were still going when the sun went down and the temperature plummeted, but eventually we struggled into an uncomfortable camp at 6400 metres. The situation was again tremendous with Chomo Lonzo, a high 7000er near Makalu, framed by the Rapiu La, the col at the foot of Everest's North East Ridge. This ridge rises in a huge sweep to the pinnacles. This is the key section which makes this route so hard to climb and where the great British climbers Pete Boardman and Joe Tasker had lost their lives 8 years before. Beside this is the glaciated face of the North Col with Everest itself poking it head up behind the col and with a savage wind creating a lengthy plume of snow from the summit. Changtse completes the circle to the right, but the face we were going to attempt it was still obscured by the mountain's own East Ridge at this point. We were now far higher than I had ever been before and I was a panting wreck, but recovered quite well after having tea and noodle soup.

I had such a bad night that the exact moment of "waking" was hard to pin down, but when the sun hit the tents I got out and wandered groggily up the hillside and round the corner to get a look at the left hand side of the face of Changtse where our planned route went. I was encouraged that it looked quite straightforward, although I knew that a big uncertainty was whether the slopes were free from avalanche risk. When I returned down to the mess tent I found our cook, Kumar, lying like a corpse in the half collapsed tent. He looked in a bad way, clearly not properly acclimatised and cold because he had left the high altitude kit he'd been issued with back down in Base Camp. This is sometimes done by local staff to keep equipment in mint condition and maximise it resale value, but although understandable it can lead to real risks of exposure, when it causes people to wear inadequate clothes on the mountain.

In the afternoon the rest of team went to have a look at the face of Changtse and when they returned later they seemed impressed by what they had seen. I wrote in my diary that Peter, who was the least experienced climber among us, looked like he'd seen a ghost. On next day several of us woke with bad headaches after another bad night. We recognised we were not yet fully acclimatised. I suggested descending to Base Camp for some rest and recuperation and returning refreshed for a summit bid. After a lively discussion, Steve decided that he and Paul should first make a reconnaissance of the face whilst the rest of us carried tents and food to set up a higher camp at the foot of the face. Steve and Paul arrived back in the evening tired but excited after having climbed to around 6900 metres. Although the face was quite steep, they reported that snow conditions were very good with crisp neve allowing cramponing with the minimum effort. Some of the team were concerned that the weather would turn and the decision to go back down will rob us of a shot at the mountain, but I was pleased for some relief from the rigours of life at 6400 metres. Here the reality of daily living is cut lips and dry skin, headaches, difficulty sleeping and lack of appetite.

Unlike over on Lhotse on the south side of the Everest group, the weather on the north is generally stable in this season, so making a later start didn't matter as long as we got down before the icy chill of a Tibetan night. After dumping some gear at 6000 metres the way down proved surprisingly hard. It was a long way and almost horizontal on the Glacier, with the moraines necessitating much up and down on energy sapping loose rocks. We arrived back down to a warm welcome in Base Camp. Liu Bin had managed to borrow the large mess tent from the departing Italian expedition and had even managed to bring down a pigeon with his catapult the day, although this had upset the Nepalese cooks who, as Buddhists, considered the Rongbuk valley a sacred place where all life should be protected. Julius contributed a bottle of Chinese Red Wine and Liu

Bin had prepared a fine Chinese banquet of mushrooms, two types of shredded potatoes, sliced lamb and rice. The air felt thick now we were back down and everyone looked forward to getting their first good night's sleep for several days. It was a wild and stormy night necessitating an exit to make repairs to the fly sheet at one point. The 14th dawned overcast and grey with light snow falling steadily. It had been a fortuitous time to descend, but chances of making the summit did not look good now. Everyone was worried that we had left our heavy double boots up at 6000 metres to save effort walking down across the rocks of the moraines. Now we realised we would have to go back in light boots in 10 centimetres of fresh snow. It was as if the season had changed from autumn to winter in the space of two days. The morning was spent on an extended breakfast and multiple games of cards. The next day dawned sunny, but we had agreed this would be rest day. I was able to wash myself in the morning; topless in the snow, but the radiation of the sun was powerful enough to warm my skin despite the very low air temperature. Contemplating the climb ahead, I felt a mixture of apprehension about the steepness and difficulty of the final Face and somehow irritation on the amount of discomfort necessary to get back up to make the final push. I was used to Alpine climbing where two or maybe three days were spent on the mountain before a retreat to the comfort of the valley. On an expedition, the effort and the discomfort was continuous and spread out over weeks rather than days, with the tents of Base Camp providing only a relative comfort. Greater mental endurance was required and it was necessary to conserve strength and rest when possible. At least I knew that whatever happened, our next excursion up the mountain would be the last.

On the 16th October, the day Soviet climbers were attempting to reach the summit of Lhotse, we started back up the mountain from Base Camp. The new snow which had fallen on the 15th accentuated the long distance we had to cover and we risked cold feet from doing this in light trekking boots. To make matters worse, we lost our way amongst the ice towers of the glacier and a sort of mood of crisis overcame the team with some wanting to go back down. After some discussion everyone kept going, gritting their teeth for the hard graft of getting up the glacier. It was a tough struggle and when I arrived at the equipment dump where we were going to camp I went straight into a tent to try and warm my feet up. When it was time to move to Steve and Kumar's three man tent for supper both my feet and boots still felt like block of ice and I had to hobble the 20 metres to the other tent with my boots half on. Steve helped me warm my feet up and life returned to some parts of them, but other parts remained without feeling and some mild frostbite was diagnosed as likely. I spent a cold and uncomfortable night worrying about my feet.

In the morning we completed the route back up to the Advanced Base Camp, close to the foot of the final face of Changtse, which would provide the first real climbing of the expedition. The next day I was loaded down by a heavy back with two Russian 11 millimetre ropes and some climbing gear added to my equipment. After ascending the moraine, the mood changed dramatically as we finally stepped onto the snow covered part of the glacier. This upper part of the East Rongbuk Glacier is a flattish basin about a kilometre across and hemmed in by the North East Ridge of Everest, the North Col and Changtse. As dots on this great white playing field we now followed bamboo wands on a path through the crevasses to reach the upper plateau where the face of Changtse lay before us. A large buttress of rock splits the low half of the Face from the complex rock architecture of the wall leading up to the East Ridge. Our planned route lay up a couloir to the left of this buttress before breaking out onto the open upper part of the Face, which led to the small trapezium formed by the twin summits of the mountain.

As I arrived with my load, Steve was already negotiating the bergschrund to reach the Face. He followed the slope above to the foot of the buttress where he started fixing ropes. I found the step over the bergschrund and the lower part of the face satisfyingly steep after all the time spent on the almost horizontal East Rongbuk Glacier. The plan was to have a caterpillar of climbers moving up the ropes that Steve was fixing and hauling up a second line which Steve would then continue to fix above. But the plan worked better in theory than in practice. I was left fairly low down, not knowing when to climb and when to haul the rope and in the end we didn't manage to fix as much rope as we'd hoped. But it was still a fantastic day and we had reached a point level nearly level with the North Col. The next morning we ate and drank as much as possible before shouldering heavy packs to move up to a Camp on the glacier directly below the face of Changtse. Kumar was supposed to bring up a large can of water to save some of the effort melting snow, but Jerry and I struggled to get him to overcome his fear of the snow covered part of the glacier. Camp I consisted of four mountain tents laid out in 2 rows facing each other so that cooking duties could be shared between pairs of tents. In practice the operation of passing food and drink between the tents proved cumbersome and we ended up just taking turns with the stoves. It was comfortable until the sun went down and then suddenly bitterly cold even with full mountain kit on inside the sleeping bag. I didn't manage to sleep and the altitude caused my mind to wander onto all sorts of things except the mountain itself. It was a strange sensation almost like a fever, but with a fuller awareness of what is going on, although no more control over the direction of one's thoughts.

On the steep lower section of the South-East Face of Changtse (Camp I is circled on the glacier below).

On the 20th October we were woken up in the early hours by the most violent wind I had ever heard. Although it only came in blasts, these were strong enough to lift us off our feet. You could actually hear a gust coming with a sort of sonic boom over the North Col while it was still calm at the camp, knowing that seconds later the tent would be violently shaken. I sat cowering in my frost covered sleeping bag hoping that Steve, who had gone out to test the weather, would not announce a summit attempt that day. It was decided we should stay put for at least a day. Andy and Jerry, who had gone down to ABC to collect supplies, returned with the worrying news that our cook Kumar had abandoned the camp. Frightened after the wind of the previous night, he had simply, rolled everything up and put it in barrels before descending alone.

The next night was equally noisy, but in the early hours there was a strange calm and, scarcely believing our luck, we realised that this was our chance for a summit bid. We set to work brewing drinks to get as hydrated as possible and fill the water bottles. Getting cold feet was my biggest fear, so I did everything I could to reduce the risk, massaging my feet to increase circulation, sleeping with my inner boots clutched to my chest and the outer ones inside the sleeping bag. I even used plastic bags between two pairs of thick socks as a vapour barrier. Once out on the mountain, the glory of the morning allowed me to forget my feet. We started to climb up the fixed ropes, sliding our jumar clamps up the line. By 12.30 the whole team had reached the top of the couloir where the angle eased and the fixed ropes ended. The slopes above looked straightforward and we started to believe we would reach the summit. We took our harnesses off and set off un-roped up the upper slopes. We moved at a funeral pace, but slowly and surely we ate up the ground. The view was incredible with Everest huge now that we were above the North Col and Kangchenjunga, yellowed by the distance rising above the Rapiu La. I felt lucid, although I could only manage 10 or 15 steps before needing a pause to get my breath back. But as we ascended the wide slope, the snow conditions started to worsen. There was a hard crust, which broke under our weight, and a deep layer of ball bearings of powder snow underneath. This was not only very hard work to ascend, but also meant a difficult to quantify risk of wind slab avalanche. We knew that this type of avalanche, where a whole wide area of slope can slide off if the slab is fractured, had killed three people on the nearby slope of the North Col just over a month before. We stopped at 7200 metres to discuss what to do. Andy was about 6 metres above the rest of us, fighting thigh deep in the snow and not wanting to give up. It was an agonising decision, but it was clear there was no choice but to retreat. As I turned back after taking a few photos I felt no emotion. After long weeks in getting there, it might seem that there should be disappointment at turning back or satisfaction at the achievement of getting that far, but there was neither. This emotional numbness seems common at high altitude. Russ on the other hand was sat disconsolate in the snow 50 metres further down and Jerry and I sat either side of him and tried to cheer him up. The descent went quickly, sliding rapidly down the fixed ropes and in little time we were lying exhausted and somehow feeling empty in Camp I. One of the discouraging dimensions of high altitude climbing is how quickly you can lose height which has cost so much effort to gain.

As we packed up the top camp, Steve accidently let go of an inner tent which flew at the speed of a racing car diagonally upwards onto the slopes of the North East Facet of Everest far above. Wearily we descended the glacier and moraine to ABC. We congregated in the damaged mess tent for an inadequate dinner. Tortured by a sore tongue and lips, I slept little that night, but it wasn't regrets which were keeping me awake. The next morning with no cook and limited working stoves it was important that we got back down to Base Camp. Since our first visit to ABC the weather had changed and it was clear that winter was drawing near. Before we collected water from a drip from the rocks which was steady in daytime, but now it was frozen solid and we had no choice but to hack off water ice and go through the slow process of melting it. The long descent back down the glacier was done on auto-pilot driving our tired bodies forward one more time to get to Base Camp and the gradual return to civilisation. That was the end of our attempt on Changtse. It was obviously in a different class as a mountaineering objective to the South Face of Lhotse, but still a very high Himalayan mountain.

At the same time on the other side of Everest, the Soviet team was taking stock after the first attempts on the summit. The work done by Turkevich's group was critical in giving access to the upper part of the Central Pillar and he and Kopeika were still fit enough to go up for another attempt. But before they got another shot it would be the turn of others. First Evgeni Klinetski led a team comprising of Nikolai Totmyanin, Sergey Tarasov and Vladimir Obichod. They started from Base Camp on the 6th October and by the 11th were in at the top snow cave. They spent the next two days battling to try and make progress on the final section of the Central Pillar with its enormous snow mushrooms. There were a number of falls during this attempt with Klinetski flying 20 metres, but fortunately not suffering serious harm. Klinetski's team failed just like Turkevich's had before. Although the end of the Pillar seemed to provide the logical way to the summit, it was starting to be in doubt whether they could actually make it that way. At least their foothold on the upper part of the mountain was gradually become firmer. A new, larger snow cave had been dug at 8350 metres and ropes were fixed in the most difficult stretches up to it. Meanwhile they heard from Elizabeth Hawley in Kathmandu that there would be very strong winds on the 15th. The same winds that delayed our summit bid on Changtse for a day, although we did not have the forecast.

The next group to try was made up of Vladimir Karataev, Sergey Bershov and Viktor Pastukh. Karataev was a Ukrainian. At the time of the expedition to Lhotse he was 35 and had been climbing since his youth. He had also done cave diving and acrobatic skiing and had been a champion climber in the Soviet Union. He had performed strongly on Kangchenjunga and so had been an obvious choice for Lhotse. On October 13th Bershov, Karataev and Pastukh reached Camp VII at 8350 metres. Pastukh had done a tremendous amount of work to try and consolidate the route to the summit, but now had a high fever. He was in no fit state to be trying for the summit and was probably starting to have pulmonary oedema, one of the most dangerous forms of altitude sickness. He also was apparently suffering from kidney failure. At the camp they met the Klinetski group who were burnt out from their unsuccessful attempts to climb the final ridge. With seven of them crammed into the snow cave, they had an uncomfortable night on the 13th, with space so limited that they had to sit all night rather than lie down. Pastukh was delirious and as the night wore on his condition worsened. He asked for help, but the others were half asleep and did not realise the seriousness of the situation until Pastukh pushed Bershov and demanded a drink. Bershov gave him his water bottle and tried to return to sleep, but Pastukh said he wanted something warm. Again Bershov mumbled something and dropped back to sleep, but when Pastukh declared that he thought he was going to die, Bershov finally understood how grave things were and woke with a start. They got the stove going and gave the patient warm drinks and an injection of strong anti-biotics, which Pastukh had self-prescribed. In the morning Pastukh was able to descend together with Klinetski's team.

The night before, Klinetski had talked to Bershov and Karataev about their experience on the section above the cave. He advised them that the upper section of the Central Pillar was very problematic because of the huge snow mushrooms and instead recommended that they traversed into the couloir to the left of the Pillar. So the next day Bershov and Karataev went out to investigate the suggested alternative route. The weather deteriorated, with strong winds and visibility down to a few metres, and they realised it was not realistic to attempt the summit that day. So they returned to the snow cave and spent the rest of the day there. The cave was more spacious than the one in which Turkevich's group had spent a terrible night there on the first summit attempt. It also made a big difference that they had a stove which allowed them to stay hydrated, but it didn't change the fact that they were above 8300 metres and at this height the physical condition can only deteriorate, even when resting. On the morning of the 15th the weather started to improve and the wind blew the clouds clear. They set off and traversed 45 metres down and left into the couloir as suggested by Klinetski. They quickly realised that this would provide a viable route to the summit and explored some way up the couloir. But they were too late in the day to make it to the summit and back before dark, so once again they returned to spend another night in the snow cave. But they knew they couldn't spend much longer at such a height and on the following day they would have to make a summit bid or abandon the attempt.

Meanwhile back down at Base Camp, the climbing leader Shevchenko had called a meeting of the remaining climbers. He was concerned that no-one was left on the mountain to provide back up for the lead pair if they got into difficulty. It was also senseless to leave quite so much equipment in the high camps. Shevchenko asked who was willing to go back up. Early in the expedition there would have been no shortage of willing volunteers, but now there was a deadly silence in response to Shevchenko's request. The effect of months of hard work at altitude, of sickness and injuries, had reduced the expedition's human resources to the bare bones. However Kopeika and Turkevich, recovered after the ordeal of their attempt with Pogorolev and Khitrikov, were keen to go and have a try at the summit themselves. They had difficulty in persuading anyone to join them. In the end, Peter Kozachok agreed, although he made it clear he would not go further than Camp V.

From the snow cave, Bershov and Karataev set out for the summit on the 16th October at 8.00 am following the route they had identified the day before. They knew that they should really have left earlier, but the extreme cold, around -40° C, prevented them. Fortunately there was no wind – otherwise the wind chill factor would have made it seem even colder. They still had two cylinders of oxygen left – enough to last for five hours if put on the minimum rate of flow. In the couloir they found the situation very different from that on ridge. Instead of the huge snow mushrooms they found themselves facing steep but straightforward snow initially. Climbing with two ice axes and placing protection they overcame the first 40 metres before a 10 metre rock wall blocked the couloir. After climbing that, they faced another 40 metres of steep snow before reaching the last obstacle at the head of the couloir - a 60 metre rock wall.

Bershov was in the lead and was a highly skilled rock climber – he had been national speed climbing champion in the USSR for four consecutive years during the 1970s. But the situation was vastly different from climbing warm limestone faces in the Crimea. Here there was little air, and he had a heavy rucksack, big boots and crampons. But despite the lack of oxygen he felt lucid and determined. He was climbing a tricky section when without warning he found himself gasping for breath. He had a bizarre feeling that some stranger was watching him and that he was trying to argue with this man, but did not manage. He looked at the gauge on the oxygen set and saw that it read zero. He ripped off the mask and the hallucinations disappeared. He discarded the oxygen bottle – apart from anything else that saved 3 kg in weight – and then carried on climbing. He tried to get a piton into the rotten rock, but it proved impossible and he climbed on without protection. From below Karataev shouted to him that there were only a couple of metres of rope left, but by then Bershov had reached a safe ledge at the top of the wall.

It had taken them eight hours to climb the eight pitches to the summit ridge where they arrived at 4 pm. As he made it up on to the ridge, Bershov saw Everest facing him, enormous and looking unfamiliar from an angle he'd never seen it from before. Of course he had stood on the summit eight years earlier in the night with Turkevich. He wanted to shout with elation, but the strength of the wind blowing from the North took his breath away and almost knocked him off his feet. He fixed the rope and shouted for Karataev to come up and join him, but it took Karataev a long time to climb that pitch. Bershov tried to contact Base Camp by radio but there was no reply. Probably the battery was too cold. Whilst fiddling with the radio he lost one of his mittens, but fortunately he had some spare woollen gloves. He took photographs looking down towards the Western Cwm, which was almost obscured, and Everest. He could see the bright spots of old tents on the South Col, but he knew there was no-one there – the climbing season was over on Everest. In fact the only other team still present on the whole Everest massif was our expedition on Changtse to the North. Although they were later in the day than he would have liked, he knew that it was a straightforward snowslope to the summit. Bershov waited an hour in the cold wind until Karataev arrived and they set off to climb the final 50m stretch together. There was little emotion despite the magnitude of their achievement, they were simply too tired. By the time Karataev arrived on top it was 17.55. They only spent 5 minutes there – it was getting dark and they knew they had a difficult descent ahead of them in the bitterly cold night. Their only comfort was that the wind had dropped – this saved Bershov from severe frostbite and quite likely saved the life of Karataev. Of course Bershov had been very high on these mountains in the night before and this experience was priceless now.

The descent was a nightmare with Karataev moving very slowly and complaining of difficulty breathing. When they reached the end of the fixed ropes Bershov went ahead to start making tea, but even he was struggling badly. The hardest section was the 45 metre rise out of the couloir to back onto the Central Pillar. Bershov had two failed attempts to get up this slope before finally managing to gather all his remaining strength to overcome it. He waited at the top of this rise until he was sure that Karataev was able to overcome it too and then carried on over the final horizontal section. It was 3am when Bershov dived into the snowcave. It was no warmer inside than the outside, but he immediately set to work making tea and got into his sleeping bag and tried to warm his frozen fingers. He waited and waited and still Karataev did not arrive. Bershov knew it was useless to shout for him because he would not hear as the route went round a bend, but he did it all the same. Finally at 5 am Karataev arrived completely exhausted and threw himself down on a sleeping mat in the entrance of the snow cave. As the morning sun started to shine through the entrance of the cave, Karataev was so disoriented that he asked whether the moon had risen. Bershov had to explain to him that it was already morning. Bershov had to warm up the radio battery on the stove before he was able to radio Base Camp to report their triumph. He also warned them that about the state of Karataev, which meant they would need help on the descent. During the descent Karataev had lost his mittens, although he had had a spare pair of gloves. Bershov tried to remove these, but the skin was stuck to the gloves. Bershov had had a similar experience on Everest when he and Turkevich had assisted Myslovsky in the descent, at first not realising the seriousness of his frostbite.

In the meantime Turkevich and Kopeika were getting ready to attempt the summit themselves from Camp VI. They were in good shape and great spirits and expecting to be able to reach the summit the next day. During the day they had been regularly in contact with Base Camp so they knew that Bershov and Karataev were attempting the summit, but because the summit team's radio was not switched on, they did not know whether they had succeeded. However they kept their radio in receiving mode and the next morning from the snatches of conversation they heard it was clear that Bershov and Karataev had reached the summit only at nightfall and that the latter was in a bad way. Without even exchanging words, Turkevich and Kopeika began to repack their rucksacks. They knew that with a rescue operation to undertake, their chances of making the summit were minimal. The priority was of course to help their teammates and so they packed all the things which could be useful – oxygen, a stove and fuel, food, a first aid kit and so on. They had mixed feelings because they knew that the expedition had been a success, but at the same time understood that they personally were going to miss out on reaching the top of this great wall. Whereas on Everest the Soviets had managed to place 11 climbers on the summit and on Kangchenjunga pretty much the whole team, on Lhotse the margin of success had been much narrower. Getting two men to the top and back down, barely alive was all that was going to be possible.

Turkevich and Kopeika climbed the already familiar part of the route and by 1pm were at the ice cave. Above was a complex rocky area on which ropes had been fixed. As they were resting before starting up these, they heard Bershov shouting. He told them to wait whilst he came down to join them. Then he explained that Karataev was sick and badly frostbitten. Bershov asked Turkevich and Kopeika whether they would continue to the summit, but without hesitation Turkevich said "What summit?" Bershov knew they were capable of doing it and how much it would mean to them, particularly to Turkevich with whom he had summited Everest eight years before. It seemed the Soviets felt a sense of comradeship, national pride and team spirit which allowed them to sacrifice their personal success in a way that Western climbers would not always do. The distinction made by Karataev on this point is probably too great – the majority of Western climbers would have done the same as Kopeika and Turkevich in the same circumstances and there are stories of great heroism involving complete strangers. But regrettably there are also an increasing number of cases, particularly on Everest, where the desire for the summit is put above all else, including assisting another climber in difficulty.

Karataev was moving very slowly, but on this steep rocky section it wasn't practical to give him assistance, so they simply had to wait for him to manage alone. By the time he joined the others it was already 5 pm and they immediately started administering first aid to Karataev. When they gave oxygen to Bershov this immediately improved his condition greatly and he was able to descend without assistance, but the situation of Karataev was much more severe. His slow progress meant that the four climbers were forced to spend another night in the lower snow cave at 8300m rather than descending to 8100 metres where they had a tent. 200 metres at this height it is a significant difference. In the snow cave they had a cold night - Kopeika found it even worse than their first night there on the earlier attempt. He did not sleep a wink all night and his teeth chattered continuously. At least they had a stove, oxygen and food, but the weather had worsened and there was a strong wind.

The next day Karataev was again very slow. They generally proceeded with Kopeika in the lead, followed by Bershov and then Karataev with Turkevich coming at the rear as anchor man. They did not have fixed ropes on all of this upper section of the climb, so they had to organise ropes to protect him and this slowed things down further. That day, the 18th, they only managed to descend 200 metres to the top camp covering a horizontal distance of only 400 metres, but they now felt closer to safety and despite the fact they were all very tired, being in a tent lifted their spirits. But the next morning they started to understand the gravity of the situation. As Turkevich was preparing breakfast, the sunlight shone through the orange fabric of the tent, refracted by the steam from the boiling tea. Karataev was inspecting his hands which had already turned black down to the third joint. The plaster they used to tape them hastily earlier was now peeling off together with the skin. The others tried to tell him that everything would be alright and that frostbitten fingers were just a price climbers had to pay for the life they chose to live. But they knew that there was no chance to save Karataev's hands and feet and the best they could hope for was to avoid further complications and infections and try to get him to hospital as quickly as possible.

Getting down the fixed ropes was extremely problematic. From the camp at 8100 metres they had 140 rope lengths to descend, each anchored at both ends and each with four or five intermediate anchors. This meant something like 600 places where it was necessary to move the descenders on and off the rope. Karataev's fingers wouldn't bend so he couldn't grip his descender. Kopeika had to pull the rope through the descender for him and then let him slide five and sometimes 10 metres down the rope. Sometimes they couldn't stop him swinging upside down and he just had to slide down like that. Then Kopeika descended himself to the same place and repeated the process. They had to go through this cycle time and again during three days of descent. Kopeika and

Turkevich were amazed at the courage and determination of Karataev during the descent – it showed the sheer strength of a human's will to live.

Bershov was frostbitten too, but was in much better condition and was able to descend largely unaided. When they reached Camp 4 where Peter Kozachok was waiting in support, it was clear that Karataev would not be able to make it down to Base Camp that day. They decided that Bershov should continue his descent with Kozachok, whilst the others stayed to continue to help Karataev descend. Since there was a lot of valuable equipment left on the route they wrapped some of it up in tents and threw it down to the bottom, although they only managed to recover some of the bundles. On the 21st October at 9pm Bershov reached the foot of the wall. They crossed the avalanche cones to find quite a crowd consisting of trekkers, team members and Russian journalists there to meet them. Makarov filmed Bershov as he pulled off his boots to reveal the first joint of his left big toe black from frost bite. Bershov was playing to the camera and joking about his feet being an advert for Himalayan climbing. Once they got Karataev to nearly the bottom of the Face and he could see the rescuers a hundred metres below, it seemed that his will finally deserted him and he sat down in the snow and said he could go no further. They had to carry him down the final section. The doctor Pastukh immediately put him on a drip and shortly afterwards he was evacuated by helicopter to Kathmandu and then by plane to Moscow. There he faced many months of treatment, the amputation of fingers and toes and terrible pain.

They had pulled off the ascent, but it had been a narrow thing and Karataev in particular had paid a heavy price. On the previous two Soviet expeditions to Everest and Kangchenjunga they had managed to get multiple teams on the summit. This time they had managed only two people on the summit and to do this they had had to push to the very limits of what was reasonable and possible. This made the achievement of Tomo Cesen all the more remarkable. A few hours after the arrival of Karataev, Profit, Beghin and his wife Annie went to visit the Soviet camp. Things were much more relaxed than they had been at their tense meeting up at 7600 metres when the French pair had encountered the Soviet fixed ropes. But the Soviet team were not very joyful despite the victory; probably they were too preoccupied by the condition of Karataev. The French wanted to pay him a visit, but the Soviets weren't keen. Beghin talked to Bershov who, despite his frostbitten hands, hadn't lost any of his usual vivacity. He explained to Beghin that "you know, the altitude is a trap. It anesthetises the brain so that you don't appreciate what's happening to you. Nevertheless the facts are simple: the longer you stay up high, the more you are exhausted, the more you are exhausted, the slower you move. And the slower you are, the more time you end up spending more time at high altitude than is reasonable. It's a real infernal circle."

Beghin clearly had great respect for the achievement of the Soviets, but the development of Himalayan climbing pre-occupied him. The growing wealth of the Western World was bringing more and more expeditions to the Himalayas. He even wondered if rules should be set with fines for those who put up fixed ropes and didn't take them down again or who left empty oxygen bottles. Beghin recognised that in the last 10 years some fantastic climbs had been achieved in a very lightweight style: climbs like his own climb on Makalu's South Face, that of Kurtyka and Robert Schauer on the South West Face of Gasherbrum IV, the British climbers Mick Fowler and Vic Saunders climb on Spantik, Bohigas and Lucas ascent on the South Face of Annapurna and Wielicki's solo on the East Face of Dhaulagiri. But above all he pointed to the solo ascent of Cesen which was the epitome of the modern style. A climb like that required a great commitment, but it meant that the challenges would wait unclimbed until someone was confident, courageous and capable enough to make this commitment. This was the same appeal as Al Rouse had made a few years when citing the Slovenian's 1981 Lhotse climb. He felt they had used a style which overcame a challenge which was best left for a future generation in a lighter style. Although Profit and Beghin hadn't been successful on their route, they had left only 2 pitons in place. If someone else wanted to come and face the same challenge they would find their route unspoilt.

Mikhail Gobarchev awarded honours to 17 members of the expedition including the prestigious Order of Lenin to Karataev. But the Soviet Union was already breaking apart and less than a year after Karataev and Bershov reached the summit of Lhotse, Ukraine, from where they both came, declared itself an independent country. As with the Yugoslavs and the Czechoslovaks before, a major route on Lhotse's South Face was made by an expedition representing a now defunct country. Although independence was declared on 24th August 1991, a Ukrainian expedition had already raised the blue and yellow flag of the country on the summit of Manaslu in May 1991 after climbing a very hard route on the East Face. Bershov was a member of that expedition, although Turkevich had turned down the chance to take past, saying he was no longer interested in heavyweight expeditions. The three summit climbers, Makarov, Sverhun and Pastukh were all members of the 1990 Lhotse team.

Chapter 16 – What Proof is Needed?

The Soviet ascent of the South Face was a spectacular and epic achievement, but ultimately one that paled into insignificance by comparison with Cesen's climb. The Soviets had a large team, used fixed ropes and oxygen and spent many weeks on the face. They had climbed a harder line than Cesen, but they did it by the skin of their teeth. Beghin rated the Soviet ascent as one of the finest achievements in Himalayan mountaineering up to that time and commented on the close and selfless teamwork they had demonstrated. But he also wrote that "l'alpinisme, ce n'est pas la guerre!", perhaps meaning that they had pushed too far, sacrificed too much, to achieve their goal.

When the Soviets returned to Kathmandu after their expedition they held a press conference. Bershov seemed to claim the first ascent of the Face and cast doubt on Cesen's climb by saying "you would have to be superhuman to make the ascent solo". Beghin, who had got to know the Soviets at the foot of the South Face, was present at press conference, spoke up to say "but what about Cesen?", Bershov replied that he had not reached the summit. "But what about his photo of the Western Cwm?" asked Beghin – you would need to reach the top of the Face in order to look down into the Western Cwm. Bershov replied that you can't see the Western Cwm from the summit of Lhotse. The photo that Beghin was referring to had appeared in an article in the French climbing magazine Vertical accompanied by a caption which said "on the summit Tomo had just enough time to photograph the Western Cwm of Everest to authenticate his ascent". When the Soviets clarified their doubts, it was clear that these centred on the 300 metre long, heavily corniced ridge which separated the point at which Cesen's route hit the main Nuptse-Lhotse crest and the actual summit. Knowing the difficult and time consuming nature of climbing on the upper part of Lhotse at first hand, Bershov seemed to find it more plausible that Cesen had completed his route to the ridge crest and then turned back down without reaching the highest point. Bershov was careful not to say that Cesen's ascent was definitely false and instead made the comment that "I am not saying he didn't reach the top, but if he did he is a superman".

But the seed of doubt had been sown, albeit perhaps unintentionally. When Cesen was nominated for membership of the prestigious French climbing club, the Groupe de Haute Montagne, several members objected to his entry on the grounds that his ascents had not been supported by sufficient proof. The most vocal critic was Yvan Ghirardini, an Italian born Frenchman who had grown up climbing around Marseille. Ghirardini had pulled off some fine solo climbs in the Alps during the 1970 and 80s including the first winter solo of the North Face of the Grandes Jorasses. He then went on to become the first man to climb the three great Alpine North Faces solo in one winter. He had been with Pierre Beghin on the large French expedition which had failed on the South Ridge of K2 in 1979 and, like Beghin, had got high on the mountain but ended up disillusioned by the experience. The next year he organised a solo expedition to Mitre Peak, a spectacular 6000er close to K2. He succeeded on this and then attempted the South ridge of K2 itself, a route for which he had tried, but failed to obtain a permit. He was able to use some of the equipment left by the national expedition the year before and made decent progress up the ridge before giving up at Camp III during a storm. Two years later he attempted an even more ambitious climb – the West Pillar of Makalu alone and in the winter. He overcame the snow arête at the base of the Pillar after three bivouacs, but he realised that to attempt the actual upper part of the Pillar itself would be tantamount to suicide given the severity of the winter conditions – 150 kmph winds and temperatures of -40 to -50 ^{O} C. After this failure, Ghirardini withdrew from top level climbing.

Ghirardini gradually became disillusioned with the European climbing scene. At the beginning of 1991 he wrote an article in the French climbing magazine "Vertical", which accused Cesen of lying about climbs such as those on Lhotse and Jannu for material gain. Ghirardini pointed out that on his own solo climbs he had always carried two cameras in case one of them malfunctioned. Since Cesen was a professional climber financed and sponsored by magazines and gear manufacturers, the Frenchman thought he should be obliged to provide incontestable proof of his climbs. To believe in his ascent of Lhotse, Ghirardini wanted to see clearly identifiable pictures of Cesen above the difficulties between 8000 metres and the summit. He even suggested that there should be a verifying commission which was "independent of sponsors, specialised magazines and other commercial interests" which would assess claims to have climbed a route.

Cesen hit back saying that Ghirandini had gone too far and that his idea of a verifying commission was absurd. He painted an image of Ghirandini as president of the commission following Cesen in a helicopter to check on the latter's climbs. He also criticised the Soviets saying that they had no idea of what modern Alpinism was like and that their climb on Lhotse had been a backwards step in the history of Alpinism. In effect he criticised their heavyweight style, which contrasted sharply with the way he had done the climb. The contrast in styles is undeniable, but the criticism of the Soviet climbers less fair. They had pulled off some fantastic ascents and when the Soviet Union ended, many of the top climbers showed they were equally capable of climbing hard routes in alpine style.

Perhaps the attack of Ghirandini was weakened because he wasn't necessarily the easiest character to get along with. Michael Kennedy, the editor of the American magazine, "Climbing", had been trekking on the Baltoro Glacier in 1980 when he heard accounts of how Ghirandini had fought with his porters, fired one liaison officer and accused another of trying to proposition his wife. Beghin, who climbed with Ghirandini on K2 in 1979, wrote that in a team of individualists, Ghirandini was individualist to excess. He was a strict vegetarian, accused his teammates of being neo-Nazis when he saw them eating meat and said that abattoirs were worse than concentration camps. Beghin saw him as an ambiguous character, who was able to inspire sympathy and mistrust at the same time. Stephen Venables, the British climber who has made some spectacular ascents including notably a new route on the East Face of Everest that he finished solo and without oxygen said the attacks of Ghirandini were "the sour grapes of a bitter man who never quite made the top grade". This is somewhat unfair. Ghirandini certainly did make some very hard climbs and the admiration of Beghin for his performance on the 1979 K2 expedition is clear. But Ghirandini hadn't been content to climb at the top level. Instead he had aimed to make climbs, like his attempted solos of K2 and Makalu, which went boldly beyond what anyone had achieved at the time. And he failed. This is no discredit, but merely the reality of someone who set his sights higher than anyone had done at the start of the 1980s, who dared to dream, and who failed to achieve these very ambitious goals.

The parallels with the climbing career of Cesen are surprisingly close. They both made hard solo climbs in the Alps, with the trilogy of North faces being a high point. They had both had their first experience in the Himalayas with a large expedition, but had then changed their focus to solo climbs. They had both attempted a couple of very hard climbs on large peaks. Ghirandini had been beaten back on K2 and on the winter attempt on the West Pillar of Makalu. Cesen had also tried K2 and also turned back, although he had completed a new route up to where it joins the Abruzzi Ridge. He then set out with a similarly ambitious programme on Jannu and Lhotse and claimed success. So were Ghirandini's complaints motivated by jealousy due to the fact that Cesen had succeeded in making the great leap forward in climbing standards that he himself had tried but failed to do? It is possible of course, but we must also recognise that Ghirandini was someone who had attempted climbs of similar difficultly to Cesen's and who knew what it was like to attempt an extreme Himalayan route solo. Could it even be possible that the temptation to fake an ascent crossed his mind in the desperate moments alone and cold on Makalu's West Pillar in winter and that he believes that Cesen gave into the same temptation he resisted? There was some history of tension between Tomo Cesen and the French. Three years before his Lhotse climb he was on a Slovenian expedition to Lhotse Shar which had been sharing the route with a French team leading to arguments about the French using the Slovenians fixed ropes. Both teams criticised each other in the accounts of these expeditions. But Ghirandini was always an outsider from the mainstream of climbing and it seems his indignation at what he believes was a fraud from Cesen was largely a personal view.

Cesen's claims got support from the American climbers Wally Berg and Scott Fischer. They climbed Lhotse by the normal route a month after Cesen's ascent. When they returned to Kathmandu they were interviewed by Liz Hawley, who is a Reuters correspondent based in Nepal who has for many years acted as an unofficial chronicler of Nepalese mountaineering. They discussed the summit area with Hawley including the presence of an old orange oxygen cylinder on a platform just below the summit. Cesen said he had seen the same cylinder. Berg also commented on the instability of the final snow cone which he and Fischer had climbed roped, but which he agrees would not have made sense to ascend unroped as Cesen was. Berg could not shed any light directly on the controversy about whether the Western Cwm could be seen from the summit because the summit was in cloud and the only feature they could faintly see was second horn, the subsidiary summit of Lhotse which lies across the other side of the West Face couloir. Berg pointed out that, from this point, which Cesen would have had to cross to get to the summit, there would probably be a clear view down into the Western Cwm. So the mystery of the photo down into the Cwm could have been solved by it having been taken there rather than on the main summit. Berg came away from this interview convinced that Cesen had made it to the same place as he and Fischer.

Not everyone saw this as conclusive. Reinhold Messner pointed out that there had been many ascents of Lhotse and Cesen could easily have learnt some basic facts about the summit by talking to someone else. Messner had originally been a strong supporter of Cesen, seeing him as a visionary, leading a leap forward in the standard and style of Himalayan climbing much as he had done 15 years earlier. He nominated Cesen for the 10,000 dollar Snow Lion prize which he had instituted for outstanding achievements in mountaineering. In his 1991 book "A Free Spirit" he dedicated a chapter to Cesen's exploits and explained that he viewed his ascent of the South Face as one of handful of defining moments in the history of mountaineering. In 1992 Cesen gave a talk in Vienna where he showed slides and the film which Ravnihar had made about the climb. This was the first time Messner and Cesen had met and things did not go well for the Slovenian. Messner found there were inconsistencies in Cesen's account. He spoke about storms, but his photos and Ravnihar's film only showed perfect weather. It was also hard for Messner to believe that Cesen had not used belays on the upper part of the Face. "From all his answers I had the feeling something was wrong" said Messner, who withdrew his nomination of Cesen for the Snow Lion prize. Given Messner's reputation in world mountaineering, this was a serious blow for Cesen's credibility.

Cesen picked up another opponent when Viki Groselj, a member of the 1981 Lhotse South Face expedition, came by chance across a copy of the article Cesen had written for the French magazine Vertical three years before. Groselj was very surprised to see that the article was supported by photographs, even though everyone in Slovenia had understood that he had taken no photos during the climb. Cesen had even declared in local press interviews that "my word is my only proof". Groselj was even more surprised when he realised that two of these pictures had been taken by him. One was a shot from over 8000 metres taken from the South Face during the 1981 attempt. The other, which showed the view down into the Western Cwm, had actually been taken by Groselj from the other side of the mountain and some distance below the summit, when he had climbed the ordinary West Face route in 1989. It turned out that Cesen had visited Groselj's wife Cveta whilst Groselj was away on an expedition and asked to borrow some slides to illustrate the route on Lhotse for one of his sponsors. Since Cesen was a friend of the family, Cveta let him take the photos he wanted without asking too many questions.

Groselj, who had viewed Cesen as the star of world mountaineering, now started to have his doubts. There was a third photo supposedly taken at around 7500 metres, which although not one of his, Groselj suspected had been taken by another member of the 1981 expedition. The photo showed cornices with a very similar structure to how they appeared on his own photos. It seemed very unlikely these snow formations would still look the same 9 years later. When confronted by Groselj, Cesen admitted he had borrowed and used the photos, but he denied he had ever claimed they were his own, saying that the mix up was the fault of Vertical's editors for wrongly labelling them as being taken by Cesen. To Groselj's questions as to why he didn't point his error out straight away when the photos were published he had some answers, but they didn't convince Groselj. Groselj tried to raise his doubts with his climbing club in Slovenia, but he was discouraged from publicising them. It seemed too damaging for the reputation of Slovenian mountaineering. Despite this pressure, Groselj decided to go public with his complaints. Cesen then issued a public statement and appeared on Slovenian TV saying that he had no photographs from the summit, that he had never claimed to have any and that there was nothing suspicious about his use of Groselj's photos. However people noted that this account seemed to be potentially inconsistent with some comments he had made in 1991 to defend himself against the doubts of the Soviet team. In some interviews he referred to a summit photo (i.e. the one taken by Groselj) saying "many people have seen this photograph. It poses no problem, it is at the disposal of all who wish to examine it".

Unfortunately some of Cesen's actions seemed to only serve to increase the scepticism about the ascent. For example he seemed to change his account during the ongoing controversy about the photos. There have been few doubts about Cesen's climb on K2 or his solo of Broad Peak and none about the climb on Yalungkang. So he has proved his ability in top level Himalayan mountaineering. The question is whether he was head and shoulders above the rest as he would have needed to be to climb the routes he claimed on Jannu and Lhotse. Greg Child, the Australian climber who has made some very fine ascents in the Himalayas, wrote an article setting out the facts related to Cesen's claims and the resulting disputes. The position of Child is that it is difficult to either confirm or refute Cesen's claim.

There was a robust reaction in defence of Cesen from some parts of the Slovenian climbing community. Dusica Kunaver, the widow of Ales Kunaver, the leader of the 1981 expedition who had died in a helicopter crash in 1984, was particularly vocal in this debate in support of Cesen. In Slovenia the controversy rumbled on with Dusica Kunaver and Viki Groselj exchanging letters in the local climbing journal.

In considering whether Cesen's claim is credible it has been pointed out that other lightweight climbs on the Face such as those of Profit, Beghin and Fauquet and Fine had got quite high. However this merely shows that there is no reason why a climber of Cesen's ability shouldn't be able to reach the upper part of the Face. It is equally relevant that some very strong climbers with excellent credentials, including Wielicki, Kukuczka, Zaplotnik, Stremfelj and Hajzer had got to this point in expedition style and then failed to finish the route. As Krzysztof Wielicki said "the real problem of Lhotse South Face is above 8000 metres". None of those – except Cesen - who had tried in very lightweight style even reached this height.

Initially most leading climbers appeared to believe Cesen's claims, but many have subsequently had serious doubts. The briefness of his accounts of the climb is a cause for concern. Quite soon after the climb, he published accounts in many of the leading mountaineering journals including Mountain Magazine, the Himalayan Journal and the American Alpine Journal, but these are all similar and quite brief. The summit day, which should be the climactic moment in one of the greatest achievements ever in mountaineering, is covered in a couple of paragraphs. Four lines describe the crux 60 metre section at 8200 metres. Above this, although he writes that there was a long way to go, there is little description of this remaining part of climbing. The terrain is described quite vaguely. Of course a lack of detail doesn't necessarily mean that the climb didn't happen, but the question might be asked why Cesen didn't provide more detailed descriptions of the climb, given the absence of photographic proof. A book was subsequently published in a number of languages including Slovenian and Italian, but not in English. It might be thought that a book format would have given Cesen the chance to flesh out his account, but actually few if any extra details are given. For example the description in the book of the section from the top of the crux to the summit is covered in about 120 words in the book (Italian version) and almost the same account of the same length is given in his American Alpine Journal article. Of course writing styles vary between climbers, but this is unusually succinct for the climatic part of such an important climb. By contrast he covers the summit day on Yalungkang in much more detail in the same book.

The speed at which Cesen managed to climb the last section is perhaps also of concern. It seems that Cesen left his bivouac at 8200 metres at 5am. He then had to climb up to the crux section which must have taken around an hour, before spending 3 hours to overcome this section. From the top of what he still had around 150-200 metres height to gain and something like 500 horizontal metres to cover. He therefore had taken something like 5 hours to cover this section. This might not sound very quick, but we should remember that Turkevich's team had spent a whole trying to climb the upper part of the Central Pillar from a point much closer to the summit and had still not made it to the top. Cesen told Greg Child that he had traversed the ridge on its South side to stay out of the wind. Child points out that all his mountaineering experience – which is considerable – taught him to avoid climbing below cornices on the lee side of a ridge. Such areas have danger of windslab avalanche or deep unconsolidated snow. The latter conditions are exactly what a subsequent Japanese team found when exiting from the Face, although admittedly in a different season. The steepness and difficulty of this ground is clear from their photos and the ridge involves crossing a number of ups and downs as well as a rocky pillar (the second horn of Lhotse). We should remember also that this was similar terrain to that which Matijevec and Knez had had such a desperate time on when they exited from the Face in 1981. This part of the account can be seen as lacking credibility and whether he traversed the ridge was exactly the point which Bershov questioned in Cesen's ascent.

So what actually did happen? There are four main scenarios. The first of course is that he did exactly what he said and made the greatest climb ever achieved and has been cruelly misjudged by the doubters. The only criticism of Cesen would then be for reporting a climb without sufficient supporting information. The second is that the climb was a complete and premeditated fraud. As Greg Child says it would mean he just went and hid behind a rock for a few days and came back saying he had done the climb. Some people have reached the conclusion that this is exactly what happened. "We all know what happened on Lhotse," Viki Groselj told the American journalist Ed Webster, "but nobody wants to talk about it anymore. We all know he cheated. He had an intentional plan to con the world. I'm sad about that. Because my biggest wish is that Slovenians do this face."

Would anyone, particularly someone who had achieved very hard climbs like his ascent of Yalungkang really make such a premeditated fraud? If the fraud had been deliberate and premeditated, wouldn't he have gone to the effort to construct a better, more robust and more consistent story? If it was all a fraud, wouldn't he have come up with an excuse for not having photos rather than trying to borrow photos and pass them off as his – something which would have been very risky if he had a guilty conscience.

The third possibility is more intriguing, which is that Cesen did climb a long way, although not to the summit. Suppose Cesen had got very high on the Face, perhaps even to the summit ridge as Bershov had suggested. If he had achieved this, the climb would remain one of the greatest ever achieved in the Himalayas, whether or not he had reached the summit. If he gave a convincing account of such a climb, people might well accept this and in some way he could salvage his reputation amongst the doubters. Of course it would make no sense for him to "admit" to having got high and turned back if, in fact, he had made it to the summit. The fourth one is a variant on the third in which a half-hearted attempt was made on the Face. It would certainly be possible for a climber of Cesen's ability to climb the lower section solo fairly quickly as Batard and Profit had done before. But maybe at some of the more difficult sections at mid-height or perhaps even at the crux which stopped the first summit attempt in 1981, he decided it was all too risky and turned back. Perhaps he realised, as Ghirandini had before him, that he had reached his limit, but he simply didn't want to admit it.

Greg Child pointed out a number of facts which don't quite fit in Cesen's account. It also needs to be asked why Cesen returned down the South Face instead of descending the normal route on Lhotse. For the Soviets descending the same way was an obvious choice because they had a line of fixed ropes and camps to within a couple of hundred metres of the top. Cesen on the other hand had neither and was obliged to descend the whole face with very limited equipment in situ. For a climber like Cesen descending the ordinary route should have been relatively straightforward. There were several large expeditions present on the South Col route on Everest at the same time (including an American team which also climbed Lhotse a couple of weeks later) so he could have quite easily got help if he needed it. Furthermore, he could have lost height quickly and got out of the wind in the West Face couloir rather than having to recross the exposed summit ridge. So why didn't he traverse the mountain and descend the easier way? This would have not reduced in any way the value of the ascent. Several of the climbers who had attempted South Face in lightweight style before had had this plan in mind including Jaeger, Fine and Fauquet, Batard, Kukuczka and Hajzer and Wielicki.

During the research for this book I have spoken to several of those who have been high on the Face. Some of them are very dubious about Cesen's claims, but few are willing to say outright that Cesen lied about his ascent. Despite the scepticism from many I do not believe it is to say that Cesen definitely did not complete the climb. Mark Twight, who at one stage contemplated an attempt on Lhotse South Face, concluded an analysis of Cesen's claims by saying he felt that more substantial evidence was needed than has been provided to refute a climber's word. He quotes another brilliant Slovenian climber, Marko Prezelj as saying "when climbers publicize their climbs, our belief is based on trust and respect. I believe Cesen, but I have no proof for that that and I don't want to convince anybody". It is true that he lacks concrete proof that he did it, but his detractors lack proof that he didn't. Vladimir Karataev made either the first or the second ascent of Lhotse from the South depending on whether you believe Cesen's claims. And Karataev paid for his victory dearly with the loss of the end joints of all of his fingers and many years rehabilitating. One might have thought he would be inclined to doubt Cesen's ascent, but when asked in 2008 whether he believed in Cesen's ascent Karataev said "Why not believe him? Perhaps even I could have climbed it alone".

With the passage of time the Cesen controversy has lost some of its sting, but it is certainly not forgotten and strong feelings are held. Mountaineering should be an honourable pursuit and it would be nice to be able to believe people merely based on their word. This is not going to be enough for everyone and unless he produces some dramatic new evidence in his favour Cesen will always have his doubters, but also some who are willing to give him the benefit of the doubt. For those who liked clear historical records, we have to say that the Ukrainian pair must be considered the first to have made a confirmed ascent of the Face.

Chapter 17 – The End of the Golden Age

The events of 1990 on Lhotse South Face can look, with retrospect, like the closing chapter in the golden era of Himalayan Mountaineering. The 1980s saw far more new routes on 8000 metre than any other decade before or since, with more than 50 new routes climbed. Since then, Himalayan climbing activity seems to have become more and more focused on simply reaching the 8000 metre summits, although of course there have still been some fine climbs. Probably a variety of factors were involved in this change. The simplest one is that the 1980s was just the era in which the most obviously feasible, reasonably safe and logical new routes were available to be climbed. Once the obvious lines were taken, the routes remaining to climb were either very hard, very dangerous routes or not very interesting and sometimes a combination of all three. Another strange factor was the fall of the Berlin Wall, which slowed the flow of Polish and Czechoslovak expeditions. Some of the artificial economic factors which had allowed the financing of so many expeditions disappeared. It was no longer possible to buy electric equipment at artificially low prices in Poland to sell it in India or bring back home scarce goods on which good profits could be made. There were also far more interesting things to do back home than there had been under Communist rule. This wasn't an immediate, nor a complete change, climbers like Wielicki and Wanda Rutkiewicz continued to be very active in the 1990s, but several climbers did give up and there were less new entrants to the game. After Lhotse South Face, the era of the huge Soviet expeditions was over, but climbers from the ex-Soviet countries became much more active in the Himalayas than before and made some of the most impressive climbs.

Another factor slowing the number of new routes was that standards had probably risen too fast and the temptation to push the limits of what was risked more and more had maybe been too great in the 1980s. In the 1970s improvements in ice climbing equipment like better front point crampons and curved ice axes made steep made routes like the Slovenian one on Lhotse significantly easier than they would have been with the traditional ice tools available at the start of the 1970s. Alessandro Gogna made the point to me that this was one reason why the Slovenians had been able to tackle the central part of the Face which the Italians avoided. But although equipment kept improving, there was not such a big change between the 1980s and 1990s. This made it hard to keep up the speed of increase in climbing standards. One way was to break through psychological barriers of what had been felt too difficult or dangerous before. But of course this required excellent judgement on when it was possible to go on and when things had really become too risky and it was necessary to give up. The very best climbers like Messner, Doug Scott and Krzysztof Wielicki had often turned back on routes when they felt that they had stepped up to this invisible edge and these people were survivors. In a thoughtful article published in the American Alpine Journal in 1991, Andrej Stremfelj pointed out the intense psychological pressure of a difficult alpine style ascent. He says that "after such an ascent, climbers are often not capable of performing an ascent of that difficulty again for several years, or perhaps ever". He also raises the question of to what extent an ascent can be judged important when huge objective risks are run. Stremfelj was of course another man who had achieved great things but turned back on Lhotse when he felt things had simply got too extreme.

Ever more expeditions visit the 8000 metre peaks, but most have the goal of following the ordinary routes so that the chances of reaching the summit are maximised and the risks minimised. The same is true on 4000 metre peaks of the Alps where the vast majority of climbers climb the ordinary routes on well-known peaks. Also in the Himalayas many have concentrated on peak-bagging and for climbers who want to collect 8000 metre peaks, the South Face of Lhotse is definitely a bad place to do it. But for those who still wanted to achieve hard new climbs on high peaks, Lhotse still presented challenges. One such challenge was the unclimbed summit of Lhotse Middle. Lhotse Middle is a knife edge rise on the ridge between the Main Summit of Lhotse and Lhotse Shar. Like Lhotse Shar, Lhotse Middle is not classified as an independent mountain, but it was the highest unclimbed significant point in the world for many years and became of particular interest for Russian mountaineers. The man who really stoked up interest in Lhotse Middle for the Russians was Vladimir Bashkirov, who first suggested trying to reach the peak. The two most obvious ways to reach it are the very difficult ridges from the neighbouring peaks of Lhotse Main or Lhotse Shar, both of which can be reached by relatively easy routes. Tragically Bashkirov died during the very first attempt in 1997 due to heart failure when descending from the main summit of Lhotse after only looking at the route along the ridge from there.

The next year Bashkirov's friends organised an expedition to try and reach Lhotse Middle from Lhotse Shar. Although they managed to reach the latter summit, they were not able to make progress along the intervening ridge. In 2000 there were two more expeditions. In the spring a Russian-Georgian team again tried via the summit of Lhotse Main. Then a Russian team tried quite a different route, which was the first attempt to climb Lhotse Middle directly. They intended to climb the South Face to reach the Cauldron below the three peaks of Lhotse and then climb the very steep face of Lhotse Middle from there. The team from the Russian Ministry of Emergencies was the brainchild of Misha Turkevich, who had put so much work into the 1990 Soviet expedition to Lhotse's South Face, but had to sacrifice a summit bid to assist in the descent of Bershov and the badly frostbitten Karataev. He had been badly affected by this setback and struggled to get the South Face out of his mind. Going back with the goal of a first ascent of Lhotse Middle gave the chance to settle his score with the Face and reach a major unclimbed summit.

Turkevich at first considered following the Central Couloir, the route attempted by Beghin and Profit, which was a fine line, but the Russians decided in the end that it was too dangerous. Instead they followed the route used by the Czechoslovaks and the Poles on the lower section. They set up Camp I at 5800 metres on the same site used by the Poles. Although more than 10 years had gone by since the Poles were last there, the Russians found gas canisters and stoves there which they could still use. They also established Camp II and went someway above this, but on 24th September Vladimir Bondarev was hit by an avalanche in the vicinity of this camp and knocked down the mountain. A search was made, but only found his rucksack and jacket. After the accident Turkevich and team wanted to continue with the expedition, but received a message from Moscow recommending them to abandon the attempt. There was some criticism about the decision of Turkevich to attempt the peak by a very difficult route, but this was characteristic of the man and his vision on the 1990 Lhotse South Face expedition.

Further attempts to climb Lhotse Middle via a traverse by Spanish and Korean teams failed in 2001 and in the end it was climbed by another Russian team by quite a different and very ingenious route. This approach reached the South Col between Everest and Lhotse and then traversed around the left hand side of Lhotse's North Ridge to reach the upper part of the unclimbed North East face of Lhotse, from where they were able to climb spectacularly unstable snow to the summit.

As well as conquering the few remaining unreached summits and harder routes, first winter ascents remain another significant challenge in the Himalayas. The same year that Lhotse Middle was climbed, a Japanese expedition set out with the goal of climbing Lhotse South Face in winter. This was a strong group from the Tokai Section of the Japanese Alpine Club. In 1997 this Section had climbed a very hard route on the West Ridge of K2 and was looking for a new challenge. The leader, Osamu Tanabe, had also been involved in the first winter ascent of the South West Face of Everest in 1991-1993. They knew that stable periods of weather in the winter tended to be short and it was necessary to move quickly to exploit them. They were already in Nepal in the autumn to acclimatise on Cho Oyu, where seven of the team members reached the summit. Another of the climbers reached the summit of Dhaulagiri, but he suffered severe frostbite and had to withdraw as did two of the Cho Oyu climbers due to illness. This left the expedition with only five climbers, a small team for what they were undertaking.

After establishing Base Camp in mid-November, they started establishing the route and by the 23rd November had reached their planned site for Camp I at 6400 metres. But they decided that it was threatened by stone fall and placed the camp lower. They engaged their Sherpas only until the end of November with the idea that they would not carry loads beyond Camp I. Load carrying after that would be done by the Japanese. They had at first planned a new variant starting well to the left of the 1981 Slovenian route, but they realised this route was exposed to rockfall and so followed a line close to that of Slovenian one. By 1st December they had established Camp I, but now the winter had really set in. Above Camp I they passed a rock band before reaching the long snow ridge followed by the Slovenians and Fine and Fauquet. The narrowest section of this ridge between 6400 and 6600 metres was particularly exposed to stonefall and three members suffered bruises after being hit. They ended up starting at 4am in the morning to reduce the risk of stonefall. The Slovenians had done the same thing, but in winter this meant dealing with the extreme cold. They continued to follow the Slovenian route and on the 6th December established Camp II at 7100 metres by cutting a platform in the fluted snow wall. For the next section they divided into two teams: an A team of Ohtani, Hanatani and two Sherpas, Dawa Tshiri and Tshiring Dorje, and a B team of Tanabe himself with Miyoshi and the Sherpas Mingma Tshiri and Nima Gyalzen. The A team managed to advance the route to just above the col where the Slovenians had placed their Camp IV. The B team then overcame the critical section of the Slovenian route which involved climbing the "Throat", the narrow chimney which acted as a drain through which all powder snow from the upper snow field descended. In this section they found three old wire ladders left by the Slovenians – a testimony to the struggle they had faced.

Up to this point, the weather had been fine, but on the 15th December, snow clouds veiled the Face and they had snowfall for the first time since establishing Base Camp. It was bitterly cold at Camp II and they had to wait until the sun struck the tents before leaving them, which inevitably slowed progress. On the 18th December the B Team reached 7600 metres, just before the Yellow Band which crosses the face, which was to prove the highest point they reached. They found that the wide slope above the throat was incessantly peppered by falling rocks from the upper slopes. As they were descending, Tanabe was hit and bruised. On the 19th December and again the following day, the B Team tried again to make progress, but were driven back by gale force winds. The team was exhausted and knew that they did not have the strength for a further try and decided to abandon the expedition.

Tanabe felt they had learnt many things during this attempt and that it was feasible to climb the Face in winter during an 18 day push. He noted that there were pros and cons of tackling this route in winter. The cold and potentially high winds made climbing difficult, but they had less problems with avalanches than the expeditions in the pre- and post- monsoon seasons. The Japanese returned in 2003. Tanabe wanted to learn the lessons from the earlier expedition to give the team the best chance of success. He judged that maintaining physical fitness and health was critical and so went with a small team of only 5 climbers in peak condition. They acclimatised by climbing Shisha Pangma, after which the team members returned to Kathmandu or Japan to rest. They also started the expedition earlier to try and give a chance to make bid at the summit before the most severe winter conditions had set in. When they arrived at Base Camp on the 14th November, they were surprised to find the bottom third of the Face quite bare of snow, although the upper part was loaded. Nevertheless, their familiarity with the route allowed them to make rapid progress and they set up three camps in similar positions to the previous attempt with a provisional Camp III placed at the site of the Slovenians' Camp IV. They found conditions on the wall better than in 2001 with less stonefall, but there was still the ever present danger of being struck by one of these shrieking bullets which appeared out of the blue sky with just a few instants warning. They stayed alert to these risks and continued to make good progress, passing their 2001 high point on December 5th. Four days later they set up Camp III at 7850 metres, which was lower than they had hoped and rather low to launch a summit push from. All the same, at this point Tanabe was confident that they would be able to reach the summit, but as with many of his predecessors, he had underestimated the difficulties of the upper part of the Face.

They decided not to go directly up Cesen's route which looked difficult and would leave them with a long traverse along the summit ridge, which would be very exposed to the savage winter winds. Instead they descended 200 metres down to the right into the couloir which lay to the left of the Central Pillar climbed by the Soviets. Bershov and Karataev climbed the top part of this couloir, although it seems the Japanese were not aware of this. Tanabe felt that this couloir could be a reasonably straightforward way to the summit, but carried some risk of avalanche. However he judged the risk pretty low because of the very limited snowfall they had had during the expedition and Tanabe decided it was justifiable to try that way. Contrary to what they had hoped, the couloir proved far from easy. There was a delicate traverse just to arrive into the couloir and once there they found a number of difficult pitches of climbing. For the next five days, two parties, one led by Tanabe, the other by Toshiyuki Kitamura, continued to make progress up the couloir. It was slow work and although they reached 8250m, they still had another 250 metres to go to the summit. Furthermore the Sherpa team had suffered a number of incidents due to rockfall and frostbite and could no longer provide much support. Tanabe's group left Base Camp for a final attempt on the 18th December. The following night the weather forecast predicted snowfall on the day they would reach the summit couloir. They expected this couloir to be at high risk of avalanche after fresh snowfall and felt they had no option but to retreat, a couple of hundred metres below the summit. This was a fine achievement in the bitter winter cold. Tanabe rightly considered the safe return of the team to be an achievement in itself. Although 8 out of the 20 climbers who had been on the wall had been hit by stonefall, there were no serious accidents.

In 2007 they were ready to try again. The driving force behind the expedition was again Osaumu Tanabe. They left Japan in September and first made an autumn ascent of Shisha Pangma to gain acclimatisation to over 8000 metres.

Despite heavy snow, all team members made it to the summit and, after a rest in Kathmandu, proceeded to the usual Base Camp at the foot of Lhotse's South Face. When they arrived they found a Korean expedition led by Lee Choongjik, which was working on the Face at the same time. The two teams agreed to work together and share the effort of fixing ropes. They had brought 6 kilometres of ropes and in the end they fixed all but 300 metres of this.

They'd encountered heavy snowfall on Shisha Pangma and consequently they found a lot more snow on the Face than when they had been there three years before. They started climbing on the 18th November and manged to establish Camp 1 at 5900 metres, but after that the strong winds hampered progress – even though they weren't yet as savage as could be found in mid-winter. Two of the climbers, Atsushi Senda and Toshio Yamamoto were blown of their feet and 10 metres into the air, but were saved by being attached to the fixed ropes. The winds also caused powder snow avalanches and rock fall which troubled the Sherpas carrying loads.

Nonetheless by 1st December they had managed to establish a second camp at 7100 metres and five days later a provisional third camp 200 metres higher. They climbed a tricky section above this camp, but then the strength of winds halted progress for five days. The normal weather pattern in the Himalayas is for extreme cold and violent gales to make climbing almost impossible after Christmas and so the Japanese had expected to have to finish by Christmas. But progress had been slow and they needed more time to have a decent shot at the summit. Fortunately, the monsoon had come late that year and this seemed to also delay the onset of the most severe winter weather. Tanabe believed one of the reasons for their failure in 2003 had been the placing Camp III 150 metres lower than planned. This time Tanabe, together with Takahiro Yamaguchi and Ngawang Tenzi Sherpa managed to forge the route up to 8000 metres and place Camp III there. This was high enough to try and make the route to the summit.

With Camp III established Atsushi Senda, Noriyuki Kenmochi and Pema Tsering Sherpa together with Ahn Chiyoung of the Korean party set off for the summit on 21st December. Tanabe hoped that three days would be enough to reach the summit. Senda's group descended into the couloir to the left of the Central Spur which had been climbed by the Soviets in 1990, although they had only reached the gully much higher up. They made progress in the gully, but after 3 days they had only reached 8200 metres and retreated, leaving Tanabe's group to take over the lead.

On Boxing Day 2006, Tanabe's group managed to climb 200 metres above the other group's high point and nearly to the top of the gully. They found traces of gear and ropes in the couloir which puzzled them because they believed that no-one had gone that way before. They thought the couloir would lead to the summit ridge just to the left of the summit, but at the top of the couloir they found a 20 metre rock with no cracks that they judged impossible to pass. The only feasible line seemed to them to be to traverse the left hand side of the couloir on fragile rock. They knew that this would take them on to the summit ridge to the left of the summit and require a long traverse of the ridge to reach the highest point. They advanced the route by one 50m pitch and then returned to Camp III to rest up ready to attempt the final section on the 27th. On this day Yamaguchi led a very bold pitch traversing across the final wall. They carried on up finishing on a very difficult snow face with almost vertical glassy powder snow, before stepping up onto the summit ridge. It was 3.30 pm and Everest was facing them directly across the Western Cwm trailing snow streamers and looking huge.

For Tanabe it was an emotional moment to conquer this wall after dedicating three winters to trying. They had arrived on the summit ridge 200 metres to the west of the summit and decided not to complete this final section. This made sense since it was winter with short days and extremely cold nights and they were very tired. Tomo Cesen would, according to his account, have arrived on this summit ridge significantly further away than this. The fact that the Japanese turned back from closer makes his claim to have traversed this last section of ridge less credible. Greg Child wrote that he was told by Cesen that he had traversed under the south side of the ridge, but photos taken by the Japanese from this part of the ridge shows this as being very steep and probably unconsolidated snow – Tanabe described this as being vertical powder snow. It was the Cesen's claim to have traversed the long summit ridge which Sergey Bershov had questioned following his own ascent. Tanabe himself was apparently doubtful about the validity of Cesen's climb and thought it should be erased from the record books.

Tanabe, Yamaguchi and Ngawang Tenzi thus became – if we credit Cesen's ascent - the fifth team after Knez and Matijevec in 1981, the Czechoslovaks on

Lhotse Shar in 1984, Cesen and Bershov and Karataev in 1990 to reach the top of this enormous wall. Eight men have looked down on the Western Cwm from the upper part of Lhotse having approached from the South (this wouldn't apply to the Czechoslovaks because Lhotse Shar doesn't overlook the Cwm). An interesting postscript to the report of the Japanese surrounds the fixed ropes they found in the upper part of the couloir. Their report says that these were probably left by one of the three Polish expeditions, but this does not seem correct because the Poles were following a line further right than this and in particular to the right of the Central Pillar of the Soviet route, which Wielicki and Hajzer reached but did not follow. It seems that these ropes were left by Bershov and Karataev as they climbed the upper part of the Face. Tanabe states that the traces of the forerunners ran out at the foot of the crux section and he presumably thought this was the high point of the Poles. We know that Bershov and Karataev actually managed to overcome this section, but Bershov's account mentions that he had difficulty placing any protection, so it may have just been the case that he left no trace. It seems that the Japanese took a line slightly to the left of that followed by Soviets, reaching the ridge at a point further from the summit.

The ascent by Tanabe's team was a magnificent achievement, one of the most difficult winter climbs ever made. Sadly he was killed on by an avalanche whilst low down on easy ground on Dhaulagiri in 2010. Apart from the ascent and attempts of the Japanese and Turkevich's attempt on Lhotse Middle, there has been very little activity on the Face in the 25 years since the first ascent. In 2007 a Korean expedition climbed Lhotse Shar by its South Face putting three Koreans and a Sherpa on the summit. The leader and one of the summiteers was Um Hong Gil who with this ascent became the first man to climb not only the 14 8000ers but also the two most significant subsidiary peaks Lhotse Shar and Yalungkang. In 2010 the Spanish climber Jordi Tosas who had repeated some of the hardest routes in the Himalayas, attempted the South Face of Lhotse, but turned back due to bad conditions.

Generally the face has been much quieter than when it was the focus of World mountaineering in the 1980s. Of the main participants from that period, those who made it to the summit, all are still alive. In the wake of all the controversy about his ascents of Jannu and Lhotse, Tomo Cesen retired from Himalayan climbing. He returned to the sport of rock climbing still living in his home town of Kranj and organising one of the events on the world tour of sport climbing as well as training one of Slovenia's leading sports climbers, Martina Cufar. Perhaps inevitably, given the storm of publicity surrounding the Lhotse climb, Cesen has kept a low profile in recent years.

Vladimir Karataev had to go through a painful process of rehabilitation. He spent the best part of 5 years in hospital and on occasions was close to death. He also got support from his partners from Lhotse like Victor Pastukh and Sergey Bershov who invited him to spend periods living at their homes. Once he was full recovered, he took up paragliding and in 2009 even went back to Nepal and climbed Pumori, a beautiful 7000er. Bershov on the other hand climbed a number of 8000 metre peaks following Lhotse including climbing Everest twice more and the South Face of Annapurna.

Of the other men who made it to the top of the wall, Francek Knez and Vanja Matijevec are still alive and living in Slovenia. Knez, without ever promoting himself as a climbing superstar, has had a fantastic career climbing very hard rock routes in places such as Patagonia and the Trango Towers in Pakistan. He was awarded the Order of Merit by the President of Slovenia in 1990. When I visited him in 2013, Matijevec was 67, but still looks in great physical shape. We met in a café in a commercial centre outside Kranj and it seemed an incongruous place to be discussing what happened in such a remote and savage place 22 years earlier. But his description of the events was so vivid that I felt transported away to that desperate night in the storm at 8000 metres trying to descend back across those collapsing snow ridges. He is retired and no longer climbs, although he still skis and plays golf.

Of the three Slovenian climbers who got highest on the face, Andrej Stremfelj has gone on to have a brilliant climbing career in the Himalayas. Highlights included the first ascent of Everest by a married couple and a difficult new route on the South East side of Kangchenjunga with Marko Prezelj. Nejc Zaplotnik, the most charismatic of Slovenian climbers, died in an avalanche on Manaslu only two years later. Pavel Podgornik was tragically killed with his girlfriend whilst climbing a hard route in the Julian Alps of Slovenia when they were hit by very bad weather and after a second bivouac they died from hypothermia and exhaustion. He and his twin brother Peter had climbed a hard new route on the 3000 metre high South Face of Aconcagua a few months after the Lhotse expedition. Peter still lives in Nova Gorica close to the border with Italy where I met him in 2013. When I met him he showed me his hands with the end joints of several fingers missing –the price for that icy lead on Lhotse many years earlier. But despite this he is still doing hard rock climbing and new routes at the age of 55.

Several of the other major actors in this drama died tragically, paying the prize for embracing the risky activity of Himalayan climbing for too long. Pierre Beghin and Christophe Profit had formed a very strong partnership on Lhotse and the following year they made a brilliant new route on the North Ridge of K2. On their way they had passed through Moscow where they met some of the members of the Soviet expedition. The tensions which had arisen when their routes crossed on Lhotse were now forgotten. The French pair reached the summit of K2 at twilight in very cold conditions, the lights of their head torches seen by trekkers on the Baltoro Glacier 4 kms below. The next year Beghin planned to return to attempt a new route on the South Face of Annapurna, again with a two man team. Profit could not join him this time and so he asked Jean-Christophe Lafaille, an ambitious young guide who had made some impressive ascents in the Alps. The first time the pair had ever roped together was when they passed the bergschrund at the foot of the face. The start of the climb was delayed because of indifferent weather and illness and then they found that an avalanche had completely buried the cache of gear which they had left at the foot of the Face. Beghin started talking about ordering a complete new set of gear from Kathmandu and trying to work out what delay that would involve. Lafaille instead started digging in the snow like a mad dog and after several hours found the end of a rope from which he was able to pull clear all the rest of the gear like a loose thread on a jumper. After a few days' rest, the two climbers set off again and reached 6900 metres below the rock barrier which goes across the Face where they bivouacked. They decided to pass the day there, protected from rockfall and resting, since it was dangerous climbing in the heat of the day and the weather seemed fine and settled. They knew that passing the rock band would not be straightforward and left at 4am the next day, but it proved even harder than expected and they had no choice but to continue traversing to the left trying to find a weak point where they could break through. They were so focused on the difficult climbing on very steep ground and that they did not fully take in that bad weather was arriving. They were forced to make a hanging bivouac at 7400 metres with no chance to open the tent and only managing to melt some water through very difficult manoeuvres with the stove between Beghin's knees. Despite a difficult night and no improvement in the weather, they decided to try and carry on and cross the very difficult band of compact schist. After Lafaille climbed 25 metres of difficult, hard to protect ground, Beghin joined him on the belay. The weather was looking bad again with a dark sky and violent wind and without much discussion it was clear they needed to head back down. They started to prepare the abseils to go down, 40 metres by 40 metres, struggling to get reliable pitons into the compact rock. At one critical point, Beghin had already abseiled down a rope length and Lafaille decided to double up a poor piton placement with one of his iceaxes. It was simply placed in the ice, but provided reliable extra security. But when Lafaille got down the rope length, he realised he had made an elementary error and that it would have been much more prudent to keep both axes. They started to prepare the next abseil from a snowy ledge the size of a fridge door. Beghin placed only a single friend in a crack without a backup. Friends act as camming devices with a trigger which can open them, but when they come under pressure from the rope the cams get wider and stick firmly into a crack. They are generally very safe and reliable belays and made some previously unprotectable climbs much safer when introduced in the 1980s. But if poorly placed in an uneven crack, a Friend can "walk" out of the crack by shifting from side to side and working its way out. At this stage they still had plenty of equipment, but most of it was in Beghin's sack. As Beghin positioned himself on the rope ready to descend, his ice axe, which was attached to his harness, got caught between his legs. He unclipped it and gave it to the younger climber telling him to give it back later. Beghin descended the first couple of metres without problems then a small overhang brought greater tension onto the rope. This caused the Friend on which he was abseiling to work out of its crack and sent him, the ropes and everything flying into the void of 2000 metres. Lafaille watched in horror as the face of his companion, looking at him and without a cry, disappeared into the mist. He had absolutely no chance. Twenty years of top level climbing, frequently testing his limits had caught up with one of the most brilliant Himalayan climbers ever. Lafaille then had an odyssey to reach the foot of the Face taking five days. For the first section he did not even have a rope. Then he had his arm broken by rock fall, before he finally struggled to the bottom. Christophe Profit largely gave up extreme Himalayan climbing after K2, although he continued to climb at a high level and be active as a guide in the Alps where he has climbed the North Face of the Eiger 10 times with clients.

Misha Turkevich died in much less dramatic circumstances after a sudden illness in the Black Sea resort of Sochi, cutting short in its prime the life of one of the Ukraine's finest climbers. His actions to renounce from reaching the summit on Lhotse certainly saved the life of Karataev, but it appears that Lhotse South Face was a burning ambition for him and it was a great regret of his that he didn't make it to the summit. The story of Artur Hajzer is even more poignant. Hajzer, after a hugely successful period of climbing in the 1980s, effectively withdrew from Himalayan climbing after the death of Kukuczka. In the mid-2000s, after a break of 15 years he returned to the sport. According to Hajzer, it was his wife who encouraged him to do it saying "My wife, she comes down to the kitchen table and says, Artur you are getting old and fat. Go back to the mountains and come home a skinny boy." After his return from retirement he climbed three 8000 metre peaks, Dhaulagiri, Nanga Parbat and Makalu. He also made a number of attempts to climb some of the remaining 8000 metre peaks which had not had a winter ascent. But in June 2013 after failing on an attempt on Gasherbrum I, he fell whilst descending the Japanese couloir and was killed. No one spent more effort in trying to crack Lhotse's South Face than Hajzer and he should be viewed as one of the greats of Himalayan climbing.

A few weeks earlier there was one of the most senseless losses of life ever in Himalayan climbing. A group of 20 terrorists, believed to be part of the Pakistan Taliban attacked Nanga Parbat Base Camp at night, tied up all locals and killed 10 foreign climbers in cold blood. The murdered climbers included three Ukrainians from Kharkiv, the base of many of the key members of the 1990 Lhotse South Face expedition. One of those killed was Ihor Sverhun who had been in the second team to attempt the summit in 1990.

Hajzer's partner on Lhotse, Krzysztof Wielicki, went from the strength. Although little known by the public outside of Poland, his pedigree as a Himalayan climber is second to none. He is the 5th man to climb all 14 8000 metre peaks, achieving this feat in 1996 just a few weeks after Carlos Carsolio, another veteran of Lhotse's South Face. Like his compatriot Kukuczka, Wielicki ascents weren't just peak-bagging repeats of the ordinary routes. Five of the peaks he climbed solo, he climbed at least three new routes as well as repeats of classics like Annapurna South Face and K2's North Ridge. He is also unquestionably the greatest ever winter Himalayan climber, having made the first ascent of Everest in winter as well as the first winter ascents of the third and fourth highest mountains in the world. At the time of writing K2 has still not had a winter ascent.

Does the story of the South Face of Lhotse give us an answer to why humans climb? The answer is yes and no. At one level there are as many answers as there are climbers who've ventured onto the face. Each person has a somewhat different way to rationalise and put into words an inner desire which they may themselves struggle to understand. I believe that in some way this is the same inner desire which determined the success of the human species. A desire to explore new places, to see round the next corner, over the next ridge, to become master of the landscape before one's eyes. This same desire to explore allowed a species originating in Eastern Africa to spread out over the whole planet, to cross the icy Bearing Straits and reach the Americas and then descend to the furthest tip. This desire to explore is an important part of what we are as humans and we naturally respect those who are willing to strive hard, to take risks and make sacrifices to try and realise their dreams.

The lives of these men are running or have run their course, but the South Face of Lhotse remains. Despite the continuous effects of erosion which see ice and storms wearing it down wall daily, it is as massive as ever. Whilst gravity and weather break the mountain down, the pressure of the Indian subcontinent against the Asian plate pushes it further up. The challenge of climbing it will remain for future climbers, but it is unlikely to ever become routine in the way that happened to some of the once great challenges of the Alps. The progression for a route from being the "last great problem" to eventually becoming "an easy day for a lady" was noted by the great British climber of the late 19th Century, Alfred Mummery. This golden rule seemed to apply in all previous phases of the development of mountaineering. The Eiger North Face went from being a fearsome challenge to being a routine ascent. The ascent of Everest was the most sought after in the World before 1953, but is now climbed by virtual novices. But with Lhotse's South Face the rule seems to be broken and is still just as much a challenge as when it was first climbed 25 years ago. It very much looks as if the hardest routes on the highest peaks will never become routine and Lhotse South Face above all epitomises this.

Vanja Matijevec told me that tackling the huge triangular overhanging face above the Slovenian route could be a challenge for the future, but at the present moment it is not one that anyone is taking up and maybe they never will. Perhaps this Face is simply too high, too steep and too dangerous to be within the capability of humans, like running the 100 metres in 8 seconds. Maybe there will never again be a period so rich climbing lore as that which I have described in this book and the two decades from 1970 to 1990 will be a sort of mythical age of mountaineering, which fades in the memory but is never forgotten.

Acknowledgements

Since many people were involved in the attempts to climb it, no one person knows the whole story of Lhotse South Face. The memory of some events has been lost with the disappearance of the climbers involved. That I have gained a good understanding of the events is in great part thanks to the generous help I have received from many of the participants and their friends and relatives.

I would particularly like to thank Helene Jaeger, who shared with me her memories of her father and let me search in the archive she has kept of his photos at her vineyard in Chablis, as well as letting me taste some of her excellent wine. Several other people helped piece together the story of the last expedition of Nicolas Jaeger including Nicolas Berardini, Jean-Francois Mazeaud, Bill Rosser, Claude Deck and Brian Hall.

Also great thanks are due to Marie-Odile Fine who showed fantastic hospitality to my son Arthur and me and shared her memories of her husband Vincent together with their son Renaud, himself a talented climber. Frederic Potie also shared with me his memories of Vincent, who could have been one of the greatest Himalayan climbers and deserves to be better known.

I spent a fascinating day in Katowice with the Poles Janusz Majer, Ryszard Pawlowski and Krzysztof Wielicki, who played such a central part in the attempts to climb the Face. Steve Boyer also took time to speak to me and generously sent me copies of his diaries of the 1987 expedition.

I also greatly enjoyed meeting Peter Podgornik and Vanja Matijevec in Slovenia who shared with me their memories of the 1981 expedition.

I had some very interesting discussions with Alessandro Gogna in Milan about the 1975 expedition and his reflections on a long and rich climbing career.

Josef Rakoncaj provided useful help from the Czech Republic as did Rinat Khaibullin in Kazakhstan.

Tamotsu Nakamura of the Japanese Alpine Club provided a lot of assistance and sent useful material to me on the Japanese expeditions.

I also received help from Isabelle Chassin at the Archive of the FFCAM in Paris and Monique Tesi of the CAF Marseille Provence.

Friends including Claude Goussot and Dominic Clark have helped with suggestions. If I have forgotten others who have helped they should accept my apologies.

Whilst researching this book I came to realise that it was an almost unfinishable task. That I have decided to publish this edition now is for a variety of personal reasons, but I do not see the work as finished and I intend to continue with the research and publish a fuller account. This will hopefully give a chance to meet the other people who have generously offered to talk to me, but who I did not yet find time to visit.

Sources and Selected Bibliography

Ballu, Yves – Solidarlhotse, Vertical 25 (French)

Batard, Marc – Les Sorties des Cimes (French)

Batard, Marc – L'envers des Cimes (French)

Batard, Marc – Le Sprinter de l'Everest (French)

Beghin, Pierre – Hautes Altitudes (French)

Bershov. Sergey - Yes, you will avoid avalanches (Russian)

Bershov, Sergey – Lhotse South Wall (Russian)

Cassin, Riccardo and Nangeroni, Giuseppe – Lhotse '75 (Italian)

Cesen, Tomo – Solo (Italian)

Child, Greg – Postcards from the Ledge

Eggler, Albert – The Everest Lhotse Adventure

Falco-Dasal, Miroslaw – Kazdemu Jego Everest (Polish)

Fauquet, Michel – La Plus Haute Paroi du Monde (French) AlpiRando 85

Fine, Vincent – Lhotse (French) – Calanques et Montagnes 1986

Galfy, Ivan – Ceskoslovenska Expedicia Lhoce Sar 1984, Vysoke Tatry 1/85 (Slovakian)

Groselj, Viki – Giants of the Himalayas

Hajzer, Artur – Atak Rozpaczy (Polish)

Kammerlander, Hans – Malato di Montagna (Italian)

Hinkes, Alan – 8000 Metres

Kanji, Kamei – Lhotse 1976, Himalayan Journal

Knez, Francek – La Pietra Infuocata (Italian)

Kukuczka, Jerzy – My Vertical World

Kunaver, Ales - Lhotse, Juzna Stena (Slovenian)

Majer, Janusz - Poludniowa Sciana Lhotse, Taternik 1985 (Polish)

Mariani, Fulvio – Tempete sur L'Objectif (French)

Mcdonald, Bernadette – Freedom Climbers

Messner, Reinhold – Spostare Le Montagne (Italian)

Messner, Reinhold – The Challenge

Pawlowski, Ryszard – 40 Lat W Gorach (Polish)

Pawlowski, Ryszard – Smak Gor (Polish)

Rakoncaj, Josef - Czechoslovak Expedition to Lhotse Shar, 1984, Himalayan Journal

Rakoncaj, Josef - Tulákem ve větru Himálaje (Czech)

Stejskal, Jarýk and Vranka, Milan – Zabudni na Everest 1989 (Slovakian)

Wi, Osamu – Lhotse South Face Winter Ascent ~ The Dream Comes True Alpine Journal 2007

Uchida, Ryohei – Lhotse 1973, Himalayan Journal 33

Warecki, Ryszard – Lhotse South Face Tragedy AAJ 1990

Wielicki, Krysztof – Poludniowa Sciana Lhotse, Taternik 1987 2 (Polish)

Wielicki, Krysztof – La Corona Dell'Himalaya (Italian)

Wielicki, Krysztof – Lhotse South Face Attempt American Alpine Journal 1990

Zaplotnik, Nejc – Pot (Slovenian)

The Top 600 Metres of Lhotse

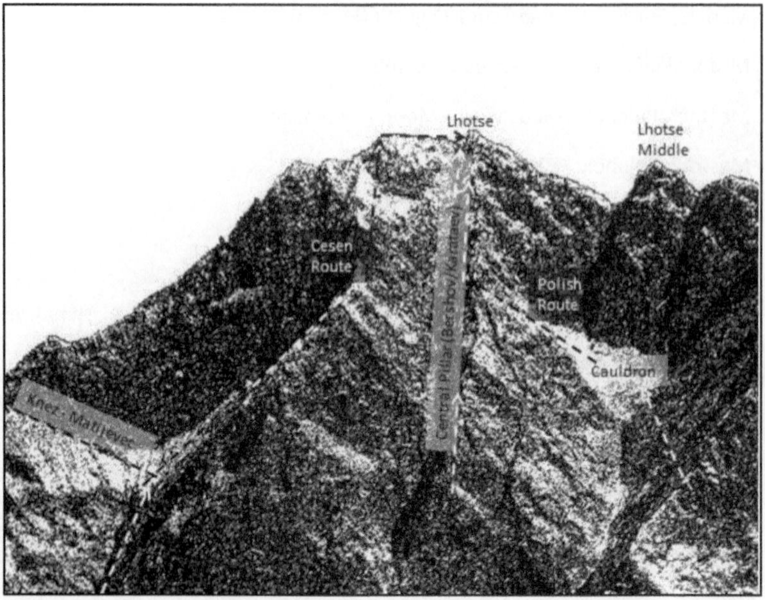

Abalakov, Vitaly ... 241
Aconcagua63, 173, 304
Afanassief, Jean 58
Aiguille Verte 63
Alpamayo....... 58, 213
Ama Dablam 29, 64, 65, 119
Anderson, Rob 253
Ang Kami, Sherpa 235, 236
Ang Phu 78
Ang Puri, Sherpa .. 207
Anghileri, Aldo38, 39, 40
Annapurna 8, 13, 15, 16, 20, 33, 40, 50, 74, 95, 146, 148, 149, 159, 167, 171, 174, 175, 179, 186, 207, 235, 283, 304, 305, 307
Arizzi, Michel 181, 182, 183
Audobert, Louis.... 203
Avila, Elsa148, 160, 197
Axt, Wolfgang 169
Bahuguna, Harsh.. 170
Baintha Brakk....... 132
Ball, Gary 188
Ballu, Yves 190, 193, 195, 196, 312
Balyberdin, Vladimir 241, 242, 243
Barbacetto, Sereno 39, 41, 44, 45, 46, 47
Baruntse 65, 70
Bashkirov, Vladimir296
Batard, Marc 202, 203, 204, 205, 206, 207, 208, 209, 210, 212, 293, 294, 312
Baxter-Jones, Roger96
Bayens, Ingrid 177
Beghin, Pierre 231, 232, 233, 234, 235, 236, 237, 238, 239, 244, 245, 246, 248, 249, 250, 251, 255, 263, 264, 265, 266, 267, 282, 283, 285, 286, 287, 291, 297, 305, 306, 312
Belak, Stane 74, 78
Bell, Steve 252, 267, 268, 269, 275
Bence, Filip 81, 82, 83, 84, 85, 214, 219
Bennett, Bill 252
Berardini, Nicolas 62, 63, 64, 65, 68, 70, 310
Berg, Wally........... 288
Bergant, Borut 78, 84, 85, 214, 215, 216
Bergar, Drago... 75, 76
Bershov, Sergey 6, 241, 242, 243, 248, 255, 256, 262, 276, 277, 278, 279, 280, 281, 282, 283, 285, 292, 293, 297, 300, 302, 303, 304, 312
Bettembourg, Georges 62
Bhagirathi II.......... 177
Bianchi, Marco 151
Biscak, Bogdan 217
Boardman, Peter 50, 62, 95, 118, 268
Bohigas, Nils 174, 175, 283
Bonatti, Walter....... 57
Bondarev, Vladimir297
Bonington, Chris 13, 14, 15, 49, 50, 57, 73, 74, 80, 159, 208
Bourillon, Alain..... 206
Boyer, Steve 159, 161, 310
Bozic, Stipe 78, 79
Bozik, Peter 104, 105, 106, 110, 111, 125, 128, 231
Braithwaite, Paul (Tut) 50, 206
Bretin, Gerard 238
Broad Peak 49, 62, 122, 126, 127, 145, 153, 217, 218, 290
Brugger, Alois 152, 154, 155, 156, 157, 158, 160
Buhl, Hermann 16, 49, 74, 151, 236
Cadot, Michel248, 249
Carsolio, Carlos 148, 149, 160, 161, 163, 187, 197, 307
Cassin, Riccardo 33, 34, 35, 36, 37, 38, 39, 40, 41, 42, 43, 44, 45, 46, 47, 48, 162, 220, 312
Castelnuovo, Floriano 190, 192, 194, 197
Cerro Torre........... 177
Cesen, Tomo 213, 214, 215, 216, 217, 218, 219, 220, 221, 222, 223, 224, 225, 226, 227, 228, 229, 231, 244, 249, 251, 256, 282, 283, 285, 286, 287, 288, 289, 290, 291, 292, 293, 294, 300, 302, 303, 304, 312
Changtse 5, 6, 8, 10, 28, 179, 252, 253, 254, 255, 268, 269, 271, 275, 278
Charlet, Armand57, 58
Child, Greg 290, 292, 293, 302, 312
Chiyoung, Ahn...... 301

Cho Oyu 173, 189, 204, 228, 254, 298
Cholda, Rafal 123, 124, 127, 129, 131, 137, 139, 142, 152, 164, 199
Chrobak, Eugeniusz 116, 120, 124, 187, 189
Cichy, Leszek 116, 117, 124, 177, 178
Conti, Mario..... 42, 47
Cormier, Bruno181, 182, 183
Coudray, Jean 232
Cufar, Martina...... 304
Curnis, Mario39, 43, 44
Czech, Leszek 194
Czok, Andrej 118, 120, 143, 144
Dawa Tshiri, Sherpa298
Decamp, Erik........ 246
Deck, Claude.......... 59
Demjan, Zoltan 106, 107, 108, 109, 110, 111, 125, 128
Desmaison, Rene . 203
Devouassoux, Gerard208
Dhaulagiri 123, 125, 143, 212, 234, 236, 244, 245, 283, 298, 303, 307
Diemberger, Kurt59, 96
Dornisch, Paul252, 269
Drlik, Zdislav..104, 109
Dyhrenfurth, Norman 21, 22, 23, 24, 169, 170
Edwards, Jeremy 252, 267, 271, 272, 273
Eiger8, 13, 14, 15, 35, 48, 176, 306, 308
Elliot, Andrew252, 272
Elliott, Andrew 273
Estcourt, Nick. 50, 206
Evans, John 169
Everest 5, 7, 8, 10, 13, 16, 20, 21, 23, 24, 26, 27, 28, 29, 33, 45, 47, 49, 51, 52, 53, 54, 55, 58, 59, 60, 67, 68, 69, 70, 74, 76, 78, 79, 80, 83, 88, 91, 94, 95, 101, 103, 116, 118, 119, 120, 124, 133, 143, 147, 148, 151, 153, 159, 169, 170, 174, 177, 179, 181, 185, 186, 188, 189, 197, 201, 203, 204, 205, 206, 207, 208, 209, 210, 225, 228, 231, 238, 239, 240, 241, 245, 246, 252, 253, 254, 255, 267, 268, 269, 271, 273, 275, 278, 279, 280, 282, 285, 287, 293, 297, 298, 302, 304, 307, 308, 312, 313
Falco-Dasal, Miroslaw 126, 128, 129, 130, 131, 138, 139, 140, 141, 142, 154, 155, 156, 157, 158, 159, 161, 162, 163, 164, 166, 167, 168, 177, 186, 187, 189, 312
Fargeas, Xavier 238
Fauquet, Michel 132, 133, 134, 135, 136, 137, 139, 140, 141, 142, 151, 168, 209, 212, 227, 251, 291, 294, 312
Fiala, Ivan 98
Fine, Vincent 132, 133, 134, 135, 136, 137, 139, 140, 141, 142, 151, 156, 168, 209, 212, 227, 251, 291, 294, 310
Fischer, Scott 288, 289
Fowler, Mick......... 283
Fresafond, Jean-Pierre 202
Fuit, Walenty 116, 127, 128, 130, 138, 153, 154, 156, 157, 159
Galfy, Ivan 98, 99, 100, 101, 102, 103, 104, 106, 107, 108, 110, 312
Galfy, Robert 108
Gardzielewski, Miroslaw 186, 187
Garrido, Fernando 246
Gasherbrum 21, 36, 48, 49, 52, 74, 75, 76, 98, 115, 116, 122, 148, 151, 173, 202, 203, 217, 218, 220, 283, 307
Gasherbrum II 122, 173, 203
Gaurisankar.......... 123
Ghersen, Alain248, 249
Ghillini, Rene 175
Ghirandini, Yvan 204, 232, 286, 287, 288, 293
Godio, Sandro 245
Gogna, Alessandro 37, 38, 39, 41, 43, 44, 45, 46, 47, 295
Grand Jorasses . 35, 88
Graux, Julien........... 70
Grézat, Philippe...... 70
Groselj, Viki 76, 85, 86, 217, 289, 290, 291, 292, 312
Guenot, Roland 209

Gyachung Kang 254
Habeler, Peter 48, 49, 52, 53, 74, 174, 176
Hajzer, Artur 123, 124, 125, 127, 128, 129, 130, 131, 138, 139, 140, 141, 142, 143, 144, 148, 149, 150, 152, 154, 160, 161, 163, 164, 165, 166, 167, 169, 172, 179, 180, 181, 182, 183, 184, 185, 186, 187, 188, 189, 199, 259, 291, 294, 303, 307, 312
Hall, Brian .62, 96, 310
Hall, Rob 188
Hanatani, Yasuhiro298
Harlin, John...... 14, 15
Haston, Dougal 14, 15, 16, 50, 171
Heinrich, Zygmunt 113, 114, 115, 118, 120, 187, 189
Herrligkoffer, Karl 16, 17, 19, 50, 116, 145
Hillary, Edmund 21, 24, 210, 211
Hindu Kush97, 117, 140
Hinkes, Alan 160, 161, 163, 312
Huascaran...60, 61, 62
Imam, Sherpa....... 205
Island Peak 66, 134, 191, 196, 209
Jaeger, Helene 60, 62, 71, 72, 310
Jaeger, Nicolas 56, 57, 58, 59, 60, 61, 62, 63, 64, 65, 66, 67, 68, 69, 70, 71, 72, 73, 94, 95, 116, 133, 187, 206, 207, 294, 310
Jakes, Karl107, 108, 109
Jakiel, Czeslaw 156, 157, 160, 199
Jannu 96, 97, 220, 221, 224, 226, 238, 239, 244, 245, 246, 286, 288, 290, 303
Just, Jozef............. 206
K2 7, 8, 33, 36, 62, 95, 100, 106, 109, 115, 118, 122, 123, 124, 144, 145, 159, 178, 198, 217, 218, 219, 231, 232, 233, 234, 236, 245, 246, 286, 287, 290, 298, 305, 307
Kammerlander, Hans 146, 147, 172, 173, 174, 180, 181, 182, 183, 184, 312
Kamuro, Hironobu 244
Kangchenjunga 7, 21, 62, 95, 99, 118, 123, 143, 144, 154, 186, 213, 244, 246, 247, 248, 255, 256, 273, 276, 280, 282, 304
Kanji, Kamei ... 51, 312
Karakoram 48, 115, 122, 153, 202, 216, 234
Karataev, Vladimir 6, 255, 256, 257, 276, 277, 278, 279, 280, 281, 282, 283, 294, 297, 300, 303, 304, 307
Kenmochi, Noriyuki301
Khabibulin, Rinat 256, 261, 262
Khan, Laskar......... 231
Khitrikov, Vladimir 258, 262, 277
Kitamura, Toshiyuki300
Klinetski, Evgeni 275, 276, 277
Knez, Francek 88, 89, 90, 91, 92, 93, 214, 292, 302, 304, 312
Kodalj, Janko 221, 222, 224, 225, 226
Konopka, Piotr 154, 155, 156, 157, 158, 161, 162, 163, 164, 166, 167
Kopeika, Gennardy 258, 259, 260, 261, 262, 275, 277, 279, 280, 281
Kopys, Tomasz 191, 192, 193, 195, 197, 198, 200
Kotnik, Ivan 78, 81
Kovac, Rajko 82
Kozachok, Peter277, 282
Krissak, Milan......... 99
Kryc, Ladisclaw..... 102
Kukuczka, Jerzy 117, 118, 119, 120, 121, 122, 123, 124, 126, 128, 129, 131, 136, 137, 138, 140, 141, 142, 143, 144, 145, 146, 147, 148, 149, 150, 151, 152, 153, 154, 160, 164, 169, 179, 186, 187, 189, 190, 191, 192, 193, 194, 195, 196, 197, 198, 199, 200, 201, 209, 245, 260, 291, 294, 307, 312
Kulej, Michal 193, 195, 196
Kunaver, Ales 73, 74, 75, 78, 79, 81, 82, 83, 84, 85, 86, 87, 88, 89, 90, 92, 93, 94, 95, 96, 98, 101, 162, 213, 248, 291, 312
Kunaver, Dusica.... 291
Kungang Chhish 112, 138, 139
Kurtyka, Voytek 112, 113, 122, 124, 143, 144, 148, 149, 153, 283
Lafaille, Christophe 305, 306

Latallo, Stanislaw . 114
LeCable, Nathalie . 133
Lee, Russell ...252, 273
Leviti, Aldo 39, 40, 41, 43, 45, 46
Lho La76, 186, 187, 188, 189
Lhotse 5, 8, 9, 10, 12, 16, 20, 21, 23, 24, 26, 27, 28, 29, 30, 31, 36, 37, 38, 40, 43, 44, 47, 48, 49, 55, 56, 61, 62, 64, 65, 66, 67, 68, 69, 71, 72, 73, 74, 77, 78, 79, 83, 91, 93, 94, 95, 96, 99, 101, 102, 103, 105, 110, 111, 112, 113, 115, 117, 118, 120, 122, 123, 124, 125, 126, 127, 128, 133, 134, 135, 139, 141, 142, 143, 147, 148, 152, 153, 154, 157, 159, 165, 167, 169, 174, 176, 177, 178, 179, 183, 184, 185, 186, 187, 189, 190, 191, 195, 198, 205, 206, 209, 210, 211, 212, 213, 217, 219, 224, 225, 226, 228, 231, 236, 241, 244, 246, 248, 250, 252, 255, 265, 267, 269, 270, 275, 276, 280, 283, 285, 286, 287, 288, 289, 290, 291, 292, 293, 294, 295, 296, 297, 298, 301, 303, 304, 305, 307, 308, 310, 312, 313
Lhotse Middle 26, 27, 101, 105, 219, 296, 297
Lhotse Shar 22, 26, 27, 28, 31, 66, 69, 71, 99, 101, 105, 127, 180, 206, 207, 219, 226, 265, 288, 296, 303
Liu Bin 254, 269
Liu Jun Hui.....254, 269
Lorenzi, Fausto. 39, 47
Loretan, Erhard 245
Losso, Roland 182, 183
Lucas, Enric 174, 175, 178, 180, 181, 182, 184, 212, 251, 283
Luchsinger, Fritz 24, 25, 26, 113, 118
Machnik, Andrzej . 144
Macintyre, Alex 95, 122, 174
Majer, Janusz 123, 131, 139, 140, 152, 187, 189, 312
Makalu 20, 31, 73, 75, 78, 79, 88, 99, 102, 110, 122, 128, 143, 146, 147, 150, 174, 197, 204, 209, 210, 213, 231, 248, 268, 283, 286, 287, 307
Makarov, Alexei 256, 257, 261, 282, 284
Manaslu 37, 47, 146, 148, 149, 236, 245, 283, 304
Manfreda, Marjan 74, 76, 84, 86
Marciniak, Andrzej 187, 188, 189
Mariani, Fulvio 176, 177, 179, 180, 181, 182, 190, 192, 196, 197, 313
Martine(Fine), Marie-Odile 133, 134, 142
Martis, Jindra 107, 108, 109
Masip, Ana 212
Matijevec, Vanja 78, 81, 88, 89, 90, 91, 92, 93, 302, 304, 308
Matterhorn 7, 13, 37, 48, 176
Mauri, Carlo 171
Mazeaud, Jean-Francois 68, 69, 70
Mazeaud, Pierre 59, 68, 171
Mellet, Bernard 20, 231, 232, 234
Messner, Reinhold 17, 18, 19, 30, 33, 37, 38, 39, 40, 41, 42, 43, 44, 45, 46, 47, 48, 49, 50, 52, 53, 54, 55, 59, 61, 62, 64, 67, 73, 74, 91, 94, 96, 118, 119, 120, 122, 123, 128, 132, 145, 146, 147, 148, 150, 152, 167, 169, 171, 172, 173, 174, 176, 177, 178, 179, 180, 181, 182, 183, 184, 185, 186, 187, 188, 190, 191, 212, 213, 231, 233, 234, 237, 244, 245, 289, 296, 313
Mingma Tshiri, Sherpa298
Miyoshi, Manabu . 298
Monaci, Daniel 232
Mont Blanc 13, 35, 57, 58, 72, 134
Mosca, Jean-Claude232
Mount McKinley... 117
Muller, Bernard 234, 235, 236, 237, 238, 239
Mummery, Alfred 57, 308
Mutschlechner, Friedl147
Myslovsky, Eduard 241, 242, 243
Nairz, Wolfgang......53

Nanga Parbat 7, 13, 16, 17, 20, 33, 37, 49, 54, 55, 74, 91, 98, 100, 117, 119, 122, 123, 128, 148, 178, 189, 197, 234, 236, 244, 307
Ngawang Tenzi, Sherpa 301, 302
Niepce, Janine 56, 65, 68, 71
Nima Gyalzen, Sherpa298
Norton, Edward53, 245
Novak, Igor....102, 106
Nowak, Jan....129, 177
Nuptse 13, 21, 26, 27, 29, 31, 38, 43, 44, 47, 62, 68, 77, 113, 285
Obichod, Vladimir 275
Ohtani, Hisao 298
Oklek, Witold 196
Olland, Pierre-Louis212
Onggel, Sherpa 204, 205, 209
Orolin, Michal 98
Osika, Andrzej 154, 156, 157, 159, 161, 163, 164
Otreba, Waclaw ... 187
Palenicek, Leopold 102, 104, 107, 110
Pasang Norbu....... 116
Pastukh, Viktor 276, 282, 284, 304
Pawlikowski, Maciej 156, 157, 163, 164, 190, 191, 192, 194, 195, 197, 198, 200
Pawlowski, Ryszard 126, 129, 131, 136, 138, 153, 154, 159, 161, 190, 193, 194, 195, 196, 197, 198, 199, 200, 313
Pema Tsering, Sherpa301
Pemba, Sherpa..... 209
Piasecki, Przemek 143, 144, 192, 193, 194, 195, 196, 197, 198, 231
Piotrowski, Tadeus 114, 144, 145, 146
Pitra, Alexander261, 262
Piussi, Ignacio .. 41, 43
Podgornik (Brothers), Peter, Pavel 81, 82, 83, 84, 85, 86, 88, 214, 304
Pogolorev, Alexander 258, 261, 262
Potie, Frédéric...... 133
Profit, Christophe 176, 178, 180, 181, 182, 183, 184, 212, 219, 231, 234, 250, 251, 255, 263, 264, 265, 266, 267, 282, 283, 291, 293, 297, 305, 306
Pumori 254, 304
Rakoncaj, Josef 100, 103, 104, 105, 106, 107, 109, 110, 111, 313
Ravnihar, Tomaz224, 289
Reiss, Ernst 24, 25, 26, 113, 118
Roberts, Jimmy169, 171
Roche, Jean-Noel.. 245
Rosser, Bill 63, 64, 66, 67, 68, 69, 70, 71, 310
Rouse, Alan 62, 94, 95, 96, 97, 167, 219, 248, 283
Rusiecki, Jacek...... 113
Rutkiewicz, Wanda 116, 150, 151, 160, 161, 295
Schubert, Karel.......99
Scott, Doug 50, 62, 95, 118, 167, 296
Seigneur, Yannick 20, 62, 203, 204, 231, 232
Senda, Atushi 301
Senn, Ernst21, 22, 23, 24
Shevchenko, Alexander 255, 277
Shisha Pangma 12, 95, 146, 148, 152, 154, 160, 161, 254, 299, 300, 301
Skarja, Tony76, 78, 213
Smid, Miroslav 102, 104, 106, 107
Steinmann, Brigitte 62, 63, 65, 68
Stejskal, Jaromir 101, 103, 104, 105, 106, 107, 109, 110, 111, 313
Stremfelj, Andrej 75, 76, 77, 78, 79, 82, 86, 87, 217, 219, 242, 291, 296
Stryczynski, Wojciech113
Sundare, Sherpa 203, 204, 205, 208
Sustersic, Miro 84
Sverhun, Ihor 261, 262, 284, 307
Tanabe, Osamu 298, 299, 300, 301, 302, 303, 313
Tarasov, Sergey 275
Tasker, Joe 62, 95, 118, 268
Tavernier, Sylvianne 181, 183
Teare, Paul 253
Tedeschi, Yves......220

Tien Shan 247
Tomazin, Iztok........87
Tosas, Jordi 303
Totmyanin, Nikolai275
Trango Towers..... 304
Troillet, Jean 245
Tshiring Dorje, Sherpa298
Turkevich, Misha 241, 242, 243, 248, 255, 258, 259, 260, 261, 262, 275, 276, 277, 278, 279, 280, 281, 282, 283, 292, 297, 303, 307
Uchida, Ryohei 29, 30, 32, 313
Uli Biaho 234
Um Hong Gil......... 303
Vaucher, Bernard. 151
Vaucher, Michel and Yvette 171
Venables, Stephen 287
Villaret, Bernard... 203
Walde, Kurt 152, 157, 159, 163
Warecki, Ryszard 123, 124, 148, 150, 160, 190, 196, 313
Whillans, Don 13, 16, 40, 57, 170, 171
Wielicki, Krysztof 116, 117, 123, 124, 128, 129, 130, 131, 138, 139, 140, 142, 143, 144, 146, 150, 151, 152, 153, 154, 155, 157, 159, 162, 163, 164, 165, 166, 167, 169, 172, 177, 178, 179, 180, 181, 182, 183, 184, 185, 189, 199, 209, 217, 259, 283, 291, 294, 295, 296, 303, 307, 310, 313
Wilson, Peter........ 252
Wroz, Wojciech 116, 120, 124, 231
Yalungkang 216, 247, 290, 292, 293, 303
Yamaguchi, Takahiro 301, 302
Yamamoto, Toshio301
Zaplotnik, Nejc 74, 75, 76, 77, 78, 79, 81, 86, 87, 88, 242, 291, 304, 313
Zawada, Andrzej 112, 113, 114, 115, 116, 117, 119, 120, 121, 138, 139, 153, 177